A PEOPLE'S MUSIC

C000279059

A People's Music presents the first full history of jazz in East Germany, drawing on new and previously unexamined sources and eyewitness accounts. Helma Kaldewey chronicles the experiences of jazz musicians, fans, and advocates, and charts the numerous policies state socialism issued to manage this dynamic art form. Offering a radical revision of scholarly views of jazz as a musical genre of dissent, this vivid and authoritative study marks developments in the production, performance, and reception of jazz decade by decade, from the German Democratic Republic's beginning in the 1940s to its end in 1990, examining how members of the jazz scene were engaged with (and were sometimes complicit with) state officials and agencies throughout the Cold War. From postwar rebuilding, to Stalinism and partition, to détente, *Ostpolitik*, and *glasnost*, and finally to its acceptance as a national art form, Kaldewey reveals just how many lives jazz lived.

HELMA KALDEWEY (Ph.D., Tulane University) is a musicologist, historian, longtime teacher, and researcher in the history of jazz. She has written and produced films about New Orleans' music culture in partnership with German public media.

NEW STUDIES IN EUROPEAN HISTORY

Edited by

PETER BALDWIN, University of California, Los Angeles
CHRISTOPHER CLARK, University of Cambridge
JAMES B. COLLINS, Georgetown University
MIA RODRÍGUEZ-SALGADO, London School of Economics and Political Science
LYNDAL ROPER, University of Oxford
TIMOTHY SNYDER, Yale University

The aim of this series in early modern and modern European history is to publish outstanding works of research, addressed to important themes across a wide geographical range, from southern and central Europe to Scandinavia and Russia, from the time of the Renaissance to the present. As it develops, the series will comprise focused works of wide contextual range and intellectual ambition.

A full list of titles published in the series can be found at:
www.cambridge.org/newstudiesineuropeanhistory

A PEOPLE'S MUSIC

Jazz in East Germany, 1945–1990

HELMA KALDEWEY

Tulane University

CAMBRIDGE
UNIVERSITY PRESS

CAMBRIDGE
UNIVERSITY PRESS

University Printing House, Cambridge CB2 8BS, United Kingdom

One Liberty Plaza, 20th Floor, New York, NY 10006, USA

477 Williamstown Road, Port Melbourne, VIC 3207, Australia

314-321, 3rd Floor, Plot 3, Splendor Forum, Jasola District Centre, New Delhi - 110025, India

103 Penang Road, #05-06/07, Visioncrest Commercial, Singapore 238467

Cambridge University Press is part of the University of Cambridge.

It furthers the University's mission by disseminating knowledge in the pursuit of education, learning and research at the highest international levels of excellence.

www.cambridge.org
Information on this title: www.cambridge.org/9781108731928
DOI: 10.1017/9781108645638

First published 2020
First paperback edition 2021

A catalogue record for this publication is available from the British Library

Library of Congress Cataloging in Publication data
Names: Kaldewey, Helma, 1962- author.
Title: A people's music / Helma Kaldewey.
Description: New York : Cambridge University Press, 2020. | Series: New studies in European history | Includes bibliographical references and index.
Identifiers: LCCN 2019029220 | ISBN 9781108486187 (hardback) | ISBN 9781108486187 (ebook)
Subjects: LCSH: Jazz--Germany--20th century--History and criticism. | Jazz--Germany (East)--History and criticism. | Jazz--Social aspects--Germany--History--20th century. | Jazz--Political aspects--Germany--History--20th century. | Music and state--Germany--History--20th century.
Classification: LCC ML3509.G3 K3 2020 | DDC 781.650943/1--dc23
LC record available at https://lccn.loc.gov/2019029220

ISBN 978-1-108-48618-7 Hardback
ISBN 978-1-108-73192-8 Paperback

Contents

Figures

Preface

In May 2009, I had just returned to Berlin when a friend of mine, a music journalist, broke the news: Werner Sellhorn had just passed away. To students of East German history, Sellhorn was something of a mystery. During previous research work years earlier, I had learned that he was an established figure in the East German jazz scene and, in his role as emcee and promoter, he had also, in fact, been an occasional informant to the state security agency, the *Staatssicherheit* (hereafter STASI). Prior to my arrival in Germany, we had spoken on the phone, and he had been friendly, asking if I had read his discography of East German jazz. We had arranged to meet, and I was looking forward to our in-person encounter, hoping he could fill some gaps in my understanding of the era. Sadly, we never got the chance to meet as his funeral took place the day after my plane landed at Tegel Airport.

Around eleven o'clock that May morning, still jet lagged, I entered Georgen-Parochial-Friedhof I cemetery in Prenzlauer Berg and walked through the rows of monuments and gravestones, not entirely sure where to go. Fortunately, the cemetery was not large, and soon I spotted a crowd of people in front of a small church. Well over a hundred people had assembled outside, with many more packed inside: even from a distance, I could feel that this was an extraordinary gathering, so I was slightly nervous about approaching the crowd. Over the next several hours, first at Sellhorn's memorial service at the church, then at the gravesite, and finally at a local restaurant for an informal gathering, my unease only grew stronger. His friends and admirers shared a deep familiarity, a cama- raderie and intimacy that made me feel almost like an intruder. Under the circumstances, I could neither act like a researcher with notebook in hand, nor bring out my expensive new camera purchased just for this purpose. In fact, cordial as the mourners were, I found it difficult even just to introduce myself and explain my presence. This difficulty only would have increased had I realized just who was gathered: internationally recognized musicians such as Conrad Bauer, Ulrich Gumpert, Ruth Hohmann, Friedhelm Schönfeld, and Klaus Lenz, all of whom had played pivotal roles in the world of East German jazz. It was a relief, therefore, when at last I spotted a familiar face: the promoter Karlheinz Drechsel just said a quick hello, turned away, and disappeared back into the crowd of guests. At that moment, another familiar face, Uschi Brüning, showed me much-needed social grace, introducing me to Drechsel's son; however, I could not help but wonder if she was diverting me from the other luminaries present, such as her husband, the great saxophonist Ernst Ludwig Petrowsky.

After the service, Petrowsky and Brüning were among the first to arrive at the gravesite, where the depth of their grief over Sellhorn's passing was clear. So, too, were the expressions of many other attendees, whose identities and relationships I could only imagine. In the restaurant later that night, after only a few perfunctory conversations it seemed best for me to leave. The farewell to Sellhorn had its public component, but something else was undeniably going on. The people gathered here – most of them at that time in their sixties and seventies – were not just remembering their departed friend, rather they were also commemorating a shared past. Each of those mourners was linked by a life in their youth that barely resembled their lives in the present. Indeed, this funeral meant far more than a mere farewell to a longtime friend. Rather, it was a commemoration of a life in jazz in the former German Democratic Republic (GDR).

This book seeks to tell that story. *A People's Music* chronicles the history of jazz in East Germany over its forty-year history, from the end of WWII to the collapse of the Berlin Wall. The first book of its kind to detail jazz history over the entire lifespan of the GDR, as opposed to examining the genre through isolated moments or trends, this book argues for a revised understanding of the role and significance of the vibrant jazz culture in socialist Germany. Tracing the origins of the jazz reception in Germany prior to WWII, examining the politicization of post-war reconstruction efforts, and documenting decade by decade both individual and institutional participation in jazz until the country's collapse, this book offers a new history of a genre of music that, to date, has not been adequately studied about this time and place.

Concurrent with its basic historical investigation, this study challenges the common claim that jazz in East Germany was a cultural form perpetually in opposition to state ideology; rather, this research takes the premise that in the communist worldview jazz was "a music of the people" and, therefore, at a basic level in ideological accordance with

Marxist cultural politics. In general, Marxist theories viewed jazz primarily as African American music rooted in the experience of enslavement and oppression under imperialist capitalism and, thus, interpreted jazz history through the lens of exploitation by commercial interests. This does not suggest that over four decades jazz in East Germany flourished free of state repression – far from it. Indeed, jazz scenes were controlled and restricted at various times and for various reasons, making the history of jazz in the GDR a complex story. Cultural conflicts, geopolitical tensions, social prejudice, and fears of racial and cultural transgression all informed the turbulent history of the music. This book shows just how state management of jazz changed decade by decade, even (at times) year by year, as a result of national and global political circumstances. Overall, the traditional account of jazz as strictly a tool of underground resistance movements requires revision.

Part of this revision involves a reconsideration of the role of the East German state. In contemporary discourse, the GDR is often denounced as "the illegitimate state," "the East German totalitarian state," or characterized as "the second German dictatorship." Such assessments generate perceptions of East Germany as an illegal, totalitarian autocracy exerting total control over its society. Yet those who made their careers in East Germany or who held state positions often feel incriminated by such retrospective, partial judgments. During interviews with musicians, writers, jazz fans, and cultural functionaries conducted over the last ten years, proponents of the East German jazz scene actively cultivated their image as advocates for jazz, claiming to have fought for the music's recognition within a state that typically opposed Western culture. Despite some discrimination and victimization by state actors or ideologues, many of these interviewees (appearing in nearly every chapter of this book) were in fact able to work toward greater acceptance of jazz, to the point that by the end of the GDR, the state had become one of the primary sponsors and benefactors of the music.

In the Anglophone world, the historiography of jazz in the Cold War era is largely one-sided, with scholarly accounts examining the role of jazz primarily from a Western perspective. Most recent works – such as books by Penny von Eschen and Ingrid Monson – have detailed how the United States Department of State used jazz as a political tool to propagate the socio-political model of capitalism and liberal democracy. The present study deepens our understanding by looking at jazz propaganda from the Communist side, detailing how Soviet policy makers utilized jazz as propaganda before western (US and British, West German) policymakers used it for their ideological purposes. As a result, *A People's Music* contributes to the field of Cold War historiography in four key ways.

First, this book explores the process of cultural transfer, wherein socialist policy promoted transracial music as a vital part of cultural life in Soviet-occupied Germany. Where Nazi racist ideology had championed the superiority of one race, under the new regime, jazz, a "negro music," became a central tool of the socialist agenda to reeducate its populace as well as to engage in an ideological contest with the United States. Here, analysis of Allied policymaking concerning African American music and musicians in occupied Germany offers insight into this battle over core socialist issues of class and race. This book places these developments in the context of Cold War cultural rivalry, revealing the complex, shifting dialectic between jazz as a political tool and as popular entertainment, deepening and complicating the story told by most other scholars.

Second, this book explores the process of cultural formation, wherein jazz gained status as an emancipated genre fully in line with Germanic musical heritage. In her study, *Composing the Canon in the German Democratic Republic* (Oxford University Press, 2014), Elaine Kelly explored socialist views of eighteenth- and nineteenth-century classical music, detailing how these works encoded the founding mythology of East Germany. On the other hand, jazz, a transracial and transnational music, belonged in some ways to a bourgeois value system and played a complicated role in East Germany's quest for cultural identity. Remarkably, despite some detractors, East German cultural criticism came to interpret Beethoven and Louis Armstrong alike as prototypes of ideal socialist citizens, ultimately integrating jazz into the socialist canon by the 1960s. Such a move deconstructed previous cultural hierarchies and elevated the jazz music to socio-political acceptance.

Third, this book deepens our understanding of totalitarianism, in particular, what the scholar Mary Fulbrook has defined as a "participatory dictatorship." Contesting the notion of "top-down" political structures, Fulbrook has explored the impact of public sentiment and engagement on Socialist Party doctrine, arguing for a communicative exchange between citizens and state officials that actively shaped the shared cultural environment. Such insights complement the findings of this study: that proponents of jazz helped to shape jazz culture in East Germany by directly negotiating with state authority as well as by institutionalizing jazz. Jazz musicians, writers, and impresarios were able to pursue remarkable careers, enjoying extraordinary privileges and, in many cases, acting as emblems of the state not only by representing East Germany's jazz on international stages but also by holding high positions in state cultural organizations. This reality upends the notion of jazz solely as a resistance to oppression, especially in the last two decades of the GDR.

Finally, this book deepens the study of Cold War cultural diplomacy, a field that has grown considerably in recent years. Works by Frederick Starr and Wolfgang Schivelbusch (echoing Michael H. Kater's work on the Nazi era) have all explored the way in which culture and the arts played a role in the politics and conflicts of this era, but none of these works have addressed the role of jazz in the overall political history of the GDR. Rather, they address jazz at individual moments or in other geographies. Similarly, works by Rainer Bratfisch, David Caute, and Mike Heffley that explore jazz and socialism are limited either by their methods or by their disciplinary bounds, typically neglecting the role of the state as an active, generative participant in the creation and management of jazz culture. Since no one has yet examined the history of jazz across those forty years or consulted primary sources that detail how cultural policies toward jazz production and consumption developed, this study seeks to map that terrain.

In order to make these contributions, this book draws on new primary sources as well as extant sources, which are explored here in new contexts and perspectives. These sources fall under five major categories: government documents, oral histories, STASI archives, private records, and visual records of the time. Together they offer a much more robust portrait of jazz in its time. First, this study examines documents East German officials produced from 1945 to 1989, representing the full hierarchy of the state power structure. These include the ruling Socialist Party's Central Committee resolutions, party convention protocols, Cultural League correspondence, reports of the State Commission for the Arts (and its successor, the Ministry for Culture), assessments of mass organizations, such as the Cultural League and Free German Youth, as well as petitions of jazz fans to local functionaries. These agencies represent the full sphere of state authority, from those at the center of power to those who represented jazz fans at the grassroots level. The information in these documents, archived today at the *Bundersarchiv* (German Federal Archives) in Berlin-Lichterfelde, makes clear the importance authorities attached to jazz, puts the oral history narratives in perspective, and reveals the discrepancies between official state positions on jazz at the time and the retrospective, at times errant views of interviewees that came later.

Second, the scholars Lutz Niethammer and Dorothee Wierling have argued that oral histories comprise a key method of understanding life in the GDR. Informants here represent a wide variety of members of the East German jazz scene: musicians, fans, cultural functionaries, theater promoters, record producers, critics, writers, and musicologists. These histories encompass memories from across the forty-year period that spans the immediate aftermath of WWII until the fall of the Berlin Wall. As noted above, these accounts must be put into the context of post-war debates of guilt, blame, and complicity, and must be interpreted in the light of retrospective emotions. Nevertheless, they illuminate individuals' experiences of jazz in that era, revealing key moments that sparked a lifelong passion for the music. By their own admission, most of these interviewees had never participated in oral history projects before, nor had they been questioned about their experiences regarding a contested cultural form. As survivors of the era are rapidly aging, this research reflects a critical knowledge base from which historians must draw before the opportunity is lost.

Besides government documents and oral histories, reports of the Ministry for State Security (*Ministerium für Staatssicherheit*, MfS or STASI) reveal a third dimension of the GDR jazz scene. In the 1950s, the STASI had begun a program of active surveillance of cultural activities by recruiting unofficial collaborators within the scene. Werner Sellhorn, described above, was but one of hundreds. These documents, also housed at the Federal Commissioner for STASI Archives in Berlin, suggest that not only did such recruits benefit from collaboration, but that the mutual relationship between informants and STASI agents actually shaped jazz activities and the jazz scene at large in direct ways – a key finding of this book. The STASI's strategy of rewarding its collaborators made jazz activities possible, bolstered the careers of musicians and writers, and influenced the very discourse on jazz in the GDR.

Fourth, this book examines a wide variety of materials from private holdings, including the personal letters, photographs, musical diaries, and memorabilia of members of the jazz scene, as well as rare, irreplaceable documents such as *samizdat* publications and programs of jazz lectures. These materials reveal the importance the actors in the music scene attached to contemporary musical experiences, such as live concerts or broadcast jazz programs, and offer unparalleled access to their opinions, perspectives, and feelings about the music while living in a largely isolated country.

Fifth and finally, while some of the visual materials of the era are well-known, such as photographs from Louis Armstrong's tour of the GDR in 1965, many of the images shown in this book have never been published. Among them are images drawn from the collection of Otto Sill, an East

German photographer and musician. Interestingly, these materials represent mostly contact prints, giving insight into the photographer's gaze while framing a shot. In many cases, images came from private photo albums taken by amateurs, giving further insight into the immediate moment of their experience. Concert programs and posters came from private sources as well as the Bundesarchiv Berlin-Lichterfelde, which in 2010, received several large private collections that, until recently, have not been investigated.

In considering sources and methods, it is important to note not only the scope of this book, but also its limitations. First, this study does not present an overview of the vast music production in the four decades of jazz history in the GDR: save for a handful of modest references, it does not detail the physical processes of recording, producing, and distributing jazz music in that time. Also, it does not aim to critically assess the work of jazz musicians within their genre. This book is more interested in compositions in the context of East German cultural politics than in the context of a composer's own oeuvre. Third, this book does not provide a musicological analysis of the formal qualities of jazz, either in East German or in Western styles. Finally, for simple reasons of space, this research does not examine jazz in every region of the GDR, but focuses primarily on Berlin, given its role as the capital city of jazz in Germany both before and after WWII, and with additional emphasis on Leipzig and Dresden. Room for all those explorations is left to future scholars.

To set the stage for jazz in East Germany proper, the book opens with a brief historical account of jazz in Germany prior to the creation of the East German state. Chapter 1 examines jazz in Germany after WWI, offering an overview of the Weimar and the National Socialist eras. These years include the introduction of jazz into the defeated German empire, its ambivalent reception by the bourgeoisie, and the questions that jazz posed about national cultural identity. Under the twelve years of National Socialism, these questions deepened because Nazi propaganda unequivocably ostracized jazz as an emblem of racial transgression, yet also recruited the popularity of the music for propagandist purposes throughout the regime, even until its collapse.

Following this background, Chapter 2 explores jazz in the years of Allied occupation in Germany from the end of the war in 1945 to the founding of the GDR in 1949. Berlin, the former capital of Nazi Germany, served as center stage for its occupying powers to engage in a battle of ideologies. During this time, culture, music, and jazz were key tools of the postwar rebuilding effort by both Soviet and Western Allies, but jazz also quickly became a political tool intended to sway audiences toward democracy or socialism. This chapter details the propagandistic role Soviet policymakers assigned to music of African American descent and shows how jazz served as entertainment for troops in the British and American sectors. Prior to detailing the creation of the GDR, this chapter also discusses the personal experiences of German jazz fans in the late 1940s, documenting racial segregation in the American sectors as well as chronicling Soviet propaganda of the time.

Chapter 3 examines the years 1949–1961, the first years of the GDR and the period during and after Stalin's regime. According to Communism, culture under Capitalism was shaped by exploitation, which communist perceptions of jazz history reviled. The chapter explores Marxist perceptions of jazz from both sides of the Atlantic that informed socialist-realist doctrine, as well the repressive methods of the State Commission for the Arts that sought to "protect" German cultural values against American cultural "decadence." This chapter then analyzes the East German jazz discourse of the late 1950s that rehabilitated the music, a process that linked it to the German bourgeois tradition of *Hausmusik*. Finally, the chapter explores the prolific West Berlin jazz scene, sponsored by Western funds, that sought to attract fans from East Berlin and beyond. At this time, the STASI initiated its surveillance of the jazz scene, empowering secret informants that proved pivotal in shaping East German jazz life. Alarmed by the increasing numbers of defections to the West throughout the 1950s, East German officials eventually responded by building the Wall, dividing the city and the country in two. This act had severe implications for the spread of jazz activities and resulted in the formation of a jazz scene specific to the GDR.

Chapter 4 examines the 1960s, following the building of the Wall in 1961. After the country's partition, which resulted both in increased jazz activities in the East and the smuggling of jazz materials across the border, the party leadership issued a pivotal "jazz resolution" that steered the course of jazz in the socialist state. This resolution, examined in detail, posited that jazz constituted a genuine folk tradition and demanded support for jazz as an art form that protested racial oppression. The chapter also examines Louis Armstrong's famous 1965 tour in the Eastern Bloc, which the United States likely sponsored but the GDR used to demonstrate its solidarity with the civil rights movement in America by portraying one the of world's most famous jazz musicians not just as an outspoken critic of American racial policy but as an ideal socialist-realist artist. Examining the legacy of this tour in such events as the Dixieland Festival in Dresden, this chapter argues that the Armstrong tour enabled

a broader social acceptance of jazz in East Germany, signifying a key turning point in the trajectory of the genre.

Chapter 5 examines jazz in the 1970s, a time of growth and innovation
in jazz in the GDR. Throughout this decade, East German cultural critics
saw free jazz as an outgrowth of the Black Power movement, interpreting
it as music protesting social grievances and echoing class warfare in the
United States. By contrast, jazz made in the GDR, a genre that trumpeted
its own new, original compositions, became an emblem of an art form in
harmony with socialist society. Yet despite this interpretation of the music,
its incorporation into state culture, and its subsequent flourishing, jazz
retained its countercultural aspect, a dimension this chapter also explores.
Fans who experienced the music live noted an "oppositional" atmosphere
at concerts and festivals, yielding an ambiguous dynamic between individual and state. At such events, performers and audiences repeatedly
found ways to repudiate the socialist state, even as diplomats elsewhere
recruited jazz to represent socialist Germany on the global stage.

In the final years of the GDR, contemporary jazz rose to an acknowledged art form receiving generous state sponsorship, a legitimization that
Chapter 6 explores in detail even as it charts the decline and fall of the
East German state as a whole. In the 1980s, key East German musicians
became established in both the Eastern and Western Blocs, turning free
jazz "made in the GDR" into a prestigious export item and projecting the
image of an open-minded, progressive socialist East Germany. In 1985, the
GDR held its first national jazz festival in Weimar, a city that represented
East Germany's humanist and democratic heritage. Despite this symbolic
choice, and the popularity of jazz as a "national" art form by this time,
larger political currents would see the collapse of the GDR a few short
years later. To conclude this history, this chapter describes the personal
accounts of the fall of the Berlin Wall by most of the members of the jazz
scene interviewed for this book. The epilogue marks the final paradigm
shift in the history of East German jazz, looking at the transition between
the fall of the Wall in 1989 and formal reunification of East and West
Germany in 1990.

Many hands were involved in the writing of this book. In New Orleans,
I would like to thank my graduate research committee in the Department
of History at Tulane University: Marline Otte, Samuel Ramer, John
Joyce, and Emily Clark. I am also grateful to Bruce Boyd Raeburn, Lynn
Abbott, Lawrence Powell, George Bernstein, and Benjamin Morris for
their expertise, as well as the late Linda Lasky. I am indebted to the staff of
Howard-Tilton Library, the Amistad Research Center, and the Hogan Jazz

Archives for their help in locating valuable materials. While at Tulane, I received several awards and fellowships from the School of Liberal Arts that enabled the beginning of this research. I am especially grateful to the administrators of the Tulane/Free University Berlin exchange program, who granted me a year of archival work in Berlin.

Outside of New Orleans, my interviewees generously gave their time and materials as I sought to chronicle life for jazz fans in the GDR. They supplied memories, material, advice, contacts, and even friendship. My thanks to the following: Karlheinz Drechsel and his wife, Annemarie; Ulf Drechsel; Gerhard Hopfe; Renate Heinicke; Herbert Flügge; Walter Cikan; Rainer Haarmann; Rolf Reichelt; Helmut Eickermann; Klaus Schneider; Erhard Kayser; and the late Alfons Wonneberg, Roland Mooshammer, Martin Linzer, and Klaus Jürgen Heinicke. I would also like to thank Volkmar Andrä, Konrad Bauer, Ulrich Blobel, Rainer Bratfisch, Matthias Brüll, Katja Deim, Jost Gebers, Wolf Glöde, Josef Graczynski, Ulrich Gumpert, Reinhard Heinemann, Günter Heinz, Ruth Hohmann, Jürgen Laartz, Theo Lehmann, Klaus Lenz, Meinhardt Lüning, Bert Noglik, Vera Oelschlegel, Jürgen Schitthelm, Friedhelm Schönfeld, Jürgen Schweinebraden, Gabriele Staamann, Gerhard Steincke, and Jörg Stempel.

Much of this research came from materials in archives across Germany, and I am deeply thankful to staff at the following institutions: Anouk Jeschke (Academy of the Arts, Berlin), Sylvia Gräfe (Foundation Archives of Parties and Mass Organizations of the GDR in the Federal Archives, Berlin-Lichterfelde), Lars Amelung (Federal Archive, Koblenz), and Maya Buchholz (Film Archive of the Bundesarchiv Berlin-Lichterfelde). I am particularly grateful to Ursula Jaensch and Raphela Schröder, Federal Commissioners of the Records of State Security Service of the former German Democratic Republic (BStU, Berlin), for their help throughout this research. My thanks as well to the staff at the German Broadcast Archive, the Library of Humboldt University, the Library of the Freie University, and the City Library, all in Berlin.

Lastly, I am grateful to my family, more than I can say. My husband Sanford Hinderlie, a marvelous jazz composer and musician himself, not only endured countless late nights working, but also accompanied me through my many research trips abroad, serving in more roles than I can name and making this research possible in ways both large and small. My family in Germany have all been wonderful sources of encouragement and support throughout this long process. I could not have told this story without their love and support.

Chronology

1918	End of WWI, German Reich becomes a republic
1920s	Jazz dance guide published in Berlin, performances by Josephine Baker, Paul Whiteman, and others, including the premiere of *Jonny spielt auf*
1933	Nazi rise to power
1938	Degenerate Music (*Entartete Musik*) exhibition in Düsseldorf
1939	Germany invades Poland, beginning of WWII
May 1945	Germany surrenders to the Soviet and Western Allies
June 1945	American delegation arrives in Berlin
February 1946	First US Information Center (*Amerikahaus*) opens at Kleiststraße
March 1946	Founding of the Free German Youth (*Freie Deutsche Jugend*)
April 1946	Founding of the German Youth Activities program
August 1946	Soviet military administration founds Lied der Zeit publishing company
February 1947	Soviet House of Culture opens at the Palais am Festungsgraben
March 1947	Lied der Zeit establishes Amiga and Eterna labels
1948	Soviets leave the Allied Control Council; Soviet Military Administration (SMAD) prohibits swing circle gatherings; Hanns Eisler returns to Berlin
1948–1949	Berlin Blockade and the Berlin Airlift; Rex Stewart's performance in Berlin
June 1948	Currency Reform
July 1949	Walter Ulbricht becomes Central Committee (ZK) General Secretary

August 1949	First elections of the Federal German Parliament
September 1949	Founding of the Federal Republic of Germany (West Germany)
October 1949	Founding of the German Democratic Republic (East Germany)
1951	Fifth annual meeting of the ZK; founding of State Commission for the Arts, *Staatliche Kommission für Kunstangelegenheiten* (STAKOKU)
March 1953	Joseph Stalin dies
June 1953	Workers' revolts in many East German cities
April 1956	IV Jugendforum in Treptow
August 1956	Premiere of *Vom Lebensweg des Jazz* at Leipzig Fair
1958	Berlin Crisis begins; Soviet premier Nikita Khrushchev demands the withdrawal of Western troops from West Berlin
December 1958	STASI recruits Werner Sellhorn as an informant
1959	First Bitterfeld Conference
August 1961	Berlin Wall constructed
December 1961	ZK Jazz Resolution developed and issued
1962	Jazz lift by Erhard Kayser, delivering records to East Berlin
March–April 1965	Louis Armstrong tours the GDR
December 1965	Eleventh Plenum of the ZK
1967	Student uprisings in West Berlin triggered by murder of Benno Ohnesorg
1968	First Total Music Meeting in West Berlin
1971	First Dixieland Festival in Dresden; Erich Honecker succeeds Ulbricht as first General Secretary of the ZK
1973	Both East and West Germany join the United Nations as full members
	Release of LP *Just for Fun* by E.L. Petrowsky Quartett (FMP, West Berlin)
June 1973	First jazz workshop (*Jazzwerkstatt*) in Peitz
1974	Both East and West Germany establish permanent representations in each other's capital cities
1976	First Leipziger Jazztage
1978	Committee for Entertaining Arts (KfU) founds jazz committee

1979	Jazz Now Concert Series, East German Musicians perform at Akademie der Künste in West Berlin
Early 1980s	Economic situation in Eastern BLOC deteriorates
1980	Release of LP *Touch the Earth* (FMP, West Berlin) featuring East and West German musicians
1985	Mikhail Gorbachev becomes General Secretary of the Communist Party of the Soviet Union
1985	First Weimar Jazz Festival; founding of the National Jazz Orchestra
October 1989	Demonstrations in Leipzig
November 1989	Fall of the Wall
December 1989	Second Weimar Jazz Festival (largely unattended)

Abbreviations

ADK	Academy of the Arts, *Akademie der Künste* (DDR)
AFJ	Anti-fascist Youth Organization, *Antifaschistische Jugend*
AGITPROP	Agitation and Propaganda Commission of the Central Committee
BMiB	Federal Ministry for Intra-German Relations, *Bundesministerium für innerdeutsche Beziehungen* (West German)
BRD	*Bundesrepublik Deutschland*, West Germany, Federal German Republic (English acronym: FGR)
BZA	*Berliner Zeitung am Abend* (newspaper)
COMINTERN	Communist International, *Kommunistische Internationale*
CPUSA	Communist Party of the United States of America
DDR	*Deutsche Demokratische Republik*, East Germany, German Democratic Republic (1949–1990) (English acronym: GDR)
DIAS	Wire Broadcast in the American Sector, *Drahtfunk im Amerikanischen Sektor*
DJF	German Jazz Federation, *Deutsche Jazz Föderation* (West Germany)
DS	Writers Association, *Deutscher Schriftstellerverband*
DSF	House of the German–Soviet Friendship, *Haus der deutsch-sowjetischen Freundschaft*
EUCOM	United States European Command
FMP	Free Music Productions (West Germany)
GDR	East Germany (1949–1990) or German Democratic Republic, *Deutsche Demokratische Republik*

GYA	German Youth Activities, program of United States Armed Forces
FDJ	Free German Youth, *Freie Deutsche Jugend*
FGR	Federal German Republic, *Bundesrepublik Deutschland* (BRD) West Germany
ICS	Information Control Service (United States)
JCL	Jazz Club Leipzig
KB	Cultural Alliance, *Kulturbund*
KfU	Committee for the Entertaining Arts, *Komitee für Unterhaltungskunst*
KGD	Agency for Concerts and Touring, *Konzert- und Gastspieldirektion*
KPD	Communist Party of Germany, *Kommunistische Partei Deutschlands*
LDZ	Lied der Zeit
MfK	Ministry for Culture, Ministerium für Kultur
MfS	Ministry for State Security, *Ministerium für Staatssicherheit*
NJCB	New Jazz Circle Berlin (West Germany)
NSDAP	Nationalsozialistsche Arbeiterpartei Deutschlands
RIAS	Radio in the American Sector, *Rundfunk im Amerikanischen Sektor*
SBZ	Soviet Occupation Zone [of Berlin], *Sowjetische Besatzungszone*
SED	Socialist Unity Party, *Sozialistische Einheitspartei Deutschlands*
SFB	Radio Free Berlin, *Sender Freies Berlin* (West Berlin)
SMAD	Soviet Military Administration, *Sowjetische Militäradministration*
SPD	Social Democratic Party, *Sozialdemokratische Partei Deutschlands* (West Germany)
STAKOKU	State Commission for the Arts, *Staatliche Kommission für Kunstangelegenheiten*
STASI	*Staatssicherheit*
STÄV	Permanent Representation of the Federal Republic of Germany, *Ständige Vertretung der Bundesrepublik* (West German entity located in East Berlin)
URANIA	Society for the Publication of Scientific Knowledge, *Gesellschaft zur Verbreitung wissenschaftlicher Erkenntnisse*

USIC   United States Information Center, informally *Amerikahaus*

VDK   Association of German Composers and Musicologists, *Verband Deutscher Komponisten und Musikwissenschaftler*

ZK   Central Committee of the SED, *Zentralkomitee der SED*

ZKM   Central Commission for Music at the Cultural Alliance, *Zentrale Kommission für Musik beim Kulturbund*

CHAPTER I

Jazz in Weimar and Nazi Germany, 1918–1945

Introduction

Just as many different musical cultures gave birth to jazz in the early twentieth century, the emergence of jazz had a reciprocal impact on musical cultures across the world. This was as true of Germany in the 1920s and 1930s, key years for the growth and development of jazz, as it was of anywhere else in the West. To understand the impact of jazz during those decades, it is necessary to begin this inquiry in the politically turbulent, yet culturally creative, Weimar era – an era that was scarred by the traumas of conflict, revolution, inflation, and political fragmentation. One way to enter this time period is alongside someone who experienced it firsthand, Erika Mann, the daughter of novelist Thomas Mann, recalled the following about the era:

> After the War, there was deep disillusionment everywhere, and a nihilism created by this disillusionment. Everyone felt like they had been cheated. Young people everywhere sought compensation for the hardships of the "great times" that had just passed. Everywhere they immersed themselves in violent pleasures and excesses. New and wild music coming from America was intoxicating, but it was no longer intoxication for a "cause" (as, for instance, patriotic fervor for "the fatherland"). It was intoxication without reason, for no cause at all. In order to intensify it, all methods were allowed: music, alcohol, marijuana, morphine, and cocaine. In the back rooms of Berlin's nightclubs, narcotics were sold just like in the harbor salons of Marseille or in the nightclubs of Harlem. The "inflation-devaluation" of monetary values that took place in Germany and France alike had its moral equivalent in all countries after the War. Suddenly anything and everything was permissible. ... Girls wore skirts that showed their knees if they preferred not to dress like young men in the evening. It was considered chic to be erotically perverted, to have just some slight peculiarity. But most of all, it was considered foolish, if not indecent, to believe in something, in *anything*. "We had been so terribly cheated by this

War," young men all over the world cried out. "From now on, we just won't believe in anything." And they were proud of their nihilism. That was the atmosphere of the twenties.[1]

The experience of war and the collapse of the German monarchy demystified familial and state authorities, causing a radical break with Wilhelmine values and social norms. Young people abandoned the beliefs of previous generations and entered a time of moral, emotional, and spiritual vacuum. Renouncing traditional roles in society and the life of restraint and obedience, this generation openly demonstrated their indulgence in unconventional pleasures: the deaths of millions caused a hunger for life, in which any stimulation was welcome. At this key moment, this "wild new music" arriving from the United States met fertile ground. Reading Mann, this music – jazz – appears to have been perfectly compatible with "intoxication without reason" or with the willingness to abandon oneself. Jazz had the power to transcend the "old times," for its content had no links to the past. As such, this new genre presented something unheard of in European musical traditions, carrying zero historical baggage, for the culture of jazz offered an antithesis to the militaristic demeanor and Wilhelmine respectability found in Prussian marches, a sound that had once filled the streets of imperial Berlin. By the 1920s, this aesthetic revolution had discarded the old musical system and its heartbeat of collective obedience; instead, the ease and lightness of syncopated rhythms became the predominant feature of musical entertainment.[2]

Like Mann, the journalist Hans Siemsen also described the narcotic effect of jazz in the era. Recollecting pre-war encounters in Paris, he wrote in 1921 that "This music, with its irrational rhythms, has the same effect as drugs and alcohol." In his words:

> Jazz has another likable characteristic: it has absolutely no dignity. It defeats any attempt at comportment, correct posture, edginess, [or] the stiff-collar. No one who is afraid of making fun of themselves can dance jazz. The schoolmaster can't dance it. The Prussian reserve officer can't dance it.

---

[1] Erika Mann, "Don't make the same mistakes," in *Zero Hour, A Summons to the Free*, ed. Vincent Benet, Erika Mann, and McGeorge Bundy (New York, Toronto: Farrar & Rinehart, 1940), 25–26.

[2] By the mid-1920s, syncopated rhythms dominated "entertaining music" (*Unterhaltungsmusik*). Cf. Peter Jelavich, *Berlin Cabaret*, Studies in Cultural History (Cambridge, Mass.: Harvard University Press, 1993). Cornelius Partsch, *Schräge Töne: Jazz und Unterhaltungsmusik in der Kultur der Weimarer Republik*, M & P Schriftenreihe für Wissenschaft und Forschung (Stuttgart: J. B. Metzler, 2000).

If only all ministers, privy councilors, professors, and politicians were obliged to dance jazz in public! How cheerfully they would shed their dignity. How human, how jolly, how comical they would be!...If the Kaiser had danced jazz, none of this ever would have happened. It's too bad he never learned it. It is easier to be the German Kaiser than to dance jazz.[3]

Recalling his experience of a jazz performance, with its humorous and seemingly outrageous approach, Siemsen praised the absence of Wilhelmine demeanor as one of jazz's finest qualities. Indeed, throughout the 1920s, critics praised jazz as an American element of renewal within European musical traditions. After the critic Frank Warschauer heard Paul Whiteman's Symphonic Jazz Orchestra, he gushed that "jazz is the most entertaining and vital phenomenon in contemporary music... jazz filled with the youthful energy of America, it is the pregnant outburst of a changed, optimistic feel for life, and it sings a different *Lied von der Erde*, the song of a new generation."[4] In his review, Warschauer contrasted jazz's vitality as a refreshing impulse to "old" Europe's music, here exemplified by the composition of Gustav Mahler. This motif of rejuvenation permeated the positive jazz reception. But while some critics greeted and appreciated the music of a "new generation," others regarded the transnational and transracial music as an intrusion into German musical culture.

Prior to detailing the history of jazz in the German Democratic Republic (GDR), this chapter outlines the trajectory of jazz before the founding of the GDR, from the Weimar era in the 1920s until the end of the Nazi regime in 1945. The way in which jazz met fascination on the one hand and disapproval and revulsion on the other reflects the spectrum of the ideological paradigms of this period, which makes a closer look at the German jazz experience prior to 1945 essential for understanding the history of jazz in communist East Germany. In this chapter, Section One ("Jazz in a Defeated Nation") explores the defeated former German Empire's first encounters with jazz, and Section Two ("Americanization and the Crisis of Culture") illustrates the music's controversial reception within the cultural criticism of the Weimar era. Section Three ("Cultural Identity and *Bildungsbürgertum*") explains the anxieties of the bourgeoisie

---

[3] Hans Siemsen, "Jazzband," *Die Weltbühne*, 1921, 278–79, 17. Jahrgang, erstes Halbjahr.
[4] Martin Jay Anton Kaes and Edward Dimendberg, *The Weimar Republic Sourcebook* (Berkeley: University of California Press, 1994), 571. Warschauer draws an analogy with Gustav Mahler's composition *Lied von der Erde* to allude to the music of the late-romantic period as the music of "Old Europe."

that most strongly identified with German musical traditions, traditions they felt that jazz violated. Then, moving forward into the wartime years, Section Four ("National Socialism, War, and Defeat (1933–1945)") explores the ambiguous, and at times contradictory, relationship of the Nazi state to jazz as a component of popular culture.

Jazz in a Defeated Nation

While one might assume that cultural life in Germany was characterized by isolation, alienation, and stagnation after the nation's defeat in WWI, the reality is far more complicated. In the immediate post-war period, Berlin's entertainment industry was eager to connect with international trends, not least because of the massive influx of foreign visitors. The capital of the former Wilhelmine Empire, which once centralized the powers that threatened the world, was of great global interest after the defeat of imperial Germany. Historian Wolfgang Schivelbusch has compared Berlin after WWI with Paris after the fall of Napoleon, arguing that both cities in their eras became a "mecca of civilization."[5] Even before the WWI, Berlin had flourished as a metropolis of international standards, offering an abundance of venues for entertainment: dozens of theaters, variety houses, and cabarets that increasingly competed with hundreds of movie theaters. The expansion in this sector was complemented by growth in Berlin's gastronomic life, with the city offering thousands of restaurants, cafés, and bars to ravenous patrons. Nor did defeat in the war curtail Berlin's nightlife, as it continued to offer everything nearby London and Paris had as well, and its restrictions on public entertainment were loosened by the abolition of preliminary censorship.[6] Visitors from the United States, France, and Great Britain flocked to the city for its culture, with sharp increases in tourism by the mid-1920s.[7]

In his recent book, *The Jazz Republic*, historian Jonathan Wipplinger has argued that there is no "singular genealogy of jazz" in the Weimar Republic.[8] Examining the years 1919–21, he has argued for a distinction

---

[5] Wolfgang Schivelbusch, *Die Kultur der Niederlage: Der amerikanische Süden 1865, Frankreich 1871, Deutschland 1918*, Erw. Lizenzausg. ed. (Frankfurt a. M.: Fischer-Taschenbuch-Verl., 2003).

[6] Jelavich, *Berlin Cabaret*, 154. Cf. also Ute Scheub, *Verrückt nach Leben* (Hamburg: Rohwolt, 2000).

[7] Michael H. Kater, *Different Drummers: Jazz in the Culture of Nazi Germany* (New York: Oxford University Press, 1992).

[8] Jonathan Wipplinger, *The Jazz Republic: Music, Race, and American Culture in Weimar Germany*, Social History, Popular Culture, and Politics in Germany (Ann Arbor: University of Michigan Press, 2017), 22.

between the situation in Berlin and occupied zones along the Rhine River, as well as against other cities such as Cologne, Bonn, Koblenz, and Wiesbaden. He stated that "though the word jazz enters simultaneously in Berlin and in the zones of occupation, Weimar jazz culture proceeds initially at least along slightly different paths within these two spaces with the greater contact with foreign citizens, soldiers and musicians more quickly producing encounters with jazz bands than in Berlin."[9] Aiding this outward spread was the fact that the emergence of jazz coincided with the invention of the technical reproduction of sound. For the first time in history, music was able to reach a large number of people in different places at once via modern recording technology. The conservation of sound was essential for the dissemination of jazz and made the genre available to audiences in disparate geographies, as well as across disparate borders of nationhood, class, and race.[10]

Jazz entered Berlin first as a dance around 1919, launching a post-war dance craze given that dancing had been prohibited during the years of the war. To ensure Germans were ready for the trend, a guide to new dance styles, *Jazz und Shimmy: Brevier der neuesten Tänze*, promised to prepare local enthusiasts for jazz. This guide, published in 1920, claimed that jazz had come to Berlin via Paris and, ever since, jazz enthusiasm had reached epidemic scale. In his introduction to the publication, the editor furthermore expressed his concern that Germans were falling behind international standards but that the *Brevier* would provide the remedy.[11] The guide consisted of three main aspects: giving step-by-step instructions for different styles, explaining the terminology involved, and citing both positive and negative opinions on the genre. Interestingly, not only did this text quote Siemsen's article, but it also suggested that jazz was a genre whose dances were, in large part, subject to individual, personal interpretation.

Despite such instructional texts, strict definitions of jazz in this time can be elusive, but contemporary accounts describing early German jazz

---

[9] Ibid., 30–31.

[10] As the historian Thomas J. Saunders has argued, "It was the interwar years that witnessed the convergence of the media which made music as ubiquitous as print or still photography or the moving picture." See Thomas J. Saunders, "The Jazz Age," in *A Companion to Europe, 1900–1945*, ed. Gordon Martel (Malden, Mass.; Oxford: Blackwell Pub., 2006), 352. In the United States, the first jazz record – *Tiger Rag* by the Original Dixieland Jazz Band – was released in 1917, selling over one million copies worldwide and establishing the term "jazz" in the public lexicon. See Scott DeVeaux and Gary Giddens, *Jazz*, 2015 ed. (New York and London: W.W. Norton & Company, 2009).

[11] F.W. Koebner, ed., *Jazz und Shimmy: Brevier der neuesten Tänze* (Berlin: Dr. Eysler und Co., 1921), 4.

bands identify rhythm and spontaneity as predominant features, imitating the original American styles of the early 1920s. In the absence of adequate equipment, rhythm was produced by beating on a variety of obscure instruments such as bells, tin cans, or any object able to produce loud and pervasive sounds. Indeed, according to some accounts, the mere presence of a bass drum seemed to have certified musical ensembles as operating jazz bands.[12] Such imaginings of jazz culture not only made it interchangeable with earlier representations of African American music in Germany such as ragtime and minstrelsy, but also created a demand for the clownesque and grotesque, reminiscent of vaudeville entertainment.[13] To convey the impression of spontaneity, trained musicians concealed their sight-reading abilities and shunned sheet music to demonstrate their skills of improvisation.[14] This eagerness to comply with the new fashion disclosed the willingness to break with musical traditions by rejecting dictation, discarding the mere disciplined reproduction of notated music in corporate settings – again, all vestiges of the Wilhelmine era.

Berlin swiftly became a magnet for the international jazz scene. By the mid-1920s, foreign jazz musicians found a lucrative market in Germany because of its new, stable currency, the *Rentenmark* introduced in 1923. The opportunity to experience jazz of international provenance also drew many German jazz players to the capital, which soon elevated Berlin into Germany's first city of jazz.[15] Here, fans could hear African American pianist Sam Wooding and his orchestra, for instance, accompanying the Chocolate Kiddies Negro Revue in the Admirals Pallast in May 1925.[16] Jazz icon Josephine Baker first performed on New Year's Eve in 1925 on Kurfürstendamm, and the Englishman Jack Hylton's Big Band became popular and remained so well into the 1930s.[17] Paul Whiteman had introduced symphonic jazz with Gershwin's *Rhapsody in Blue*, touring Berlin

---

[12] Horst H. Lange, *Jazz in Deutschland* (Berlin: Colloquium, 1966).

[13] Rainer E. Lotz, *Black People: Entertainers of African Descent in Europe and Germany*, Limited ed. (Bonn: Birgit Lotz Verlag, 1997).

[14] Heinz Pollack, *Die Revolutions des Gesellschaftstanzes* (Dresden: Sibyllen, 1922).

[15] Cf. Kater, *Different Drummers*. Partsch, *Schräge Töne*. Jonathan Wipplinger, *The Jazz Republic: Music, Race, and American Culture in Weimar Germany* (Ann Arbor: University of Michigan Press, 2006).

[16] Martin Lücke, *Jazz im Totalitarismus*, Populäre Musik und Jazz in der Forschung (Münster: Lit Verlag, 2004), 53. See also Jonathan Wipplinger, "The Aural Shock of Modernity: Weimar's Experience of Jazz," *The Germanic Review* 82 (4) (2007): 309.

[17] For an excellent analysis of Baker's reception in Berlin, see Nancy Nenno, "Feminity, the Primitive, and Modern Urban Space: Josephine Baker in Berlin," in *Women in the Metropolis: Gender and Modernity in Weimar Culture*, ed. Katharina von Ankum (Berkeley: University of California Press, 1997).

Figure 1.1   Rehearsal of the jazz band Weintraub's Syncopators with ballet in Berlin. From *ullstein bild* via Getty Images. Editorial #549701947

in 1926.[18] In this environment, German ensembles such as the Weintraub Syncopators, who were featured in the film *Der blaue Engel* with Marlene Dietrich, directly emulated American jazz music and adopted its iconography (Figure 1.1).

In these years, the "hyperactive Weimar media" and entertainment industry propelled jazz into a catch-all buzzword, laden with images of free-swinging American lifestyles.[19] In its so-called golden years, the term "jazz" was associated with a wide range of musical offerings from American popular music, including the work of Paul Whiteman's symphonic jazz, the hot "jazz" of Louis Armstrong, and even that of the Guy Lombardi Orchestra, famed for its "sweet," slow, muted dances.[20] Whatever the public conception of the music had been in its early years, by the mid-1920s the wide array of offerings under the umbrella term "jazz" had led musical

[18] Cf. Joshua Berrett, *Louis Armstrong & Paul Whiteman: Two Kings of Jazz* (New Haven, Conn.; London: Yale University Press, 2004).
[19] Cf. J. Bradford Robinson, "Jazz Reception in Weimar Germany," in *Music and Performance during the Weimar Republic*, ed. Bryan Randolph Gilliam (Cambridge University Press, 1994).
[20] Lange, *Jazz in Deutschland*, 35.

qualities such as syncopated rhythms to dominate popular music. This aspect alone sharply differentiated it from nineteenth-century traditions. As one observer noted in 1926: "Just as operetta is defined musically by the three-quarter time of the waltz, the revue is characterized by two-quarter time, and more precisely by syncopation. A revue without syncopation seems almost unthinkable to us today."[21] Composer Kurt Weil made the same observation, noting: "A gaze into the dance culture demonstrates that jazz is an expression of our times, just as the waltz was for the late nineteenth century."[22] Critically, syncopated rhythms became synonymous with the music of a new age, a linkage that remained throughout the 1930s and 1940s. But this linkage would bring with it a particular kind of baggage: the notion of a non-European, transracial music ignited fierce controversy in listeners and critics, stirring fears of Americanization and the decline of German culture. As detailed in the next section, such friction would set the stage for the recruitment of jazz as well as its politicization throughout the following decades.

Americanization and the Crisis of Culture

As noted above, in the post-WWI era, America permeated the imagination of Weimar Germany. Images of United States offered connotations of lands of boundless opportunity, industries boasting modern innovation and efficiency, developments in the arts and culture, and burgeoning economic and technological strength. Such visions served as the antipode to the traditional European, agricultural, hierarchically organized society.[23] As historian Detlev Peukert has explained, "After the defeat in the war and more especially after the achievement of economic and political stability under the aegis of the United States in 1924, a mythicized version of America that had already been gaining currency in the earlier years of the century now emerged as a symbol of modernity."[24] America's function as a role model in the Weimar imagination thus provided fertile ground for the reception of many American cultural styles, jazz included. As the scholar Thomas Saunders has noted of the era, "Whether one refers to

---

[21] Jelavich, *Berlin Cabaret*, 169.

[22] Kim Kowalke, *Kurt Weil in Europe, 1900–1935* (Ann Arbor: University of Michigan Press, 1979), 95.

[23] Cf. Detlev Peukert, *The Weimar Republic: The Crisis of Classical Modernity*, 1st American ed. (New York: Hill and Wang, 1992); Adelheid von Saldern, "Überfremdungsängste," in *Amerikanisierung: Traum und Alptraum im Deutschland des 20. Jahrhunderts*, ed. Alf Lüdtke, Inge Marssolek, and Adelheid von Saldern (Stuttgart: F. Steiner Verlag, 1996).

[24] Peukert, *Weimar Republic*, 179.

clothing and hairstyles, music and dance, or media and advertising, America figures as the primary foreign element in Germany's development."[25] Yet such images provoked ambivalent and contradictory responses, leading to heated debates about the Americanization of Germany.[26] Peukert has suggested that the discourse about Germany's Americanization was "heterogeneous and inconsistent," for it was not a simple question of for or against changes of modern life. Rather, on this view, "America served as a mirror for Germany's own transformation to modernity," negotiating a complex web of embrace and rejection and representing a specific version of modernity already apparent in Germany.[27] Yet during the crisis-stricken interwar years, Peukert admits that such debates on modernity and modernization became "both more intense and ironically more inconclusive."[28] Within this discourse the term "jazz" served both to represent a general youth culture that defied Wilhelmine values and to enable a rhetoric ostracizing of this "intruder" in derogatory racist, anti-Semitic, anti-socialist, and anti-capitalist terms. This was not limited to hard-line reactionary voices. On the contrary, in the 1920s and 1930s, the moderate bourgeoisie engaged in a vigorous campaign against jazz in all its variations, reflecting the anxieties engendered by Germany's transformation into a twentieth-century modern society. To give but one example, the affinity of urban youth for jazz worried one Protestant clerical educator, Günter Dehn:

> Earning money and enjoying themselves are the twin poles of their existence, their enjoyments taking in both the high-minded and the squalid: primitive sexuality and jazz.... The nation's thinking has become indeed Americanized, through and through, ... it is not socialism but Americanism that will be the end of everything.[29]

In Dehn's view, Americanization had become the predominant ideology of Germany's youth, which he assessed as a greater threat than socialism. The emancipation of women, the rising acceptance of sexual freedom, trends toward secularization, increased mobility among economic classes, and the

---

[25] Thomas J. Saunders, "How American Was It? Popular Culture from Weimar to Hitler," in *German Pop Culture: How "American" Is It?*, ed. Agnes C. Mueller (Ann Arbor: University of Michigan Press, 2004), 352.

[26] See Mary Nolan, *Visions of Modernity: American Business and the Modernization of Germany* (New York: Oxford University Press, 1994). As well as Frank Trommler and Joseph McVeigh, *America and the Germans: An Assessment of a Three-Hundred-Year History*, 2 vols. (Philadelphia: University of Pennsylvania Press, 1985). Cf. also Anton Kaes.

[27] Peukert, *Weimar Republic*, 179.

[28] Ibid.

[29] Günter Dehn, *Proletarische Jugend*, Berlin, 1929. As cited in: Peukert, *The Weimar Republic*, 178.

culture of leisure were all blamed on America's influence and particularly
on jazz, commonly juxtaposed with the term "primitive sexuality."

While some critics decried modern lifestyles – and its emblem, jazz – as
a negative influence on German youth, others voiced their fierce opposition against jazz's intrusion into the realm of highbrow culture. For in the
1920s, jazz did not just enter saloons and barrooms, but instead entered
operas, concert halls, and institutions of higher education. Between 1927
and 1930, a new genre of opera, *Zeitoper* (contemporary opera of the time),
competed with traditional ones and incorporated attributes of modern life
such as new technologies and jazz elements.[30] One of the most successful works was Ernst Křenek's *Jonny spielt auf,* which thrived on German
stages as a "jazz" opera. One of the reasons for *Jonny's* success was that
it touched the nerve of contemporary debates about the transnational,
transracial impacts on European music by presenting a story of conflict
between an African American and a European musician. Furthermore,
the set for the opera presented up-to-date, modern technology such as
loudspeakers and film projection. Music critics were outraged – the opera's
enormous popularity seemed to confirm the scenarios of cultural demise
recently promulgated by Oswald Spengler, in his famous *The Decline of
The West* – leading right-wing organizations to instrumentalize fears of
the alleged decline of German operatic culture.[31]

This tension manifested in other ways as well. When the American
conductor Paul Whiteman introduced crossover experiments between
jazz and orchestral sound in Berlin in 1926, his performances ignited
further controversy.[32] Whiteman disconnected jazz from dance halls
and reintroduced it into a concert-hall setting, thereby violating a space
reserved undisputedly for highbrow nineteenth-century orchestral works.
The legendary Aeolian Hall concert in 1923, premiering Gershwin's
Rhapsody in Blue, was described as "an experiment in modern music"
and attempted to bridge modern genres with the classics. Yet the idea of
connecting tradition to modernity by fusing symphonic sound and jazz
kicked off a firestorm: critics denounced Whiteman's experiment for a
variety of reasons, not least because jazz was seen as intruding into the
stronghold of Germanic orchestral music.[33]

---

[30] Cf. Susan C. Cook, *Opera for a New Republic: The Zeitopern of Krenek, Weill, and Hindemith*
(Ann Arbor: University of Michigan Press, 1988).
[31] Eckhard John, *Musikbolschewismus: Die Politisierung der Musik in Deutschland, 1918–1938*
(Metzler, 1994), 295–303.
[32] Cf. Berrett, *Louis Armstrong & Paul Whiteman.* For Whiteman's performance in Berlin, see
Wipplinger, *The Jazz Republic,* 93.
[33] *The Jazz Republic: Music, Race, and American Culture in Weimar Germany,* 86–102.

Moreover in 1927, Bernhard Sekles, director of the Hoch Conservatory in Frankfurt, introduced jazz as part of the academic program, triggering a storm of indignation and igniting smoldering debates about the relationship between music and race as well as the division between high and low culture.[34] The outrage reached a climax when the Pilgrim's Chorus of Wagner's *Tannhäuser* resounded in syncopated rhythms.[35] Remarkably, the magazines *Zeitschrift für Musik* and the *Allgemeine Musik-Zeitung* called for government intervention in the institution.[36] Many writers – among them the theorist and critic Theodor Adorno – denounced such handling as disrespectful, trumpeting their outrage at hearing Wagner's and Beethoven's themes as "jazzed up" alterations.[37] According to Adorno and others, what Siemsen had once called the "amicable character" of jazz here destroyed the music's sacral solemnity and mythic grandeur, its syncopation distorting the carefully composed emotional structure of the music. Jazz arrangements thus deceived an expected musical experience, violated cultural hierarchies, and demystified the revered classics – a sentiment that, as described in later chapters, would prevail for many decades. For just these reasons in the 1950s the East German jazz band Melodia Rhythmiker were denied the chance to record a bebop arrangement of Bizet's *L'Arlésienne Suite* for Radio Leipzig.[38] Also in the late 1960s, East German officials denounced the French vocalists the Swingle Singers due to their scatted versions of J. S. Bach's fugues.[39]

In dialogue with these developments, Theodor Adorno provided one of the first sociological analyses of jazz (namely early jazz and swing), a position that would heavily influence later Marxist ideologues.[40] In his view,

---

[34] For more about the debate over Whiteman in the Weimar press, see ibid., 102–14.

[35] Peter Cahn, *Das Hoch'sche Konservatorium in Frankfurt am Main* (Frankfurt a. M.: Kramer, 1979), 262.

[36] John, *Musikbolschewismus*, 294.

[37] Theodor W. Adorno, *Abschied vom Jazz*, vol. Gesammelte Schriften, Band 18, Musikalische Schriften V (Frankfurt a. M.: Suhrkamp, 1933/1997–2003).

[38] Melodia Rhythmiker/Wolfgang Muth, "Letter from Gerhard Dopleb to Wolfgang Muth, December 22, 1988" (1980–1990).

[39] VI. Parteitag der SED. Cf. H.P. Hoffmann, "Unsere Kunst in der DDR," *Melodie und Rhythmus* (7/1967). A record of the Swingle Singers was released by the GDR label ETERNA (820596), which added to the controversy over the release. ETERNA only published so-called "classics," which in this case stoked the debate.

[40] Although theorists in the GDR had been aware of Adorno's anticapitalist view on jazz, his work was not directly referenced until later in East German jazz discourse given that he had distanced himself from Soviet Communism early on. For the inclusion of his ideas in East German discourse in the 1980s, see Bert Noglik, *"Rezeptionsästhetische Aspekte des zeitgenössischen Jazz"* in: Informationen der Generaldirektion für Unterhaltungskunst, 5/86, Beilage zur Zeitschrift "Unterhaltungskunst" Oktober 1986.

the function of music in capitalism was strictly that of a commodity whose value was dictated by the market, a dynamic that causes an estrangement between music and people.[41] In this account, musical production is split between the forms that submit to market rules and the forms that withdraw from them.[42] Adorno regarded twelve-tone music as the latter kind; however, jazz constituted the former kind alongside the genre of "easy listening" (*leichte Musik*), genres that are unable to accomplish genuine musical innovation.[43] In his largely dismissive view, Adorno rejected the notion that jazz had any regenerative effect on European music – suggesting instead that the jazz industry fed off the European classical tradition by emulating its creativity, such as harmonics within French expressionism.[44] To Adorno, jazz's improvisation and rhythmical complexity represented merely ornamental accessories functioning as embellishments upon simplistic patterns and primitive formulas.[45] As a result, listeners who were permanently exposed to such formulas would eventually lose their ability to realize and appreciate true innovation; indeed, Adorno doubted that "genuine" African American folk music, which may have harbored true artistry, had much in common with the popular genre marketed as jazz that audiences demanded.[46] In sum, while his conclusions were not universally accepted, Adorno's critique nevertheless anticipated ideas of later East German theorists, providing a key theoretical groundwork to discuss the authenticity and commercialization of the genre. As the next section details, this critique would echo the fears of the German bourgeoisie as the 1930s took shape, a decade that would witness increasing ambivalence to jazz.

Cultural Identity and *Bildungsbürgertum*

In general, the fear among the German bourgeoisie about the dilution of its culture by American influence stemmed from its long identification with its national musical heritage. As scholars such as Celia Applegate

---

[41] Theodor W. Adorno, *Zur gesellschaftlichen Lage der Musik*, vol. Gesammelte Schriften, Band 18, Musikalische Schriften V (Frankfurt a. M.: Suhrkamp, 1932/1997–2013), 729.

[42] Ibid., 733.

[43] Ibid., 734.

[44] Adorno, *Über Jazz*, vol. Gesammelte Schriften, Band 18 (Frankfurt a. M.: Suhrkamp, 1936/1997–2003), 82.

[45] *Zur gesellschaftlichen Lage der Musik*, Gesammelte Schriften, Band 18, Musikalische Schriften V, 774–75. In a later essay he elaborates on these ideas. See *On Popular Music*, ed. Max Horkheimer, vol. IX/1941, Zeitschrift für Sozialforschung (München: Kösel-Verlag, originally published by the Institute of Social Research, Morningside Heights, New York City, 1941, 1941/1970).

[46] *Über Jazz*, vol. Gesammelte Schriften Band 17, Musikalische Schriften IV (Frankfurt a. M.: Suhrkamp, 1936/1997–2003), 83.

and Pamela Potter have detailed, in the course of the nineteenth century no other art form had embodied what it meant to be German more than music.[47] Indeed, the notion that music was linked to German identity permeated the middle class in German-speaking countries long before the geopolitical manifestation of the German empire in the late 1800s. Even, and especially, after WWI – the revolution, inflation, and instability of the Weimar Republic – music in Germany remained its primary cultural capital, weathering upheaval and change and promoting eternal intellectual values. Unsurprisingly, such notions of German cultural hegemony also generated notions of superiority: on this view, an ideal German music contrasted with an inferior American music, nurturing binaries of the external and internal, the physical and metaphysical, and the body and spirit that permeated much of the anti-jazz discourse. As the historian Bernd Spohnheuer has suggested, German music contained a spiritual value absent in its American counterpart, which was seen as more commercially oriented. Popular music styles such as ragtime, foxtrot, and jazz allegedly lacked soul, with terms such as *seelenlos, ohne Seele,* and *entseelt* functioning as the dominant *leitmotifs.*[48]

At the time, the threat jazz posed to these "spiritual" dimensions of German music manifested primarily within the social groups that upheld such cultural values as *Bildung* (education). The *Bildungsbürgertum,* the educated bourgeoisie, feared the deterioration of its cultural capital and demonized American culture, not least because the bourgeois youth indulged in the jazz scene, ostensibly betraying their own origins. As Erika Mann – a member of the bourgeoisie herself – illustrated above, within the political and moral vacuum of the 1920s, German youth adapted to a culture that they saw not just as American but as modern and embraced the culture of the exotic or "primitive" racial Other. On this view, jazz as a hybrid music form projecting both primitivism and modernity served as a vehicle to oppose traditional nineteenth-century values, appealing to a new generation seeking to break radically with its past.[49]

---

[47] Celia Applegate and Pamela Maxine Potter, "Germans as the 'People of Music': Genealogy of an Identity," in *Music and German National Identity,* ed. Celia Applegate and Pamela Maxine Potter (University of Chicago Press, 2002).

[48] Bernd Sponheuer, "Reconstructing Ideal Types of the 'German' Music," ibid., ed. Celia Applegate and Pamela Maxine Potter, 37. See also Partsch, *Schräge Töne,* 69.

[49] For more on modernity and primitivism in jazz in Weimar-era popular culture, see Nenno, "Feminity, the Primitive, and Modern Urban Space."

If debates about jazz looked westward to America, they also looked eastward to newly communist Russia, emboldened and volatile after its violent revolution. In the second half of the 1920s, jazz debates engaged not only Americanism but also Bolshevism, which supports Peukert's claim that cultural criticism of the day grew both fiercer and more inconclusive, resulting in a space in which "real and imagined dangers became ever more indissolubly blurred."[50] In this domain, with respect to jazz, Americanism and Bolshevism became oddly compatible constructs, each evoking notions of the people's sovereignty in their own way. Jazz bands were simultaneously associated with democratic societies on the one hand and with socialist "collectives of artists," or "Kapellen-Kommunismus," on the other, showing to what extent political concerns permeated cultural discourses.[51] As later chapters detail in different ways, there was never a moment in East Germany's history wherein jazz was not a contentious musical form – jazz was always in some way political – but it is revealing to see here how early such associations began.

By the end of the 1920s, and especially after the world economic crisis that began in 1929, anti-jazz debates took on an increasingly anti-Semitic tone. In Germany, the ascendant National Socialist Party (NSDAP, Nationalsozialistische Arbeiterpartei Deutschlands) instrumentalized fears of cultural decline, blaming the commercial interests of Jewish impresarios and promoters for the popularity of jazz. By the end of the 20s, Nazi-organized anti-jazz agitation was in full swing. Performances of Ernst Křenek's popular jazz opera *Jonny spielt auf* provoked massive rightwing protest and propaganda efforts both in Germany and in neighboring Austria, and the star performer Josephine Baker, who had launched her sensational *La Revue Nègre* in Berlin just a few years earlier, encountered numerous disturbances during her shows in Berlin and other German cities from 1928 onward.[52] In Vienna, the National Socialists summoned citizens to mass demonstrations against such "Jewish-negro defilement."[53]

In 1930, a representative of the German Nationalist-Imperialist Party used revealing language in the Prussian state parliament during a debate on Weimar's politics of theater. The speaker, a member of the clergy,

[50] Peukert, *Weimar Republic*, 184.
[51] See John, *Musikbolschewismus*, 290. John's sources are: Alfred Baresel, *Das neue Jazzbuch* (Leipzig: Metzler, 1929); A. v. Gizycki-Arkadjew, *Glossen zur Jazzbandfrage*, in: Der Artist 46, 1928.
[52] Ean Wood, *The Josephine Baker Story* (London: Sanctuary, 2002), 151.
[53] Pamphlet of the National Socialist Workers Party of Great Germany, January 1928 in John, *Musikbolschewismus*, 300.

denounced the experimental Berlin Kroll Opera with its production of *Jonny* as part of a "conscious plan to destroy the Christian-German culture" of the country and suggested that a "Jewish-Negro era of Prussian art" had begun.[54] Granted, not all Germans who harbored nationalist political tendencies approved of the violent racist agitation of the Nazi stormtroopers, but for many, the protection of German cultural values still lay deep in their hearts. While examples in the era were frequent, one typical moment came at the Frankfurt international music exhibition in 1927, when, in his opening speech, foreign affairs minister (and former Reichskanzler) Gustav Stresemann denounced the predominance of jazz in popular music with its "negro rhythms" and instead demanded cultural internalization.[55] Moreover, by the late 1920s, nationalist parties as well as churches of both Protestant and Catholic denominations had organized societies for the protection of German culture amid political fragmentation and economic instability.[56] Bourgeois women, in particular, seemed fearful of cultural decline, founding such groups as the *Königin Louise Verein für Deutsche Kultur* and promoting a sentimental glorification of the previous "great era" of Germany. With Hitler's rise to power, these organizations consolidated under the Nazi-umbrella organization, "Battle League for German Culture" (*Kampfbund für Deutsche Kultur*).[57]

As a result of these changes in public opinion in the later Weimar years, it became increasingly difficult for African American performers to work in Germany.[58] The worldwide economic crisis and high unemployment bred resentment against non-German competitors among professional musicians, who demonstrated for their right to work.[59] In 1930, for the first time in their history, the National Socialists received enough votes to be able to participate in regional government, winning a majority of seats in the state of Thuringia. Once in power, the National Socialists issued anti-jazz policies denouncing "jazz bands and drum music, negro dances, negro songs, and negro works, [and] the glorification of Negro culture"

---

[54] Speech of Protestant clergyman Koch, DNVP, April 4, 1930. As cited in: John, *Musikbolschewismus: Deutschland, 1918–1938*, 277.

[55] *Frankfurter Zeitung*, June 12, 1927. As cited in: John, "Musikbolschewismus," 294–95.

[56] The nationalist Deutsche Nationale Volkspartei (DNVP) organized the *Schutzverein für die geistigen Güter Deutschlands*, while the Catholic and Protestant churches supported the *Deutscher Bund zum Schutz der abendländischen Kultur*. In 1933, these organizations were integrated into the National-Socialist *Kampfbund für deutsche Kultur*.

[57] John, *Musikbolschewismus*, 206–207.

[58] Horst Lange speaks of a 1932 decree of the government of Franz von Papen that prohibited all African Americans from performing. According to Martin Lücke there is no proof of such documents. Lücke, *Jazz im Totalitarismus*, 60–61.

[59] Ibid.

as a "slap in the face of the German sense of culture."[60] Commenting on this anti-jazz agitation, the satirical press published cartoons lampooning the Nazi approach. Indeed, in the final Weimar years, jazz had become a key target in the ideological power struggle, as Nazi propaganda posters from the 1930s further reveal (Figure 1.2). Such propaganda addressed the anxieties of a deeply unsettled, crisis-ridden society stirring fears of a communist revolution. Geared toward female voters who (as the message suggests) in the event of a communist revolution would ostensibly transform into comrades, the term *jazz* here stands for the threat of a Bolshevist society that entails racial impurity, secularism, and industrial anonymization. The false contrast of "Folksong or Jazz?" (*Volkslied oder Jazz?*) could not have expressed the anti-jazz position, nor its propagandistic value, more clearly. As the next section details, in subsequent years, Nazi propaganda would continue to portray Hitler's party as the defender of German culture, ostracizing anything deemed to be non-German and targeting the problematic question of jazz in youth culture in particular.

National Socialism, War, and Defeat (1933–1945)

Swift though it was, the demise of the Weimar Republic in 1933 was the product of multiple causes. The historian Detlev Peukert has distinguished four separate processes leading to its collapse: first, the economic destabilization of hyperinflation in 1923 and the subsequent world economic crisis in 1929; second, the gradual loss of political legitimacy during the 1920s; third, the reversion to authoritarianism during that same time; and fourth, the support of elite representatives who ultimately gave Adolf Hitler the chance "of translating the destructive dynamism of the National Socialist Movement into the seizure of power."[61] Two months after Hitler's appointment as Chancellor in January 1933, the Reichstag approved an Enabling Act, which gave him the legal basis to centralize power under the leadership of the National Socialists. Over the following months, the National Socialists set to work both eliminating their political enemies and implementing racist policies.

Amid this consolidation of power, the arts played a central role in Nazi cultural politics. Nazi propaganda saw music as a vital part of representing the state's cultural legitimacy and preserving a common German heritage

---

[60] Amtsblatt des Thüringischen Ministeriums für Volksbildung, April 22, 1930. As cited in: John, "Musikbolschewismus," 303.

[61] Peukert, *Weimar Republic*, 266–67.

Figure 1.2   National Socialist propaganda, *Der Rote Krieg*, ca. 1930. "The Red War:
Mother or comrade? Human or machine? God or devil? Blood or gold? Race or
crossbreed? Folk song or jazz? National Socialism or Bolshevism?" From Bundesarchiv,
Plak 002-038-011

against everything that was seen as non-German. Yet the Nazi state's relationship toward jazz was ambiguous. Nazi Germany aimed to present itself as a modern state that appealed to the youth, and therefore did not pursue an overall restriction of popular music. Moreover, anti-jazz policies faced the problem of the lack of a precise definition of the genre. To be sure, Nazi policy aimed to whitewash jazz by trying to erase its African American element, and in March 1933, a Berlin broadcasting official announced new restrictions by simply declaring that African American roots would no longer play a role in modern dance music.[62] Such restrictions prompted Adorno to publish an essay entitled "Farewell to Jazz" in which he announced its demise, arguing that such policies only formally sanctioned what was with respect to general musical trends already consummated.[63] He again denounced jazz as "an expression of wretchedness of fabricated music" and suggested that the music's commercialization had estranged it from "real black music" (*echter Negermusik*). Furthermore – in contradiction to later theorists who would praise Louis Armstrong on just these grounds in the 1960s, as discussed in Chapter 4 – Adorno dismissed any notions that jazz exemplified the conciliation of art and entertainment (*Kunstmusik und Gebrauchsmusik*).[64]

The Nazi regime's anti-jazz position was perhaps most visible in the exhibition *Entartete Musik*. Here, Nazi jargon revived the word *Entartung* (degeneration), which had originally been used with connotations of psychopathology for new currents in the arts in the late nineteenth century and, after WWI, took on racist connotations.[65] In general, the ideology of the Third Reich used the term to derogate artistic productions that were understood as non-desirable. It was used in the title of the notorious Munich art exhibition in 1937, *Entartete Kunst*, and again in Düsseldorf in 1938 for the exhibition *Entartete Musik*, which showcased examples of musical production of the previous decades.[66] The exhibition included published music, images of stage settings, reviews, and excerpts from composers including Schönberg, Weill, Křenek, Hindemith, Stravinsky, Schreker, Eisler, Berg, Webern, Sekles, Reinhardt, Korngold, Holländer,

[62] See the press release of *Berliner Funk-Stunde*, March 8, 1933. As cited in: Wipplinger, *The Jazz Republic: Music, Race, and American Culture in Weimar Germany*, 220–25.

[63] Stefan Müller-Doohm, *Adorno* (Frankfurt a. M.: Suhrkamp, 2011), 280.

[64] Adorno, *Abschied vom Jazz*, Gesammelte Schriften, Band 18, Musikalische Schriften V, 795.

[65] Max Nordau, *Entartung* (Berlin 1892/1893). As cited in: John, "Musikbolschewismus," 20.

[66] Erik Levi, *Music in the Third Reich* (Basingstoke: Macmillan, 1994), 94; Albrecht Dümling and Peter Girth, *Entartete Musik. Dokumentation und Kommentar zur Düsseldorfer Ausstellung von 1938* (Düsseldorf: *DKV der Kleine Verlag*, 1988), 192–93.

Figure 1.3   Image produced for the exhibition *Degenerate Music* featuring caricature
of an African American jazz musician with Star of David, Düsseldorf, 1938.
Source: bpk-Bildagentur

and others. Amid the widespread defamation of musical modernism, the exhibition featured jazz as the most prominent target: a racist caricature of a Star of David-wearing, saxophone-playing black musician on the exhibition's catalog sent a clear message: blackness and Jewishness had no place in German culture (Figure 1.3). Such an image contrasted sharply with the widespread iconography of the eagle, which represented the state as the true protector and defender of Germany's music (Figure 1.4). Overall, this exhibition reflected the anti-modernist musical discourse of previous years by condemning modern music as the products of Jews, Bolshevists, and the mentally disturbed. Indeed, the entire concept of the *Entartete Musik* show sought to convince attendees that Nazism had saved "German music" from its demise, a fate for which Jews above all were to blame.

Even so, during this time, Nazi officials were forced to balance their official anti-jazz approach with the recognition that jazz music (or "rhythmically accentuated music" in occasional Nazi terminology) was, in fact, an established part of youth culture of the era. Aware of this fact and in need of recruits to serve state ideology, the Ministry for Propaganda was keen to bend to their tastes. To present an ostensibly open and tolerant Germany to international visitors during the 1936 Olympics, party officials

Figure 1.4   *Deutschland, Land der Musik*. Poster produced by Lothar Heinemann in 1938 for Deutsche Reichsbahn (German National Railway). Source: bpk / Kunstbibliothek, SMB / Dietmar Katz

loosened the restrictions on jazz, which briefly seemed to revive the local scene in Berlin.[67] In 1937, the British band the Jack Hylton Boys performed at the press ball in the capital on the invitation of Joseph Goebbels himself.[68] Nor was the sale of American jazz records restricted until the United States entered the War; even during the war years, foreign productions were available in German-occupied territories from which members of the *Wehrmacht* regularly brought them back to the Fatherland.[69]

In fact, the Ministry for Propaganda followed a policy of tolerance – and in some cases, even outright support – of jazz when it came to the needs of the Wehrmacht.[70] Wehrmacht officials had urged the German *Rundfunk* that the demand of modern rhythmic music was central to the

[67] Kater, *Different Drummers*, 36.
[68] Fred K. Prieberg, *Musik und Macht* (Frankfurt a. M.: Fischer, 1991), 178–80.
[69] Lücke, *Jazz im Totalitarismus*, 106–12.
[70] Philipp Gassert, *Amerika im Dritten Reich: Ideologie, Propaganda and Volksmeinung 1933–1945* (Stuttgart: Franz Steiner Verlag, 1997), 357. Lücke, *Jazz im Totalitarismus*, 96–97.

younger generation and that the youthful soldiers "of our time" should get what they needed.[71] Thus, Goebbels defended the use of modern dance music from skeptical party members and music critics, arguing that the well-being of the Wehrmacht was of the highest priority. In its statements, the Ministry for Propaganda defended such music as appealing to young audiences, audiences that rejected traditional music (e.g., the waltz) as anachronistic.[72] Indeed, Goebbels was willing to use anything that served his ministry's purposes, including commissioning otherwise blacklisted jazz titles using a secret propaganda band called Charlie and His Orchestra to promote German interests during the war years.[73] Eventually, however, with mounting hardships as the war dragged on, ministry officials had to weather increasing criticism concerning their permissiveness toward jazz.[74] In 1942, the practice of broadcasting jazz met the denunciation of German critics: "Jazz is dead—long live jazz," proclaimed a writer in the *Zeitschrift für Musik*, arguing that the "negro element" was still dominant in German dance culture and demanding a more melodic approach to dance music. Goebbels was forced to issue new rules. In an attempt to streamline German popular music and shun the "negro element," Goebbels decreed that "music with ragged rhythms, music with atonal melodies and the usage of muted horns" would hereby be prohibited.[75]

As noted above, the primary danger that jazz posed to the Nazi regime was its influence on the youth as an alternative culture to allegedly mainstream values. Indeed, in the late 1930s and 1940s, several new groups of nonconformist youth culture emerged such as the Edelweißpiraten, the Meuten, and the "Swing Youth," groups that refused disciplinary drills in Nazi mass organizations. These drills did not appeal to a large segment of the younger generation who sought alternative forms of leisure. Peukert has suggested that these social groups had "seized on an element of 'non-political' leisure activity, which they had then directed against the claims of Nationalist Socialist youth policy."[76] The Edelweißpiraten

---

[71] Lücke, *Jazz im Totalitarismus*, 96.

[72] Josef Goebbels, "Der Rundfunk im Kriege," *Das Reich* (June 15, 1941). As cited in: Lücke, *Jazz im Totalitarismus*, 97.

[73] Lücke, *Jazz im Totalitarismus*, 96, 102–104.

[74] Gassert, *Amerika im Dritten Reich*, 358. See also Lücke, *Jazz im Totalitarismus*, 96–97. Lücke cites "Reports from the Reich" of the Nazi Security Service, *Reichssicherheitsdienst*, between 1942 and 1943. Parts of the German population criticized the high proportion of jazz broadcast within Germany.

[75] Lücke, *Jazz im Totalitarismus*, 94–96.

[76] Detlev Peukert, *Inside Nazi Germany: Conformity, Opposition, and Racism in Everyday Life* (New Haven, Conn.: Yale University Press, 1987), 167.

and the Meuten were loosely organized groups of working-class youth who spent their leisure time biking, hiking, and singing; by contrast, the "swing youth" largely represented the bourgeoisie and its higher level of education and financial opportunity. These young people indulged in swing music and dancing and – according to the Gestapo – engaged in a "sleazy lifestyle."[77]

Restrictions against "swing youth" activities seem to have defined the movement, officials radicalizing its characteristic features such as dance styles, dress code, and behavior, and, as Peukert has argued, "...styliz-ing it into an emblem of a culture that rejected the Hitler Youth norms, stripping it of its domesticated dance-floor character in favor of hotter varieties of what in National Socialist parlance was called negro music."[78] Critically, these youth emphasized internationalism, such as using French and English languages in their gatherings, and welcomed Jews into their groups.[79]

Nazi reports on young people complained about their "'jiving and jit-terbugging,' hair 'grown down to the collar,' and a cult of 'casualness' and 'sleaziness'."[80] As Peukert notes, the rejection of the ideal of soldierhood among some teenagers may have been rooted years earlier, when "the pro-cess of childhood socialization of the swing generation took place during a period of very great disorientation within the family, as Germany was hit first by inflation and soon afterward by world depression."[81] On this view, during a period of national crisis the authoritarian male figure, the head of the household, was unable to function as a provider, resulting in a demystification of parental authority. Either way, Peukert's work on youth movements reveals that the Nazi regime, while dominant, did not in fact have a total grip on German life in the 1930s and 1940s, and that some young people still created their own cultural identity within the totalitar-ian society. Musical preferences such as jazz and tastes in international movies and culture as an alternative to bourgeois values ran contrary to "the mobilization of the people, militarized and schooled in chauvin-ism."[82] The leisure activities of these groups serve as an indicator that a generational shift took place within the bourgeoisie, "where the basis of

[77] Ibid.
[78] Ibid.
[79] Bernd Polster, *Swing Heil: Jazz im Nationalsozialismus* (Berlin: Transit, 1989), 133.
[80] Peukert, *Inside Nazi Germany*, 167.
[81] Ibid.
[82] Ibid.

Figure 1.5   Karlheinz Drechsel as a boy with his parents in Dresden, 1944. Private
collection of Karlheinz Drechsel, used by permission

National Socialist doctrines and of the authoritarian ideal of soldierliness
was concentrated."[83] Ultimately, Peukert suggests, fascist ideals did not
appeal to all teenagers of the late 1930s and 1940s.

Among these teenagers was Karlheinz Drechsel, born in 1930 in
Dresden to a middle-class family and interviewed at length for this history (Figure 1.5). Drechsel was a passionate jazz fan who rejected the
authoritarian drills of the Nazi youth organizations. As he recalled,
"I entered the *Jungvolk* grudgingly. Not because of political reasons
but because the uniforms were repulsive to me. The duty drills on
Wednesday and Saturday evenings were horrifying and I didn't like the
insignia and badges."[84] His older brother sparked Drechsel's interest in
jazz and took him to his first live jazz concert, by the Ernst van t'Hoff
band.[85] The performance Drechsel attended was undisturbed by Nazi
officials, although the van t'Hoff band had a reputation (according to
some reports) of being "*total verjazzt.*" Informants to Nazi officials had

[83] Ibid., 167.
[84] Ulf Drechsel, *Zwischen den Strömungen. Karl Heinz Drechsel: Mein Leben mit dem Jazz*
(Rudolstadt: Greifenverlag, 2011), 12.
[85] Ibid., 10–11.

complained about the jazzing up and rhythmical alterations of popular songs, which turned into "nigger dances."[86]

Fortunately for Drechsel, his brother owned a large collection of popular music that he was able to expand during the Nazi years. Drechsel's brother was stationed on the Western Front, from which he regularly brought the latest records including swing from the United States.[87] By 1944, his collection comprised over 500 titles that gave the fourteen-year-old Drechsel exceptional access to and knowledge of jazz, which he was glad to share with friends and eventually transformed his lifelong passion into his career. As he recently recalled, "Back then, between 1940 and 1945, I often took the gramophone to our local public pool. Many young folks gathered around me to listen to music they would never have heard otherwise. Before I put a record on, I would announce the name of the band, even though I couldn't always pronounce it correctly."[88] Drechsel's account illustrates the scarcity of jazz at that time: as noted above, jazz had been banned from state radio, and during the war years themselves, American records were no longer available in Germany. At the time, Drechsel was proud to be able to present up-to-date and rare American jazz, but equally he was ignorant of the dangers involved with its public presentation. He recalled an incident in the fall of 1944: "One day I took my gramophone to school and played swing music for my schoolmates. When our teacher came in, he stopped us from listening. Shortly afterwards, an angry SA official entered the classroom and broke my shellac record. My mother had to come to school, and I was punished with several hours of social service."[89] In retrospect, Drechsel has admitted his naiveté, noting that "[When the SA official broke the record] I experienced where I was living, and suddenly felt a new kind of fear."

For most of the war, Dresden was relatively spared by Allied bombing attacks, leading its citizens to feel safe in a city famous for its historic baroque architecture and art. It was not until the nights of February 12 and 13, 1945, when Dresden, crowded with refugees from Silesia, was annihilated during the infamous two-night bombing raid. During the carnage, Drechsel and his family barely survived the bombing, both losing their house and witnessing the demise of the city firsthand (Figure 1.6).

[86] Bundesarchiv Berlin-Lichterfelde BArch R58/158. *Meldungen aus dem Reich*, 27. März 1941. As cited in: Lücke, *Jazz im Totalitarismus*, 97.
[87] Drechsel, *Zwischen den Strömungen*, 9.
[88] Ibid., 10.
[89] Ibid., 14.

Figure 1.6   Burning corpses in Dresden-Altmarkt, February 25, 1945. Fourteen-year-
old Drechsel witnessed the bombing and explored the city in its immediate aftermath.
Photograph by Walter Hahn, Deutsche Fotothek, Hauptkatalog: #0314620

In the final weeks before Germany's capitulation, Drechsel was forced to
serve in what was called the *Volksturm*, the last-ditch territorial army in
which underage and elderly men were recruited to defend the home front.
During Drechsel's service in this unit, the Red Army entered Dresden in
May 1945. Of its entry, Drechsel recalled:

> Everybody was horrified. We had heard and read so much, but nothing
> happened to children. We were able to thoroughly observe the tanks,
> trucks and horse-drawn carriages as well as the grounds where Russian
> soldiers were camping, most of them very young. But adults vanished from
> the streets, because they feared encounters with the Russians, and we also
> heard about rapes.... The Russians also took young people between 17 and
> 19 years of age captive. Many of them never returned.[90]

It was not yet the end of the war, but it was the end of the Nazi regime.
In April 1945, Hitler and his lieutenants committed suicide in their Berlin

---

[90] Ibid., 19.

Figure 1.7   Scenes at the Reichstag in Berlin showing a Russian soldier and an
American soldier with a bronze bust of Adolf Hitler atop a damaged globe as Allied
forces occupy Berlin at the end of WWII. July 14, 1945. Photo by Daily Mirror/Mirrorpix
via Getty Images. Editorial #592037722

bunker as Allied armies from both sides swept across the country and
accepted the surrender of German forces. Germany would soon be divided,
with the Soviets arriving in Berlin in May 1945, several weeks before the
Western forces, and before the long process of rebuilding would begin
(Figure 1.7). The capital city would soon be divided into four occupation zones: Soviet, American, British, and French. While new national
anthems would shortly appear on local radio stations, the sounds of jazz
would once again accompany them as countless work crews attempted to
repair and rebuild the ravaged cities. But as the next chapter shows, these
jazz tunes were far from serving as just music: they, too, were tools in the
rebuilding process and in the newfound confrontation of the Cold War.

CHAPTER 2

Jazz in the Soviet Zone, 1945–1949

Introduction

In the later years of WWII, with the advance of Allied forces against the Axis powers, the devastation that the Nazi regime had first brought to Europe turned back onto Germany itself. Between 1940 and 1945, Allied bombers destroyed over one thousand cities and parishes, eradicating Germany's medieval urban centers. For the generation of German youth born around 1930, air raids and firebombing were routine childhood experiences – just as disorder, fragmentation, and struggle under the post-war military occupation defined their teenage years. Compounding the wreckage of the conflict, the German winters in those postwar years were some of the coldest in recorded history, with living conditions plagued by insufficient food and an absence of heating materials.[1]

These were formative years for the generation of Werner Sellhorn, Gerhard Hopfe, Alfons Wonneberg, and Karlheinz Drechsel, all key figures of the jazz scene in years to come. Sellhorn, a journalist and jazz enthusiast, had witnessed the annihilation of his hometown of Hamburg. Gerhard Hopfe and Alfons Wonneberg (who would become a celebrity bandleader) had both experienced the destruction of Berlin. And as discussed at the end of the last chapter, fourteen-year-old Karlheinz Drechsel had barely survived the firebombing of his native Dresden in February 1945. After the war and the collapse of the Nazi regime, many of these future members of the GDR jazz scene took part in reeducation programs established by the Soviet Military Administration (*Sowjetische Militäradministration*, SMAD). Like the majority of youngsters in the Soviet zone of occupation, they joined the Anti-fascist Youth (*Antifaschistische Jugend*, AFJ). Communist teachings shaped their view of Germany's recent past, offering

---

[1] Cf. Jörg Friedrich, *Der Brand. Deutschland im Bombenkrieg 1940–1945* (Berlin: List Verlag, 2004). See, for example, Chapter II of Christoph Kleßmann, *Die doppelte Staatsgründung: Deutsche Geschichte 1945–1955* (Göttingen: Vandenhoeck und Ruprecht, 1982).

ideologically colored explanations for war, destruction, and racism. Within the network of the AFJ, Russian authorities typically supported the youngsters' enthusiasm for jazz and assisted them in organizing jazz clubs – the consequences of these efforts would play out over decades.

This chapter examines jazz in postwar Germany from 1945 to 1949, looking particularly at the central role jazz played in the propaganda efforts of the Soviet authorities in the eastern zone of occupation, as well as the cultural contest between the Soviet and American occupying powers in Berlin. Section One ("'The Show Must Go On': Rebuilding German Musical Life in Soviet Germany") shows how the Soviets resurrected cultural life in their zone of occupation, beginning with brick-and-mortar establishments key to German civic and artistic identity. Sections Two and Three ("African American Music in the Worker's Revolution" and "The Politics of Race at the Berlin Philharmonic") detail the Communists' recognition of African American music as a propaganda tool, both prior to WWII as well as in the postwar era, a recognition that included supporting musicians of African descent. Section Four ("Cold War in the Arts: Socialist Realism versus Cultural Freedom") sheds light on a specific ideological competition beginning in 1947, when East and West battled over notions of socialist realism and cultural freedom. Section Five ("German Jazz Is 'Up to Date'") details grassroots activities that resulted in the revival of East Germany's jazz scene, and Section Six ("'Shades of Uncle Adolf' and *Air Lift Stomp*") shows how American forces on the ground propagated jazz in schools within the Soviet zone of occupation.

"The Show Must Go On": Rebuilding German Musical Life in Soviet Germany

On the afternoon of June 22, 1945, General Floyd L. Parks, commanding general of the United States Headquarters in the Berlin District, landed with a party of a dozen officers at Tempelhof Airfield. At the time, greater Berlin was occupied by Red Army troops, as the Soviets had conquered the city in early May. Traveling to the city as a member of Parks' preliminary reconnaissance party, Colonel Sheen, one of the officers in the American detachment, reported what he saw:

> The bomb damage in the heart of the city is difficult to describe. In certain areas the stench of unburied dead is almost overpowering. From Tempelhof to the Wilhelmstrasse not one undamaged building is standing; roofs, floors, and windows are gone, and in many cases the fragments

of only one or two walls are standing. Many of the streets remain pass-
able, but rubble covers the sidewalks and large numbers of streets are still
blocked off because of bomb craters and debris.[2]

Seeing the ruins of what once was Berlin's vibrant center, the Americans
were astounded to hear the sounds of their homeland being broadcast
from the Soviet-occupied Berlin Radio, as if the Red Army wanted to lay
out a welcome mat for the Americans. To their amazement, "plenty of
jazz" was being broadcast from the station of the former *Großdeutscher
Rundfunk*, which the Soviets had taken over and kept on the air. On June
23, *Stars and Stripes Magazine* reported:

> Berliners living in the ruins of their city had one thing for which to thank
> the Red Army. This was Berlin radio, which in a few short weeks had been
> changed from a frantic propaganda mill to a bright, entertaining broad-
> casting station. Observers from the German capital reported that Berlin
> radio was on the air for 19 hours out of 24. Its programs abounded with
> items Germans have not heard for ten years. There was, in addition to
> German classical music including that of the Jewish composers, plenty
> of jazz and swing – eliminated by the Nazis long ago as detrimental to
> German youth.[3]

Observers at *Stars and Stripes* did not miss the fact that cultural offerings were interspersed with communist propaganda, strangely equated to
advertisements in American broadcasts. "Interlarded with this musical fare
were interviews with enthusiastic Berlin house-wives, and a little straight
propaganda. So artful is the combination, said one observer, that Germans
will undoubtedly accept the propaganda as the price of good entertainment, much as Americans accept 'Krispy-Krunch' announcements along
with Jack Benny and the Boston Symphony." Facing the Soviets' skilled
broadcast, fully functioning in June 1945 mere weeks after the National
Socialists' surrender, these reporters recommended that the Americans and
the British "would have to work hard and fast to keep good listener ratings
in the Reich."

Jazz music was from the very beginning of Soviet occupation a key
component of Russian broadcast policy. Indeed, only fourteen days after

---

[2] Memo, SHAEF G-2, CI Sub Div., for Brig Gen T. J. Betts, sub: Report of Visit to Berlin, June
27, 1945, in SHAEF G-2, GB I/CI/CS/091.1–4. As cited in: Earl F. Ziemke, *The U.S. Army in
the Occupation of Germany, 1944–1946*, Army Historical Series (Washington, D.C.: Center of
Military History, United States Army, 1990), 298.
[3] *Stars and Stripes Magazine – Weekly Supplement*, June 23, 1945.

the end of the war, Russian officials had assembled the Radio Berlin Tanzorchester (RBT) and began to broadcast swing music.[4] Jazz, a wartime symbol of anti-fascism for the Allies, was now being used to celebrate the victory over Nazi Germany, produced and broadcast directly from what had been Hitler's most effective propaganda machine.

Such promotion of jazz took part within an enormous cultural renewal effort that the Soviets orchestrated in their zone of occupation (*Sowjetische Besatzungszone*, SBZ). In contrast to their Western Allies, Soviet authorities immediately recognized the importance of cultural propaganda in occupied Germany, and due to Russian organization, music returned to theaters and concert halls within a few months after the end of the war. In the middle of Berlin's ruins, the SMAD erected the magnificent House of Culture, representing the alleged socio-economic prowess of the Soviet system as well as symbolizing the value that Soviet power attached to the arts. Therefore, their zeal in rebuilding the SBZ not only represented the Soviet state as a cultured people cherishing the cultural heritage of a defeated Germany, but simultaneously offered the Soviets an advantage in the cultural competition with the West.

In both of their zones, however, Soviet and Western forces alike were committed to extirpating Nazism, making anti-fascism the common denominator in this unified approach. At the Potsdam conference in July–August 1945, their directives for the arts postulated guidelines of anti-nationalism, anti-militarism, modernism, and internationalism. In the immediate postwar era, Soviet directives for the arts differed little from their Western counterparts, except for using the term "reactionary" – a combative term expressing the antithesis of socialist progressiveness, an issue that will be discussed below.[5] In the first months of its occupation, moreover, Red Army cultural officers had no specific directives concerning music. It was not until August 1945 that SMAD department of

---

[4] Joachim Schütte, "Discographie des RBT-Orchesters und der anderen Formationen des Berliner Rundfunks," *Jazzfreund-Publikation Nr.3,* Menden 1977. As cited in: Rudolf Käs, ed. *Hot and Sweet: Jazz im Befreiten Land, So viel Anfang war nie: Deutsche Städte 1945–1949* (Berlin: Siedler Verlag, 1989), 253. The orchestra was led by Michael Jary.

[5] In: Ministerium für Auswärtige Angelegenheiten, *Um ein antifaschistisches-demokratisches Deutschland. Dokumente aus den Jahren 1945–1949 (Kapitel 2, Tulpanov Direktiven)* (Berlin: Staatsverlag der DDR, 1968). As cited in: Toby Thacker, *Music after Hitler, 1945–1955* (Aldershot; Burlington, Vt.: Ashgate, 2007), 26.

propaganda under Colonel Sergei Tiulpanov gave the first official guidelines for the arts. They called for:

> a) the full liberalization from Nazi, racist, militarist, and other reactionary ideas and tendencies, b) the active employment of artistic materials in the struggle against Fascism, and for the reeducation of the German people in a logically consistent democratic manner; c) an opening up to the values of international and Russian art.[6]

Denazification, however, proved as problematic in the arts as in other realms of society, engendering widespread discontent caused by its contradictory and bureaucratic approach. This was not least because the immediate needs of musical entertainment interfered with the process of denazification, with decisions of licensing and authorization often being made in arbitrary fashion. The patronage of high-quality professional music frequently included the widespread practice of censorship.[7]

Although similar in their general claims of anti-fascism, the Western Allies and Soviet planning for musical control was based on opposing political traditions. Planning for cultural renewal in the Soviet zone was part of a unified political vision in which the arts were assigned a propagandistic role within the broader workers' revolution. This renewal was also intended to make German citizens understand the superiority of the humanistic and progressive Soviet spirit, embracing the people's cultures of the world. This process was all the more essential given how the Nazi regime had denigrated Soviet culture as a product of inferior "Judeo-Bolshevik" civilization.[8] By contrast, while socialist ideology subjugated cultural production in the SBZ, cultural policies in the western zones were based on liberal traditions that tended to divorce the arts from politics. British and American authorities sought to portray themselves as champions of cultural freedom, ordering censorship to be subtle and pragmatic in order to avoid being labeled as regulation-heavy or repressive occupiers. Under the banner of internationalism and modernism, Germans in the western zones were afforded choices in selecting acceptable music.

As Wolfgang Schivelbusch has detailed, the Soviets, as the first conquerors of the former Nazi capital, ruled uncontested for two months,

---

[6] Thacker, *Music after Hitler*, 26.

[7] Ibid., 43–44.

[8] Norman M. Naimark, *The Russians in Germany: A History of the Soviet Zone of Occupation, 1945–1949* (Cambridge, Mass.: Belknap Press of Harvard University Press, 1995), 398–99. As noted, right-wing organizations in the Weimar and Nazi periods attached terminology such as "Judeo-Bolshevik" to jazz.

laying the foundation of all future cultural activity along guidelines of opening up instead of restricting.[9] Well aware of the value of propaganda, Russian officials also believed in the necessity of entertainment to counter the apathy of the demoralized German populace. SMAD quickly organized cultural institutions under Communist leadership, whose efforts of renewal – their encouragement, apparent tolerance, and zealous support of the arts – amazed the other Western powers during their respective occupations of the Berlin territories in the summer of 1945. Overcoming great difficulties, the Russians cleared rubble away from theaters and reopened them for Berlin audiences.[10] The US-led Information Control Service (ICS) kept close watch on these activities. As early as July 1945, Henry C. Alter, an Austrian emigrant working for American intelligence, reported weekly on cultural activities in bombed-out Berlin, relaying details of film, theater, and music productions. Alter illustrated the Russian cultural renewal effort in one of his reports:

> The current situation of Berlin's movie, film and music-life is the result of…targeted Russian politics, which have been emphatically conducted.…Immediately after their takeover of Berlin the Russians brought theater directors, actors and stage workers together and demanded the re-opening of theaters.[11]

These efforts led to remarkable results. As noted above, within days of Hitler's death, the Soviets restarted transmissions from Radio Berlin, in the building of the former *Großdeutscher Rundfunk* on Masurenallee in Charlottenburg, broadcasting eclectic programs including classical music and jazz. On May 13, 1945, the Berlin Chamber Orchestra gave an open performance to the public in Schöneberg's city hall.[12] The Berlin Philharmonic performed its first postwar concert on May 26th, conducted by Leo Borchard in the Titania-Palast.[13] By September, they

---

[9] Wolfgang Schivelbusch, *In a Cold Crater: Cultural and Intellectual Life in Berlin, 1945–1948* (Berkeley: University of California Press, 1998), 37.

[10] Brewster S. Chamberlin, ed. *Kultur auf Trümmern: Berliner Berichte der amerikanischen Information Control Section, Juli-Dezember 1945* (Stuttgart: Deutsche Verlags-Anstalt, 1979), 20. See also: Friedrich Luft, *Berliner Theater* (Hannover, 1961); Karl Laux, *Nachklang* (Berlin, 1977).

[11] Recommendations of Film, Theatre and Music Sub-Section, Henry C. Alter (FTM) to ICS Officer Berlin District, July 18, 1945: OMGUS 5/242–3/13. As cited in: Chamberlin, *Kultur auf Trümmern*, 60. Alter reported as an MFT officer (music/film/theater) to the ICS.

[12] Winfried Ranke et al., *Kultur, Pajoks und CARE-Pakete. Eine Berliner Chronik 1945–1949* (Berlin: Nishen, 1990), 50. As cited in: Maren Köster, *Musik-Zeit-Geschehen: Zu den Musikverhältnissen in der SBZ/DDR 1945–1952* (Saarbrücken: Pfau, 2002), 19.

[13] Chamberlin, *Kultur auf Trümmern*, 16. See also: Ruth Andreas-Friedrich, *Der Schattenmann* (München: Rheinsberg-Verlag, 2000), 200. Matthias Sträßner, *Der Dirigent Leo Borchard. Eine unvollendete Karriere* (Berlin, 1999), 215–17.

had re-opened and controlled four leading theaters.[14] Soviet officials even managed to set up a successful music library, and by April 1946, more than one hundred theaters were operating throughout the territory of the SBZ.[15] By comparison, it seems that the other Western powers merely observed the "atmosphere of excitement and accomplishment" that arose from the Soviets' deep commitment to their mission.[16]

In Berlin, the Soviet House of Culture on Friedrichstraße (No. 176–179 Berlin Mitte), a splendid building with an elaborate interior featuring art exhibitions and musical performances, became a source of envy for the Western Allies, who at this point had little comparable to offer.[17] The House of Culture dazzled one British cultural affairs officer, R. E. Colby, who reported jealously that the institute

> surpasses anything the other allies have done and put our poor little effort right in the shade. ... It is most luxuriously appointed – good furniture, much of it antique, carpets in every room, a brilliance of lights, almost overheated and everything newly painted. ... [This is a] grandiose cultural institute which will reach the broad masses and do much to counteract the generally accepted idea here that the Russians are uncivilized. This latest venture is depressing as far as we are concerned – our contribution is so small – one information center and a few reading rooms which have had to be closed down because of lack of coal! ... We should be spurred on by this latest Russian entry into the *Kulturkampf* to answer with an equally bold scheme for putting over British achievements here in Berlin.[18]

In his report, Colby vividly describes the effect that the House of Culture had in what he calls the *Kulturkampf* in postwar Berlin. Amid the rubble, the House of Culture projected Soviet power in a glorious light, as a place of abundance in a desolate city where everything was scarce.[19]

Not only had Russian officials outpaced the Western Allies in their immediate efforts at cultural renewal, but they had also gained ground in the race for cultural credibility through their artistic imports. German audiences received works by Russian composers, such as Tchaikovsky and

[14] Naimark, *The Russians in Germany*, 426.
[15] Ibid., 424.
[16] Chamberlin, *Kultur auf Trümmern*, 399.
[17] Frances Stonor Saunders, *Who Paid the Piper? The CIA and the Cultural Cold War* (London: Granta Books, 1999), 18–19.
[18] R. E. Colby, British Control Commission, Berlin, to Montague Pollock, March 19, 1947. As cited in: ibid.
[19] P. Wladimir und Alexandr O. Tschubarjan Koslow, ed. *SMAD-Handbuch: Die Sowjetische Militäradministration in Deutschland 1945–1949* (Walter de Gruyter, 2014), 269–71.

Shostakovich, with great appreciation.[20] The RBT gave a jazz concert to benefit German war veterans and raised funds for soldiers, including prisoners of war, returning from Russia.[21] In a way, this propagated a double lesson in moral reeducation: by deconstructing the idea of racial superiority, jazz, the music of an allegedly "inferior" race, was here used to benefit German soldiers defeated by another racially "inferior" people, the Slavs. Moreover, the Soviet-licensed daily paper *Berlin am Mittag* proclaimed a "Peace agreement with Jazz" in 1947, praising the synthesis of modern concert music and jazz, and claiming jazz as part of the socialist music culture that bridged genuine folk music with the modernism of Igor Stravinsky.[22] Elsewhere, commentators denounced the racist notions of Germany's postwar society: the periodical *Aufbau* condemned anti-jazz polemics in 1946 as a phenomenon of German arrogance, alluding to National Socialism.[23]

While the Russians were successful both in rebuilding musical life and in disseminating their musical culture, in the western zones, music making decreased considerably. It seems, in the immediate postwar era, the American administration was prepared neither to allocate basic needs for musical life nor to provide scores for highbrow, contemporary American music. Moreover, the Americans utilized opera houses primarily as movie theaters for troop entertainment.[24] Amid the tremendous Soviet reconstruction effort, these insensitive dealings with signifiers of German high culture fed into the German perceptions of the United States as an uncultured nation, and it worked only toward the advantage of the cultural credibility of the Soviets.

Watching these developments resentfully, American officials soon began to feel politically outmaneuvered; thus, they sought to reconsider their cultural policies. Their dilemma was twofold: on the one hand, strict denazification policies restricted German artists from working, and on the other hand, entertainment offered by cultural activities such as concerts

---

[20] Unauthored article, "Sowjetische Musik ist stark gefragt," *Melos*, no. March (1948). As cited in: Thacker, *Music after Hitler, 1945–1955*, 95; Naimark, *The Russians in Germany*, 430.

[21] "Jazzmusik und Heimkehrer," *Berlin am Mittag* (February 24, 1947).

[22] Heinz von Cramer, "Friedensschluß mit dem Jazz. Moderne Musik für zwei Klaviere," ibid. (April 28, 1947). Cramer referred to the "6th Evening of Contemporary Music," presented by the Kulturbund and organized by Hans Heinz Stuckenschmidt, reviewing *Concerto per due-piano-forti soli* by Stravinsky, in which according to the article the composer fused jazz and boogie-woogie elements.

[23] Paul Höffer, "Jazz-Musik," *Aufbau* (May 1946).

[24] Thacker, *Music after Hitler, 1945–1955*, 93–95.

and operas were prohibited by their own orders.[25] Facing these discrepancies, Colonel F. N. Leonard, head of the ICS, stated in 1946 that "it was a vital error of American occupation policy to misrecognize the advantage of cultural propaganda."[26] Such an assessment reflected not only the failure to see the advantages of cultural propaganda, but also the difficult question of what specifically American culture to send to Germany in the presence of such overwhelming Russian cultural offerings. Meanwhile, American officials observed the Russian politics of "the show must go on" with equal parts admiration and suspicion.[27] Alter's report, cited above, encapsulates the Russian attitude, while simultaneously shedding light on the deficiency of American cultural policies in occupied Berlin:

> At the core of Russian policy is an almost fanatical worship of art and artists, paired with the belief that artistic activity is in itself good and necessary for the people in time of uncertainty and suffering. They seem to consider them (the artists) a different species who are hardly to be held accountable... they were summoned to come out of their hiding and start working again.[28]

Such assessments matched the reality on the ground. Strategies of the Russian *Kulturkampf* included the widespread physical dissemination of jazz. According to historian Uta Poiger, more jazz records were produced 1946–1948 under Soviet supervision in the SBZ than in all the western zones.[29] Much of this prowess can be attributed to the two main entities in the SBZ, the Russian-controlled record label Amiga and the publishing company and distributor Lied der Zeit (LDZ). Prior to the founding of the East German state in 1949, Amiga released over 100 jazz records – an astounding number.[30] LDZ, controlled by SMAD and managed by actor and singer Ernst Busch, championed socialist educational ambitions. After being liberated from Nazi imprisonment, Busch enjoyed the support of Russian officials such as Alexander Dymschitz, who saw the political value of the popular performer. Enjoying a successful career during the Weimar Republic, then later victimized by Nazism and connected with

[25] Chamberlin, *Kultur auf Trümmern*, 26.
[26] OMGUS, 5/35–3/6: Interview with Col. F.N. Leonard, November 1946. As cited in: ibid., 20.
[27] Henry C. Alter: Empfehlungen der Film-, Theater-, und Musik-Abteilung, 18. Juli 1945 in: ibid., 60.
[28] Ibid., 60–61.
[29] Uta Poiger, *Jazz, Rock and Rebels: Cold War Politics and American Culture in a Divided Germany* (Berkeley: University of California Press, 2000), 42; Horst H. Lange, *Jazz in Deutschland*. Colloquium, 1966, 153.
[30] Mathias Brüll, *Jazz auf Amiga: Die Schallplatten des Amiga-Labels von 1947 bis 1990* (Berlin: Pro Business, 2003).

leftist intellectuals through his involvement in the Spanish Civil War, Busch was a perfect vehicle to propagate the socialist cause in the SBZ.

In 1947, Busch's LDZ held the monopoly of shellac (78 rpm phonograph) record production in the Soviet zone, after having its competitors expropriated by SMAD. Under Dymschitz's protection, Busch managed LDZ 1946–1953.[31] Predominantly interested in the promotion of Busch's own music – socialist battle songs – the company had to recoup the deficits raised by such productions with moneymaking products, yet in the late 1940s, recordings with an ideological message seemed to have lost their luster. To promote the sales of Busch's recordings, customers were obligated to buy titles with a socialist message if they wanted to purchase popular music. Annoyed by these regulations, customers broke shellac records of "educational value" to return them to Amiga to recycle the scarce material.[32] Tired of ideological lecturing, young people preferred the ease of popular swing music, such as the leading German big bands RBT under Horst Kudritzki and the Swingband des Berliner Rundfunks under Walter Dobschinsky. Most recorded titles were adaptions of contemporary swing hits, many of them of American origin. In January 1947, the RBT recorded a version of Glen Miller's "Chattanooga Choo" with a German version on the B-side titled "Kötzschenbroda Express," which at first glance satirically reflected the hardships of train travel in postwar Germany.[33] But these adapted lyrics to Miller's upbeat tune allude to more than just overcrowded trains and uncomfortable conditions. Lines such as "At night in Wusterhausen [a village near Berlin] one must delouse and lose one's head" convey the hardships millions of people had to endure.[34] Refugees, displaced individuals, and soldiers returning from the war were all trying to reach German soil, a journey that many did not survive.

Indeed, alongside Busch, Alexander Dymschitz – the leader of SMAD's cultural division – and his colleague Sergej Barskij, who was responsible for music activities, expertly helped to orchestrate the SBZ's cultural renewal.[35] The work of individuals like Dymschitz and Barskij reflected their bourgeois upbringing on the one side, and their commitment to Soviet Union on the other. Multilingual and well-versed in German

---

[31] In 1953, Busch was removed from his position and the company was transformed into the state-owned VEB Deutsche Schallplatte. Jochen Voit, *Er rührte an den Schlaf der Welt: Ernst Busch. Die Biographie* (Berlin: Aufbau Verlag, 2010), 182–83.

[32] Ibid., 197.

[33] Brüll, *Jazz auf Amiga*, 31–32. Amiga Sonderklasse 1109, AM 519.

[34] *Nachts in Wusterhausen muss man sich entlausen und verliert den Kopf leider dabei.*

[35] See the description of Barskij's work for SMAD: Köster, *Musik-Zeit-Geschehen*, 54–67.

literature and music, they also embraced the art associated with the workers' movement; their appreciation for Thomas Mann was compatible with their support of Berthold Brecht, Hanns Eisler, and Ernst Busch. Bringing leading German intellectuals into the Soviet camp was a top priority in the competition for cultural credibility; a stance that also illustrated the early Soviet leniency toward politically compromised artists of the time – in their vigorous reconstruction of German musical life, Russian officials did not recoil from supporting the reemployment of musical celebrities who once represented Nazi Germany, such as Hermann Abendroth, orchestra conductor, who was appointed musical director of the Weimar Symphony Orchestra. Though German communists protested his rehabilitation, shortly after the founding of the GDR in 1949, Abendroth was honored with the *Nationalpreis der DDR*.[36]

Finally, Soviet officials knew that the secret to their ideological project lay in cultivating new generations of young people; thus, they steered numerous efforts to that end. Communist postwar planning included the formation of the AFJ, which SMAD had organized in July 1945. With its bipartisan approach propagating peace and democracy, the organization drew members from various political camps. At the same time, Soviet officials founded the Central Youth Committee (*Zentraler Jugendausschuss*) in Berlin representing all political parties, but it was dominated by the Communist Party of Germany (*Kommunistische Partei Deutschlands*, KPD). Communist control became overt in 1946, when the AFJ became the *Freie Deutsche Jugend* (FDJ) chaired by Erich Honecker, who in the 1970s would rise to become overall party chair in the GDR.[37] It seems that in the formative years of the GDR, youth organizations did face requirements to be registered and authorized but did not suffer immediate restrictions in terms of Western popular music. Rather, their members enjoyed copious amounts of "Anglo-American music" broadcast regularly by the Soviet-controlled Berliner Rundfunk.[38]

One of the early members of the AFJ, Karlheinz Drechsel, has recalled the postwar years in recent interviews. As a fifteen-year-old, he wanted to initiate a *Swingzirkel* and had no difficulties having his activity permitted. Soviet officials seemed to have supported Drechsel's project and

[36] Naimark, *The Russians in Germany*, 431.
[37] *Jugend nach dem Krieg*, hrsg. v. Bundeszentrale für politische Bildung und Robert-Havemann-Gesellschaft e.V., letzte Änderung September 2008, www.jugendopposition.de/index.php?id=2852.
[38] Ulrich Mählert, *Die Freie Deutsche Jugend, 1945–1949* (Paderborn: Schöningh, 1995), 196.

allocated facilities for the jazz gatherings of several dozen teenagers, who met weekly to listen to and discuss jazz recordings:

> By the end of 1945 I had the idea of founding a swing circle, so I went to the Office of the Antifascist Youth in Dresden-Neustadt. The officials there were open-minded and allocated a facility, which was a vandalized workshop. In the spring of 1946 we moved to a small historical building badly affected by bombing at Palaisplatz. For days we had to clear up the debris and clean the place, before I could put up my portable gramophone to listen to swing. Within a short time, solely by word-of-mouth, our swing circle grew to about forty people.[39]

According to Drechsel, most of the members were genuinely interested in the music alone, but others were intrigued by its American dimensions in a Soviet-controlled world. For these young people, jazz here signified a Western counterculture as it had in the Nazi years. Even under the protective umbrella of the AFJ, however, the jazz meetings could not be held for long. Anti-Western propaganda intensified in the late 1940s, and by the end of 1948, authorities prohibited the *Swingzirkel* meetings[40] (Figure 2.1).

In sum, the renewal of German cultural life was central to Soviet-occupation politics, signaling the superpower's shrewd appreciation of the arts of the defeated nation. Soviet officials were aware of the effects of their engagement in the revival of German musical life. In contrast to the Americans, the Russians presented themselves as a cultured nation, defying prior German notions of Russia as uncivilized. For Germans in the Eastern Zone, the restoration of many theaters by 1946 served as a Soviet act of great benevolence, bringing back the arts that the Germans had been deprived of and reconnecting them to their cultural heritage prior to its abuse by Nazi racial ideology. In this sense, the Soviet effort helped not only to physically rebuild theatres and opera houses, but also helped to reinstate a sense of German cultural identity in the midst of the ruins of what once were Germany's historical centers.

This immense Soviet effort overshadowed the Western forces' paltry attempts to present the cultural achievements of their respective nations. The American's disregard of cultural propaganda and the resulting lack

---

[39] Ulf Drechsel, *Zwischen den Strömungen. Karl Heinz Drechsel: Mein Leben mit dem Jazz* (Rudolstadt: Greifenverlag, 2011), 25.
[40] Interview with Karlheinz Drechsel, 2009. See also: ibid., 25–26.

Figure 2.1 Young jazz entrepreneurs Karlheinz Drechsel (right) and Berthold Hinze (left) in Dresden, December 1947. Private collection of Karlheinz Drechsel, used by permission

of a humanistic presence within the occupied territory meant that the United States was not able to present itself as a cultured nation. Moreover, American policies dealt crudely with the cultural heritage of the defeated, but still artistically proud, German nation. Such insensitivity provoked German resentment and fostered the notion that American influences posed a threat to German cultural identity, especially when American popular culture and arts, including jazz, was becoming increasingly popular among young Germans. Thus, the growing popularity of jazz occurred under unfavorable auspices: in contrast to the jazz propaganda and reception in the Soviet zones, jazz in the western zones initially carried the aura of a lack of culture, serving merely as troop entertainment. Indecent, disreputable, and lacking cultural and educational value, it was thus seen as an offense to the continuity of German musical heritage.

African American Music in the Worker's Revolution

As the historian Frederick Starr has detailed, a vibrant Russian jazz scene reflected the liberalization of Soviet musical life during WWII, a scene that embraced contemporary Western musical developments.[41] Russian propagandists promoted jazz for different reasons at different times. During the war, while the Soviet Union and the United States were allies in the war against the fascist powers, jazz predominately represented an anti-fascist position. In the years after 1945, however, African American music broadcast under Soviet control conveyed an additional message; for in the communist view, it represented the voice of an oppressed people within the capitalist system – a message whose significance in this period cannot be overstated.

To fully understand the political role jazz played in the post-war era, it is important to understand the role it had played before the war as well. Indeed, the recruitment of African American music to propagate the socialist world revolution dated back at least to the 1920s. The Communist International (*Kommunistische Internationale*, COMINTERN) recognized the revolutionary potential of the black working class and endorsed African American self-determination within the broader goal of the worldwide liberation of the proletariat in the late 1920s.[42] To bring American racism to public awareness, the COMINTERN's publication *International Press Correspondence* monitored violence against African Americans.[43] Focusing on the American South, communist organizations such as the International Labor Defense (ILD) brought public attention to lynching, as witnessed in Scottsboro, Alabama, in the early 1930s, when nine African American teenage boys had been accused of raping two white girls.[44] Because of

---

[41] Frederick S. Starr, *Red and Hot: The Fate of Jazz in the Soviet Union, 1917–1980* (Oxford; New York: Oxford University Press, 1983), 181–203; Ziemke, *The U.S. Army in the Occupation of Germany, 1944–1946*.

[42] Steven Garabedian, "Reds, Whites, and the Blues: Lawrence Gellert, 'Negro Songs of Protest,' and the Leftwing Folksong Revival of the 1930s and 1940s," *American Quarterly*, no. 57, 1 (2005). See also: COMINTERN Electronic Archives: KOMINTERN, "Biulleten´organizatsii 'The African Blood Brotherhood'," ed. op.1 F.515, d.91 (December 1921). Robbie Lieberman, *My Song Is My Weapon: People's Songs, American Communism, and the Politics of Culture, 1930–1950* (Urbana, IL: University of Illinois, 1995).

[43] For example: E. Siminell, "Der Ku-Klux-Klan," *Internationale Presse-Korrespondenz, COMINTERN* (November 19, 1921).

[44] The ILD was a branch of Willie Münzenberg's International Workers Relief. Hugh Wilford, *The Mighty Wurlitzer: How the CIA played America* (Cambridge, Mass.; London: Harvard University Press, 2008), 13. See http://law2.umkc.edu/faculty/projects/ftrials/scottsboro/scottsb.htm.

the involvement of the ILD, the accused were eventually given a trial instead of being lynched. In 1935, at its Seventh World Congress in Moscow, the COMINTERN proclaimed a new global policy against fascism. Amid the rising power of fascism in places such as Germany and Spain, the anti-fascist cause was a noble reason to join the Popular Front. In America, many intellectuals, celebrities, students, and African Americans, who were sympathetic to left-wing activity, joined the Popular Front affiliated with the Communist Party of the United States (CPUSA).[45]

Communists made use of African American folk music as a weapon in the fight against racism, which they saw as one of the pillars of the capitalist system. For over a decade beginning in the 1920s, American folklorist Lawrence Gellert, a committed activist in the struggle for black social and economic justice, collected hundreds of black vernacular songs from field workers, miners, and chain gangs.[46] A selection of these songs first appeared as *Negro Songs of Protest* in the journal *New Masses* in 1930 and was later published in 1936 by the American Music League, a Popular Front-affiliate of the CPUSA. Gellert's aim was to present examples of black folk music "reflecting a level of intellectual and social consciousness that exposed the fundamental conceit of white racism."[47] As he later stated: "I wanted propaganda. I wasn't interested in just music for its own sake but rather as a weapon in the service of black freedom."[48] After 1945, American critics denigrated his collection as mere fabrications, representing white left-wing propaganda rather than black vernacular creativity of discontent and protest.[49] Nevertheless, it is clear that Gellert enjoyed a rare opportunity to record examples of a provocative side of African American lyricism, never meant for white listeners.[50] Fearing white reprisal against them, Gellert had to keep the identities of his performers strictly anonymous.

Ideologically driven, Gellert's approach was selective, searching out songs that featured clear and direct expressions of social protest, including open invocations of black rebellion and murder. This was in contrast to folklore collectors John A. and Allan Lomax who followed a less socio-critical, more populist approach by collecting broader, at times apolitical

---

[45] Ibid., 12–13.
[46] Born in Budapest, Hungary, Gellert (1898–1979) moved in the 1920s to Tyron, North Carolina, where his collection process began.
[47] Garabedian, Reds, Whites, and the Blues, 184.
[48] Gellert interview by Reuss, March 28, 1968, and September 11, 1969. As cited in: ibid., 182.
[49] Ibid.
[50] Ibid.

representations of African American folklore. Gellert's efforts quickly gained ground in the socialist world. The writer Langston Hughes initiated a Russian translation of Gellert's work through contacts he made during his Soviet travels in 1932. After WWII, the *Protest Songs* were republished in East Berlin: *Negro Songs: Protestlieder des Amerikanischen Negerproletariats. Aus der Sammlung von Lawrence Gellert* was published by LDZ in the SBZ/GDR in 1949.[51]

The star German singer Ernst Busch and the musicologist G. M. Shneerson, formerly comrades in the International Brigades during the Spanish Civil War – Shneerson had composed melodies for Busch's battle songs in the war – collaborated on the German edition of *Negro Songs* (Figure 2.2). To show solidarity with African Americans, the volume was dedicated to singer and "fellow combatant" Paul Robeson.[52] In his preface to the anthology, Shneerson pointed out that the songs Gellert collected demonstrated for the first time that black people were not limited to praying or hoping for redemption and happiness in the afterlife. Instead, these

Figure 2.2   Title page of *Negro Songs*, from Lawrence Gellert, *Protestlieder des Amerikanischen Negerproletariats*, Lied der Zeit: Berlin, 1949; ROBA/Hamburg

[51] Ibid., 179. See also Lawrence Gellert, ed. *Negro-Songs: Protestlieder des Amerikanischen Negerproletariats* (Berlin: Lied der Zeit, 1949).
[52] The dedication: *"Dieses Buch ist unserem Freund und Mitkämpfer Paul Robeson gewidmet."*

songs served as expressions of African American self-determination, verbalizing resistance against oppression. Shneerson stressed the lyric's social-revolutionary potential, stating: "The oppressed proletariat of the Negroes reveals in these songs an increasing sense of anger and strengthening combat spirit."[53] The examples in these lyrics addressed a wide spectrum of grievances, many general in nature, but also specific cases such as the arrest and trials of the Scottsboro boys. Four out of the eighteen songs call for active resistance against white cruelty and a summons to fight back. The song "Sistren an' Brethren" (*Schwestern und Brüder*) demands revenge for lynching:

> Your head tain' no apple
> Fo' danglin' from a tree
> Yo' body no carcass
> Fo' barbacuin' on a spree.
> Stand on yo' feet,
> Club gripped 'tween yo hands
> Spill their blood too,
> Show'em yo's is a man's.[54]

The anthology ends with a song by Busch entitled "Black and White," calling for workers' solidarity and the unity of people of all races against exploitation. The song's call and response form changes into a stirring battle song in march rhythm, as if leading to a path out of misery. It urges the listener not to moan and pray, because redemption will not come from heaven but will instead come about through the union of blacks and whites, who together will liberate the world from oppression.[55]

> Join in the fight, o Negro comrade.
> Join in the fight, o struggling Comrade.
> O hard pressed comrade.
> Black and white, we'll rebuild the world.
>
> O brother, don't you weep, don't you pray.
> Salvation isn't coming that way.
> All together let's press on the fray:
> Black and white, we'll rebuild the world.

---

[53] Gellert, *Negro-Songs.*
[54] Ibid., 23.
[55] Ibid. Written by Ernst Busch. First stanza: *"Gib uns die Hand, Mein schwarzer Bruder! Gib uns die Hand, Mein armer Bruder! Gib uns die Hand, Mein starker Bruder! 'Black und White' werden ändern die Welt."*

While jazz and protest songs played a central role in Soviet anti-racist propaganda, providing a fertile ground for the music in the SBZ, the music
encountered a very different reception in the western zones of occupation,
where numerous incidents of opposition to jazz arose. Here, jazz music
met with disapproval, as a controversy about dance music programs of the
Nord-West Deutscher Rundfunk indicates.[56] While in the aftermath of the
Nazi regime German jazz musicians and bandleaders sought to connect
to international developments in popular music, the majority of German
audiences preferred dance music free of jazz elements. Conservative listening habits still dominated, rejecting such musical techniques as the
"jazzing up" of popular melodies. Public opinion found the sound of saxo-
phones and vocal jazz intonation undesirable, with audiences preferring
traditional aesthetic concepts such as string-dominated sounds. Moreover,
the majority of listeners rejected jazz because of the way in which it evoked
fears of racial transgression, fears expressed in terms of *Negermusik* (Negro
music) that defied bourgeois standards. Resurrecting Nazi terminology,
some listeners of the time equated jazz with the music of the "abnormal
and retarded."[57] In Frankfurt, a jazz concert had to be interrupted because
of right-wing rioting, the troublemakers shouting "*der Führer hat es verboten*" (the Führer prohibited this) and demanding German operatic hits
such as "*Berliner Luft*," whose song lyrics praised the city's genteel qualities
of the Wilhelmine era.[58]

    In the same vein, an article in the *Frankfurter Rundschau* of September
29, 1949, reported on right-wing threats to a jam session presented by
the Jazz Club Hamburg: "... the German Party had threatened to send a
'mobile commando' (*Rollkommando*) to prevent the jam session. The jus-
tification was that the participation of Negroes in the Band was irrecon-
cilable with the ethics of the German race."[59] This disapproval of jazz was
not just a grassroots phenomenon, but to some extent seems to have been

---

[56] "Blech an die Wand gedrückt," *Der Spiegel* (3/1948).
[57] Hot Club Journal Stuttgart, July 1948. As cited in: Käs, *Hot and Sweet*, 254. "*Viele Musikliebende
beiderlei Geschlechts werden mir darin einig sein, wenn ich behaupte, dass Jazz das geschmackloseste
Produkt misshandelter Musikinstrumente darstellt, das der Jugend jedes Interesse für gute, anständige
Musik nimmt. Wenn man sich solches Getöse anhört, hat man den Eindruck, als wenn Geisteskranke
auf Musikinstrumenten ihr 'überdurchschnittliches Können' nachweisen wollten.*"
[58] Hot Club News Frankfurt, July/August 1947. As cited in: ibid.
[59] *Frankfurter Rundschau*, September 27, 1949: "*Deutsche Partei und das Germanische Lebensethos:
Auf einer von jungen Journalisten und dem Jazzclub in Hamburg veranstalteten 'Jam-Session' wurde
bekanntgegeben, die Deutsche Partei habe gedroht, ein 'Rollkommando' zu entsenden, um die Jam-
Session zu verhindern. Als Begründung habe sie angegeben, das Auftreten von Negern in der Band des
Kubaners Jose Camino sei mit dem 'Lebensethos der Germanischen Rasse unvereinbar'.*"

institutionalized. Echoing these racist sentiments, the finance authority in West Berlin rejected the application of the Hot Club Berlin to be approved as a public charity by responding "in the name of the German people." As they claimed, "In the view of the majority of the German people, jazz music is not a cultural product. Jazz is a kind of music that is alien to the German perception of art and that the majority of the German people reject."[60] These statements, which portray jazz as outside the realm of culture, clearly reflect a perception of cultural hierarchy based on racist ideology. Moreover, they stand in stark contrast to socialist perceptions of race and culture in which jazz was embraced as a music of the people and understood as a contribution of an ethnic group to world music – something that, whatever its origins, transcends racial categorization or cultural hierarchy.

In sum, lingering tensions aside, the international communist organizations engaged in the struggle for African American self-determination recognized the revolutionary potential of black music early on. Utilizing jazz as a tool of propaganda prior to WWII, they continued to propagate African American music after 1945 in the SBZ. While promoting the "voice of the oppressed," the Soviets not only stressed their accusations of racism in American domestic policies, but also sought to demonstrate the social and political superiority of the Soviet Union, which portrayed itself as a system overcoming not just class but racial and cultural barriers as well. The Soviets allowed a greater cultural plurality than the Western Allies in their respective zones, providing a liberal climate in which a prolific jazz scene flourished. The broadcasting of jazz and the production of new records and publications, such as *Negro Songs*, exemplified the Soviet championing of African American music at a pivotal point in Germany's postwar rebuilding. In this respect, jazz was quickly becoming much more than just a genre or a style of music, a transformation that would continue in new ways.

The Politics of Race at the Berlin Philharmonic

American attitudes favoring European high culture stemmed from the notion of culture as hierarchically organized, a notion common to American class-based society in the nineteenth century. As historian

---

[60] Hans Blüthner, private archive. As cited in: Käs, *Hot and Sweet*, 255.

Lawrence Levine has shown, the notion of European (and specifically German) music as intellectually and aesthetically superior informed cultural categories of the highbrow and the lowbrow in a time when genres associated with African American "inferior" culture such as ragtime and jazz characterized popular music.[61] Among American officials, these elitist perceptions persisted into the first half of the twentieth century and influenced policies for postwar Germany, simultaneously excluding popular music with its currents of jazz, and gearing cultural transmission toward a more highbrow Eurocentric culture.[62] This hierarchy would only begin to shift in the second half of the twentieth century, when jazz gravitated from the fringe of society to its center, being chosen to represent American culture abroad – and, by the end of the twentieth century, becoming formally recognized as an indigenous American art form.[63]

By contrast, socialist conceptions of culture had theoretically resolved such delineations. Culture in the proposed one-class society operated at a higher level than in other societies, demonstrating the superiority of Marxism-Leninism. The Soviet concept of culture yoked the highest standards of the classics to popular culture such as folk music, dance, and film.[64] The concept of Soviet mass culture ostensibly made bourgeois categorizations obsolete, sublimating cultural divisions in terms of race and ethnicity. From the communist perspective, American blacks were victimized by imperialist repression, such that their artistic expressions – blues and jazz – were directed against capitalism and its inherent racism.[65] As described above, the fight for black freedom had been on the agenda of the COMINTERN since 1929.[66] That there was "plenty of jazz" on Berlin radio in July 1945 represented not only the openness of Soviet cultural policies, but also served as an implicit indictment of America's racial politics: with respect to jazz, it could be said that the Cold War began at this moment.

It was not until the summer of 1945 that the Western Allies considered including jazz in their policies. Before that, American and British cultural

---

[61] Lawrence W. Levine, *Highbrow Lowbrow: The Emergence of Cultural Hierarchy in America* (Cambridge, Mass.: Harvard University Press, 1988), 171–242.

[62] Ibid.

[63] www.congress.gov/bill/100th-congress/senate-concurrent-resolution/23.

[64] Naimark, *The Russians in Germany*, 398–99.

[65] According to Marxist-Leninist ideology, imperialism, as embodied by the socio-political order of the United States, was the last phase of capitalism, a description of its aggression toward socialist countries and the catalyst for world revolution. To describe cultural products as "imperialist" was to claim their power to "manipulate intellectual abilities and paralyze the revolutionary combat power of the people." See, for instance: "Imperialismus," in *Kleines Politisches Wörterbuch* (Berlin: Dietz, 1969/1973).

[66] KOMINTERN; Garabedian, Reds, Whites, and the Blues.

policies did not promote popular music in their reeducation plans. Strictly following elitist guidelines in March 1945 (with the fall of the Nazi regime imminent), American and British officials stated that there would be no promotion of jazz, making a distinct division between entertainment and art.[67] However, in July 1945, a few months after entering Berlin, they reconsidered this position and toned down their approach, as directives called for adding music from popular genres. Jazz would henceforth be included and represented by composers such as Duke Ellington and Cole Porter.[68] This change in policy was a direct response to the encounter with Russian cultural practices, inducing a divergence from Eurocentrism toward more Americanized concepts of culture. At the same time, American officials also began to realize that black artists could be recruited for propaganda purposes, to two ends: first, to represent a democratic America to counter Soviet accusations of racism, and second, to counter racist concepts of white supremacy directed against the defeated Nazi regime. Indeed, in 1946, Robert McClure, the head of the US Psychological Warfare Department, recommended an emphasis on American music, including African American artists, in postwar cultural engagement to foster the equality of races. This would send a strong anti-racist message to the Germans and Soviets, challenging the myth of white superiority and projecting a vision of a multi-racial democratic America in which distinction was open to all through merit.[69] McClure's instructions for American contributions in the realm of music emphasized the inclusion of "negro" artists, recommending the African American opera singers Marian Anderson and Dorothy Maynor to perform in Germany.[70]

One of the first concerts featuring an artist of African American descent took place with the Berlin Philharmonic Orchestra on September 2–3, 1945. At the time, the orchestra was under the American military administration.[71] The circumstances of this concert are important, for it was not the Americans who were responsible for this extraordinary event that caused both excitement and provocation. Rather, a Soviet cultural

[67] The National Archives (London, England) 1049/71, Draft Notes on Music for Germany. As cited in: Thacker, *Music after Hitler, 1945–1955*, 25.

[68] IfZ/OMGUS 5/243–2/1, Annex 'A'. As cited in: ibid.

[69] The National Archives (London, England) 946/57, untitled memorandum signed McClure, May 14, 1946. As cited in: ibid., 96.

[70] IfZ/OMGUS 5/348–3/4, Report of Meeting on February 15, 1947. As cited in: ibid., 95–96. Cf. David Monod, *Settling Scores: German Music, Denazification, and the Americans, 1945–1953* (Chapel Hill: University of North Carolina Press, 2005).

[71] The program listed the following pieces: Carl Maria von Webern, *Oberon Overture*; William Grant Still, *African-American Symphony*; Peter I. Tchaikovsky, *Symphony No. 6*. www.berliner-philharmoniker.de/en/konzerte/calendar/details/6369/.

officer had introduced conductor Rudolph Dunbar to Russian-born Leo Borchard, the conductor of the Berlin Philharmonic, who that summer had replaced celebrity Wilhelm Furtwängler after a brief vacuum of leadership (Furtwängler had fled from Vienna to Switzerland the previous January).[72] Borchard had originally organized these performances with Dunbar but had been accidentally killed that August, when his driver failed to see an American road blockade and the guards shot at the vehicle.[73] Meanwhile, the Philharmonic had moved to the Western sector under the jurisdiction of the American military administration, with Dunbar's concerts taking place in the Titania-Palast in Berlin-Steglitz. After Dunbar had rehearsed, the American authorities gave him permission to perform, causing vivid discussions among the officials. A report to the ICS depicts the commotion among American officers over his performance: "There was great excitement about the performance of Rudolph Dunbar, the young colored conductor and the Philharmonic orchestra. Even before there had been fierce debates whether it would be reasonable for him to conduct. From now on, the discussion about Dunbar's abilities will be continued ad nauseam."[74] Although the informant did not specify exactly what caused the excitement, it is likely that the conductor's performance was seen as highly provocative. The fact that a black man was conducting the Berlin Philharmonic not only flew in the face of Nazi racist ideology, but also helped to dismiss charges of the American promulgation of white supremacy. Moreover, Dunbar's choice of program represents a political statement further challenging Eurocentrism, featuring a German, a Russian, and an African American piece: The *Afro-American Symphony* by William Grant Still, was performed alongside Carl Maria von Weber's *Oberon Overture* and Tchaikovsky's *Symphony No. 6*.

Such instances in those years were rare but meaningful, and as noted above, Soviet authorities tended to promote African American music for its social revolutionary potential in the Cold War effort. American officials strictly directed their cultural policies toward showcasing high culture, ostracizing black cultural contributions as outside the realm of culture and respectability. In contrast, Soviet ideology defied conceptions of white superiority, not just by their support of jazz, but also by their initiative to

---

[72] Sam H. Shirakawa, *The Devil's Music Master: The Controversial Life and Career of Wilhelm Furtwängler* (New York: Oxford University Press, 1991).

[73] Andreas-Friedrich, *Der Schattenmann*, 385–89.

[74] Semi-Weekly Report No.18/19, Edward Hogan, John Bitter, Robert Joseph (FTM) to ICS officer Berlin District, September 5, 1945; OMGUS 5/242–3/13. As cited in: Chamberlin, *Kultur auf Trümmern*.

deploy a conductor of African descent for an orchestra once symbolizing Aryan superiority. Policy changes toward jazz and the American acquiescence to Dunbar's performance did signal some shifts in official opinion, but as the next section details, by the late 1940s, divergent aesthetic conceptions of socialist realism on the one side and cultural freedom on the other solidified Eastern and Western positions on jazz.

Cold War in the Arts: Socialist Realism versus Cultural Freedom

In the ideological competition of the Cold War, diverging cultural concepts emerged in force by the late 1940s. American officials took up the cause of cultural freedom pushing for modernist art, while Soviet authorities promoted the concept of socialist realism, shunning modern works representing abstract styles and instead emphasizing a nationalist approach to art rooted in folk traditions.[75] Soviet leadership had propagated socialist realism during the 1930s, demanding that Soviet art and literature must have educative responsibilities and apolitical art could no longer be tolerated. Works of art, in this view, were to be freed from outside influences expressed in such terms as "formalism," "bourgeois decadence," or "cosmopolitanism." Over the following years, cultural purges spearheaded by Andrej Zhdanov targeted numerous Soviet artists whose works allegedly embodied these qualities: the ramifications of Zhdanov's directives, entrenched with nationalism, xenophobia and anti-Semitism, would set the direction of cultural politics – including jazz policies – in the SBZ and later GDR.[76]

Soviet authorities disparaged undesirable tendencies in music as "non-artistic," "confused noise," "alien to the normal human ear," or "formalistic distortions inimical to the people."[77] Not only did Russian music such as that of Stravinsky and Shostakovich fall under this verdict, but ideologues

---

[75] The United States policymakers showcased Stravinsky's work and were reluctant to feature experimental music such as that by John Cage. Cf. Wilford.

[76] Andrej Alexandrowitsch Zhdanov: Rede auf dem 1. Unionkongress der Sowjetschriftsteller 1934. In: A. Zhdanov, Über Kunst und Wissenschaft, Berlin 1951. As cited in: Daniel Zur Weihen, "Die Kunstkommission und die Komposition zeitgenössischer Musik," in *Die staatliche Kommission für Kunstangelegenheiten (1951–1953) – eine Kulturbehörde "neuen Typus,"* ed. Jochen Staadt (Frankfurt a. M.: Peter Lang, Internationaler Verlag der Wissenschaften, 2011), 283.

[77] Beschlüsse des Zentralkomitees der Kommunistischen Partei der Sowjetunion (KPdSU) (B) zu Fragen der Literatur und Kunst (1946–1948), 25–32. As cited in: David Pike, *The Politics of Culture in Soviet-Occupied Germany, 1945–1949* (Stanford, Calif.: Stanford University Press, 1992), 465–66; ibid.

lashed out at twentieth-century European modernity in general, deprecating French expressionism and the atonality of the Schönberg circle alike. Atonality violated the principles of melodious Russian folk music and, therefore, could not be brought into accordance with the national interests "of the people." Zhdanov's cultural policies, mingling Russian nationalistic chauvinism with anti-Western xenophobia, sought to popularize socialist realism while also denigrating Western culture to prevent the ideological contamination of Soviet artists. Proponents legitimized cultural isolation by outlawing the foreign influence of the "seditious" West.[78] Moreover, strong anti-Semitic tendencies entered this discourse under the epithet "cosmopolitanism," which as the historian David Pike notes became a euphemism for Jewishness.[79] In the Soviet view, true internationalism flourished only when national art prospered. As Zhdanov argued, "[Those] who ignored this simple principle by allowing themselves to be influenced by modern artistic innovations or experiments of the West were therefore not internationalists at all, they were 'homeless cosmopolitans' whose patriotism and race was as suspect as their politics."[80] The term "enemy of the people" derived from this rhetoric and was later used by policymakers in the GDR. In extreme instances, certain forms of artistic expressions were outlawed because they were conceived as manifestations of national betrayal, falling into the category of criminal offences such as treason.[81]

As mentioned above, the German music discourse after WWI, terms such as decadence and degeneration suggested deviations from civilized bourgeois respectability and were used to fight works, or conduct, seen as racially transgressive. As explored in Chapter 1, beginning in the 1920s, buzzwords such as "cultural bolshevism" stirred fears of "leftist revolutions," "Jewish conspiracies," and cultural infiltration in the form of jazz. Such rhetoric only gained significance in the 1930s and 1940s when the National Socialists condemned modern art and music as evidence of racial decline. After the war, both Soviet and German Communists utilized a similar vocabulary to denounce modern art and Western popular culture, crystalized in the term "cosmopolitanism," in contrast to national-ethnic art, which the Soviet authorities were eager to protect from outside influences. Both these pejoratives of "cultural bolshevism"

---

[78] Ibid., 200–45.
[79] Ibid., 467.
[80] Zhdanov, "Fragen der sowjetischen Musikkultur," *Neue Welt*, 11 (1948): 3–18. As cited in: ibid., 470.
[81] Ibid., 460–72.

and "cosmopolitanism," one used primarily by Fascists in the 1930s and 1940s and the other primarily by Stalinists in the 1950s, targeted modern and Western cultural tendencies.

In the late 1940s, authorities in the SBZ directed the term "cosmopolitanism" against jazz as an American cultural product – but, importantly, not against it as an African American music. This ambiguity complicated both the ideological use of jazz and the Communists' efforts to streamline their position on the music. On this perspective, jazz fulfilled socialist demands via its perceived ethnic origin and its popularity, but in the late 1940s, as ideologies hardened, officials simultaneously rejected it as both an American and a "cosmopolitan" influence. This would eventually turn jazz into a problematic propaganda tool for the Soviets: in the immediate postwar years they politicized jazz, aiming it against the injustices of capitalist America, but by the late 1940s, the rising popularity of American pop music among the youth undermined these efforts to exploit its potential as propaganda.

Though cultural officers such as Dymschitz had first tried to dampen Moscow's harsh dogmatic tone in order to pacify German artists and intellectuals, by the late 1940s, such officers were increasingly inclined to function as ideological mouthpieces, propagating the dogma of socialist realism and employing proven dictatorial methods.[82] The rhetoric used to condemn various forms of artistic expressions echoed that of Nazi propaganda almost embarrassingly. Historian David Pike has suggested that "Dymschitz knowingly used fascist terminology to denounce modern art in hopes of pandering to currents of public opinion that shared his revulsion, however different the reasons might have been."[83] Moreover, Pike argues,

> Dymschitz referred contemptuously to "influences alien to the essence" of art (*wesensfremde Einflüsse*) and extolled the struggle for its deliverance from the perils of capitalism, which endangered art's supposed "innermost essence." He then suggested that the formalist direction in art risked causing artistic creativity to "degenerate" (*entarten*) and represented a "direct attack upon the essence of art."[84]

The employment of such rhetoric distinguished Soviet cultural politics from that of their rivals by suggesting that under Soviet leadership "decadent" American influences would be contained and true national

[82] Ibid., 201–45.
[83] Ibid., 534.
[84] Ibid.; Alexander Dymschitz, "Über die formalistische Richtung in der deutschen Malerei. Bemerkungen eines Außenstehenden," *Tägliche Rundschau* (November 19 and 24, 1948).

art could flourish. To draw on nationalist, right-wing Nazi rhetoric was most likely a populist-driven decision, taking into consideration the fact that the majority of German citizens preferred conservative aesthetic concepts. One signifier of this was that, in general, the notion of jazz was associated with fears of Americanization and racial transgression in postwar Germany.[85]

With an emphasis on "collective work" and "central regulation," a group of musicians and composers, supported by the Socialist Unity Party (*Sozialistische Einheitspartei Deutschlands*, SED), which was the Communist Party in the SBZ, worked on defining a Marxist-Leninist theory of music for the future socialist German society. The guidelines for music and society worked out in the late 1940s by Ernst Hermann Meyer and his colleagues Max Butting, Karl Laux, and Nathan Notowicz constituted the blueprint for the subsequent musical politics of the future GDR.[86] Meyer, who is discussed in more detail in the next chapter, had been active in the émigré Free German Cultural League in England during the war and had developed a range of Marxist ideas about music and its role within socialism. Although he had a considerable reputation as a composer, broadcaster, and musicologist, his aspirations to help reconstruct musical life in the British zone were rejected by British authorities because of his open commitment to the Communist Party.[87]

However, after the Nazi era, German-leftist composers and musicologists, in general, questioned modernist concepts of music anew. In their view, the catastrophes of genocidal war, the mass murder of civilians, and the devastation across Europe demanded a collective effort to build a new and humane society, which they assumed would have to be socialist. Ready to serve the socialist cause, they shunned musical works that were considered unable to educate the masses. These individuals, such as Hanns Eisler, a prominent composer who would go on to compose the East German national anthem, supported the notion of socialist realism.[88]

The importance of Eisler's arrival at this key moment cannot be overstated. In postwar Berlin, the leftist musical community anxiously awaited his return from exile in the United States; Eisler finally arriving in October 1948. The fact that Eisler had dedicated his work to the

---

[85] Timothy L. Schroer, *Recasting Race after World War II: Germans and African-Americans in American-Occupied Germany* (Boulder: University Press of Colorado, 2007). See also Poiger's work on the same topic.

[86] Thacker, *Music after Hitler, 1945–1955*, 114–17.

[87] Ibid., 26–27.

[88] Köster, *Musik-Zeit-Geschehen*, 80.

socialist cause during the 1930s made his presence of great significance to the efforts to build a new socialist music culture. During the Weimar era, Eisler had employed popular music and jazz to engage the masses and to raise social consciousness of American racial politics in compositions such as op. 18/6 from 1930 and the "Ballad of Nigger Jim" (*Ballade vom Nigger Jim*), a work that vividly portrayed segregation in the United States.[89] In a press conference that October in East Berlin, he spoke about his experiences during his exile. Questioned about racism in the United States, he answered by relating an experience he had had in New York: "I was in a bar having my beer, when a black man came in and ordered one as well. Instead of serving the man, the bartender filled up a glass with beer and smashed it on the bar in front of him."[90] It seems that in the 1940s, attempts to break through the color line, even in a northern city, could still elicit outbursts of hostility. During that same press conference, the German publisher of Howard Fast's novel *Freedom Road* asked if Eisler could confirm that Fast was still incarcerated in the United States. "Yes," Eisler responded, "Howard Fast is in prison. The House Un-American Activities Committee put him in jail for six months. He committed the following crime: he refused to release the names and addresses of Spanish freedom fighters to Franco's regime. He did not want to jeopardize people in Spain."[91] As is clear, such accounts tended not only to advance notions of America as the imperialist adversary, but also suggested its direct connections to fascist powers such as Franco's Spain.

Furthermore, during that press conference, Eisler revealed his view on African American musical culture:

> The most talented musicians in the United States are African-Americans.... Their methods of performance, their precision should be envied by any symphonic orchestra. I admit, they are used as musical shoe shiners, their music is played in late-night bars where they have to churn out a kind of entertaining music. But the skill, the talent and the originality, the wit and vigor is so remarkable that I daresay the real great American composer will be an African-American.[92]

Eisler's deep admiration of African American musical talent languishing under the framework of capitalism echoed his view of the low artistic

---

[89] The derogatory term "nigger" here illustrates the practice of segregation. On jazz in Eisler's work see Monika Tibbe, "Volkstümlichkeit als Problem des Komponierens," in *Hanns Eisler* (Berlin: Argument-Verlag GmbH, 1975).
[90] Hanns Eisler, *Hanns Eisler Archiv, Akademie der Künste, 7152 AVM* (October 25, 1948).
[91] Ibid.
[92] Ibid.

level of symphonic orchestras in the United States, reflecting common European notions of the uncultured nation. As he said: "I see in the mediocre performances of Beethoven in American cities a frightening deficiency of talent."[93] Pressing the point against the myth of white superiority, Eisler portrayed black music as more original and suggested that black talent laid idle because it was trapped within capitalist music production, even observing about the entertainment industry: "Yes I say, this is filth and trash, but in this the negroes are showing their talent and originality, and a connoisseur sees in a filthy little piece of pleasure real virtuosity and talent."[94] Eisler's views were unambiguous: American society engaged in racist practices that permeated all realms of life, the American government backed fascist interests, and the talents of its most creative musicians were wasted because the capitalist entertainment industry misused them. In subsequent years, Eisler would go on to express his overt appreciation for jazz: his approval would bestow great cultural credibility on the form, and throughout the following decades, jazz fans in the GDR would refer to Eisler to vindicate their position on the music.[95]

After a brief period of cultural plurality in the mid-1940s, by the end of the decade, Soviet and Allied forces had established competing ideologies of socialist realism versus cultural freedom. In its efforts to postulate guidelines for artistic production, socialist doctrine denounced modern and Western influences and, using fascist rhetoric, drew on concepts of populist traditions that were determined more by ethnicity or nationality rather than by other markers. Moreover, German-leftist musicians and theorists were convinced that their participation in the cocreation of a German socialist music at this turning point in history was of critical importance. They believed that their task was to create works for the masses; therefore, they eagerly awaited guidelines from Soviet ideologues.[96] Eisler, who in the GDR was believed to be the founding father of the German socialist music culture, represented the paragon of such a composer. His view encapsulated the dilemma over jazz within socialist discourse in the 1950s and most of the 1960s. African American music was believed to be tainted by a profit-driven industry, which exploited the musical talent of a people. On the one hand, jazz stemmed from the ingenious creative force of a people whose history was one of suppression and discrimination in the capitalist world, and

[93] Ibid.
[94] Ibid.
[95] "Hanns Eisler über den Jazz," *Berliner Zeitung* (April 18, 1956); *Musik und Politik*, ed. G. Mayer (Berlin, 1973).
[96] *Hanns Eisler Archiv, Akademie der Künste, 7152 AVM.*

on the other, it nevertheless represented popular American music culture. To overcome this predicament, East German jazz discourse would develop notions of the music that created further polarized terms such as "true jazz" and "corrupted jazz."

German Jazz Is "Up to Date"

In the late 1940s, Berlin gradually reconnected to its once-prosperous jazz scene. After the restrictions of the Nazi years, many Germans found it exhilarating to hear American popular music legally on the radio, played by channels such as Armed Forces Network, the British Broadcasting Corporation (BBC), *Drahtfunk im Amerikanischen Sektor* (DIAS), which was the predecessor of *Rundfunk im Amerikanischen Sektor* (RIAS), and not least the Soviet-controlled Berliner Rundfunk.[97] Jazz fans founded the so-called Hot Clubs in major German cities such as Frankfurt, Düsseldorf, Hamburg, Leipzig, and Berlin. The Hot Club Berlin, founded in late 1945 by Hans Blüthner, drew its members from diverse wartime (and pre-war) jazz organizations.[98] Proponents of the Hot Clubs advocated the appreciation of what they regarded as "pure jazz," as opposed to noisy, rowdy music. In the view of these purists, pure jazz was the music of small improvisational New Orleans-style ensembles, which they preferred over pre-arranged big band swing.[99] Some of the first jam sessions in Berlin were held in June 1947, and they drew professionals and amateurs from all zones of occupation.[100] Chief of Production Konstantin Metaxas, working for the Soviet-controlled record company Amiga, was responsible for the recording of these sessions, calling its various constellations the "Amiga All-Star-Band."[101]

To explore these new musical opportunities, numerous dance orchestras and jazz ensembles formed in the late 1940s across the SBZ. They predominantly featured swing music but also showcased styles such as bebop. To name but two, the RBT under Horst Kudritzki and the Swingband des Berliner Rundfunks under Walter Dobschinsky did studio work and

---

[97] The Russians occupied the building of the former Großdeutscher Rundfunk on Masurenallee until the early 1950s, leading the Americans to improvise a broadcasting system via telephone cables, named *Drahtfunk*, or wire broadcasting.

[98] Lange, *Jazz in Deutschland*, 151.

[99] Program of a "Jazz Jamboree" dated May 8, 1949, and organized by the Hot Club Berlin. As cited in: Käs, *Hot and Sweet*, 250.

[100] Lange, *Jazz in Deutschland*.

[101] Wolfgang Muth, "Jazz Made in Germany 1919–1949" (Private Collection Hopfe, 1962/1963).

recorded for Amiga. The first years after the war also witnessed a dance craze in Germany: during the years prior to currency reforms in 1949, dance events were widely popular and generally sold out, because dancing had been prohibited by the Nazi regime since February 1943 after the battle of Stalingrad.[102] One indicator of the postwar craze was dance marathons, serving as an emotional release valve for the pent-up demand of the war years. Ensembles such as the Melodia Rhythmiker in Halle, the Heinz-Kretzschmar-Sextett in Dresden, and the Joe Glaser Quintet in Berlin revived the scene, elaborating on postwar modern impulses in jazz.[103] By 1949, there had been 130 Sunday jazz matinees presented in the Friedrichstadt-Palast in Berlin. Also by that time, the divided nation had become a political reality. Cold War battles were fought on-stage with audiences choosing sides in so-called "battles of the bands" via ballot cards: a surviving program of one such concert dated November 13, 1949, announces "Berlin Bands against guests of the Eastern Zone and prominent jazz bands from West Germany and Berlin."[104]

Around the turn of the decade, the East German jazz scene was vital and up to date, here exemplified in a letter describing the concert of the Melodia Rhythmiker. On June 7, 1949, Hans Lothar Hoffmann from Halle in the SBZ wrote a letter to his sister, Efi: "Dear Efi! On Whitsunday (*Pfingstsonntag*) there was a Matinee of the Melodia Rhythmiker in the Steintor Variety Theater under the direction of Horst Hartmann. It began at 10:30. As a matter of course it was totally sold out. I was sitting close to the orchestra. And then it began. ... It was excellent!"[105] Hoffmann's account offers great insight into concert practice and reception, which challenges recent scholarly views on the German jazz scene in the late 1940s. These views argue that, because of Germany's relative isolation during and after the war, Germans had missed recent musical developments in the United States. Yet the Melodia Rhythmiker and their fans seem to have been well aware of the latest developments and were able to differentiate between various jazz styles.[106] The "Melodias" – as the fans called

---

[102] Käs, *Hot and Sweet*, 250.

[103] See also Lange, *Jazz in Deutschland*; Drechsel; in *Jazz in Deutschland*, ed. Wolfram Knauer (Darmstadt: Wolke Verlag Hofheim, 1996); Muth, Jazz Made in Germany 1919–1949; Manfred Raupach, "Swing in Görlitz: Ein musikalischer Rückblick auf die ersten Jahre nach dem 2. Weltkrieg," *Der Jazzfreund*, no. September (1996).

[104] Program of the 130th battle of the bands, "Jazz on Sunday Mornings." Private archive of Hans Blüthner. As cited in: Käs, *Hot and Sweet*, 251.

[105] Hans-Lothar Hofmann, "Letter to his sister Efi," (1949).

[106] Poiger, *Jazz, Rock and Rebels*, 42; Michael H. Kater, *Different Drummers: Jazz in the Culture of Nazi Germany* (New York: Oxford University Press, 1992), 203.

them – were dressed in dark suits that morning as they performed in the Steintor, one of the oldest variety theaters in Germany with 1,200 seats.[107] As a popular dance band, they featured swing tunes of Duke Ellington, Count Basie, Tommy Dorsey, and Glenn Miller; some of the arrangements for big band swing had been obtained by one of the band members during his time as an American POW. According to jazz researcher Wolfgang Muth, the Melodias' baritone-saxophonist "copied a fundamental part of the classical [swing] arrangements of Glenn Miller, Benny Goodman, etc."[108] (Figure 2.3).

Figure 2.3   Melodia Rhythmiker at Naumburg 1951, with band lineup. Private collection of Wolfgang Muth/Gerhard Hopfe, used by permission

[107] www.steintor-variete.de/das-steintor-variete/.
[108] Muth, *Jazz Made in Germany 1919–1949*.

Most of the band members had enjoyed a professional musical education and were able to transcribe big band arrangements by ear in the absence of sheet music sources.[109] Their knowledge of recent developments in jazz and their ability to master modern arrangements and harmonies made the Melodias sound like an up-to-date postwar big band. As Muth noted, the orchestra had a modern presence "with sweeping arrangements and unorthodox harmonic progressions following Stan Kenton's work."[110] Interestingly, the Melodias' postwar repertoire up to 1949 featured only Latin and American titles. Comparing the Melodias' song list from the immediate postwar era to that featured at the Steintor Variety Theater, it is striking that titles of American compositions were featured in German translation in 1949, for in the late 1940s, the band eschewed their American appearance in favor of a more Germanized look due to anti-Western policies. Moreover, after the founding of the East German state, they renamed the band to Tanzorchester Horst Hartmann and dropped almost all the song titles of American origin to ensure the granting of a performance license.

In his letter, Hofmann informed his sister of every detail of the concert including song titles, names of composers, arrangers, and soloists, occasionally rendering and coediting titles. Besides American songs, the Melodias featured a variety of German wartime and post-wartime songs typical for that era with their escapist quality, a common aspect at the time.[111] These melodies were arranged for big band, a practice established since the early days of jazz. Among these titles were: *Ein kleines Lied soll uns verbinden* ("A little song should connect us," 1943) and *Musst nicht traurig sein* ("Don't be sad," 1941) by Werner Kleine; *Komm' mit mir nach Tahiti* ("Come with me to Tahiti," 1947) by Friedrich Schröder; and songs by Gerhard Winkler, the composer of the famous *Capri Fischer* song. During the war, the catchy tune *Ein kleines Lied soll uns verbinden* had been featured regularly in a popular radio program.[112] Hofmann comments: "(Composer) Werner Kleine would have not recognized his songs, because of their jazzy arrangements."[113] The band had managed to arrange these foxtrots and waltzes for big band. The audience expressed excitement after each piece and reacted not just by

[109] Gerhard Dopleb and Wolfgang Muth, December 22, 1988. Ibid.
[110] Ibid. Some of the musicians who later pursued a career in the Berlin Rundfunk were educated at the private music school *Stadtpfeife* in Görlach.
[111] See also: Raupach, Swing in Görlitz.
[112] Probably the most important radio series of this kind was *Für jeden etwas. Zwei bunte Stunden.* See Konrad Dussel, *Deutsche Rundfunkgeschichte* (Konstanz: Verlagsgesellschaft Konstanz, 2004), 114; Hans-Jörg Koch, *Das Wunschkonzert im NS-Rundfunk* (Köln, Weimar: Böhlau Verlag, 2003), 158.
[113] Hofmann, Letter to his sister Efi.

applauding, but also by stamping their feet and clanging cowbells, rattles, and tinkles, which were common accessories for jazz concerts. The resulting noise was probably perceived as a sign of misbehavior and "American-influenced" rowdiness of the era, given that such conduct was historically uncommon in German concert halls. Adaptations of Kenton's titles such as "Eager Beaver" and "Artistry Jumps" earned long applauses, according to Hofmann, who labeled them "new progressive jazz." Two arrangements were in bebop style, one of which was given as an encore titled "Hurricane," after well over a thousand young people demanded more bebop. A later account of these Berlin concerts acknowledges that high-energy, loud pieces were more successful with audiences than more reserved ones. "We had great success, but also the Berlin audience chose loud and noisy titles over our subtle arrangements."[114] Indeed, the band was invited in 1949 and 1950 to a battle of the bands contest in West Berlin's Titania-Palast and won first place both times[115] (Figure 2.4).

Figure 2.4   The Titania-Palast, Berlin, 1955, advertising Karl Walter Band on marquee. Photo by Marche/ Getty Images. Editorial #542374925

[114] Letter from Gerhard Dopleb to Wolfgang Muth, December 22, 1988. Muth, *Jazz Made in Germany 1919–1949*.
[115] Gerhard Hopfe, *Melodia Rhythmiker im Titania-Palast, Berlin; 137 Kapellenwettstreit, 9 April 1950* (1950). Cf. Letter from Gerhard Dopleb, December 22, 1988, Muth, *Jazz Made in Germany 1919–1949*.

At one point, the Melodias had the opportunity to record with Radio Leipzig, but the producer rejected their modern jazz arrangements of George Bizet's *L'Arlésienne Suite*, likely because of the deconstruction of the solemn dignity of Bizet's work.[116] Such a response recalls similar reactions in the 1920s to the "jazzed-up" versions of nineteenth-century European classical music, which disturbed the emotional codex. The rhythmic syncopation disrupted an emotional world conjured by nineteenth-century classics. As Lothar Hofmann had mentioned to his sister, the Melodias' jazz adaptations altered well-known tunes almost beyond recognition. Even in the late 1940s, swinging interpretations of European classics caused great indignation, recalling similar reactions to Paul Whiteman's jazzy arrangements of nineteenth-century German music in the 1920s.

The example of the Melodia Rhythmiker is key to understanding the musical performances of German jazz bands, their reception by young Germans, and the practices of German broadcasting and production at the time. The Melodias' musicians were eager to connect to recent developments from America: at the same time as they were reaching out to contemporary streams of jazz, their big band arrangements recalled the recent past by utilizing popular wartime melodies. Yet this was not the only exposure to American music that young audiences had. For German youth, especially for young people living in the SBZ like Gerhard Hopfe, a native of Berlin born in 1933, the introduction to jazz came from an unlikely source. Hopfe had grown up in the Falkensee in the western part of Berlin, a neighborhood that had been part of the Russian sector since the spring of 1945. In a recent interview, Hopfe recalled his first encounter with jazz at the age of fourteen in the winter of 1947–1948, which was one of the hardest in recent years. Temperatures dropped well below average, and lakes remained frozen far into the spring. Severe food shortages caused high fatality rates. Hopfe remembered American troops at his school, which the students would only visit to get food and hand in their homework, because the schools themselves could not be heated:

> One day we were asked to stay a little longer, because the Americans wanted to show a movie. A GYA truck drove into the schoolyard and they set up a film projector and screen in the auditorium. And what did we see? The Glenn Miller movie *Sun Valley Serenade* ... and the entire Glenn Miller Air Force Band in uniforms, and our eyes and ears were opened. What music was that? We had never heard anything like this before, and were aroused with interest.[117]

[116] Letter from Gerhard Dopleb to Wolfgang Muth, December 22, 1988.
[117] Gerhard Hopfe (2010). Interview with the author.

As Hopfe noted, jazz was propagated locally within the United States Armed Forces German Youth Activities (GYA) programs, although official GYA reports do not account for this. In early 1948, GYA officials showed jazz films in conjunction with food distribution programs for schools in and around Berlin, reaching those areas that were occupied by the Soviets. American food distribution in Berlin's schools – mostly Army provisions – continued until the division of the municipal administration of Berlin in November 1948. Just as the Soviets had organized the AFJ, the Americans tried to engage youngsters in programs of the GYA offering numerous activities to foster democratic reorientation. Supplying basic needs for their visitors, Americans opened GYA centers in Berlin in close proximity to the Soviet zone, offering entertainment such as the screening of *Sun Valley Serenade.* This movie featured some of the swing era's biggest hits such as "In the Mood" and "Chattanooga Choo-Choo," with stunning dance performances by African Americans Dorothy Dandridge and the Nicholas Brothers. Granted, some censorship was still in effect: according to Hopfe, the scenes with African American performers were not featured in the version he viewed in the spring of 1948. Since the United States Armed Forces were still segregated, it seems that the "white" version was used in this context.

The United States European Command (EUCOM) had established the GYA in April 1946 under the name "Armed Forces Assistance Program to German Youth Activities." The program was never an official part of the Office of Military Government for Germany (OMGUS) but was partially financed by funds from the Government Aids and Relief in Occupied Areas (GARIOA).[118] Official reports documenting the GYA programs do not account for the deployment of jazz entertainment in German schools nor at the GYA centers in the American zone.[119] Nevertheless, GYA officers used the screening of this film to great effect with minimum effort by concealing the act of propagating American culture within food distribution. Without a doubt such propaganda in the SBZ in the late 1940s was extremely disturbing to the Soviet administration, which already had criticized the GYA as corrupting the ideology of young Germans. In November 1947, Marshal Vasily Sokolovsky, head of the SMAD and

---

[118] Hermann-Josef Rupieper, *Die Wurzeln der westdeutschen Nachkriegsdemokratie: Der amerikanische Beitrag 1945–1952* (Opladen: Westdeutscher Verlag, 1993), 156.

[119] "The US Armed Forces German Youth Activities Program, 1945–1955," published by Historical Division Headquarters, United States Army, Europe 1956. https://archive.org/details/UsArmedForcesGermanYouthActivitiesProgram1945–1955_927.

member of the Allied Control Council (*Alliierter Kontrollrat*), accused the GYA of being a subversive cover-up for the military training of German youth.[120]

The discrepancies between the official and unofficial activities of the GYA become obvious on a closer examination. In 1956, the United States Army published an assessment of the GYA's success, giving an overview of its work in the past decade. The report mentions evening entertainment: "One of the most popular activities with young Germans – though much criticized by their parents – was the program of evening dances."[121] The GYA report does not specify what kind of music was played at these dances, but it is likely that popular swing music was the preferred genre. Such GYA activities had caused resentment among parents and church officials, stirring fears of the "Americanization" of youth through these coeducational and cross-denominational activities.[122] As noted at the beginning of this chapter, in the immediate postwar period, American officials initially did not intend to use jazz for reeducation purposes. Rather, the dissemination of jazz in occupied Germany occurred primarily through channels intended for Army entertainment. The screening of *Sun Valley Serenade*, initially intended for American troop entertainment but then screened in front of German schoolchildren, can be understood as an initiative on the ground to serve both practical and ideological purposes. Over sixty years later, Hopfe recalled not only his fascination with big band swing, which he had never heard before, but also the military attire of the musicians symbolizing American power. Musical pleasure was combined with respect for the occupying American authority in a playful, sympathetic manner featuring pop music appealing to teenagers. There is no doubt that American troops on the ground used films such as this to curry respect and admiration among German youth. While Soviet jazz propaganda aimed to raise social consciousness against the American model, the American approach to jazz propaganda foregrounded fun, not ideology.

If the GYA served as one route to jazz for German youth, another route was just as effective: the United States Information Center (USIC) or, informally, *Amerikahaus* (Figure 2.5). For the teenage Hopfe and his schoolmates, "The *Amerikahaus* was a treasure chest: Books, magazines,

---

[120] Historical Division United States Army, *US Armed Forces German Youth Activities Program 1945–1955* (1956), 29.
[121] Ibid., 34.
[122] Poiger, *Jazz, Rock and Rebels*, 39.

Figure 2.5   Amerikahaus Berlin, Einmerstraße am Nollendorfplatz, June 1949.
Getty Images. Editorial #542394111

records, movies and American newsreels. We were there constantly on weekends but also after school during the week. When there was something going on, after school we went straight to the *Amerikahaus*."[123] Although the *Amerikahäuser* did not feature live jazz performances until the mid-to-late 1950s,[124] they nevertheless held a magical appeal. Everything American was associated with the sense of life represented by swing music. In recent interviews, Hopfe recalled numerous trips from Falkensee into Berlin's Western Zone to visit the *Amerikahaus* in the late 1940s. Having already been exposed to jazz via *Sun Valley Serenade*, the teenager and his friends were drawn to the *Amerikahaus*, located then at Nollendorfplatz, where they could learn more about the country associated with their beloved music. One of their geography teachers, who had

[123] Gerhard Hopfe (2010). Interview with the author.
[124] Ingrid Monson, *Freedom Sounds: Civil Rights Call Out to Jazz and Africa* (Oxford: Oxford University Press, 2007), 113–20.

been a POW in the United States, was fond of jazz and informed them about the newest trends. Hopfe recalled:

> We had a geography teacher who had come from war imprisonment in the US. He had brought swing LPs and instructed us that there was not only Glenn Miller, but also Tommy Dorsey and Jimmy Dorsey and so on. One of our classmates brought a gramophone and the teacher presented his records. We wanted to know so much![125]

In schools in the SBZ, it was still possible for teachers to include jazz in their programs. Hopfe continued: "Then our school had a new director who had come back from a Soviet prison camp. He was a Stalinist. He gave speeches against the bourgeoisie and about the rebuilding of the GDR, whereby no philosophers were needed."[126] For people like Hopfe, the new political course in the East became manifest in discrimination against those who were not representative of the workers and peasants classes. Indeed, Hopfe, the son of an architect, was prohibited from earning a high school diploma and was forced instead to learn a trade because his family had no working-class background. Such repressions against families with educated backgrounds reveal the East German system's effort to recruit proletarians and penalize formerly privileged families. A few years later, when Hopfe was in his early twenties, GDR authorities accused him of working for the Eastern office of the West German Social Democrat Party (SPD), and he was imprisoned for several years (Figure 2.6).

In any case, American officials established *Amerikahäuser* in major German cities in all three western zones after 1945.[127] Twenty-seven centers altogether, initially housing libraries and reading rooms, offered access to international culture. While outright jazz promotion in the *Amerikahäuser* in the form of concerts and lectures or the support of West German jazz clubs would not arrive until the late 1950s, Germans were still able to obtain contemporary American literature as well as information about art, politics, and science that had been inaccessible during the Nazi era. The goal was to represent America not only as a country of high culture, but also as one devoid of social grievances.[128] American translation programs

---

[125] Hopfe, *Melodia Rhythmiker im Titania-Palast, Berlin.*

[126] Ibid.

[127] Daniel Haufler, "Amerika, hast Du es besser? Zur deutschen Buchkultur nach 1945," in *Amerikanisierung und Sowjetisierung in Deutschland: 1945–1970,* ed. Konrad H. Jarausch and Hannes Siegrist (Frankfurt a. M.; New York: Campus, 1997), 396; On censorship on cultural products see Wilford, 99–122.

[128] Saunders, *Who Paid the Piper? The CIA and the Cultural Cold War,* 19–20.

Figure 2.6   Gerhard Hopfe with his audio equipment, 1966. Private collection
of Gerhard Hopfe, used by permission

supported works with a clear anti-communist message and increasingly
banned writers and works with leftist tendencies and Communist affili-
ations, including works native to America that described or denounced
racism and crime in the United States. Communist writer Howard Fast's
Freedom Road was prohibited from translation outright.[129] A German
translation of Fast's novel, though, still circulated in the Soviet zone: the
FDJ-affiliated publisher *Neues Leben*, which specialized in literature for
youth, published the first edition of the German translation in 1948. Fast's
novel was widely distributed by the FDJ and, therefore, became well-
known among the GDR youth.[130]

In sum, while American policymakers pondered how to culturally represent their country in occupied Germany, one of the most potent weapons
in the Cold War was unwittingly placed at their disposal: popular music.

---

[129] Haufler, Amerika, hast Du es besser? Zur deutschen Buchkultur nach 1945, 393–94.
[130] Howard Fast, *Strasse zur Freiheit* (Berlin: Neues Leben, 1948).

Disseminated through American troop entertainment, the demand for jazz influenced the cultural reorientation of many young Germans after WWII. The desire for entertainment and dance in the immediate postwar era was met in the formation of hundreds of bands, which were well-versed in contemporary American styles. Even so, American policymakers refrained from outright jazz promotion because they perceived it as counterproductive to the propagation of the American democratic model. Rather, in the late 1940s, efforts to streamline American cultural representation manifested more readily in anti-Communist activities. While American cultural centers refrained from outright jazz promotion, jazz promotion on the ground was in full swing – occasionally in surprising settings, as the next section details.

"Shades of Uncle Adolf" and *Air Lift Stomp*

> My worst anxieties became certain when I was told that my first concert was at two a.m. in the practically deserted Delphi-Palast located on a ruined Berlin street, and would be lit only by two carbide lamps. The invitation to the event read, 'In view of the power cuts, each guest is requested to bring a candle.' To my surprise, the lack of lighting turned out to be an asset. It was a stunning sight to look out into the pinpoints of fluttering candlelight. Furthermore, the big crowd of jazz buffs, both German civilians and American soldiers, greeted us with tumultuous applause. Because I had expected so little, this concert is one I will never forget – an outstanding page in my book of memories.[131]

This is how Rex Stewart recalls his experience in Berlin in July 1948. He had just left Duke Ellington and was touring France and Germany with his own ensemble and about to record in Berlin. Yet the setting for such an event could not have been more tense.

By the end of the 1940s, the former war allies were split into two hostile camps with incompatible ideologies. Rather than celebrating their common victory over fascism, the superpowers were now trying to preserve and expand their spheres of interest within Europe. Western initiatives of the late 1940s and early 1950s included such efforts as the Truman Doctrine, the Marshall Plan, and NATO to contain Communist influence on the

---

[131] Rex Stewart, *Boy Meets Horn*, ed. Claire P. Gordon, *The Michigan American Music Series* (Ann Arbor: University of Michigan Press, 1991).

one hand, but as Thomas Borstelmann has argued, they also fostered colonial interests and racial inequality on the other. The Truman Doctrine of March 1947 opposed potential dangers on the left but not those on the right—European colonial powers, such as Britain and France, who ruled much of the world. The Marshall Plan of June 1947 funded those governments' efforts to preserve white rule against indigenous independence movements in Asia and Africa. As Truman was leading the United States into the Cold War, trying to project the American liberal-democratic and capitalist order as the most humane, he not only had to preserve relationships with British and French colonialists, but also with Southern segregationists.[132] At the onset of the Cold War, "democracy" and "freedom" for some populations remained only token concepts; moreover, in the wake of the Holocaust and the downfall of the Nazi regime, the concept of white supremacy had been irrevocably damaged. After WWII a new era began, one that slowly dislodged notions of racial hierarchy. In the United States, this shift engendered violent racial unrest provoked by segregationist Southern whites, generating headlines across the world. On the other side of the Atlantic, Soviet propagandists eagerly focused on these racial tensions, denouncing segregationist practices as imperialist and fascist.[133] Soviet propaganda had demanded the overthrow of colonialism and the end of legislated segregation all along, given how they believed that racially oppressive systems were inherent to capitalism.

In Germany, the political calculus was shortly to change even further. In March 1948, Allied communication and planning about Germany's future came to an end, as Soviet officials left the Allied Control Council in West Berlin and retreated into their eastern territory. On June 18, 1948, currency reform was implemented first in the Western Zone and then a few days later in the East, splitting Germany into two economic regions that made a political division inevitable. The Soviet Union responded with the blockade of Berlin to coerce the Western powers into rescinding the fiscal reform in West Berlin, with the ultimate goal of subsuming the Western island surrounded by the Soviet-occupied zone. Famously, the American government countered with the Berlin Airlift, providing over two million West Berliners with basic goods via cargo planes from the

---

[132] Thomas Borstelmann, *The Cold War and the Color Line: American Race Relations in the Global Arena* (Cambridge, Mass.; London: Harvard University Press, 2001), 47–48.
[133] Ibid., 75.

West German territory.[134] During that time, Hans Blüthner, cofounder of the Hot Club Berlin, wrote:

> Berlin is the world's center of attention. Once again the inhabitants of the city are in a sorrowful, nerve-wracking crisis. Nevertheless they have kept their unwavering optimism and their belief in a better future. To keep our spirits up the *Luftbrücke* has helped, providing for the city, the mediator of art and culture of the outside world. ... What's more, in the world of jazz, after a hiatus of twenty years a real proponent of this art form has come to Berlin – Rex Stewart![135]

Stewart, who had been touring in France, had arrived in the German capital. The American magazine *Down Beat* reported from occupied Berlin: "Rex Leads by Candlelight: German jazz comes out of hiding. At 2 a.m. in the half-deserted Delphi-Palast in Berlin's ruined Kantstraße, a mixed band holds forth by the light of two smoky carbide lamps."[136] Stewart had arrived on the invitation of the special services branch of EUCOM, but while performing in the American sectors, he still had to act according to US Army law with its segregationist policies (Figure 2.7). The long arm of Jim Crow extended even into American-occupied Germany. *Down Beat* critic Ernest Bornemann noted: "Paradoxically enough, to meet the terms of the contract which EUCOM offered him, he had to shelve the good, little [racially] mixed band he had in France and replace it with an all-colored group recruited in England."[137] To act in accordance with policies prohibiting mixed bands on stage in American zones, Stewart performed with an all-black band, which was haphazardly assembled and whose members came from places such as Trinidad and Ceylon. Stewart continued to recall the summer days of 1948: "A few days later I recorded with some of the German jazz musicians. We did 'Blue Lou' and 'Muskrat Ramble' and a couple of my original tunes. I often wondered if any of these records still exist."[138] (Interestingly, in the 1960s when Stewart was writing his memoirs, these records did still exist and had reached legendary status among East German jazz fans – for not only had Amiga released more jazz records than the West, it had also produced the first record of an African American jazz artist in the post-Nazi era.) The Stewart event

---

[134] Roger G. Miller, *To Save a City: The Berlin Airlift, 1948–1949* (Texas A&M University Press, 2000).

[135] Blüthner's account as cited in: Käs, *Hot and Sweet*, 251.

[136] Ernest Borneman, "Rex Leads by Candlelight: German Jazz comes out of hiding," *Down Beat*, no. October 6, 1948 (1948): 13.

[137] Ibid.

[138] Stewart, *Boy Meets Horn*, 216–17.

Figure 2.7 *Down Beat* magazine, October 6, 1948, reporting on Rex Stewart's concert in Berlin. Used by permission

serves as an early example – of which many more would follow – of the appreciation of African American jazz artists in socialist Germany. Yet alert to the racist politics of their "democratizers," German musicians commented on the situation, comparing such practices with Nazism. Bornemann again: "'Shades of Uncle Adolf,' as the Germans, not unaware of such things, remarked smirkingly when they heard of EUCOM's latest essay on in how-to-teach-those barbarians-some-democracy in action."[139] Such comparisons were fully warranted at the time: Truman had ordered the desegregation of US forces that year, and by 1955, under Eisenhower, the American military had become more integrated.[140]

Interestingly, an intra-zonal collaboration brought about Amiga's Rex Stewart recordings. The Hot Club Berlin (West), which had organized jam sessions regularly in 1947, also organized Stewart's concert on July 9th at the Delphi-Palast, causing a sensation because it was the first time since the Nazi years that such a prominent American jazz musician had

[139] Borneman, Rex Leads by Candlelight.
[140] Borstelmann, *The Cold War and the Color Line*, 91.

played in Berlin.[141] On July 7th, Hot Club members had arranged a party where Stewart met Konstantin Metaxas, one of Amiga's producers. They arranged a jam session with German musicians that was recorded on July 14th at the *Amerikahaus*, then located on Kleiststraße.[142] The racial mixing in these jam sessions were *de facto* violations of US Army segregationist policies, but some of the Germans were professional jazz musicians such as trombonist Walter Dobschinsky and pianist Helmut Wernicke, who impressed Bornemann with their musicianship. Indeed, the *Rex Stewart Hot Club Berlin Session* recordings represent, according to Lange, the first of their kind featuring black artists in Germany since 1927.[143] The fact that Stewart had performed as part of a vaudeville show a few days earlier in front of American soldiers in the Titania-Palast in a segregated setting only added to the tension. The desegregated show in the Delphi-Palast defied American racial hierarchies and exemplified how African American jazz musicians were engaged in cold war rivalry. On the other hand, at the time of the Berlin Blockade and the American support for the city, titles such as *Air Lift Stomp* likely annoyed Soviet officials, for this title was later published instead as *Amiga Stomp* (Figure 2.8).[144]

Overall, the intra-zonal cooperation of the Rex Stewart sessions and record productions illustrate the ways in which proponents of jazz were able to negotiate a position outside the ideological polarizations of the two superpowers. On the one hand, *de facto* violations of the color line were one way to protest racist policies and expose the double standards of American morality in "democratizing" Nazi Germany. On the other hand, the title *Air Lift Stomp* represents a rebellious attitude against Soviet measures in Berlin, which were trying to cut off supply lines to the Western part of the city. In the main, however, even amid the high-level conflict between the superpowers, the production of these and other collaborations show that for the jazz community of Berlin, music could supersede ideology.

Such conditions could not last. After the monetary reform, it was only a matter of time before the political separation would follow. The SMAD instructed SED leaders to shape the party strictly after the

---

[141] Lange, *Jazz in Deutschland*, 153.

[142] Bornemann dated the Rex Stewart session on July 14th and Lange on July 15th. Ibid. Amiga Sonderklasse 1163, 1164, 1165. Brüll dated the recording one day later than Bornemann. Brüll, *Jazz auf Amiga.*

[143] Lange, *Jazz in Deutschland*, 153.

[144] Brüll, *Jazz auf Amiga*, 51. Cf. Poiger, *Jazz, Rock and Rebels*, 59.

Figure 2.8   Record of Rex Stewart "Hot Club Berlin" Session, *Air Lift Stomp*, Amiga Sonderklasse AM1163, 1948. Rereleased as *Amiga Stomp*, Amiga Sonderklasse AM1050, 1948. Lied der Zeit, Berlin; ROBA/Hamburg

Marxist-Stalinist framework and to erect a political order in the Soviet zone modeled after the "people's democracies."[145] The SED had hoped to get a green light from Moscow to proclaim the German workers' and peasants' state, but on their first effort, Stalin checked their zeal. In a meeting in Moscow in December 1948, the Soviet premier ordered them not to declare the founding of an East German state before the West had created a *fait accompli*. The following year, on August 14, 1949, the West German population elected the first German parliament, and on September 15th, Konrad Adenauer became the first (West) German Chancellor. The East German delegation – Walter Ulbricht, Otto Grotewohl, and Wilhelm Pieck – traveled to Moscow again and anxiously awaited Stalin's orders. On September 27th, Stalin agreed to the founding of the East German state. Otto Grotewohl became Ministerial President (*Ministerpräsident*) and Wilhelm Pieck became President.[146] With these results in hand, the total economic and political separation of postwar Germany was complete, and on October 7, 1949, the German Democratic Republic (*Deutsche Demokratische Republik*, hereafter GDR) was born.

---

[145] See Naimark, *The Russians in Germany*, 251–317.
[146] For a detailed account of the founding of both Germanies see Kleßmann.

Conclusion

In recent histories of the era, certain scholars have claimed that jazz was exclusively a tool of American propaganda.[147] However, it was the Soviets who first politicized jazz. While American perceptions of cultural hierarchy consigned jazz to the fringe of the cultural realm, excluding it from reeducation programs, in the Marxist view, jazz represented a music of a people harboring social-revolutionary potential. Just as COMINTERN had supported the struggle for African American self-determination by propagating African American music from the 1920s onward, it continued to do so after 1945. In occupied Germany, African American music became an important dimension of the Soviet cultural renewal and reeducation effort, one that defied conceptions of racism and white superiority. In this respect, such propagation not only functioned as an ideological statement against Nazism, but also against American-style capitalism. In this sense, the Soviet propagation of jazz began in the immediate postwar era, in June 1945, when the American delegation reached Berlin only to hear jazz broadcast from the very facility that had been part of Hitler's propaganda machine. In subsequent years, the socialists' explicit anti-racist position and their politics of cultural plurality facilitated a far more prolific jazz scene in the SBZ than in the western zones.

Unlike the Western occupying powers, the Soviets showed more initiative in dealing with cultural traditions of the defeated German nation. With the revival of musical life in the SBZ, the Soviets accommodated the need for entertainment, but also appeared as a cultured nation by showing their appreciation of German arts, defying Nazi prejudices of an uncultured Russia and of a racially inferior people. In a Germany of ruins and rubble, the revival of musical life helped to reinstate a part of the German cultural identity reaching beyond the catastrophe of the war and Nazi crimes by connecting to its historic humanist roots. By presenting German as well as Russian orchestral works, Soviet cultural policy aimed to propagate a cultural kinship, thus nurturing the understanding and friendship of both nations after the carnage of the war.

Conversely, the American disregard of the importance of cultural propaganda led to occupation policies that seemed to have affirmed German

---

[147] Penny M. von Eschen, *Satchmo Blows Up the World: Jazz Ambassadors Play the Cold War* (Cambridge, Mass.; London: Harvard University Press, 2004); Lisa E. Davenport, *Jazz Diplomacy Promoting America in the Cold War Era* (Jackson: University Press of Mississippi, 2009).

traditional perceptions of an uncultured America. Its insensitive approach to the culture of the defeated nation, disrespectfully handling icons of German cultural identity, contributed to notions held by many Germans that America's influence constituted a threat to Germany's cultural heritage. Because of these contrasting approaches, within the different occupied German territories the image attached to jazz was antithetical. In the West, jazz was associated with an American occupation army who utilized opera houses for military entertainment. The music's growing popularity among German youth seemed to threaten the continuation of a German cultural tradition. In the East, however, the jazz promotion by Soviet policymakers had a different effect: the music was of an ethnic as well as a working-class provenance presented by a cultured nation with a deep appreciation of the German arts. Here, jazz was presented not as a threat to German culture, but as one enrichment within a broad spectrum of cultural offerings.

Over these four years, American and Soviet policymakers engaged in a gradually evolving dialectic. American policy changes in the late 1940s would facilitate jazz music, a clear shift from the prior position of favoring highbrow culture. These shifts reflected changing paradigms of cultural hierarchy and identity in both the United States and Soviet Union. While Germany served as a field of cultural contestation between the American and the Soviet model, both superpowers defined themselves against the defeated Nazi regime. In the late 1940s, the popularity of jazz among German youth bolstered the American cultural presence, while in the Eastern Zone, jazz became problematic, as the music's popularity proved unserviceable for propagandistic purposes. Its ambiguity evoked multiple contrasting notions, far beyond merely informing social consciousness: on the one side, jazz contributed to the fascination with America and its respective way of life, and on the other, it grew in reputation as being un-German.

Eventually the Communist use of African American music induced an American counter-response, as exemplified in the unofficial jazz activities of the GYA. The popular entertainment of the American occupying forces, rather than official American cultural offerings or reeducation programs, steered the musical reorientation of many young Germans. Yet overall, these years of foreign occupation in Germany laid the foundation for the ambiguous role of jazz in the GDR. While jazz was promoted in order to raise social consciousness, the music's increasing popularity was nevertheless understood as an overpowering aspect of American influence, threatening socialist progress and mitigating the role-model function of the Soviet Union. As the popularity of jazz rose among young Germans, Soviet cultural dogmatism demarcated a "national" or "ethnic" culture from "Western" influences in the late 1940s. The next chapter, which explores the period from the founding of the East German state to the construction of the Berlin Wall, examines in detail how this concept of socialist realism informed the position of jazz in the GDR.

CHAPTER 3

Jazz in the Founding Years of the GDR, 1949–1961

Introduction

On the evening of November 8, 1957, seventeen-year-old Helmut Eikermann, a technical apprentice at Radio DDR, and his girlfriend were on their way from their homes in East Berlin to West Berlin expecting a great show – Duke Ellington and his Orchestra were performing in the Deutschlandhalle.[1] That night, as they had done many times before on trips to the West, visiting jazz events or the *Amerikahaus,* they took the underground to Stalin Allee and from there a train passing Schönhauser Allee. There, they heard the announcement "you are leaving the democratic sector of Berlin." These trips were illegal for the couple, since their employment contract at Radio DDR prohibited visits to the West. At the Deutschlandhalle, they met their friends – all members of the Jazz Club East Berlin.[2] These fans had held meetings in the FDJ clubhouse at Gartenstraße, Prenzlauer Berg, until they were shut down in May 1958 (Figures 3.1 and 3.2). Shortly afterward, they regrouped and met in private homes to continue listening and performing. Once the immediate prohibition had passed, they then reformed at the House of the German-Soviet Friendship (*Deutsch-Sowjetische Freundschaft,* DSF), also called the Franz Club, hoping to operate under the radar of the FDJ and the agents of the Ministry for State Security (MfS, or Staatssicherheit, STASI).[3] These agents had been regulars at the Gartenstraße meetings, easy to detect by their eager note-taking on the content of jazz lectures for their reports.

For some time after the partition in 1949, East Berlin jazz fans not only frequently visited the West but maintained close contact with West

---

[1] A large event hall in Berlin Charlottenburg/Wilmersdorf, destroyed during WWII, reconstructed after the war, and finally demolished in 2011.

[2] The term Jazz Club Berlin here refers to the East Berlin jazz club, which had various names, also referred to as Interessengemeinschaft Jazz Berlin and Jazz Circle Berlin.

[3] Eikermann interview with the author, 2010.

Figure 3.1   Jan Eikermann (trumpet) and friends retreated into basements of private homes for jam sessions in Berlin-Karlshorst, 1957. Private collection of Jan Eikermann, used by permission

Figure 3.2   Jan Eikermann and friends, 1957. Private collection of Jan Eikermann, used by permission

Berlin jazz clubs. In fact in 1955, some thirty East Berliners were official members of the West Berlin-based New Jazz Circle Berlin (NJCB),
which was organized within the German Jazz Federation (*Deutsche
Jazz Föderation*, DJF) based in Frankfurt and held its meetings in the
Amerikahaus Berlin.[4] NJCB president Wolfgang Jänicke had helped those
East Berliners organize the tickets for the Ellington concert. Eikermann,
the Radio DDR apprentice, served as the contact between East and West,
receiving tickets from Jänicke and distributing them among his friends in
the East.[5] Everybody had anticipated a fantastic musical experience, but
this evening's delight was tempered: when the East German fans browsed
through the concert program, they saw their own names in print. The
official newsletter of the NJCB had been inserted into the program and
distributed several thousand times that night in the Deutschlandhalle.
For the East Germans, this would have felt as though a spotlight had
been directed onto each person individually. The newsletter not only
announced the recent prohibition and reformation of the East Berlin Jazz
Club, but it also published the names and addresses of all its members.
The East Germans – who had hoped they had operated under the STASI's
radar following the formation of the new club – now had to worry not
only about the publication of their names and activities, but also about the
public evidence of their connections to the West Berlin NJCB. With this
act, the anonymity they saw as indispensable was violated, and they feared
that the STASI could have direct access to their homes, including their
record collections, which traditionally had been private spaces in which
enthusiasts could play and perform with a measure of freedom (Figure 3.3).
Most of the records in these collections were purchased in the West,
purchases which were prohibited.[6]

Forty years later, when the STASI archives opened, their informant was
revealed – Werner Sellhorn, the jazz enthusiast and impresario codenamed
"Zirkel" but whom everybody knew as "Josh." In retrospect, club members reckoned that "Josh" had played both sides of the fence, informing on
Eastern as well as Western organizations. Since his days as a student, Sellhorn
had cooperated with the STASI, but in late 1957, he entered into a long-term
relationship with state security, exemplifying what Charles S. Maier has

---

[4] See West Berlin daily paper: "Hier wird Jazz ernst genommen: Zu Gast im Amerika Haus –
'Swingheinis' lernen um – Krach oder Kunst?," *Der Tag* (September 13, 1955).
[5] For more on Jänicke and the NJCB, see Siegfried Schmidt-Joos, *Die Stasi swingt nicht: Ein
Jazzfan im Kalten Krieg* (Bonn: Bundeszentrale für politische Bildung, 2016).
[6] Interview with the author, November 2013.

Figure 3.3   Staged image of Karlheinz Drechsel with Winnie Büttner, Dresden, Radeberger Straße, 1952–53. Private collection of Karlheinz Drechsel, used by permission

called the "double distortion" that socialism yielded in practice: "It transformed the public sphere into one of negotiated bargains, while it twisted the idea of a private sphere into a domain of complicity and secrecy."[7] Sellhorn's cooperation with the STASI both made it possible for him to participate in the vibrant West Berlin jazz scene – he was a regular at the *Amerikahaus* – and, ironically, allowed him to emerge as one of the most prominent jazz promoters in East Germany until the late 1980s. The relationship was mutually beneficial: his STASI connections enabled him to launch a career as a jazz writer and critic, even as the agency profited from his networking skills and his information about the East German jazz scene. In his writings, Sellhorn's rhetoric emphasized the sociological aspects of jazz from a Marxist-Leninist point of view, something that sharply distinguished his work from Western publications.[8] As indicated by the NJCB publication in Duke Ellington's concert program, his services were utilized not just by East Germany's security agency, but also when the United States officially turned to jazz promotion as an ideological tool in the late 1950s and began to feature jazz events in the *Amerikahaus*. The East and West Berlin jazz scenes became embroiled in a conflict in which Sellhorn functioned as a double agent.[9]

The many layers of this incident reflect the overall tenor of jazz in this decade, the first full decade of the GDR's existence. This chapter explores the position of jazz in the GDR in the 1950s: the decade of Stalin's last years, Stalin's death in 1953, the cultural Khrushchev Thaw, and the building of the Berlin Wall in 1961. Section One ("Art for World Peace") examines the position of jazz in the view of Marxist theorists, who portrayed jazz as a musical form emerging out of its history of capitalist exploitation, categorizing styles of jazz in polarized terms of "true" and "corrupted." Section Two ("*Hoten Verboten*: In Search of a National Dance Culture") shows how in the early 1950s a newly formed Stalinist State Commission for the Arts attempted to control the jazz scene under the auspices of combating American decadence, including attempting to establish a national dance culture. Section Three ("Jazz: The People's Music") examines how after Stalin's death in 1953 debates about jazz reevaluated the genre as the "music of the people" according to Marxist theories, while nevertheless shaping

---

[7] Charles S. Maier, *Dissolution: The Crisis of Communism and the End of East Germany* (Princeton University Press, 1997), 47–49.

[8] Joachim Ernst Berendt, *Das Jazz Buch* (Frankfurt a. M.: Fischer, 1953).

[9] Ingrid Monson, *Freedom Sounds: Civil Rights Call Out to Jazz and Africa* (Oxford University Press, 2007), 116–20; Penny M. von Eschen, *Satchmo Blows Up the World: Jazz Ambassadors Play the Cold War* (Cambridge, Mass.; London: Harvard University Press, 2004). The Amerikahäuser did not feature live jazz until the late 1950s.

an East German jazz culture along notions of bourgeois respectability. Section Four ("The Truth about America") illustrates East Germans' attitudes toward and notions of American society and how these were influenced by socialist anti-American cultural propaganda. Finally, Section Five ("Berlin in Crisis: State Surveillance and the Building of the Wall") elaborates on these accounts to further illustrate how the STASI apparatus infiltrated the jazz scene.

Art for World Peace

As a historical doctrine rooted in economic analysis, Marxism-Leninism regarded National Socialism (Nazism) in Germany as an outcome of a crisis within global capitalism. According to the Dimitrov definition, Marxist leaders believed that the root of all evil was the capitalist system, of which fascism was the highest evolutionary stage.[10] From this perspective, long-term protection from further German military aggression could only be guaranteed by transforming the socio-economic system in such a way as to abolish capitalism. Operating on this assumption, the KPD demanded in June 1945 that the property of members of the Nazi party, war criminals, and large-scale landholders be expropriated. In the Marxist view, West Germany's orientation toward the American capitalist model was a continuation of fascism and aggression, as opposed to the "progressive" and peaceful social and economic development of the Eastern Bloc.[11] Thus, the GDR adopted the Soviet model as the guarantor for a humane future. In the process of building a socialist society, the arts were assigned a pivotal task. Embracing the significance of national cultures as well as aesthetic concepts of socialist realism, the state encouraged and facilitated a conservatism that dominated the cultural production of the GDR during the Stalinist years. As discussed in the previous chapter, the state strongly identified with pan-German musical treasures, historically reinterpreted according to Marxist ideology, a stance that contributed to the image of the GDR as the exclusive inheritor and custodian of German national culture after WWII.[12]

---

[10] Konrad H. Jarausch, *Die Umkehr: Deutsche Wandlungen 1945–1995* (Deutsche Verlags-Anstalt München, 2004), 97–98.

[11] Ibid.

[12] Ibid., 89–90.

East German cultural criticism set about defending German cultural traditions from a variety of contaminating influences, in particular from American popular culture and from the modernism of the Weimar era. Communists denounced modernist art as elitist and bourgeois and furthermore viewed it as having been unfruitful in the course of history, namely that the democratic system of the Weimar Republic had resulted in fascism.[13] Intellectuals and party leadership envisioned a new kind of art that would radically break with the recent past, shunning Weimar's innovative artistic production, and that would instead be guided by the cultural heritage of the eighteenth and nineteenth centuries.[14] Critics argued that realist aesthetic concepts should inform the new socialist art, both educating society on its way to a humane future and thereby ostensibly aiding the preservation of world peace.

The SED leadership's concerns about Western infiltration through popular music were articulated even before the founding of the East German state in October 1949. In a protocol of a party meeting the previous month, leaders argued that: "At cultural events an importance is to be attached to the prevention of any American cultural propaganda. Not only sensual boogie-woogie music—good jazz and negro songs are to be excepted—but also the covert and openly antidemocratic propaganda of pop singers. ...."[15] As is clear, following the Communist directive to champion African American music as folk music and to valorize it for its revolutionary potential, the SED leadership explicitly excluded "good jazz" from censorship. In contrast to the alleged "sensual boogie-woogie," "good jazz and negro songs" were not perceived as American ideological propaganda but were seen as desirable in the future socialist state. Though the terms "good jazz and negro songs" lacked definition, boogie-woogie was a clearly defined musical style that was a fad at the time. It is characteristic of SED policy that officials were specific about what was to be rejected, but just what socialist culture should include remained open to

---

[13] The "Allgemeine Deutsche Kunstausstellung" in Dresden 1946 featured German Expressionism. Most of the artists had been categorized as "degenerate" during the Nazi regime. The political purpose of the exhibition and its criticism was to suggest that Weimar art was unfruitful and that the Soviet model of realism was worth being emulated by German artists. David Pike, *The Politics of Culture in Soviet-Occupied Germany, 1945–1949* (Stanford, Calif.: Stanford University Press, 1992), 237–39.

[14] Norman M. Naimark, *The Russians in Germany: A History of the Soviet Zone of Occupation, 1945–1949* (Cambridge, Mass.: Belknap Press of Harvard University Press, 1995), 399.

[15] BArch/DY 30/J IV 2/3 52 Kleines Sekretariat der SED, "Protokoll Nr. 52" (September 12, 1949). At that meeting, the following SED members were present among others: Ulbricht, Oelßner, Baumann Wessel, Axen, Hager, and Herrnstadt.

interpretation. Indeed, in subsequent years, during the controversy over what works to include in the cultural canon, such vague definitions would characterize the approach to jazz in the GDR.

A year later, in 1950, the first President of East Germany, Otto Grotewohl, stated in a speech at the founding celebrations of the Academy of the Arts (*Akademie der Künste*, ADK) that true German art was cherished only in the GDR. He proclaimed that the deadly foes of art and culture were cosmopolitanism, formalism, and kitsch.[16] Believing in "scientific socialism," policymakers and intellectuals were convinced that strict policies against formalism would be constructive in the pursuit of an art that would foster the construction of a socialist society. Underscoring this view, the fifth meeting of the SED's Central Committee (*Zentralkomitee der SED*, ZK) in March 1951 was solemnly devoted to the arts in the future East German state. The party, meeting under the motto, "The fight against formalism in art and literature for a progressive German culture," called for a complete politicization of all artistic expression. Formalism – as apparent in abstract art or art in the Bauhaus style (*Bauhhausstil*) – was denounced in favor of a "progressive" German culture that would reconnect German society to its national humanist treasures, represented in figures such as Lessing, Schiller, Goethe, Heine, Beethoven, Dürer, and Holbein. By contrast, critics in the East decried West Germany's cultural life as deteriorating under the influence of American popular culture, which, they argued, posed a threat to Germany's cultural unity. This position depicted West Germans as being victimized, a "cultural contamination" that they insisted was causing the two states to drift apart not just politically but culturally. In this conflict, East Germany portrayed itself as the defender of national cultural identity and, with that reasserted, its national legitimacy.[17]

East German leaders believed that this culture war, or *Kulturkampf,* was an indispensable dimension of their fight for the peaceful future of mankind. Formalism was regarded as an evil that had to be dispelled in order to create a new socialist-realist art that would provide insight into and access to "real life," something that abstract art both obscured and contradicted. ZK member Hans Lauter, who invoked Zhdanov's doctrines, proclaimed: "Formalism pretends to create something new, but in

---

[16] Maren Köster, *Musik-Zeit-Geschehen: Zu den Musikverhältnissen in der SBZ/DDR 1945–1952* (Saarbrücken: Pfau, 2002), 77.

[17] Hans Lauter, *Der Kampf gegen den Formalismus in Kunst und Literatur. Für eine fortschrittliche Deutsche Kultur: Referat von Hans Lauter, Diskussion und Entschließung von der 5. Tagung des Zentralkomitees der Sozialistischen Einheitspartei Deutschlands vom 15.-17. März 1951* (Berlin: Dietz, 1951). See in particular Lauter's own article in this collection, pp. 7–41.

fact it breaks with our classical heritage, uproots our national culture, destroys the national consciousness and encourages cosmopolitanism." Therefore, he concluded that "[it] supports the American politics of war."[18] In proclaiming "the fight against kitsch," the committee denounced the "imperialist destroyers of art," who utilized "kitsch to poison the consciousness of the masses" by preparing young people to commit atrocities such as those transpiring, at the time, in the Korean War.[19] Moreover, party leaders encouraged solidarity between German artists in East and West, urging them to preserve their shared cultural heritage in the fight of the German people for peace and national unity.[20] The speeches at the 1951 ZK meeting reflected the self-inauguration of the GDR leadership as the bearer of German national culture, implying that only the socialist cultural paradigm would save the German nation from cultural decline – and, subsequently, war – further fostering visions of a Germany eventually united under socialist hegemony.

Finally, this meeting also proclaimed significant anti-jazz statements. "Jazz music," party leaders proclaimed, "contributes to spoiling the taste for beauty and to the neglect of the cultivation of old folk art and the classical cultural heritage."[21] This commentary on jazz contained a profound notion: the fear of transracial cultural infiltration under the paradigm of socialist realism. The concept of beauty appeared as an inherent dimension of German musical traditions, while jazz was allegedly incompatible with beauty and therefore functioned as a corrupting factor separating the (German) recipient from German musical traditions. Within this view, such corruption would lead to the neglect of these traditions and, consequently, their endangerment. While jazz was embraced as part of world folk traditions and thus socialist music culture, the SED still regarded it as a disturbing element within the German cultural domain. Yet these fears of cultural transfer could only be indirectly articulated given that any explicit expression of racial discrimination would break a socialist taboo.

By the early 1950s, the SED rhetoric toward jazz had clearly undergone a transformation: whereas "good jazz and negro songs" had been seen as acceptable components of socialist culture in 1949, just a few years later jazz no longer enjoyed that status. The generally inclusive anti-fascist paradigm of the mid-1940s gave way to a more exclusive position on

[18] Ibid., 13–14.
[19] Ibid., 19.
[20] Ibid., 5.
[21] Ibid., 20.

jazz, one in which German national cultural values took precedence. To defend German national cultural traditions, in July 1951, GDR leadership called for the formation of a State Commission for the Arts (*Staatliche Kommission für Kunstangelegenheiten*, STAKOKU) to oversee and enforce cultural policies as part of an effort to reform the arts, literature, and music. Party leaders envisioned this task force as a "powerful weapon" against imperialism and toward the democratic unity of Germany.[22]

As noted in the last chapter, composer and theorist Ernst Hermann Meyer emerged as an influential figure in cultural policymaking during the formative years of the GDR.[23] Meyer was a paramount example of those from the ranks of German Jewry who strongly identified with German notions of the *Bildungsbürgertum*. After joining the KPD in 1930, he studied with Hanns Eisler in Berlin, and in 1933, following Hitler's rise to power, he emigrated to Great Britain. His family fell victim to racist Nazi policies: his father died in Berlin during the *Kristallnacht*, and his mother later perished in Auschwitz. After Meyer's return from exile in Great Britain, he achieved fame in the GDR, receiving honors and acquiring an important position in the cultural life of the state. By 1951, he had received the National Award, was elected a member of the ADK, and assumed a professorship at the Humboldt University in Berlin.

Understandably, Meyer's ideas strongly influenced the discourse on jazz. In his speech to the ZK, he derogated American and English popular music, regarding it as a capitalist tool. Pained by the fact that Western pop music represented a trendsetting force in youth culture, compromising the demand for German composers and arrangers, he denounced Western dance music, including "jazz cosmopolitanism" embodied in so-called "progressive" jazz.[24] Meyer strongly believed that the humanist cultural heritage, the German classics, should serve as the foundation for a new socialist music culture. In the course of the history of the GDR, he is considered to have been one of the founding fathers of German musical realism, along with Eisler and Paul Dessau.[25]

---

[22] Ibid., 41–40.

[23] Though his musical contributions receive less attention in this book than his theoretical legacy, Meyer's compositions were still significant in East German cultural life. His *Mansfelder Oratorium* was an important work of socialist-realist art and was included in musical education in schools in the GDR (Walter Cikan, interview with the author, 2016).

[24] Speech of *Nationalpreisträger Genosse Prof. Dr. Ernst H. Meyer, Mitglied der Deutschen Akademie der Künste, Professor der Humboldt-Universität Berlin*. As quoted in: Lauter, *Der Kampf gegen den Formalismus in Kunst und Literatur*, 137.

[25] Heinz Alfred Brockhaus and Konrad Niemann, eds., *Musikgeschichte der Deutschen Demokratischen Republik, 1945–1979*, Sammelbände zur Musikgeschichte der Deutschen Demokratischen Republik (Berlin: Verlag Neue Musik Berlin, 1979).

True to Stalinist party principles, Meyer based his view on cultural history strictly on Soviet communist theories. As the founder of the journal *Music and Society* (*Musik und Gesellschaft*) and a founding member of the Association of German Composers and Musicologists (*Verband Deutscher Komponisten und Musikwissenschaftler,* VDK), he used these platforms and others to advance his views. In his book *Musik im Zeitgeschehen,* published in 1952, he applied Marxist interpretations of music history to outline the principles of future music production in the GDR, echoing those of his contemporary Theodor Adorno, whose ideas about music and society had circulated for years.[26] Capitalism's incessant drive for profits had corrupted the "true" nature of music, in which there was a primordial unity of music and society.[27] In capitalist systems, Meyer argued, economic and aesthetic disconnection forced artists into isolation from society, resulting in a contemporary crisis of music exemplified by aberrant, modernist musical movements, on the one hand, and by the mass consumption of cheap entertainment, on the other:

> The common denominator of the crisis of contemporary music in all countries ruled by imperialism is an extreme dualism, a division between the artist and the masses as we have never before seen in history. The isolation of the artists on the one hand and artistic restriction of the masses on the other embody the crisis of music in imperialism. . . . The masses do not understand contemporary composers . . . and the people's powerful needs for music are fobbed off with second-rate mass-produced offerings that appeal to the lowest human instincts.[28]

According to this view, modern developments in music, music production, and consumption – represented by avant-garde music inaccessible to broader audiences, on the one hand, and popular music made for mass consumption through modern technology, on the other – were both

---

[26] Ernst Hermann Meyer, *Musik im Zeitgeschehen,* Herausgegeben von der Deutschen Akademie der Künste (Berlin: Verlag Bruno Henschel und Sohn, 1952). Adorno describes the alienation of modern composers from society with more complexity than Meyer, but they share the view that under capitalism music is primarily a commodity whose monetary exchange value is the dominant value. Some of Adorno's views are reflected in Meyer's text, but he does not cite them by name, and he refers to them in derogatory fashion. See, for instance, Adorno, *Zur gesellschaftlichen Lage der Musik,* Gesammelte Schriften, Band 18, Musikalische Schriften V. Rather, this omission may be due to Adorno's distancing himself from Soviet Communism, a distance that Meyer found politically unacceptable. For similar ideological principles, see G. Shneerson, *Musik im Dienste der Reaktion,* Musik und Zeit (Halle (Saale): Mitteldeutscher Verlag, 1952).

[27] Meyer, *Musik im Zeitgeschehen,* 110.

[28] Ibid., 139.

Figure 3.4   Ernst Hermann Meyer at the J.S. Bach Festival, July 28, 1950, photo by Roger and Renate Rössing. The backdrop reads: *Bach's Work Is the National Cultural Heritage of All German People.* Deutsche Fotothek: df_roe-neg_0002793_002

unwelcome outcomes of a capitalist socio-economic system. This chasm between society and art was symptomatic of commercial culture in capitalism.

Elaborating on the significance of composers such as Bach, Beethoven, and Brahms for a new German socialist society, Meyer praised the old masters' "clarity of thought" and "humanity," while repudiating the "self-destructive" tendencies in modernist music.[29] The music of the second Viennese school, the Arnold Schönberg circle, represented "nihilist" tendencies serving both as an example of works of estranged artists and as a "weapon in the hand of reactionary bourgeoisie."[30] Devoted to eighteenth- and nineteenth-century German musical traditions, above all others, Meyer spearheaded the celebrations for Bach's birthday in 1950 (Figure 3.4), reconstructing music history according to socialist ideology and thereby weaving Germany's musical past into the

[29] Ibid., 187.
[30] Ibid., 151.

founding myth of the socialist German state. Ironically, Meyer's musical preferences coincided with those of a social class that ostensibly no longer existed in a classless society, namely, the German educated bourgeoisie (*Bildungsbürgertum*).[31] Championing the music associated with the German bourgeoisie and rejecting musical modernity, his writings resemble the German cultural conservatism of earlier in the century, when right-wing dogmatism rejected the complexity of modernism. Paradoxically, Meyer tried to turn the wheel of history backward in his ambitious attempt to outline the future music of a socialist society.

Meyer thought that the solution to this crisis lay in a true unity between music and society and built his ideas from Soviet writings on socialist realism. In *Musik und Gesellschaft*, he explains how such salvation could be achieved through the creativity of the people and, more particularly, by their ability to create folk songs inspired by the reality of life. In his vision of cross-fertilization, composers ought to be inspired by folk music, thus empowering them to create for the people. This collective creation of art, he argued, was the highest level of artistic activity, offering catharsis through a collective effort.[32] (The notion of artistic creation within a collective would, in the 1970s, become a central dimension of free jazz in the GDR, discussed in Chapter 5.) As an example of what he called a "direct" creation of folk song within the unity of composer, interpreter, and recipient, Meyer cited accounts from the era of slavery in the United States in which slave songs arose from physical suffering inflicted by colonial slave masters. Furthermore, Meyer stressed the significance of African American music for socialist music culture, binding socialist-realist directives for music production with an ideological message: solidarity with the African American emancipatory movement with its music enshrined as valid for social revolution.

Meyer's view of jazz both legitimized efforts to repress jazz activities and posed a dilemma that made it difficult to explore political measures against jazz. He distinguished between categories of jazz such as "Ur-Jazz," primordial or original jazz as an emerging in the American South before its commercial exploitation, on the one hand, and on the other, "kitschy" American popular music such as the "subversive" boogie-woogie style, popular around 1950. The "tidal wave of boogie-woogie" was a key source of Meyer's aversion.[33] As he argued in 1952, "Today's boogie-woogie is a

---

[31] Ibid., 138.

[32] Ibid., 81–82.

[33] Ibid. Marxist writers including Adorno believed in an authentic African American music and its commercial variants. See, for instance, Adorno, *Abschied vom Jazz*, Gesammelte Schriften, Band 18, Musikalische Schriften V. p. 795.

channel through which the barbarian poison of Americanisms invades and intoxicates the minds of the workers. This menace is as dangerous as an attack with poison gas. ..."[34] According to Meyer, the American entertainment industry conquered the nations of the world and undermined their cultural independence through what he called "Boogie-woogie cosmopolitanism."[35]

Predictably, Meyer valued this alleged Ur-Jazz and recommended that its elements be used within a new German dance culture due to its rhythmic vitality, its instrumental colorings, and its humor.[36] He also imagined that Ur-Jazz was music that evolved naturally, prior to its corruption by the profit-seeking American industry with its insatiable appetite for reproduction and distribution. In a way, this construct resembles the idea of a "Golden Age" of jazz in the 1920s and 1930s often found in writings of Western origins.[37] By contrast, however, blues represented a genre unsuitable for the building of socialism. For Meyer, blues music aroused "opium-dreams."[38] Yet ironically, according to Meyer's own theory, blues – the closest derivative of the folk music that stemmed from slavery as presented in *Musik im Zeitgeschehen* – should have served as the great example of realist music.[39] While it is unclear today why Meyer never recognized this irony or sought to engage it, given the importance of his voice in GDR musical policy-making, his opinion explains why blues was (for a time) excluded from the socialist cultural canon.

In his jazz critique, Meyer mainly refrained from pointing out specific names of jazz players, except in the case of Stan Kenton. Kenton's arrangements for big band represented the current postwar American export bought by East German jazz fans, and as shown in the last chapter, bands such as the Melodia Rhythmiker adopted Kenton's high-energy style. Meyer abhorred Kenton's music, which its fans saw as "progressive" compared to prewar swing, in that it featured up-tempo, seemingly improvised phrases,

---

[34] Meyer, *Musik im Zeitgeschehen*, 161–63.

[35] Meyer was not alone in such opinions. Of the many observing the scene, one critic, hearing boogie-woogie in the West Berlin club Badewanne, had a similar view. See Florian, "Nihilismus mit Boogie Woogie in der 'Badewanne'," *Neues Deutschland*, September 7, 1949.

[36] Meyer, *Musik im Zeitgeschehen*, 162.

[37] Cf. Horst H. Lange, *Jazz in Deutschland*. Colloquium, 1966.

[38] Meyer, *Musik im Zeitgeschehen*, 110.

[39] Ibid., 82.

deconstructing known concepts of melody. Meyer claimed, "Instead of a melody this music consists only of the repetition of meaningless phrases. Listen to the 'Jazz Fantasy' of Stan Kenton: all that is represented here is vicious, barbaric rage."[40] This verdict would have a considerable impact, for as discussed above, in their programs of the 1950s, the Melodia Rhythmiker would not feature Kenton's arrangements as they had so enthusiastically in the late 1940s.

Basing his theories on Meyer's, self-proclaimed jazz-Marxist Reginald Rudorf (1929–2008), a critic and theorist who participated in STAKOKU meetings and discussions about dance culture in the socialist state, sought to convince his peers that popular dance music was also contaminated by the products of the American music industry. He condemned the styles of swing, bebop, and sweet jazz. "True jazz," though, he argued, should influence the new dance music East Germans were to create because it represented genuine folk music.[41] Intended as an ideological guideline, STAKOKU published his ideas about aesthetics and socialism as a book (*Zu Einigen Grundlagen der Ästhetik als Wissenschaft*, or *On the Basics of Aesthetics as Science*), and in December 1952, he gave a speech at a festival of contemporary music (*Festtage Zeitgenössischer Musik*) conference about Ur-Jazz and its commercial variants, in which he more or less appropriated earlier Marxist interpretations of jazz such as those of Meyer.[42] In discussing dance music, Rudorf proposed that the New Orleans collective improvisational style should have a solid position in the GDR dance music repertoire.[43] Remarkably, his dedication to jazz tempted him to attack opponents of jazz with the gravest of accusations, calling them Fascists.[44] His zeal not only led to arguments with musicologist Georg Knepler, but also to confrontations with authorities that eventually contributed to his downfall and conviction for counterrevolutionary activities in March 1957.[45] Among the consequences of this dust-up were repressions against

---

[40] Ibid., 163.

[41] Reginald Rudorf, "Für eine frohe und ausdrucksvolle Tanzmusik," *Musik und Gesellschaft* (1952/8); "Die Tanzmusik muss neue Wege gehen," *Musik und Gesellschaft* (1954/2).

[42] *Zu einigen Grundlagen der Ästhetik als Wissenschaft* (Leipzig: Staatliche Kommission für Kunstangelegenheiten, Lizenz-Nr. 460 350/7/53, VEB E.A. Seemann, Leipzig, 1953). For an announcement of Rudorf's speech, *Ur-Jazz – Kommerzielle Tanzmusik – Neue Tanzmusik*, at the Symposium Tanzmusik at the Festtage Zeitgenössischer Musik in Berlin, see STAKOKU, BArch/DR 1/ 6133.

[43] Rudorf, "Für eine frohe und ausdrucksvolle Tanzmusik."

[44] See files of Rudorf's trial, BStU, MfS Leipzig AU 43/57, pp. 4–7.

[45] For these debates see Georg Knepler, "Jazz und die Volksmusik," *Musik und Gesellschaft* (1955/6). For the STASI's investigation into Rudorf see BStU, MfS, Leipzig AU 43/57, Reginald Rudorf.

the jazz scene that resulted in the prohibition of numerous jazz circles in the GDR.[46] Rudorf's name was eradicated from the public and from the Deutsche Film AG (DEFA) film *Vom Lebensweg des Jazz*, to whose production he was a primary contributor. The film, officially evaluated as "politically effective," was withdrawn from further distribution.[47]

Overall, however, from early in the newly formed GDR, the arts played a critical role in public education. Numerous ZK meetings discussed what kind of art should be included in the rearing of a society on its path to socialism, searching for an ideological basis that balanced Soviet socialist realism, ethnic and folk traditions, and anti-modern tendencies. East German policymakers sought a reconnection to the German humanist heritage, on one side, and a renunciation of the Weimar era's cultural heritage, on the other. Eminent twentieth-century developments such as abstract art and atonal music were condemned as formalist, contributing (according to East German theorists) to a historically unprecedented chasm between art and society, which was seen as an outcome of a capitalist socio-economic system. East German theorists believed that artistic production submitted to socialist realism would remedy and eventually overcome this chasm. From this perspective, Western cultural influences served as an ideological weapon of the class enemy, who intended to disrupt the building of socialism and, ultimately, world peace.

Thus, East German officials declared a cultural war against formalism and sought to champion the German classical heritage, exemplified in music of the eighteenth and nineteenth centuries. Such policies nurtured a cultural nationalism that explains the shift in jazz policies between the late 1940s and the early 1950s. While in 1949 policymakers explicitly demanded the inclusion of "good jazz and negro songs" to represent folk art, in 1951, they excluded jazz from their master plan for a socialist music culture, indirectly expressing their fears of racial-cultural transgression. To defend national traditions against Western infiltration, the East German leadership followed their Soviet counterparts and established a State Commission for the Arts, STAKOKU, in order to oversee and enforce cultural policies and stand against the West.

---

[46] See Schmidt-Joos, *Die Stasi swingt nicht*. For a lengthy discussion on Rudorf, see Uta Poiger, *Rock and Rebels: Cold War Politics and American Culture in a Divided Germany* (Berkeley: University of California Press, 2000).

[47] Cf. BArch/DR 1/4533 (1955–56), "Discussion about the film *Vom Lebensweg des Jazz* in the presence of high governmental officials including a minister."

Moreover, Marxist interpretations of jazz history by critics such as Ernst Hermann Meyer, Georg Knepler, and Reginald Rudorf postulated a "Golden Age" of jazz. According to their theories, original or Ur-Jazz exemplified the ideal relation between music and society: music created by the people for the people. This relationship was allegedly corrupted by the profit-oriented music industry, accused of having commercialized genuine folk music by means of mass production. In the GDR jazz discourse of the early 1950s, indictments of formalism went hand in hand with those denouncing the commercialism of contemporary Western popular music styles. This approach to jazz raised difficulties for policymakers given the influx of various styles, the practice of using the term "jazz" for a multitude of genres of American popular music, and the ignorance of these styles among critics and the general public alike – particularly in a time when the Americanization of German music culture was understood as a political threat. In this context, only a deeper invocation of tradition could help.

Hoten Verboten: In Search of a National Dance Culture

The reorientation of national musical traditions toward socialist realism and anti-formalism resulted in an unprecedented micromanaging of youth culture in the early 1950s. STAKOKU's efforts in the realm of youth culture were aimed primarily at dance music, in which American influences were the most prominent. In the early 1950s, contemporary popular dance music consisted of styles such as swing and boogie, which in the official jargon were usually grouped under the umbrella term of "jazz." To counter the Americanized dance culture, STAKOKU postulated guidelines for musical activities, instructed writers and composers, made ideological schooling for bandleaders obligatory, and even attempted to control conduct on dance floors. This section explores the extent and the ramifications of these measures.

In October 1952, STAKOKU addressed the German Writers Association with the following request: "Dear Colleagues, today we have to approach you one more time. This is about our problem child, dance music, with which we need your cooperation."[48] As noted above, STAKOKU, modeled

---

[48] STAKOKU was divided into several departments. The department for the Performing Arts and Music (*Hauptabteilung für darstellende Kunst und Musik*) controlled dance music in clubs and dance halls. For STAKOKU's letter to the German Writers' Association see STAKOKU, Hauptabteilung darstellende Kunst und Musik, BArch/DR 1/6133 (1952), "*Liebe Kollegen! Heute wenden wir uns nochmal an Euch. Es handelt sich um unser Schmerzenskind 'Tanzmusik', wozu wir Eure Mitarbeit benötigen.*"

after its Soviet counterpart, was founded to direct and control all artistic activity and, if necessary, oppress any activity perceived as out of line with cultural doctrine.[49] STAKOKU's subdivision for Performing Arts and Music was led by Rudolf Hartig, who formed the section for Tanzmusik. In their crusade, STAKOKU mobilized writers, composers, music theorists, music producers, and dance instructors in order to forge a national dance culture liberated from Western influences.[50]

Hartig turned to writers to seek their help in creating lyrics and suggested they cooperate with composers.[51] STAKOKU had set up guidelines for a "new German dance music," arguing that Western popular music was part of imperialist propaganda in the countries colonized by and dependent on the United States, and that it aimed to divide Germany's ostensible cultural unity. The rhetoric used in these debates invoked notions of "cleaning," or "cleansing," and the cultivation of vitality and optimism, in contrast to the morbidity, nihilism, and sensuality of the music of the class enemy. In their words, STAKOKU envisioned "a clean and vivid dance music" (*saubere und lebensvolle Tanzmusik*) that could guide disoriented youth.[52] Officials were convinced that this would help to nurture social consciousness and lure juveniles away from an "un-German" dance music culture often characterized by "openly erotic elements."[53] Such rhetoric against alleged eroticism in modern dancing is reminiscent of the Nazi and Weimar eras, nor was it limited to Germany. In the Soviet Union in the 1920s, Communist Party officials denounced fashionable dances and demanded a "healthy, hygienic and beautiful" mode of dancing.[54]

To combat such cultural infiltration, STAKOKU officials came up with the following strategy: first, orchestrate competitions as an incentive for the creation of "clean" dance music; second, hold conferences for bandleaders to inform them of the responsibilities they carried toward the youth;

---

[49] Dagmar Buchbinder, "Die staatliche Kommission für Kunstangelegenheiten (1951–1953) – eine Kulturbehörde 'neuen Typus'," in *"Die Eroberung der Kultur beginnt!": Die staatliche Kommission für Kunstangelegenheiten der DDR (1951–1952) und die Kulturpolitik der SED*, ed. Jochen Staadt (Frankfurt a. M.: Peter Lang, Internationaler Verlag der Wissenschaften, 2011), 44–54.

[50] STAKOKU, BArch/DR 1/6133, Resolution of *Landesvolkshochschule* of Sachsen, Meissen-Siebeneichen, *Dozentenlehrgang für Kunst und Literatur*, August 8, 1951.

[51] STAKOKU, BArch/DR 1/6133, *Gründung eines Autorenkollektivs, Hartig an den Deutschen Schriftstellerverband*, October 14, 1952.

[52] STAKOKU, BArch/DR 1/6133, *Perspektivenplan für eine neue Deutsche Tanzmusik*, September 1, 1952.

[53] STAKOKU, BArch/DR 1/6133, "Wie soll nun die neue Tanzmusik aussehen?," November 13, 1952. As discussed in Chapter 1, debates about un-German dancing date to the 1920s.

[54] Martin Lücke, *Jazz im Totalitarismus*. Populäre Musik und Jazz in der Forschung (Münster: Lit Verlag, 2004), 72.

third, publish a flyer labeled "dance music—like this" (*Tanzmusik – so*); and fourth, guide publishers as well as record producers accordingly.[55] In addition, the owners of clubs were held responsible for the "cleanliness" (*Sauberkeit*) of the featured dance bands.[56] By the end of the year 1952, STAKOKU had formed numerous committees representing various creative fields to shepherd the creation of the GDR's new dance culture.

Having established their strategy, officials began to determine how the new dance music should sound, proclaiming a reorientation toward German classical heritage and specifically denouncing the influences of the "commercialized jazz" infiltrating Europe.[57] Over the past decades, they argued, American jazz "in its commercialized form ... [had] dissolved all elements of music and led to a barbarism of sound similar to that in the arts: Futurism, Cubism and Dadaism denied tradition and created a distortion of reality."[58] As in the Weimar and Nazi eras, cultural critics in the early 1950s saw transracial culture, in particular, as distorting traditional perceptions of beauty and harmony. What critics had denounced in previous decades as degenerate art, was now violating the principles of socialist-realist aesthetics. To reinforce their arguments, officials invoked the founding fathers of socialism such as Lenin, who had allegedly made comments denouncing modern art.[59] Officials sought to reconnect youth culture to the "classical cultural legacy."[60] Therefore, melodies were to be reconstructed, avoiding chromatics: harmony should prevail over dissonance, and rhythms should be simple and "healthy" according to the natural flow of the heartbeat – particularly avoiding syncopations because "syncopal excesses spoil rhythmic proportions and symmetry."[61]

---

[55] VEB Deutsche Schallplatte was advised to produce records exclusively of GDR bands. Cf. STAKOKU, BArch/DR 1/6133, "Wie soll nun die neue Tanzmusik aussehen?"

[56] STAKOKU, BArch/DR 1/6133, Perspektivplan.

[57] STAKOKU, BArch/DR 1/6133, "Wie soll nun die neue Tanzmusik aussehen?"

[58] Ibid. *Jahrzehnte hat der Amerikanische Jazz in seiner kommerziellen Form alle Elemente des Musikalischen aufgelöst und zur Klangbarberei geführt.*

[59] Lenin's words, cited as Clara Zetkin remembered them: *"Warum sollen wir uns von dem wahrhaft Schönen abwenden und es nicht mehr als Ausgangspunkt für die weitere Entwicklung anerkennen, nur mit der Begründung, daß es eben alt ist. Warum muss man sich vor allem neuen verbeugen, wie vor einem Gott, sich nur deshalb unterwerfen, weil es eben neu ist? .... Ich kann die Werke des Expressionismus, des Futurismus, Kubismus u.a. Ismen nicht als Erscheinungen künstlerischer Genialität ansehen. Ich verstehe sie nicht, sie verschaffen mir keinerlei Freude"* (Clara Zetkin: Erinnerungen an Lenin, S.13). As cited in STAKOKU, BArch/DR 1/6133, "Wie soll nun die neue Tanzmusik aussehen?"

[60] Officials used the term *Klassisches Kulturerbe*. STAKOKU, BArch/DR 1/6133, "Wie soll nun die neue Tanzmusik aussehen?"

[61] STAKOKU, BArch/DR 1/6133, "Um eine neue Tanzmusik," November 11, 1952.

In addition, arrangements should avoid lengthy instrumental solo parts improvising on melodies, which were seen as destroying melodic integrity. All these musical guidelines were directed against jazz.

According to party officials, the ideal template for East German dance culture was found in the operettas of Strauss and Offenbach. Elsewhere, they endorsed traditional dances: baroque dances, waltz, polka, and Rheinlander, as well as the tango and foxtrot, supposedly appealing to the youth. But rumba, samba, and boogie-woogie were strictly denounced. These dances had allegedly been imported after 1945 from the United States, for "the American originators also sent instructions for erotic distortions."[62] The guidelines instructed officials clearly: "Here is our task: to mercilessly combat these [erotic distortions] and not to cultivate them."[63] STAKOKU concluded that healthy German dance music would affect the youth positively, diminishing the appeal of "imported bad dancing" and ending the "distortions of the body" (Körperverrenkungen).[64] Officials supported dances such as the tango, foxtrot, blues, and slow fox hoping to reconnect with what they considered "natural movements." The inclusion of blues into the ensemble of permitted dances suggested the discord between state officials regarding genres of African American music. While Ernst Hermann Meyer, VDK president, had denounced blues for evoking "opium dreams," here officials endorsed them as tolerable and even desirable.[65]

Interestingly, issues of "health" emerged in this discourse. Movements perceived as "healthy" in traditional dances contrasted with "distortions of the body," which were associated less with the inability to dance properly than with excessively erotic displays or even what officials regarded as mentally disturbed conduct.[66] Movements that might have been merely individually expressive were now fundamentally incompatible with notions of traditional dancing as part of a mass culture, which was envisioned as compliant, streamlined, and collectively harmonious.[67] Improvised dance, with its perceived erotic distortions, not only challenged the concept of traditional dancing, but also norms of respectability regarding gender and racial transgression.[68] Criticism of these transgressions was not expressed

---

[62] Ibid.
[63] Ibid.
[64] STAKOKU, BArch/DR 1/6133, "Wie soll nun die neue Tanzmusik ausehen?"
[65] Meyer, Musik im Zeitgeschehen, 110.
[66] STAKOKU, BArch/DR 1/6133, "Wie soll nun die neue Tanzmusik ausehen?"
[67] Max Butting, "Tanzmusik Abschlußbericht" (Berlin: Deutsche Akademie der Künste, Sektion Musik, 1952).
[68] STAKOKU, BArch/DR 1/6133, "Um eine neue Tanzmusik."

in terms of racial discrimination – again, a taboo in the socialist society – but rather in terms of physical or mental health, reflecting the rhetoric of degenerate culture from earlier in the twentieth century.

Attempting to streamline the position on jazz, other party officials worked to distinguish it from modern dance music, which by the early 1950s was dominated by styles such as rhythm and blues and boogie-woogie. The section music of the Academy of the Arts continued the debate about dance music in 1952, admitting inconsistencies and confusion regarding the nature and treatment of jazz.[69] Author of its final report was composer and later vice president of the ADK, Max Butting, who argued that these inconsistencies had been clarified within recent debates.[70] He refrained from targeting jazz and disconnected it from American dance music, which he denounced, dismissing it as predominantly based on rhythm without a necessary emotional quality. Moreover, to propagate the difference between jazz and other styles of contemporary dance music, officials launched a campaign specifically against boogie-woogie. Articles such as "Why are we rejecting boogie-woogie" in the FDJ publication *Junge Welt* denounced the style as a means of destroying German cultural integrity.[71] One reader – mentioned by name to intimidate him – had argued that dancing was part of his private sphere, a claim that evoked a wave of reactions from commenters in FDJ publications. Participants involved in the discussion argued that members of the FDJ should endorse the youth organization's values, which embodied German national cultural heritage. Demanding "good dance music," young readers expressed concern about the "cultural barbarism" of boogie-woogie and wondered why it was still being performed. Admittedly, it is speculation to say whether this backlash against boogie-woogie was fabricated by state authorities, who were encouraging protest of American dance from the grassroots, or whether at least a few East German adolescents were expressing their genuine beliefs. In any case, such campaigns likely led some juveniles to restrict themselves to more accepted styles of dancing on the dance floor.

Indeed, youth conduct on the dance floor elicited surprising levels of concern and attention to detail on the part of authorities, particularly with the emergence of a style known as "hotten."[72] A frustrated informer to

---

[69] Butting, "Tanzmusik Abschlußbericht."

[70] Ibid., 1.

[71] "Wir wollen gute Tanzmusik haben," *Junge Welt* (April 29, 1953).

[72] The term hot music originates from American music discourse of the 1920s and 1930s in which hot was contrasted with sweet. As the *Junge Welt* article indicates, in the GDR in the early 1950s, hot music was also the term used for boogie-woogie.

STAKOKU argued that "it is not so much the volume or the rhythm but the tempo of the music. When hot music is played excessively fast, then the drunk youth only engage in unrestrained dancing (*hoten*). ..."[73] Such "unrestrained dancing" was termed "hoten" (derived from the English term *hot*), which was Germanized and used as a verb *hoten* or *hotten*. The adjectival use was *hot*, and the nominal use was *der Hot, die Hotmusik*, or *das Herumhotten*. Karlheinz Drechsel claimed that the jazz scene used the term "hotten" from the 1930s until the 1950s to describe an "un-German" style of dancing to swing music. In the early 1950s, GDR youth used the term for a style of improvised intuitive dancing[74] (Figure 3.5).

Perhaps surprisingly to modern audiences, STAKOKU's approach to control and censorship enjoyed genuine support from the East German citizenry. Complaints about unrestrained dancing, or *hotten*, came to STAKOKU from persons in official positions such as municipal authorities but also from private citizens who expressed their outrage at juvenile conduct.[75] The effort to eradicate improper dancing, originally led by state authorities, was joined by citizens who wanted to help in the creation of a national dance culture. STAKOKU delegated volunteers to observe dancehalls and, if necessary, remonstrate the juveniles. The following reports from January to September 1953 offer insight into the mentality and methods of socialist educators (as well as reactions to them) that reveal a deep disconnectedness between political bureaucrats, socialist educators, and working-class youth. The informant in these reports was Paul Roll, who functioned as a *Tanzordner*. These *Tanzordner* were individuals who attended dances to intervene and speak with dancers when they danced in an unrestrained fashion (*hemmungsloses Hoten*), a description that presumably included a degree of allegedly erotic movements. Roll attended dances at the Felsenkeller, which was in a working-class neighborhood of Leipzig. Since the turn of the century, the Felsenkeller had been a traditional establishment, where decades earlier Roll had attended lectures by socialist leaders such as Rosa Luxemburg and August Bebel. Roll, whose diction clearly identifies him as educated and not working-class, repeatedly condemned excessive alcohol consumption and up-tempo, hot dance music,

---

[73] STAKOKU, BArch/DR 1/6133, Letter from Roll dated April 1, 1953. *"Meine Beobachtungen ergeben, daß es nicht so sehr auf die Lautstärke und den Rhythmus ankommt, sondern auf das Tempo der Kapelle. Wenn heiße Musik im Tempo übersteigert wird, dann gibt es für angetrunkene Jugend nur hemmungsloses Hoten und der Ordner ist der Prellbock, an dem sich alles reibt."*

[74] Email from Karlheinz Drechsel, November 18, 2013.

[75] STAKOKU, BArch/DR 1/6133.

Den Rücken gekrümmt wie eine Katze mit ge-
sträubtem Fell, tanzt dieser Jüngling auf einem
Jugendforum der FDJ. Seine knallrote Seiden-
jacke mit den Flaggen der vier Besatzungsmächte
unterstreicht die „wirkungsvolle" Figur. Auch
seine Partnerin versucht, dem peitschenden
Boogie-Rhythmus alles an unpassenden Ver-
renkungen und Grimassen abzugewinnen

Auch so kann man einen Boogie-Woogie tanzen.
Der Rhythmus ist nicht einen Takt schwächer
und die Kapelle genauso laut. Trotzdem gibt
dieses Meistertanzpaar ein Beispiel, wie junge
Menschen auch gesittet und doch temperamentvoll
Boogie tanzen können

Fotos: Eckebrecht

Figure 3.5   "Von Dir über Dich" ("From You About You"), column in *Frau von heute* (*Woman of Today*) magazine, condemning improvised dancing and propagated conventional forms of dance. The image on the left is likely a collage, ca. 1956. Bundesarchiv Berlin-Lichterfelde, BArch/DR 1/415

which induced the youth to engage in the offending styles of dance – and which in his view led unmistakably to violence, his central concern. Roll was puzzled that "these people are the same ones who have been publicly praised as above-average workers as well as activists. They are also the ones who have been given the opportunity to participate in the cultural ascendance of the GDR, but in fact they are rejecting our goals."[76] To his

---

[76] STAKOKU, BArch/DR 1/6133, Letter from Roll dated April 1, 1953.

regret, Roll's bourgeois notions of entertainment and his socialist mission to uplift working-class youth seem not to have been appreciated by their recipients. Roll sought to prohibit *hoten*, which he perceived from the perspective of the generation born around 1900 as "bad dancing" (*schlechtes Tanzen*). From his point of view, these youth were rejecting the cultural ascendance of the working class, and he complained to STAKUKO that the same youth were aware of the fact that there were no laws in place that prohibited such dancing.

With time, Roll seems to have lost his optimism in his efforts to guide working-class youth. He recorded with disappointment the response of a young man he had admonished: "My friend drank for 40 D-Marks," the young man replied, "and I drank for 20 D-Marks. For my money I should be allowed to dance however I want!"[77] While Roll regarded this remark as cynical, it could equally be construed as the honest answer of a youngster who was simply having fun. To tame "hot" dancers in the Felsenkeller, officials decided to feature proper dancing in between the performances of the popular "Karl Walter Kapelle," a group that enjoyed a large following among Leipzig's working-class youth. Unsurprisingly, performances of these proper dances invited not just ridicule, but sabotage. On one occasion, Roll reported that the electricity was cut off and the lights went out for some time, while authorities demanded that nobody leave the premises. This resulted in unrest and aggression:

> During the darkness nobody was allowed to leave the dance hall (because of the danger of theft)! Because of that measure, the disruption of electricity and the interruption of the dance, the atmosphere was fretful. Intense anxiety arose when at 11:15 p.m. the performance of the folk dance group was announced. Only after a while could we perform an English waltz. When finally we performed a tango, the youth mingled with the performing group on the dance floor.[78]

The Felsenkeller audience saw state interference as highly annoying, provoking mockery. After all, the socialist notion of educating the workers here manifested ironically in efforts to direct the working class toward bourgeois forms of conduct in their leisure time. Roll deplored such insensitive methods, warned STAKOKU about their potential consequences, and criticized its bureaucratic approach.

---

[77] Ibid.
[78] STAKOKU, BArch/DR 1/6133, Letter from Roll dated March 19, 1953. Defamation campaign against a band see: Karl Peter Fleischer, *Karl Walter und sein Orchester: Eine Dokumentation* (2004).

Over the following months, Roll seems to have become increasingly frustrated and doubtful whether East German music productions were able to counter American trendsetting influence: "The question to be asked," he wrote, "is how we should combat this open eroticism (*aufdringliche Erotik*) and pseudo-culture (*Scheinkultur*) that streams in (*einstrahlen*) from the West? Are we able to immunize our youth plagued by such poison with our own dance compositions?"[79] Roll was skeptical about the effectiveness of the party's methods of mandating a national dance culture, although several years of efforts to keep order at the Felsenkeller convinced him that the music was merely the symptom, and not the primary cause, of violent behavior. The most important cause, he argued, was alcohol. In his view, debates about the "problem child" (*Schmerzenskind*) of dance music had to include the problem of excessive alcohol consumption that led to violence; a point that party leadership had not yet addressed.[80] Roll concluded that neither the band nor its Americanized music caused violent behavior.[81] He recommended focusing on the prevention of violence, repeatedly urging officials to assess the realities of juvenile entertainment on the dance floor.[82] Roll was not alone in his assessments; reports from the obligatory bandleader meetings imposed by STAKOKU indicate similar observations.[83]

The campaigns against American dance music that over the course of that decade were increasingly dominated by rock 'n' roll must be seen in the context of the 1950s youth riots, which had shaken cities in both East and West Germanies. Uta Poiger has analyzed the "Halbstarken" riots as a youth rebellion by both working-class and middle-class youth. Born around 1940, this generation grew up in a time of great upheaval without male parental supervision. According to Poiger, these rebellions were further influenced by American "rebel" movies featuring James Dean or Marlon Brando.[84] Live jazz performances had sparked rebellious and destructive audience behavior in large venues, such as the Sportpalast (West Berlin) during a Lionel Hampton concert in November 1953, but also in smaller venues such as the Felsenkeller in Leipzig featuring the

---

[79] STAKOKU, BArch/DR 1/6133, Letter from Roll dated April 1, 1953.
[80] STAKOKU, BArch/DR 1/6133, Letter from Roll dated May 10, 1953.
[81] STAKOKU, BArch/DR 1/6133, Letter from Roll dated September 20, 1953.
[82] STAKOKU, BArch/DR 1/6133, Letter from Roll dated May 10, 1953, p. 3.
[83] STAKOKU, BArch/DR 1/6133, Letter from Butting to Pischner dated November 14, 1952. "*Die Jugend sei zum Teil in einer bedauerlichen Verfassung und ein Junger FDJ-Funktionär berichtete selbst, wie ein musikalisch harmloser 2/4 Tanz von Jugendlichen zu wüstestem Tanzen, unter Zerschlagung von Biergläsern, benutzt wurde. Zerschlagen von Stühlen sei nicht selten....*"
[84] Poiger, *Rock and Rebels*, 71–79.

Figure 3.6   Still from the film *Helden ohne Ruhm* showing young demonstrators in Leipzig on June 17, 1953. Courtesy of Schmidt & Paetzel Fernsehfilme GmbH, used by permission

Karl Walter Band.[85] Unsurprisingly, critics blamed this behavior on the influence of American popular culture on the youth, an influence that caused aggression out of keeping with social norms. Even so, such interference and oversight did not help to build confidence between state authority and the younger populace. On the contrary, it led to disturbance and anger, especially among working-class youth who were contributing to the rebuilding effort in East Germany and, in general, were supporting the socialist project. As exemplified in the Felsenkeller episodes, STAKOKU's methods exposed the state to ridicule and undermined its authority in the wake of the worker's uprising. In June 1953, the uprising spread within days throughout the country taking party leadership by surprise (Figure 3.6). Only with the help of Soviet tanks were authorities able to quell the revolt.

[85] Jazz events and youth riots often coincided. See Lange, *Jazz in Deutschland*, 154; Hermann Glaser, *So viel Anfang war nie: Deutsche Städte 1945–1949*, 1. Aufl. ed. (Berlin: Siedler, 1989). Gerhard Hopfe witnessed the Hampton concert, remembering: "Hampton started to hit people's heads at the front of the stage when the mood escalated and the rioting began. Chairs, railings, everything was demolished, and the police had to intervene" (Interview with the author, February 6, 2013). For Karl Walter Band, see STAKOKU, BArch/DR 1/6133, Letter from Roll dated March 19, 1953.

Roll ended his activities at the Felsenkeller in September 1953. Recounting his experiences in a letter addressed to Rudolf Hartig, the STAKUKO functionary, Roll explicitly argued that dance music should not be judged from the viewpoint of art – implicitly questioning not only the Commission's competence in dealing with youth, but also the state's interference in popular culture. From Roll's perspective, the social engineering effort at the Felsenkeller had failed. Despite enjoying limited support from some quarters, overall, STAKOKU's cultural tutelage and bureaucratic efforts to control popular entertainment proved widely unpopular.[86] Many intellectuals retreated into private life or escaped to the West, holding STAKOKU's repressive measures responsible for the 1953 protests.[87] State officials, though, discredited the workers' rebellion as a coup that the West had provoked. They also decried young people who preferred Americanized fashion as provocateurs, treating the rebellion explicitly as a manifestation of juvenile delinquency, thus criminalizing the behaviors they believed responsible in such disorders.[88]

Ultimately, however, the failure of STAKOKU lay in its overall bureaucratic approach of control. Conceptualized almost exclusively in terms of censorship and repression, its aim of "guidance" and "education" took the form of paternalistic didacticism. The agency was driven by a messianic approach to cultivate ideal workers by interfering in leisure activity such as dancing. STAKOKU set up an enormous apparatus to centralize control of all musical activity, including relying on local authorities to monitor dance events – leading to further complications when the GDR's administrative structure was reorganized into districts (*Bezirke*) in 1952. This administrative reorganization gave district officials increased authority, which led to drastic discrepancies in the approach to jazz within the GDR. The degree to which nonconformist culture was tolerated thus came to depend upon the personal views and whims of district officials.[89] The ZK was aware of the dysfunctional institution, had discussed its failure prior to the uprising in June 1953, and finally disbanded the Commission in November that year. Nevertheless, the ZK reaffirmed the course of socialist realism and continued to issue warnings about cultural degeneration and decline. In subsequent years, STAKOKU's successor, the Ministry for

---

[86] Buchbinder, "Die staatliche Kommission für Kunstangelegenheiten (1951–1953)," 207.
[87] Toby Thacker, *Music after Hitler, 1945–1955* (Aldershot, UK; Burlington, Vt.: Ashgate, 2007), 164.
[88] Poiger, *Rock and Rebels*.
[89] Colloquial language gave these officials the title *Landesfürsten*.

Culture (*Ministerium für Kultur*, MFK) continued this overall approach toward Western youth culture as well as toward its personnel.[90]

Unsurprisingly, party officials finally punished the Felsenkeller crowd in Leipzig for "bad dancing" in March 1954, when they banned the house band Karl Walter Dance Orchestra.[91] By the time the rock 'n' roll wave hit East Germany, officials had provided a legal basis for containing American culture by passing the Youth Protection Laws in 1955.[92] Like waltz or tango in the nineteenth century and jazz dances in the early twentieth, swing, jump blues, and boogie-woogie appeared provocative in the 1950s because of the ways in which they stretched traditional boundaries of respectability, gender, and race. In their search for a socialist culture, GDR policymakers ignored the significance of popular styles for a generation of youth seeking to define itself and identify new role models in the post-Nazi years. Furthermore, racially transgressive elements in dance styles – what was perceived as "openly erotic" – were denounced as American decadence, thereby avoiding rhetoric alluding to race altogether. Such alleged "excesses" were interpreted as the results of African American culture being manipulated and corrupted by capitalist commercialism.

Before concluding this discussion, one final illustration helps to illuminate the shift in the position on jazz in the early 1950s. By 1952, the performances of the Melodia Rhythmiker, which had been touring the GDR extensively since the late 1940s, still enjoyed a large enthusiastic following. As described in the last chapter, the Melodias displayed a preference for post-swing styles, such as that of Stan Kenton, in their repertoire, which audiences in their hometown of Halle adored. As noted above, these post-swing big band styles were denounced by GDR musicologists such as Meyer, who disapproved of the "repetition of meaningless phrases" in Kenton's "Jazz Fantasy," phrases that embodied "nothing but vicious, barbaric rage."[93]

The leader of the Melodias, Horst Hartmann, attended an obligatory STAKOKU political-educational meeting of bandleaders and functionaries

---

[90] Rudolf Hartig and Hans Pischner in the department of music remained in their posts, barely changing their views, as did Hans Georg Uszkoreit. This is discussed in Chapter 4.

[91] "Runter vom Podium Karl Walter," *Volksstimme* (March 30, 1954). "Massenprotest verhindert Karl Walters Auftreten," *Volksstimme* (March 31, 1954). See also Schmidt-Joos, *Die Stasi swingt nicht.*

[92] Poiger, *Rock and Rebels*, 67. GDR, "Verordnung des Ministerrats der DDR zum Schutze der Jugend, Gesetzblatt der DDR, Teil 1, No. 80" (September 29, 1955).

[93] Meyer, *Musik im Zeitgeschehen*, 163.

on April 22, 1952, in Halle.[94] The protocol quotes Hartmann, who seems to have been a comparatively quiet participant, and only once did he remark that consistent participation at these weekly meetings on Wednesdays was unmanageable for him, asking the committee if he could send a union representative instead. He also complained that during previous meetings about dance music the music itself was never discussed. Hartmann's remarks were not responded to because the meeting was apparently almost over, the proceedings ending with standard formulas that the music should reflect reality.[95] Indeed, it seems that Hartmann underestimated the importance of using ideological rhetoric in debating how to implement realism in dance music. The Melodias would have probably risen in the officials' estimation had he done so, but Hartmann did not adapt well to the ideological transformation of dance music that the commission prescribed. While other bands attempted to adapt to the new guidelines, the Melodias seem to have continuously provoked authorities. On October 10, 1952, the council of the University of Jena informed STAKOKU: "While the performance of Kurt Henkels was tolerable, the music of the Melodia Rhythmiker had no melodic line...."[96] The informer, a man named Federbusch, evidently preferred the sound of the former bandleader and seems to have disliked the hotter passages of the Melodias, whose style was likely influenced by bebop.[97] Federbusch continued, noting that "before the intermission they performed real American hot music [....] I think it is my duty to point out that the second part of their program drifted into degenerate, screaming atonality." Furthermore, he suggested the need for further investigation and, if necessary, the withdrawal of the Melodias' license to perform since "this kind of music spoils our youth."[98]

At the concert in Jena, Federbusch had confronted Hartmann, who responded firstly that he had to make concessions to the audience and secondly that, in other cities, nobody had complained about his music.

---

[94] STAKOKU, BArch/DR 1/6133, *Protokoll! Über die am 22.4.1952 mit den Leitern der Tanz-und Schauorchester durchgeführte Besprechung in Halle-S., Verwaltung für Kunstangelegenheiten – Sachsen-Anhalt.*

[95] STAKOKU, BArch/DR 1/6133.

[96] STAKOKU, BArch/DR 1/6133, Der Rat der Universität Jena an STAKOKU, Dezernat Volksbildung – Abteilung Kunst – und kulturelle Massenarbeit, October 10, 1952.

[97] Unlike Hartmann, Henkels, leader of the Radio Dance Orchestra Leipzig, willingly communicated with STAKOKU. STAKOKU, BArch/DR 1/6133, Letter from Kurt Henkels dated February 19, 1953.

[98] STAKOKU, BArch/DR 1/6133.

This annoyed Federbusch, who commented: "The reason for his kind of ignorance is to avoid a clear position on the matter."[99] Federbusch suggested that examples of programs for dance music should be sent out to all districts, so that those officials responsible for venues would be able to avoid such "degenerate" material from the outset. In any case, given the lack of recordings of such performances, it is unclear what elements of the show would have upset officials. As suggested earlier, the high-energy style of Stan Kenton had been accused of destroying melodic integrity by the dogmatist Meyer; what was portrayed here as screaming atonality was most likely modern jazz harmonics. Nevertheless, Federbusch employed a rhetoric that permeated STAKOKU correspondence and was reminiscent of the discourse over *Entartete Musik* (degenerate music) in the Nazi era.

STAKOKU's bureaucratic methods of imposing socialist-realist guidelines are apparent in the public image changes of numerous big bands and dance orchestras in the GDR, including that of the Melodia Rhythmiker.[100] For their concert in Magdeburg on Carnival Day 1953, the Melodias had adopted a new name, Dance and Entertaining Orchestra Horst Hartmann, and by that time, the band had to submit itself to stricter measures of control, such as sending concert programs to regional authorities for pre-approval. The program of the 1953 concert differed drastically from the one in 1949: the 1953 gig was strictly in German, featuring neither English song titles nor American compositions. Having featured a big band ensemble with brass and reed instruments in 1949, in 1952 the Melodias now included strings, indicating that the band represented an orchestral ensemble, not a jazz big band. The foxtrot – long outdated by the 1950s – dominated the repertoire, and the modern bebop and swing titles that featured in the program of 1949 had also disappeared. According to the 1953 program, the band seemed to have adapted to the STAKOKU guidelines, shunning the American jazz image in favor of a more Germanized approach. In any case, what was actually performed live almost certainly differed from the printed program, as even that performance on Carnival Day aroused official ire. According to internal reports, complaints about the Melodias quickly amassed, and shortly afterward on April 22, 1953, their

99 Ibid.
100 Compare the history of the Kurt Henkels Orchestra affiliated with Radio Leipzig. Gerhard Conrad, *Kurts Henkels. Eine Musiker-Biographie mit ausführlicher Diskographie* (Hildesheim, Zürich, New York: Georg Olms Verlag, 2010).

performing license was withdrawn.[101] The Melodias would not perform again for many years until they were officially rehabilitated in 1961.[102]

The experience of the Melodias suggests that mere adaptation to political and ideological correctness was not enough to guarantee a band's survival. To establish relations with STAKOKU and actively engage in discussions about ideologically appropriate dance music might have salvaged the band's career, but for how long, it is difficult to say. Hartmann seems not to have known how to cultivate his image as a committed Socialist who could present his music along political lines, or if he did know, he seems not to have cared. In contrast to Hartmann, bandleaders such as Günter Hörig not only made concessions, but engaged in ideological discussions about music and its political dimensions in a socialist society from early on, which undoubtedly contributed to his successful career.

To conclude, in the last years of Stalin's regime, jazz continued to complicate the nationalist approach to culture. On the one hand, it represented a valuable folk tradition fertilizing the socialist canon. But on the other hand, jazz, which in the early 1950s was often confused with various popular Western styles, was still understood as imperialist agitation manipulating the psyche of German youth. To counteract such influences, state authorities attempted to micromanage the GDR dance culture on an unprecedented scale. Their measures comprised direct agitation in public spaces, bureaucratic oppressive measures, and obligatory ideological schooling. In this effort to shape and forge a national German dance culture, STAKOKU enjoyed initial widespread support from regional officials and private informers.

As part of their efforts, STAKOKU sought to eradicate "improper" dances that did not fit the templates of traditional dance culture. The agency's vision of a GDR-specific one recalled antiquated styles of the late nineteenth and early twentieth centuries. Criticism of improper dancing was not expressed in terms of race as it had been in the Nazi era (a taboo in socialism); instead, in the 1950s, it was discussed in terms of "commercialism" or American ideological infiltration. STAKOKU's attempts to implement such policies shed light on the contentious relations between working-class youth and cultural-political leadership, revealing a deep disconnectedness in the wake of the 1953 uprising that ultimately contributed

---

[101] STAKOKU, BArch/DR 1/6133. STAKOKU to Deutsche Konzert-und Gastspieldirektion, signed by Uszkoreit, April 22, 1953.
[102] Unsigned Article, "Die Melodia-Rhythmiker," *Melodie und Rhythmus* (24/1962).

to the agency's closure. STAKOKU's repressive methods of curbing unde-sired conduct in public spaces engendered resistance against state authority from below, adding an important dimension to our understanding of that rebellion from the perspective of youth culture.

Apart from the effort to observe and supervise audiences, the agency also tried to "de-Americanize" the appeal of jazz bands. American titles and dance styles were Germanized or removed altogether. Critics and functionaries rebuked bandleaders whose music was judged as "degen-erate" and "terrible Hollywood music" with "screaming atonality" or "screaming trumpets." Such criticism reveals anti-American and anti-modernist rhetoric reminiscent of previous decades. In this moment, authorities expected full engagement by performers in discussions about creation of the socialist-realist music culture; those who did not comply or did not distinguish themselves in such debates had to fear negative consequences. Regrettably, the judgment of random informers in some cases had drastic consequences for musicians in the GDR, at times ending their careers. However, the Marxist interpretation of jazz still seems to have gained acceptance on a leadership level, informed by national debates about the "problem child" of dance music. These discussions had raised sensibilities toward a more nuanced understanding of jazz, which until then was loosely equated with divergent styles of American popular music. The public jazz debates of the post-Stalinist era reflect an increasing accul-turation of jazz in the GDR in the second half of the 1950s, a development discussed in the next section.

Jazz: The People's Music

"What's up with Jazz?"; "A lively valuable music"; "Jam session in the GDR"; "Jazz in Europe"; and "Jazz with genuine content" were all headlines seen between March and June 1956 in the *Berliner Zeitung am Abend* (BZA), a widely distributed and so-called "boulevard paper" in East Germany.[103] In fact, the mid-1950s were years in which East German officials launched a massive press campaign in order to correct the negative image of jazz that had evolved in the Stalinist years.[104] Cultural functionaries sought to clarify the confusion about jazz, generally associated with various styles

---

[103] See *"Was macht den Jazz aus?," Berliner Zeitung,* March 17/18, 1956; *Berliner Zeitung,* June 22/23, 1956; *Berliner Zeitung,* April 6, 1956.

[104] Articles in the *Berliner Zeitung* and *Berliner Zeitung am Abend* were also published in other daily papers. See Hauptabteilung Musik Ministerium für Kultur, BArch/DR 1/415 (1955–1957).

of popular music including rock 'n' roll, and as noted, blamed for causing youth riots and amoral behavior. In contrast to previous years, now authorities sought to develop a socialist position on jazz in the public realm that would pacify fans irritated by confusing ideological statements and inconsistent measures of control. These debates mark a major turn in the discourse on jazz toward the reinterpretation of jazz as a people's music and, though primarily theoretical, are key to understanding broader shifts in jazz reception not just in this decade but in decades later.

These debates about jazz occurred against the backdrop of political changes in the Soviet Union following Stalin's death in 1953. In February 1956, his successor Nikita Khrushchev had denounced Stalin's "cult of personality" and crimes against the Party at the Twentieth Party Convention of the Communist Party, launching the era known as the Thaw. In August 1956, Russian writer W. Ardamatski denounced the oppression of jazz in the Stalinist years in the state news outlet *Pravda,* criticizing the negative view of jazz that Maxim Gorky had advanced earlier in the century.[105] The following year, in 1957, Soviet leadership loosened its restrictive policies on jazz by featuring an international jazz festival at the World Games in Moscow. Comparable to the efforts in East Germany at the Weltfestspiele, the Soviet Union promoted a "tamed" or Europeanized image of jazz at the World Games and they substituted instruments to limit the associations with American culture, with guitars instead of banjos and flutes instead of clarinets. East German banjo player Alfons Zschockelt, for instance, performed with a guitar accompanying an English flute (Figure 3.7). In the GDR, the 1956 press campaign tried to convince the public that jazz was not responsible for triggering violent behavior but was in fact intellectually accessible music. Disconnected from social spaces such as large concert halls with incidents of mass rioting, it was instead connected to the private sphere, associated with the German nineteenth-century tradition of *Hausmusik*. The Ministry for Culture carefully orchestrated this campaign, modifying the image of jazz for the broader public in a fashion that accorded with socialist-realist interpretations.[106]

---

[105] W. Ardamatski, "Jazz und Jazz," *Komsomolskaja Pravda* (August 22, 1956). The German translation is found in Hauptabteilung Kulturelle Beziehungen Ministerium für Kultur, Abteilung Sowjet-Union, BArch/DR 1/415 (September 9, 1956). The Office of Cultural Relations of the Soviet Union informed Vice Minister Hans Pinscher at the GDR Ministry for Culture about Ardamatski's article on September 13, 1956. Ministerium für Kultur, "Presseartikel," BArch/DR 1/415 (1955–1957).

[106] Government files contain articles about jazz from German newspapers published in both East and the West; in some cases, the same articles were published in multiple GDR newspapers under different names to create the illusion of a broader variety of opinion (1955–56).

Figure 3.7   Alfons Zschockelt's Washboard Band (*Waschbrett Band*) in Moscow in the Sixth World Games of Youth and Students, July–August 1957. Private collection of Klaus Schneider, used by permission

The political tolerance for jazz that emerged in the Thaw in fact had been preceded by publications of Marxist writers. As noted above, in the late 1940s and early 1950s, Ernst Hermann Meyer had grappled with the role of music and jazz in society. Beginning in 1953, *Musik und Gesellschaft* published a series of articles on jazz, featuring citations drawn from these Marxist musicologists. The provenance of the following articles indicates that discussions of jazz and society were informed by contributions from both sides of the Atlantic but particularly from the United States where, until the early 1950s, a strong Communist Party fueled debates about African American self-determination.[107]

Indeed, the groundwork for these ideas had been laid just a few years earlier in the United States. One of the most influential jazz histories for the political left was the 1948 *Jazz: A People's Music* by the American writer Sidney Finkelstein (1909–1974).[108] Its translation appeared in

---

[107] William Z. Foster, ed. *The Communist Position on the Negro Question* (New York: New Century Publishers, 1947).

[108] Sidney Finkelstein, *Jazz: A People's Music* (New York: The Citadel Press, 1948); *Jazz* (Stuttgart: Verlag Gerd Hatje, 1951).

West Germany in 1951 from Verlag Gerd Hatje in Stuttgart, a publishing house that had received its license after the war from the American and French military authorities. For his views, Finkelstein was forced to testify before the House Un-American Activities Committee in 1957, and from then on until his death in 1974, he worked at the jazz record label Vanguard, discontinuing his political activities. In East Germany, however, his jazz history impacted Marxist jazz criticism, and his writings, published in East German periodicals, remained an important part of East Germany's jazz discourse until the late 1980s.[109] Active in the CPUSA, Finkelstein became its leading musical and cultural theorist.[110] He argued that music production and promotion depended on the capital of the music business, which controlled the means of production and therefore the market. The music of those who perform jazz, according to Finkelstein, was typically of high quality but was bound to be corrupted by an industry that used the impulses of folk music for commercial endeavors. He assumed that distinctions between high and low culture were inherent in the capitalist system.

Finkelstein argued that jazz displayed the enormous creative potential of the people, producing music suited to the needs of the masses. Jazz therefore served as a prime example that quality music could be produced by the people and for the people.[111] He further argued that the ever-evolving styles of jazz were caused by the fact that musicians were constantly trying to withdraw their art from mass consumption and exploitation by the industry. Although published in West Germany, Finkelstein's book served as a standard work in the East, and GDR writers and scholars regularly cited it throughout the following decades. For jazz fans in Germany, Finkelstein's book offered an alternative, more politicized source to Joachim Ernst Berendt's *Jazz Buch*, published in West Germany. From a socialist viewpoint, Berendt's book represented a reactionary perception and interpretation of the music, depoliticizing jazz history. One of Berendt's most outspoken critics, Werner Sellhorn, blamed him for detaching the music

[109] Finkelstein published in the FDJ periodical *Weltjugend, Heft 1, 1956*. See Siegfried Schmidt, "Mitteilungen der 'Arbeitsgemeinschaft Jazz' in der FDJ-Organisation der Martin-Luther-Universität Halle," *Jazz-Journal* (February 1956).

[110] Born in Brooklyn, Finkelstein received a BA from City College and an MA from Columbia before becoming a renowned critic of music, literature, and the arts. In the 1940s, he joined the staff of the *Herald Tribune* and served as a music reviewer for other publications including *New Masses* and *Masses & Mainstream*. From 1951 to 1973, he served on the staff of Vanguard Records.

[111] Finkelstein, *Jazz*, 13–26.

from its socio-historical background and intellectualizing it by discussing it merely as an aesthetic dimension of modernity.[112]

In 1953, *Musik und Gesellschaft* published the article "The Future of the Negro Music" by American Abner W. Berry, organizer for the CPUSA in Harlem in 1930s and later the state education director of the Communist Party of Michigan.[113] He interpreted the development of styles in jazz history as a result of the American capitalist system and its inherent racism.[114] Berry argued that jazz was originally created by the people, both expressing life and enjoying a social function as a weapon against oppression. He dated the corruption of genuine folk music to the late nineteenth century, when it was plagiarized and commercialized by the music industry. On the one hand, white America sought to deny the contribution of blacks to American culture but, on the other, used black musical creative innovation for profit-making entertainment. Berry claimed that every new style of jazz represented a revolt against this theft by the white entertainment industry, which sought to quarantine black musicians away from the market. Therefore, black jazz musicians found refuge in increasingly complex novelty music and finally created bebop, a music that, in Berry's view, had lost its connection to the people. Basing his argument on the Stalinist Andrej Zhdanov's writings, Berry adopted the anti-formalist position that complex art could not reach the broad masses of people and therefore could not be understood as artistic progress.

In the period of the Thaw, Soviet musicologists directly engaged in these debates about jazz and society.[115] "The Legend and Truth about Jazz" by W. Konen, an article first published in the journal *Sowjetskaja musyka*, claimed that both genuine folk elements and those influenced by capitalism fused into an indissoluble entity, but nevertheless jazz emerged through the interdependency of other genres, thereby constituting a novel art form.[116] Konen, like Meyer and other theorists, idealized a "Golden Age" of jazz, imagined as taking place prior to commercial corruption.

[112] Werner Sellhorn, "Jazz im Anzug bürgerlicher Sittsamkeit," *Forum* (July 23, 1959); "Was ist eigentlich Jazz?," *Märkische Volksstimme* (August 12, 1956); "Was auch zum Thema Jazz gehört," *Berliner Zeitung* (August 20, 1959).

[113] Abner W. Berry (1902–1987). W. Abner Berry, "The Future of the Negro Music," in *The Communist Position on the Negro Question* (New York: New Century Publishers). This article was translated by H. Seeger in: "Die Zukunft der Negermusik," *Musik und Gesellschaft* (September 1953).

[114] Berry was a contributor to a key anthology on the topic (Foster, 1947).

[115] See also Ardamatski, "Jazz und Jazz."

[116] W. Konen, "Legende und Wahrheit über den Jazz," *Musik und Gesellschaft* (December 1955).

Moreover, he criticized the social position assigned to blacks by whites, citing examples in the performing arts such as minstrel shows that presented African Americans as physically, mentally, and culturally inferior. Konen concluded that with ideological conformity the creative and artistic utilization of jazz elements would remain impossible so long as society did not recognize the deep division between genuine black folk music and its exploitation in the form of commercialized jazz.

In the period of the Thaw, in the second half of the 1950s, these debates reached a larger public forum. As noted above, the campaign in the *BZA* in spring 1956 reflected a change in the party leadership's willingness to communicate with jazz fans about their musical preferences. After the period of extreme restrictions by STAKOKU in the early 1950s, young people were confused about party directives, given that jazz now seemed to be compatible with socialist ideology. Over those four months, the *BZA* published a series of articles and letters in which jazz fans participated in a discussion leading to a generally positive assessment of the genre. Comparable to West German efforts to intellectualize jazz, this new jazz discourse in East Germany projected jazz as an intellectually challenging, sophisticated art form divorced from uncontrollable mass events and dances.[117] But the reconciliation of jazz with respectability was still ideologically loaded. In these *BZA* articles, jazz fans and authorities alike reaffirmed the role of the music according to socialist ideology, applying principles of socialist realism, which – contrary to earlier interpretations – legitimized the pursuit of contemporary styles of jazz.[118]

This greater tolerance toward jazz occurred as a new genre of American music reached Germany from across the Atlantic, capturing the attention of teenagers: rock 'n' roll and, its embodiment, Elvis Presley. Concerned about its popularity, East German officials stepped up their propaganda against rock. SED General Secretary Walter Ulbricht publicly indicted its "noise" as an "expression of impetuosity" reflecting the "anarchism of capitalist society."[119] Such attacks on the music of Elvis and Bill Haley, as well as on their fans, were a prominent part of the mission to expose the degenerate works of the class enemy. In 1959, Ulbricht denounced "the ecstatic singing of Presley" with the East German press deriding the entire genre of rock 'n' roll as none other than an act of psychological warfare by

---

[117] Poiger, *Rock and Rebels*, 137–67.
[118] Ernst Hermann Meyer, "Realismus – die Lebensfrage der deutschen Musik," *Musik und Gesellschaft* (1951/2).
[119] Michael Rauhut, *Rock in der DDR* (Bundeszentrale für politische Bildung, 2002).

NATO – a move that, as historian Michael Rauhut notes, would subject rock to the same level of scrutiny by state security as jazz.[120]

Similarly, the debates in which proponents of jazz tried to divorce their genre from popular music reflect clear socialist-realist indoctrination. Günter Hörig, the leader of the Dresdener Tanzsymphoniker and who later held a professorship at the Dresden conservatory, explicitly delineated his jazz music from other influences: "We are rejecting so-called rhythm and blues jazz (music à la Lionel Hampton and Earl Bostic). We think that the instrumental effects, which within older forms of jazz were intentional expressions, are here fabricated."[121] Hörig differentiated between intentional expression (*Ausdruckswillen*) in older forms of jazz, and music that he saw as fabricated (*Mache*). Clearly his musical sensibility was informed by socialist-realist ideology, for he classified certain music as commercially produced and therefore detached from intentional expression, a term engendered by the idea of "the voice of the people" allegedly reflecting the reality of life.

In 1956, then, contributors to the *BZA* generally defended jazz as victimized by the music industry, denouncing its alleged "commercial" variants: boogie-woogie, as one reader tried to debunk the scheming of the music business, was a piano accompaniment that turned into "wild hooping," and bebop was a complex jazz style that turned into a dance lacking sense and aesthetics.[122] Just like in West Germany, jazz fans gravitated toward a more intellectual appreciation of jazz: "Not for the dance hall—listening to jazz demands attention" admonished one caption.[123] Referring to the alleged commercialization in the West, one jazz fan denounced mass dancing:

> The saddest part is this thing with the eccentric dances: jazz fans should take these seriously for they represent a rendezvous between jazz and idiocy. This does jazz no service. When jazz musicians—especially in West Germany and West Berlin—prostitute themselves by playing at jitterbug contests, they damage the reputation of jazz.[124]

While dogmatists such as Meyer in the 1950s had denounced boogie-woogie and bebop outright, this debate indicates that after the mid-1950s

---

[120] Ibid., 7. See also "Ohr an Masse. Rockmusik im Fadenkreuz der Stasi," in ed. Peter and Lothar Müller Wicke (Berlin: Ch.Links, 1996). For an analysis of rock 'n' roll in West and East Germany and gender, see Poiger, *Rock and Rebels*, 168–205.

[121] *Berliner Zeitung am Abend*, May 12/13, 1956.

[122] *Berliner Zeitung*, March 26/27, 1956.

[123] *Berliner Zeitung am Abend*, March 22/23, 1956. For a discussion on Jazz in West Germany see Uta Poiger, Jazz, Rebels.

[124] Ibid., April 10/11, 1956.

contemporary styles had been partially rehabilitated: one particular style of jazz was less likely to face repudiation than its alleged degree of commercialization. These letters expressed a conscious distancing from mass events, such as concerts in West Berlin where – as discussed earlier – the Lionel Hampton concert had ended in mass riots. While jazz had been linked to rowdy behavior and destructiveness, this debate constituted the attempt to restore its image.

Furthermore, in the *BZA*, some readers expressed regret over the lack of jazz events in East Berlin. "We can only dream of jazz events," complained one.[125] Rejecting the indirect accusation of state repression, the *Berliner Zeitung* (daily edition) countered with the article "Jam Sessions in the GDR," publicizing the name of this complainant within the article in order to intimidate and ostracize him. Moreover, indirectly hinting at the fact that East Berliners frequently visited "commercial" events in the western part of the city, this article suggests that they were spoiled by Western influence.[126] Everywhere else, however, the newspaper pointed out, many young people sought out jazz on their own:

> Everywhere in the world where American dance music is played, young people who are tired of monotonous pop music realize that once in a while, musicians of dance orchestras gather casually to play. In numerous cities amateur groups have formed, who play jazz without guidance or financial expectations in their living rooms.[127]

Conjuring an idyllic image of jazz played "at home," real jazz (*echter Jazz*) invoked the tradition of *Hausmusik*, detaching the music from the alleged cacophony and disorder of mass events. The "spirit of jazz" seems to have inspired young people, professionals, and amateurs alike to play within a communal experience of kindred spirits freed from commercially driven interests. The images in the magazine *Deine Gesundheit* ("Your Health") sharply contrasted with those of rock 'n' roll concerts in the West, revealing their propagandistic intent (Figures 3.8 and 3.9). The association of jazz with *Hausmusik* linked it to bourgeois respectability in a new politicized form. Ironically, communist propaganda denounced the bourgeoisie as a dying class, yet did not refrain from utilizing its cultural tradition. Critics adopted terms such as "contemporary house music" (*zeitgemäße Hausmusik*), declaring, "Young people gather to play jazz today just like

---

[125] *Berliner Zeitung*, March 26/27, 1956.
[126] Rainer Bratfisch, *Frei Töne* (Berlin: C.H. Links, 2005), 45. In 1959, 45,000 GDR citizens were estimated to have visited West Berlin concerts.
[127] *Berliner Zeitung*, April 5/6, 1956.

Figure 3.8   The periodical *Deine Gesundheit* (*Your Health*), April 1961 issue on "*Jazz und Jugend.*" Private collection of Jan Eikermann, used by permission

Figure 3.9   *Deine Gesundheit* montage showing a Bill Haley concert and how ecstatic enthusiasm and "improper" dancing at a rock 'n' roll concert ends in violence and disorder

they did in previous centuries, dedicated to the works of great classical composers."[128] Such analogy suggested a continuity of the nineteenth century with modern forms of *Hausmusik*, thus leveling demarcations of cultural hierarchy.

In this respect, critics contrasted "real jazz" with its corrupted variations, evoking the notions of past decades. Despite the different paradigms of Communism and National Socialism, modern forms of dance music still served as markers of the abnormal. Psychiatrist Edith Bartsch of the Institute for Social Hygiene in Berlin observed negative consequences for the youth when what she considered *"unechter Jazz"* (here exemplified as the rock 'n' roll of Bill Haley) led to excessive dancing in the "morally contaminated" West. According to Bartsch, such expressions would lead to "decline in performance," "mental dilapidation," and even "criminal activity."[129] Concerned about a questionnaire conducted in the early 1960s among students in the GDR, which revealed a widespread enthusiasm for "hot music" and jazz, Bartsch sought to redirect this preoccupation with jazz to benefit the youth. On the one hand, she demanded jazz education from an early age, and on the other, for those who "indulged in hot music and who have an inner disposition for abnormal conditions," she recommended more drastic measures – namely, to "remove them from their milieu and to teach them the appreciation of positive values."

Such rhetoric was not just common among experts of social hygiene. Proponents of jazz in the late 1950s pushed for the acceptance of the music, regarding it as a "perfectly healthy sprout" of contemporary music, as band leader Günter Hörig argued in his article "Jazz with Distinct Content" (*Jazz mit eigenem Inhalt*).[130] Hörig contended that the number of earnest jazz fans was growing even though the music was intellectually challenging, thus arguing for the contribution of jazz to this cultural ascendance of the masses. Suggesting that within a learning process, the listener would be able to distinguish between good and bad and genuine and false, Hörig boasted that his orchestra featured every style of jazz – a claim that thus defied arguments over acceptable styles. Even the title "Jazz with Distinct Content" invoked socialist-realist dogma as it suggested filling

---

[128] "... und zum Empfang Dixielandrhythmen," *Liberaldemokratische Zeitung* (April 4, 1956). "*Die Jazzmusik der Amateure entwickelte sich in den letzten Jahren immer mehr zu einer neuen zeitgemäßen Hausmusik. Die jungen Menschen unserer Tage kommen in der gleichen Weise zusammen, um Jazz zu spielen, wie man in den vergangenen Jahrhunderten im kleinen Kreise zusammenkam, um die Werke der großen Meister der Klassik schöpferisch nachzuempfinden.*"

[129] Edith Bartsch, "Jazz und Jugend," *Deine Gesundheit* (April 1961), 5.

[130] *Berliner Zeitung am Abend*, May 12/13, 1956.

various jazz forms with its "own" or "distinct" content, alluding to realist concepts of art in which content prevailed over mere formal structures. Hörig's depiction of jazz as intellectually challenging was compatible with the overall goal of engaging socialist society. In the 1950s, his Dresdener Tanzsymphoniker established itself as one of the GDR's most successful big bands, not least because of his skillful "public relations" – a sharp contrast to how the Melodias' bandleader Hartmann had handled his encounters with party officials a few years earlier.[131]

In 1956, the FDJ organized forums for the youth (*Jugendforen*) hoping to engage in a dialogue with young people. During the *IV Jugendforum* in the hall of culture of the factory Elektro-Apparate-Werke J. Stalin in Berlin-Treptow, state representatives engaged in discussions about the role of jazz in society. In the presence of Hanns Eisler and a number of cultural functionaries, young people were given the opportunity to discuss how and whether jazz could be cultivated in the GDR. Eisler is quoted as saying that, at future meetings, participants should speak less and spend more time listening to records, suggesting that even one of the GDR's leading composers thought debates on jazz could become too theoretical, something that musicians such as Hartmann of the Melodia Rhythmiker had also criticized.[132] Nevertheless, the reports of the meeting feature an astounding amount of criticism about the inconsistencies in policymaking.[133] Participants asked the following questions: Why are jazz shows being broadcast and then discontinued without explanation? Why does *Musik und Gesellschaft* not feature articles about jazz, although there are manuscripts available? Why must the pursuit of jazz be still half-illegal? Why do the authorities still raise difficulties for jazz circles in various cities? Why is the DEFA jazz film [*Vom Lebensweg der Jazz*] not released yet? To these questions, the *BZA* bluntly reported: "The audience did not get answers."

The jazz series in the *Berliner Zeitung* concluded that jazz is "a vital and precious music"[134] and proclaimed that the debate's most important goals had been achieved: after exploring the range of positions – some people

---

[131] Press release, Radio Dresden, studio recording. The article emphasizes the originality of the intellectually challenging music, produced in a collective with improvisational skills that have been forgotten in Germany. Improvisation is here presented as a lost German musical tradition. Found in Ministerium für Kultur, BArch/DR 1/415 (1955–56).

[132] The youth forum in Treptow was covered by various papers: "Unsere Leser schreiben zum Thema Jazz," *Berliner Zeitung* (April 26, 1956); "Reges Forum mit dem Thema Jazz," *National-Zeitung* (April 8, 1956); "Jazz – ja oder nein," *Neues Deutschland* (April 5, 1956).

[133] *Berliner Zeitung am Abend*, April 10/11, 1956.

[134] *Berliner Zeitung*, June 22/23, 1956. "… Jazz ist eine lebensvolle und wertvolle Musik…"

were ignorant about jazz, and associated it with "American barbarism" – jazz activities in small clubs or concerts would be supported from then on. The editors of the *BZA* assured the readers repeatedly: "We are debating with anyone who has to say something critical about jazz." This reminded the readers and contributors of the fact that they had directly engaged in a discussion with state authority, here portraying itself as receptive to a plurality of opinions. Although there was no "public sphere" in the Western sense within the GDR, these discussions show that there was occasional space for an exchange between above and below. Individuals spoke their minds to the state, shared their grievances with state officials, and thus received a sense of being active participants in shaping their cultural environment. In this sense, the GDR represented a "participatory dictatorship" as historian Mary Fulbrook has described, one that permitted these forums for collective debate "about the character and future of East German society, or for the development of different subcultures and lifestyles."[135]

By the mid-1950s, Marxist cultural criticism dominated the perceptions of jazz both in the public and the private sphere. The diaries of twenty-year-old Herbert Flügge, a schoolteacher who later would become active in the Potsdam jazz club, offer insight into the mindset of a young jazz enthusiast. His diaries are exclusively dedicated to the memory of musical experiences, such as live concerts, jazz films, and Western and Eastern radio shows. For over two years, he diligently recorded these shows, listing every title in English with its German translation including hits of the week broadcast by RIAS (Figures 3.10 and 3.11). This meticulous daily work indicates the level of appreciation Flügge had for this musical experience. By listing titles, he was able to claim a virtual ownership of this music and to recall his experiences at any given moment; at a time when recordings were typically out of reach for most people. The following entry relates to a jazz show from Saarbrücken, capital of West Germany's federal state Saarland.

> Monday, January 3, 1955. 0:05 AM. I have heard the jazz show of Saarbrücken (speaker: Ralph Günther). Quite pleasing, only two commercial recordings of Billy May and Stan Kenton ("Hot Canary"). Overall this show can be very commercial. The signature tune ("Lean Baby") played by Billy May is totally "commercial."[136]

---

[135] Mary Fulbrook, *The People's State: East German Society from Hitler to Honecker* (New Haven, Conn.: Yale University Press, 2005), 251.
[136] Flügge used the English term.

Tagebuchaufzeichnungen

Montag, d. 3. Januar 1955

...0.05 Uhr. Habe die Jazzsendung von Saarbrücken (Ansage: Ralph Günther) gehört. Ganz
nett, nur zwei kommerzielle Aufnahmen von
Billy May und Stan Kenton ("Hot Canari").
Überhaupt ist die Sendung manchmal reichlich
kommerziell gehalten. Schon die Erkennungs-
melodie "Lean Baby", von Billy May gespielt,
ist glatt "commercial"...

Dienstag, d. 4. 1. 1955

...Leichte Kopfschmerzen. Werde aber trotzdem noch Jazz hören. 0.10 Uhr SWF: "Swing
Serenade" mit Joachim Ernst Berendt...

Freitag, d. 7. 1. 1955

...Habe die 9. Folge der Sendung "Vom Lebensweg einer Musik" (Jazz) im Deutschlandsender
gehört. Jimmie Lunceford, Count Basie und
George Gershwin waren dran. Am 20. kommt die
letzte Folge...

Montag, d. 10. 1. 1955

...Radio kaputt. Ist richtige Scheiße ohne
Radio. Heute z. B. kann ich Saarbrücken nicht
hören...

Figure 3.10   Page of Herbert Flügge's jazz diary, entries from January 3 to 10, 1955, showing radio stations broadcasting from West Germany. Private collection of Flügge, used
by permission

Figure 3.11   Images from Herbert Flügge's jazz diary showing self-portraits of domesticity, respectability, and modest affluence within the private sphere, entries from April 1960

Clearly, the notion of jazz as either commercial or non-commercial heavily influenced the enthusiast's judgments about this 1955 broadcast, which in this case were entrusted to a private space.[137] Flügge's notes about another show a few weeks later seem to detract from ideological manipulation by comparing two distinctive thoughts about jazz. The statement of the young man contrasts the words of Maxim Gorky, whereby Flügge expresses his doubts about Gorky's judgment.

> Tuesday, January 25, 1955. Today I heard a wonderful show: the sixtieth show of the "Jazz Club Hamburg." A book dealer and chemist talked about how they got into jazz by presenting records: V-disc-recordings [used by the Armed Forces Network] of Coleman Hawkins, Benny Goodman, Art Tatum, Lennie Tristano, Muggsy Spanier, etc. One of the two said: It doesn't matter which style [of jazz is being played], if the sentiment, the real, genuine feeling is still there.

> My opinion is that jazz is something beautiful. I don't understand Maxim Gorky [*sic*], who called it "dirt in clear water" and the like. This man must have never truly given himself to jazz. Maybe it because he is Russian and has a different mentality, a matter of taste...

Such comments by Gorky were well-known within the jazz discourse in the GDR and, given his prestige in the Eastern Bloc, were of the highest significance.[138] Despite Flügge's difference of opinion, what is important here is his rejection of two contrasting positions, which must be set in the context of the jazz discourse of the time. At that time, jazz debates were permeated by polarizations between "real" or "fabricated" styles. Flügge denounced such positions in the Hamburg show, rejecting these classifications as qualifying criteria and instead suggesting that emotional content was of importance. Tellingly, Flügge's private criticism in 1955 of Gorky's verdict, occasioned by his devoted radio listenership and film patronage, likely precedes the official Soviet take on Gorky's critical dismissal.[139]

In sum, American, Soviet, and German Marxist views on jazz in this era differed in some details, but all agreed on its exploitation of folk traditions and estrangement between artists and society. Beginning in the mid-1950s, however, during the period of the Thaw, critics denounced the Stalinist repressions of jazz and signaled a more liberal position on

---

[137] Cf. Meyer, "Realismus – die Lebensfrage der deutschen Musik."
[138] Compare editions of *Musik und Gesellschaft* in the early 1950s. For a discussion of Gorky and jazz, see Starr, 88–94. Starr refers to the article "O muzyke tolstykh" by Maxim Gorky published in *Pravda*, April 18, 1928.
[139] Ardamatski, "Jazz und Jazz."

the music, adhering to the principles of Marxist views cherishing jazz as genuine folk music. In the years after Stalin's death, jazz fans increasingly founded jazz clubs, which organized concerts and lectures to educate the public about jazz. This initiative was met by a public dialogue with jazz fans and East German officials, including prominent musicians such as Hanns Eisler. Within these debates, fans were able to express their opinion and level their grievances, reflecting the state's disposition to engage in a communicative process and exemplifying the dynamics of the participatory dictatorship.

Importantly, these debates projected an image of the music that delineated it from the popular commercial music styles of the mid-1950s such as rock 'n' roll. Contrary to Western youth, who were seen as victimized and stupefied by American cultural infiltration, jazz music in the East inspired socialist youth engaging in music-making infused with the character and spirit "of the people." Liberated from commercial constraints, toned down, and disconnected from rowdy youth in large social spaces, jazz was envisioned as a new form of *Hausmusik*, thereby rewoven into German bourgeois music traditions. As a result, socialist-realist notions not only permeated public discourses, but also the private realm. Diaries of jazz fans, at the time, show that such views on jazz were internalized and not just publicly articulated when it was beneficial for one's career. These entries reveal the degree of ideological indoctrination, on the one hand, as well as criticism directed against cultural paternalism, on the other. Nevertheless, these broader shifts were not yet complete, as the next section details.

The Truth about America

Understandably, the reception of jazz in the GDR was linked to the image of America that was promoted by socialist propaganda, with debates over racist America permeating cultural life. The following accounts of members of jazz clubs offer insight into these conceptions, influenced by propaganda portraying a socialist utopia while attacking the capitalist system. In a 2007 interview, Helmut Eikermann, the former Radio DDR technician and member of the Jazz Club Berlin in the 1950s, recalled his experiences of the postwar era:

> My imagination about America was influenced by the Americans themselves. When I was five years old we were liberated by the Amis in Thuringia. They searched the house, were very friendly, and I wasn't afraid

at all. Later people in the GDR leveled massive attacks against the Amis, there was a magazine called *USA in Bild und Wort*, but we never took that seriously, even though the history of the blacks was very important. There was a lot of literature about that life, such as Howard Fast's *Freedom Road*, which greatly shaped our notions of America. The book was distributed by the FDJ to the youngsters and it was very popular. My copy was in fact my brother's, who was four years older than I was. He frequented the House of the Children, which was the predecessor of the House of the Young Pioneers, and was active in a theater group. There was also other literature about young black children, which of course was propaganda, but we got a fairly realistic image.[140]

In his account, Eikermann discriminated between information identified as propaganda and that which purportedly provided a "realistic image" of America. Yet when he read *Freedom Road* as a youth, he was more than likely unaware of its propagandistic purpose.[141] He continued:

These books were published in the late 1940s, when not much else was published, especially not for children, but these books were widespread. Among our generation I think everybody read *Freedom Road*; it was just part of us. We had a split image of America, which was congruent with jazz. When you compared that to the biographies of Charlie Parker or Thelonious Monk you were confronted with the social contradictions of that country.[142]

Eikermann's view of America was shaped both by real experiences, such as his personal recollection of the American occupation in Thuringia, and fictional ones, such as Fast's novel. The influence of propaganda material combined with his affinity for African American music projected a contradictory image between cultural fascination and ideological repudiation.

Images of the United States and the Soviet Union in the GDR arose from a polarized vision that was propagated in newspapers, magazines, radio and television shows, and films.[143] In publications such as *USA in Bild und Wort*, the Soviet Union appeared as the country where life was better and the people happier, while the United States appeared as an unscrupulous exploiter. But the anti-Americanism of the 1950s was not directed against the United States, as a whole, for there was still the "other America," the America of Native Americans, African Americans, Democrats, and leftist

---

[140] Eikermann also wrote under the pseudonym Jan Eik. Interview with the author, 2008.
[141] Howard Fast, *Strasse zur Freiheit* (Berlin: Büchergilde Gutenberg, 1950).
[142] Interview with the author, 2009.
[143] See P. Pawlenko, *Amerikanische Eindrücke* (Berlin: Tägliche Rundschau, 1949).

intellectuals victimized by the system. Thus, within the GDR, the image of America was itself divided, in which jazz was seen as the voice of the exploited, stoking fascination about the land of the oppressor.[144]

To illuminate the power of such images, it is worth briefly describing Fast's novel and the effects it had on a hungry readership eager to learn more about the class enemy. The German translation of Fast's *Freedom Road* was first published by the FDJ affiliate *Neues Leben* and – according to Eikermann – distributed by the FDJ network.[145] Fast's novel depicted the struggle of the African American protagonist Gideon Jackson after the Civil War in the American South. In the novel, poor whites and blacks seek to rebuild their lives working side by side, a utopian project that ultimately ends in tragedy brought about by rich white supremacists. Of course, *Freedom Road* did not "mirror democratic life" or project an "undistorted image" of America, which at the time of the novel's publication was still directing the reeducation of the Western part of the former Nazi Germany.[146] In fact, as noted above, *Freedom Road* was prohibited from German translation by the US-led Information Control Division, not least because of the author's affiliation with the Communist Party. For those Communists, though, it served as a perfect tool of ideological warfare, for it not only forcefully decried racism in capitalist America, but also it offered a political solution to remedy such grievances; a solution that also, conveniently, functioned as a corrective for the German racist past.

To make young people believe in socialist ideas required great sensitivity, for the question of guilt also affected German youth. In the view of German communists, Hitler's regime had abused German youth, and by September 1945, the KPD had proclaimed that the party was open for membership to young people who had once been part of the Nazi organizations.[147] By helping to rebuild a socialist Germany, many young people

---

[144] See Ina Merkel, "Eine andere Welt. Vorstellungen von Nordamerika in der DDR," in *Amerikanisierung: Traum und Alptraum im Deutschland des 20. Jahrhunderts*, ed. Alf Lüdtke, Inge Marssolek, and Adelheid von Saldern, Transatlantische historische Studien (Stuttgart: F. Steiner Verlag, 1996). See also Uta A. Balbier and Christiane Rösch, eds., *Umworbener Klassenfeind: Das Verhältnis der DDR zu den USA* (Berlin: Christoph Links Verlag, 2006).

[145] Fast, *Strasse zur Freiheit.*

[146] The Civil Affairs Division, affiliated with the Information Control Division, set up criteria for books fit for German translation. Authors with links to the Communist Party were prohibited from translation. See Daniel Haufler, "Amerika, hast Du es besser? Zur deutschen Buchkultur nach 1945," in *Amerikanisierung und Sowjetisierung in Deutschland: 1945–1970*, ed. Konrad H. Jarausch and Hannes Siegrist (Frankfurt a. M., New York: Campus, 1997), 393.

[147] *Deutsche Volkszeitung*, July 7, 1945. As cited in: Ulrich Mählert and Gerd-Rüdiger Stephan, *Blaue Hemden, Rote Fahnen: Die Geschichte der Freien Deutschen Jugend* (Opladen: Leske und Budrich, 1996), 25.

believed they had a chance to labor toward the "right" side of history. The story of *Freedom Road* served this notion in multiple ways, which explains the book's tremendous popularity in the SBZ and GDR, and among the broader citizenry who identified with the protagonist victimized by capitalism, fascism, and racism.

Undoubtedly, in the 1940s and 1950s, racial inequalities persisted in the United States where, in many states, the laws of Jim Crow denied blacks equal access to basic rights and opportunities. In response to these realities, the prologue of *Freedom Road* called for the fight for the emancipation of humanity and leveled an accusation at its own country of origin: "One thing is for sure: The American proponents of racism should not act as the keeper of the seal for democracy and freedom, because we know their own infamy. . . . Karl Marx assessed that the liberation of the working class and the liberation of the colored people are inextricably intertwined."[148] Repeatedly, the novel suggests that racism is inherent to the system of capitalism and portrays the peaceful coexistence of races so long as capitalist interests do not endanger them. In this socialist utopia, human beings of all races are imagined as capable of living and working together in harmony. By pointing at grievances abroad, racism in Germany's recent past was thus put in perspective. *Freedom Road* served as a corrective to the Nazi past and genocide, for such views functioned to recriminate the capitalist and fascist systems for their crimes.

Finger-pointing at American racism and the propagation of the eradication of fascism and racism in the GDR engendered very different forms of juvenile conduct. The GDR's founding mythology was based on antifascism; as the propaganda effort repeatedly trumpeted, fascism and racism remained only in the Western world, having been overcome in the East. Authorities were therefore outraged when juvenile provocation broke such taboos. One incident of racist conduct occurred around Carnival season in 1961, when adolescents in Karl-Marx-Stadt dressed up as members of the Ku Klux Klan. FDJ functionaries complained in a report to the Central Committee of the FDJ: "In the club of the youth and sportsmen in Karl-Marx-Stadt, a group of juveniles with decent manners spent Carnival evening dressed as a Ku Klux Klan gang unimpeded. That is too much. We cannot condone this."[149] Officials were enraged because apparently nobody

---

[148] Fast, *Strasse zur Freiheit*, 314–15.
[149] Zentralrat der FDJ, Abteilung kulturelle und sportliche Massenarbeit, "Bericht an das Büro des Zentralrats über die Arbeit im Wohngebiet und den Stand der kulturellen und sportlichen Massenarbeit." BArch/DY 24/1804 (April–December 1961).

intervened that evening, presumably due to a tacit agreement between those youngsters and the clubhouse leaders. Openly racist agitation was a taboo in the socialist society that, on occasion, "errant" youth sought to provoke.

But fiction was not the only means of portraying the United States in a negative racial light: musical broadcasts continued to offer numerous opportunities to drive a wedge between Western and Eastern cultures. "The Truth about America" (*Die Wahrheit über Amerika*) was a series of radio shows at the Deutschlandsender produced by Georg Friedrich Alexan from 1951 to 1953.[150] On December 12, 1951, Alexan broadcast a show about singer and civil rights activist Paul Robeson, one of the most prominent representatives of the "other" America.[151] During the McCarthy era, Robeson was blacklisted and his passport was confiscated, a move that triggered worldwide protest. The show began with Robeson's deep voice, introducing the program with the gospel song "Sometimes I Feel Like a Motherless Child." While the song continued, the clear, sincere voice of a female speaker explained: "A voice, dear listeners, which went around the world. The voice of Paul Robeson, recipient of the World Peace Prize, recipient of the Stalin Prize, recipients of the medals which were given during the Spanish war for freedom—Paul Robeson, the singer for freedom." The speaker excused the bad quality of the recording, explaining that "Robeson has no access momentarily to a studio, because the American Gestapo has condemned Robeson not to leave his hometown. But the voice of freedom is not oppressed: No!" The persona of Robeson functioned as a representative of the *other* America, as the voice of the oppressed who took on the fight for freedom in the country of the oppressor. At this point, the spirit of the music changed dramatically by featuring the "The Wall of Jericho" at an up-tempo pace, with the female speaker translating the lyrics: "One day the walls that keep us prisoners will tumble down."[152]

The show detailed Robeson's lifelong fight for peace on many fronts, represented in songs such as "Mamita Mia," alluding to his involvement in the international brigades in Spain, and "Ol' Man River" as an "unforgettable song for all friends of the true America" (*das wahre Amerika*).

[150] http://bundesstiftung-aufarbeitung.de/wer-war-wer-in-der-ddr-%2363%3B-1424.html?ID=33.

[151] Georg Friedrich Alexan, *Ein Sänger für den Frieden: Paul Robeson, Die Wahrheit über Amerika* (Deutsches Rundfunk Archiv X150, December 12, 1951). See also Michael Rauhut, *Ein Klang – Zwei Welten: Blues im geteilten Deutschland* (Transcript Verlag, 2016).

[152] Alexan, *Ein Sänger für den Frieden.*

The narrator described his youth of extreme poverty, as "he and his father and mother had to rifle through the trash dumps of the American cities to find something edible." But Robeson, listeners were assured, came to "realize the laws of exploitation transforming him into a fighter for progress and freedom," a realization that signaled the awakening of his political consciousness.[153] As portrayed in the show, Robeson had sent a message recorded in a music shop in his hometown to explain why he could not participate in person at the Weltfestspiele in Berlin. Invoking workers' solidarity, the speaker introduced Robeson's message as it had reached Berlin:

> Hear his voice with the message of the American people fighting for freedom: 'I deeply wish that I could be with you, but the temporary rulers of the American government have said no. Their revocation of my passport is part of a huge plan to try to isolate the American people from their true friends, the peace-loving masses of all lands. The bond of friendship and understanding which unites the people of the United States with forward-looking humanity the world over grows stronger everyday. And this festival serves to help make that bond unbreakable.'[154]

The proclamation of worldwide solidarity and freedom ended with a poem, "Peace Will Conquer War," which the speakers recited in both English and Russian, ending with the gospel song (and celebrated civil rights anthem) "We Shall Not Be Moved." As is clear, the persona of Robeson functioned within the anti-American propaganda of the GDR on multiple levels: his victimization symbolized the "true America" associated with the persecuted people during the McCarthy era; his race represented the masses of oppressed African Americans; his biography functioned as a symbol of anti-fascist resistance; and finally, his impressive, operatic bass fulfilled ideals of European music culture. In short, Robeson fully represented the civilized, acculturated racial other, projecting equality in every domain.

Another example of the East German effort to propagate jazz as the music of the people was represented in a program called "A musical journey around the world," broadcast on June 8, 1952. "When we talk about American music we think about jazz. In today's show we will come to know that jazz was originally a music which was close to the people, not containing eccentric sound and rhythms."[155] As well as propagating the notion of an original Ur-Jazz in contrast to more commercialized forms,

[153] Ibid.
[154] Ibid.
[155] June 8, 1952, program of Deutschlandsender and Berliner Rundfunk, DRA, Pressearchiv.

productions like these reveal two sides of anti-American propaganda: the music satisfied a need for popular music from across the Atlantic, serving as a window to the world, while simultaneously conveying the horrors of capitalism and the benefits of socialism to their listeners.

Ernst Bartsch's *Neger, Jazz und Tiefer Süden* (1956) presented a Marxist interpretation of the fight of African Americans for freedom, tracing the fate of black Americans after the Revolutionary and Civil Wars.[156] The chapter about jazz was based on various historical and musicological writings by Marxist historian Herbert Aptheker, black activists W.E.B. DuBois, Marcus Garvey, and Booker T. Washington, sociologist Frank Tannenbaum, and musicologist Sidney Finkelstein.[157] Bartsch told the stories of such leaders of slave rebellions as Toussaint L'Ouverture, Gabriel Prosser, and Nat Turner, devoting over thirty pages to African American music. Like Meyer, Konen, and Shneerson, Bartsch relied on a myth of the "Golden Age" of jazz. Like other critics, Bartsch denounced the "corruption" of the music, which he traced to New York in the 1930s, and he gave credit to jazz's positive influence on world music by citing famous composers' opinions about the genre. Bartsch cited Aaron Copland, who underlined the effect on contemporary composers by the rhythmical sense of the people of the "Dark Continent," alluding to Meyer's comments on jazz rhythms as a fruitful component of socialist music.[158]

This general view on jazz appeared again in the 1957 documentary *The History of Jazz* (*Vom Lebensweg des Jazz*) written by Reginald Rudorf among others.[159] As noted above, the filmmakers had to endure a long struggle with authorities to satisfy censors, which reflects the confusion over defining what "the people's music" really was. The participation of high-level officials in the censoring process sheds light on the importance authorities laid on the outcome of this film, which premiered in August 1956 during the fall fair in Leipzig.[160] In 1955, officials at the Ministry for

---

[156] Other titles depicting the African diaspora: Heinrich Loth, *Das Sklavenschiff. Die Geschichte des Sklavenhandels* (Berlin: Union Verlag, 1981); A.O. Schwede, *Glory, Glory Hallelujah* (Berlin: Union Verlag).

[157] Ernst Bartsch, *Neger, Jazz und tiefer Süden* (Berlin: VEB F. A. Brockhaus, 1956), 252.

[158] Ibid.

[159] The other writers were Wolfgang Bartsch and Wernfried Hübel; the producer was Heinz Rüsch.

[160] The following persons were present in the censorship discussions: *Der Minister* (no specification), Notowicz, Rebling, Schwehn, Uszkoreit, Gass, Knepler, Pinscher. See BArch/DR 1/4533 (1956), "Diskussion 'Jazz' in Anwesenheit des Ministers." For more on the making of the documentary, see Thomas Heimann, "Vom Lebensweg des Jazz," in *DEAFA Jahrbuch 2000*, ed. Ralf Schenk and Erika Richter (Berlin: 2000). Heimann relies on Rudorf's Western publications, which occasionally distort the facts. See Reginald Rudorf, *Jazz in der Zone* (Köln, Berlin: Kiepenheuer&Witsch, 1964); *Nie wieder Links* (Berlin: Ullstein, 1990).

Culture had expressed concern about the ongoing jazz debates, suspecting illegal activities that attempted to "infiltrate Western cultural barbarism," and even going so far as to recommend the removal of scenes showing swing dance.[161] The final version of the documentary began with music of the 1920s performed by African American singer Bessie Smith underneath a voiceover: "This music has never seen its blossom. Where the dollar rules, music is victimized by its laws, and now it sounds like this. ..."[162] At this moment the speaker goes quiet, giving way to examples of white swing performers who were supposed to function as a deterrent, representing the commercialization of black music. Whether viewers fell into this propagandistic trap is questionable, but swing fans in the audience probably took pleasure in these scenes. The film's overall argument is that genuine folk music – here represented by the New Orleans style, which was portrayed as "happy music" expressing the enjoyment of life, with ensembles such as the Rodauer Waschbrett Kapelle then exemplified (Figure 3.12) – had

Figure 3.12   Rodauer Waschbrett Kapelle, late 1950s, dressed in bourgeois attire reminiscent of New Orleans jazz in early 1900s. Private collection of Klaus Schneider, used by permission

[161] BArch/DR 1/4533 (1955), "Ministerium für Kultur, Hauptverwaltung Film, Ackermann an Stier, VEB DEFA-Studio für populärwissenschaftliche Filme. 23.5.1955."
[162] Bundesarchiv Berlin-Lichterfelde/Filmarchiv, Berlin: *Vom Lebensweg des Jazz.* "*Diese Musik hat ihre wahre Blüte nie erlebt: Wo der Dollar der Maßstab aller Dinge ist, macht man auch vor einer Musik nicht halt und nun klingt sie so ... Für diese schlechte Ware mißbrauchen sie den Namen Jazz. Der Jazz ist von dieser schmutzigen Flut fast verschüttet worden. ...*"

been destroyed by commercialization, suggesting that this music would have instead blossomed in a socialist society. As noted, the screening of the documentary was prohibited in February 1957 because of Rudorf's involvement in its production. Accused of counterrevolutionary agitation, Rudorf was arrested in March of that year.[163] Sentenced to prison for two years, he emigrated to West Germany following his incarceration.

While cultural offerings typically pushed such images of America from a distance, some jazz fans directly experienced America's segregated society in occupied Berlin. In a recent interview, Alfons Wonneberg, member of the Berlin Jazz Club and a well-known bandleader in a popular television show, recalled his years in 1950s Berlin.

> I played back then in a band, which performed a lot in American clubs. Back then, these were still segregated, which meant a club for whites and a club—in today's politically correct term—for African-Americans. Naturally we preferred to play in black clubs, because the cats there were more laid-back. In the white clubs we had to play hillbilly music. They came from Texas, they wanted their music when dancing with the *Fräuleins*. But the blacks liked music by Billy Eckstein ... To be honest, for me the United States was always a racist country. It started with the Indians and it did not stop with the blacks and even the Jewish were badly treated. A lot of Jewish jazz cats changed their names to not be identified as such.[164]

As a thirty-year-old white man, Wonneberg had the chance to play in West Berlin's nightclubs, which were frequented by US soldiers and where he witnessed segregation firsthand. Yet, by his own account, he preferred playing in black clubs because that gave him a chance to play with African American musicians. Wonneberg saw America's democratic mission in defeated fascist Germany as hypocritical.[165] His affinity toward African Americans within the brotherhood of all people resulted years later in an incident in the 1970s. Traveling on the New York City subway, he sat next to an African American, proclaiming without prior introduction: "I am not like the other whites, I am your brother." To his surprise, he received a hostile reaction.[166]

---

[163] BStU, MfS, Leipzig AU 43/57, Reginald Rudorf. *Einlieferungsanzeige vom 27.3.1957. Tatbestand: Rudorf hielt Anfang November 1956 als freischaffender Künstler vor den Studenten der medizinischen Fakultät der Karl-Marx-Universität Leipzig einem Vortrag über Psychologie und Jazz. Im Verlauf dieses Vortrags hetzt Rudorf vor den anwesenden Studenten gegen führende Funktionäre der Freien Deutschen Jugend und der Partei der Arbeiterklasse. Diese Funktionäre wurden von ihm als Bürokraten und Stalinisten bezeichnet. Gleichzeitig forderte er die Anwesenden auf gegen die von ihm genannten Funktionäre vorzugehen und aus der FDJ zu entfernen. Die Tätigkeit der Kulturfunktionäre vergleicht er in diesem Zusammenhang mit der Tätigkeit ehemaliger Faschisten.*
[164] Alfons Wonneberg (2009).
[165] Ibid.
[166] Ibid.

In sum, socialist propaganda constructed a polarized image of America, in which the exploiter and the exploited existed within a system that nurtured racial hatred and perpetuated oppression. Notions of a "reactionist" America appeared alongside those of the "other" America represented by leftist democratic forces. Representations of conflicts between these opposing poles stimulated notions of a socialist utopia, notions heavily propagated in socialist popular culture such as film, theater, and radio productions. Furthermore, radio programs were produced in direct response to repression in America, such as the persecution of Paul Robeson. Such programs conjured a solidarity between the GDR and the "other" America.

Moreover, cultural products that suffered American censorship were often propagated in the East. The reception of Howard Fast's novel *Freedom Road* exemplifies such practices of the opposing ideological camps, serving both as an indictment of capitalist America and as a corrective for Germany's racist Nazi past. Rudorf's documentary *The History of Jazz* (*Vom Lebensweg des Jazz*) further attempted to portray jazz as a socialist-realist art form, envisioning the New Orleans style as "the people's music" prior to its corruption by the music industry. Its effect, though, was minimal: before it could achieve widespread exposure, authorities withdrew the film from theaters because of the counterrevolutionary activities of writer Reginald Rudorf. Across the GDR, the impact of such offerings engendered diverging conduct among the youth. As in years past, within jazz circles, the polarized image of American society simultaneously informed a repudiation of its political system as well as cultural fascination with the enemy, with the ambiguity of jazz music and jazz culture eclipsing such bivalent perceptions. Such ambiguity could not be tolerated or left unchecked forever, though. As the next section details, systematic surveillance of the jazz scene preceded the climactic decision to divide the city and country in half.

Berlin in Crisis: State Surveillance and the Building of the Wall

In the 1950s, West Berlin was a mecca for jazz fans. Large venues such as the Deutschlandhalle and the Titania Palast as well as small establishments, the Badewanne and the Eierschale, regularly featured the celebrities of the international jazz world. The Festhalle at the radio tower put on a series called Jazz Meetings, which included "Jazz at the Philharmonic" produced by Norman Granz.[167] In the second half of the 1950s, the city of Berlin sponsored jazz festivals called Jazz Salons, and when the US State Department began to officially promote jazz in the late 1950s,[168] the American Cultural Centers (the *Amerikahäuser*) began to feature jazz events as well. The *Amerikahaus* in Berlin offered its facilities to a West Berlin Jazz Club called New Jazz Circle Berlin (the NJCB briefly mentioned in the introduction of this chapter) for its regular meetings.[169] At the Ninetieth Record Lecture on March 4, 1957, Wolfgang Jänicke, then president of the NJCB, presented novelties of the German jazz-record market. Among the fifteen titles showcased that night were American and German productions, such as Stan Kenton and his Orchestra's "Unison Riff," Gerry Mulligan's "Bernie's Tune," and Teddy Stauffer's "Lime-house Blues," presenting a wide spectrum of genres. Two years later in January 1959, the NJCB organized the Jazz Salon, a well-publicized multiday event at multiple locations around West Berlin, sponsored by the DJF and the city of Berlin under the patronage of mayor Willy Brandt.

The organizers of the event had two goals: first, they sought to burnish the image of jazz with intellectual sophistication, and second, they tried to lure East Germans to West Berlin, compensating their guests' expenses and distributing gifts such as jazz records.[170] Performances at the Jazz Salon called *Konzertanter Jazz, Concertino in Jazz,* and *Concerto Grosso* gave the event the appearance of a crossover of European musical traditions and American modernism. Furthermore, the programs of these events were revealing: in one lecture, jazz historian Horst Lange linked jazz to Germany's cultural history by tracing the roots of German jazz to the Weimar era, and on the same evening, a ballet group fused highbrow dance culture and jazz in a single performance. The media covered the events of the Jazz Salon extensively with broadcasts by Radio Free Berlin (*Sender Freies Berlin*) and RIAS.[171] Overall, such events, especially the Jazz Salon, functioned as a cultural bridge between East and West, a bridge that GDR authorities viewed with increasing distress. To understand

[167] Monson, *Freedom Sounds*, 79. The Jazz at the Philharmonic concert and package tours had begun in 1944, bearing the image of Norman Granz' opposition to Jim Crow. Programs for these events were costly, printed in large format and featuring a whole page photograph of Granz.

[168] von Eschen, *Satchmo Blows Up the World*; Monson, *Freedom Sounds*; Lisa E. Davenport, *Jazz Diplomacy Promoting America in the Cold War Era* (Jackson: University Press of Mississippi, 2009).

[169] Interview with Gerhard Hopfe, February 6, 2013. "ZIRKEL" (1958), 3–4.

[170] Ibid.

[171] Programmheft: Deutscher Jazz Salon Berlin 1959. Veranstalter: Deutsche Jazz-Föderation e.V./ Der Senator für Jugend und Sport Berlin/New Jazz-Circle Berlin e.V. Ibid., 37.

how this distress escalated into the building of the Berlin Wall, it is first important to understand the previous conditions: The Berlin Crisis of the late 1950s and the systematic state surveillance that fed East German paranoia over its political security and sovereignty.

In the late 1950s, during the time of the Western Jazz Salons but before the construction of the Berlin Wall in 1961, about three million East German citizens, mostly skilled workers, decided to leave their homes to build their lives in West Germany. While the mass immigration benefitted West Germany, given that it both discredited the Communist state and provided skilled labor, for the GDR, the exodus contributed to a harsh economic crisis. During these years, Berlin was once again the stage for confrontation: in November 1958, Soviet premier Nikita Khrushchev had demanded the withdrawal of Western Allied troops from West Berlin territory, as well as the delegation of sovereign rights to all GDR entryways. The Berlin ultimatum was limited to six months, by which point the Western part of the city was supposed to be a free and demilitarized zone. Allied powers rejected this demand, and the tensions over the crisis eased only when Khrushchev accepted an invitation to the United States the following year. Nevertheless, the SED leadership still sought a quick and, if necessary, forcible solution for its "Berlin problem," as the escape route for those who had fled their homes in the East had led most of them to West Berlin.

Political tensions during this crisis led to repercussions on jazz activism in the GDR, such as the prohibition of clubs and the closing of venues, but what may initially appear as intolerance and repression of jazz must be set in context. The frequent prohibition of clubs in the East German capital was not based on a political rejection of jazz itself, but rather it grew out of the political situation at the time. The East blamed the West for demagoguery, using jazz as but one of its many enticements for people to escape. After its dissolution in May 1958, the Berlin Jazz Club (in East Berlin), which had undergone name changes over the course of the decade, reformed in the spring of 1959.[172] The new meetings were then held at

---

[172] The Interessengemeinschaft Jazz Berlin was founded on December 18, 1955, meeting at the FDJ house in Gartenstraße, Prenzlauer Berg before it was dissolved on May 22, 1958. When it reformed the following year, Alfons Wonneberg, the former leader, had resigned. Elected members of the board were: Werner Sellhorn (1st chairman), Klaus-Jürgen "Lefti" Heinicke (2nd chairman), Jürgen Schitthelm and Helmut Eikermann. Cf. Werner Sellhorn, "Jazz – Jenseits des Potsdammer Platzes," *West German Publication, 1958. Presumably issued by a West-Berlin jazz club. Content: Sellhorn's information about East Berlin's jazz scene. The Publication also featured a preliminary program of Deutscher Jazz Salon as well as a jazz convention in 1959* (1959).

the DSF at Schönhauser Allee, which the STASI certainly knew about, as their agent Werner Sellhorn reported the names, ages, and occupations of some ninety members, including their political preferences and personal details.[173] The Berlin Crisis, however, doomed the existence of the jazz clubs, and their last meeting was held on May 6, 1959. Municipal authorities had decided that the present political situation demanded its prohibition. Sellhorn, always a spokesman for the group, had been in communication with municipal representatives and was prepared for the closure, justifying the measure in a speech to the members. A discussion followed, in which the regrouping of the club at a later point was proposed. The members were discontented but acquiesced in the resolution.[174] Two years later, they reorganized officially again at Humboldt University.[175] Until then, jazz fans met illegally in private venues, of which – unsurprisingly – informants also made the STASI aware. Sellhorn's reports revealed the addresses of their new meeting places as well as the identities of the attendees.[176]

If, during the Berlin Crisis, jazz suffered in the East, West Berlin still had much to offer. Jazz festivals, salons, and conventions continued to lure East German fans, particularly youth, to the western part of the city. Supported by the DJF, West German officials sent invitations in neutral envelopes so as to not arouse suspicion.[177] In fact, the federation's so-called *Ostbüro* supervised this propaganda, and it is possible that Sellhorn, working as a double agent for both East and West, had provided the necessary contact information for the invitations.[178] Facing high numbers of refugees defecting to the West each month, the SED leadership blamed Western propaganda, and the STASI evaluated the Jazz Salon as a prime event to utilize jazz as a "psychological preparation for war."[179] To stay informed of Western jazz activism, the STASI sent Sellhorn on missions

---

[173] BStU, MfS, 13412/65, "Zirkel" Werner Sellhorn [File covers 1958–1967], pp. 48–59.

[174] Ibid., p. 60.

[175] Since March 3, 1961, the STASI was informed about the reorganization of a new jazz circle at Humboldt University under the auspices of the FDJ. Sellhorn informed on around nineteen members, who had met twice. They had planned the third meeting on May 30, 1961. See BStU, MfS, "Zirkel," pp. 102–106. An article in the Berliner Zeitung encouraged the new formation of the jazz circle. See "Nicht im eigenen Saft schmoren," *Berliner Zeitung* (May 3, 1961). At this time not only did new jazz circles emerge in Berlin, but a jazz circle under the auspices of the Kulturbund was formed in Potsdam. See "Jazz – durchaus ernst zu nehmen! Interessengemeinschaft des Kulturbundes gebildet/ Experten geben Unterstützung," *Märkische Union* (February 2, 1961).

[176] BStU, MfS, "Zirkel," pp. 86–94.

[177] Ibid.

[178] Ibid., p. 27.

[179] Ibid., pp. 100–101.

to the West and provided generous benefits in Western currency – just as he had demanded. In January 1959, he informed the STASI about the organizational and financial details of the Jazz Salon, such as municipal subsidies for the festival, the kind of programming, the political content of lectures including audience reactions, and – most importantly – information about the identities of East German visitors.[180] According to his report, the promoters of the Deutscher Jazz Salon had sent hundreds of invitations to GDR jazz fans. Fearing repercussions, however, not many undertook the trip; according to Sellhorn's estimation, there were only ten to fifteen East German citizens present.[181] Under the pretense of making contacts to organize jazz lectures in the GDR, he obtained contact data from these citizens, noting that they received valuable presents such as posters, programs, photos, and records.[182] These gifts were particularly precious, since such records – purchasable only in West German currency – were beyond the financial means of most young people in the East.

Shrewd to the end, Sellhorn knew how to combine his STASI cooperation with his own ambitious jazz activities. In one of his reports, he emphasized the differences between Western clubs and Eastern jazz circles. In the GDR, jazz circles fell under the umbrella of mass organizations, such as the FDJ, the Cultural Alliance (*Kulturbund*), and the DSF. Sellhorn denounced the events of the Western NJCB as "snobbiest-bourgeois," contrasting his work in the East as being politically engaged and educationally ambitious.[183] His report to the STASI reads:

> The NJCB meets once a week at the *Amerikahaus* at the train station ZOO. ... The members are seriously into jazz—they listen to records and lectures, but do so in a bourgeois and snobbish way. ... Our jazz club at the House of the German-Soviet Friendship has a different approach. We are dealing with jazz very seriously, in particular through the lens of sociology. We try to educate our members towards progressive development by engaging them in political discussions and lectures on topics of socialist culture.[184]

---

[180] Ibid., p. 26.
[181] Ibid., p. 25.
[182] Ibid. Report about the German Jazz Salon 1959, pp. 40–43.
[183] Ibid.
[184] In the early 1950s, Sellhorn wrote a five-page report about jazz in West Germany, adopting current socialist ideology on the music and its participants. [Der] *"New Jazz Circle Berlin (NJCB), [tagt] allwöchentlich im Amerikahaus am Bahnhof Zoo. Dieser Club ist äußerst seriös aufgemacht mit Vorsitzendenglocke etc. Man beschäftigt sich zwar ernsthaft (vor allem mit Plattenvorträgen) mit dem Jazz, aber in bürgerlich snobistischer Weise. ... Die Interessengemeinschaft der Jazzfreunde im Haus der Deutsch-Sowjetischen Freundschaft (demokratischer Sektor Berlins) ist ganz anders konzipiert. Ich bin ihr 1. Vorsitzender. Wir beschäftigen uns ernsthaft mit dem Jazz, vor allem in soziologischer*

Together with jazz club member Klaus Jürgen Heinicke, Sellhorn held a forum on February 20, 1958, entitled Jazz and Literature.[185] The program featured social-critical and anti-war pieces by Erich Kästner, Berthold Brecht, and Kurt Tucholsky that were mixed with blues and jazz song titles such as "Working Man Blues" and "Revolutionary Blues," which linked the music to its proletarian roots (Figure 3.13). In an attempt to

Figure 3.13   Diary montage of Klaus Jürgen Heinecke, showing Werner Sellhorn playing records at Berlin Jazz Club, as well as conservative, intellectual attire of members (Heinecke to right of Sellhorn), late 1950s. Private collection of Klaus Jürgen Heinecke, used by permission

Hinsicht. Wir versuchen, unsere Mitglieder außerdem durch gemeinsame Aufbaueinsätze, politische Diskussionen und Vorträge über Themen sozialistischer Kultur (neben den eigentlichen Jazzvorträgen) zu fortschrittlichen Menschen zu erziehen." Ibid., p. 33. By the late 1950s, the STASI already had informants among West German citizens. In his report, Sellhorn mentions a friend who was a West German leftist jazz activist in Düsseldorf: Sellhorn writes that he was recently "in contact with the MfS (Schmidt, 533038/531), which he told me confidentially (I played dumb and told him that I would not do such thing)." Ibid., 30–31.

[185] Many years later, when STASI files were opened and Heinicke learned that Sellhorn had been spying on the club all along, he ripped Sellhorn's photograph in his photo album in half.

impart socialist-realist ideology to his listeners, the young lecturer argued: "According to our theory [...] the jazz fan who likes a particular style relives similar problems which are expressed in this style. [...] Jazz is a product of the conflict between individual longing and the demands of reality."[186] Such lectures from 1958 can be seen as the predecessor of the famed series in the GDR called *Jazz und Lyrik*, which Sellhorn also initiated and which featured noted actors such as Manfred Krug and Angelica Domröse, and singer/songwriter Wolf Biermann. This series is discussed in detail in the next chapter.

At the time of his first contact with the STASI on December 12, 1958, Sellhorn had suspended his studies in philosophy at Humboldt University in order to take various jobs. He earned only a small income since he had no professional qualifications.[187] Sellhorn's financial difficulties were perhaps his chief motive for cooperating with the STASI, but he was also driven to do so by the prospect of participating in those jazz events on which he would report.[188] He seemed to have profited from his services in multiple ways: his frequent trips to the West were legal; as a passionate jazz fan he was able to enjoy jazz concerts; and he was paid for his services regularly, sometimes even in Western currency. While his eager networking activity helped organize his lecture tours throughout the GDR, at the same time, he helped the state in its efforts to observe and control the jazz scene. In a way, Sellhorn's activity extended and even organized the GDR jazz scene under the tutelage of the STASI, which generally conceded as long he was cooperative. The STASI made Sellhorn's lifestyle possible, which allowed him to evolve not just as a ubiquitous figure on the scene, but most importantly someone who enjoyed the trust of his friends and fellow enthusiasts. The income he earned, which among friends he falsely attributed to a family inheritance, often went to maintaining and expanding his considerable library of records.[189] He seemed to have few moral scruples about informing on individuals who illegally attended Western jazz events and did not burden himself with the consequences, especially when it served his own interests.[190]

---

[186] Klaus Jürgen Heinecke and Werner Sellhorn, "IGLB – Vortrag am 20.2.1958; Jazz und Dichtung, (I) Fröhlicher Auftakt; (II) Brecht/Kästner/Prevert (III) Tucholsky und Holiday" (February 20, 1958).

[187] BStU, MfS, "Zirkel."

[188] BStU, MfS, "Zirkel," p. 23. The Finanzant, the state financial auditor, threatened to take his record player and radio.

[189] Interview with Gerhard Hopfe, 2017.

[190] BStU, MfS, "Zirkel," p. 40: "[At the jazz salon] … there were approximately twelve to fifteen guests from the GDR. I asked for some addresses (important for my travels to the GDR jazz clubs), as there are …" Sellhorn listed four names and addresses from Rostock, Görlitz, and Greifswald.

Around 1960, the STASI expressed dissatisfaction with their informant, for Sellhorn had become increasingly unreliable, often failing to show up for meetings. During that time, he also lost his party membership. Nevertheless, the STASI still needed his cooperation because, during the Berlin Crisis in the late 1950s, the ministry worried about increasing Western jazz infiltration and manipulation. Agents had received information that large amounts of jazz materials, such as literature and records, were being sent via post to the Eastern Bloc. The campaign – which its Western initiators called the *Jazzbrücke* (jazz-bridge) – was allegedly organized by the editors of *Das Schlagzeug*, a magazine published by Äquatorverlag, and the Swiss publication *Die Tat*.[191] The STASI had immediately informed its compatriot agencies in Czechoslovakia, Poland, Bulgaria, Hungary, and Romania to limit such infiltration.[192] All correspondence regarding this counteraction was classified "top secret," though the outcome must have been a disappointment for the STASI, for only in Poland did the search for records yield results. Of the 6,000 records seized, however, most were not jazz, but recordings of religious content or German folk music.[193] The STASI knew about Sellhorn's contact with the editors of *Das Schlagzeug* and sent him across the border to spy on the *Jazzbrücke*. Sellhorn reported back that records were still being sent to the East, and that instead of a mass organized campaign, more likely personal contacts between sender and receiver engendered the transfers.[194]

In May 1961, Sellhorn traveled one last time to West Berlin to obtain information about the Deutscher Jazz Salon. In the eyes of state security, the Deutscher Jazz Salon remained a key tool of Western subversion; according to STASI documents, one of the strategies of attracting East Germans was to engage East German bands, such as Günter Hörig's Dresdner Tanzsinfoniker, for performances.[195] STASI agents discovered that the orchestra had illegally signed a contract with the Jazz Salon,

---

[191] BStU, MfS, 5496/72, Jazzbrücke, p. 18. The documents represent internal ministry correspondence from Deputy Minister Erich Mielke to Department X dated October 16, 1959.

[192] Ibid., pp. 18–31.

[193] Ibid., pp. 26–27. Letter from State Department of Poland to Minister of State Security Erich Mielke, dated February 12, 1960, classified "top secret."

[194] BStU, MfS, "Zirkel," pp. 27 and 81.

[195] Ibid., p. 111.

resulting in its prohibition from traveling to the West.[196] After Sellhorn's mission in May was completed, his handlers did not contact him again until that November. In the meantime, state security officers had other work to do, work that demanded their full attention: fortifying the border between the two Germanies.

As noted, by the late 1950s, many East Germans believed that trips to the West would not be possible for much longer, and in July 1961, some 30,000 GDR citizens relocated to West German territory.[197] SED leadership reacted nervously, continually denouncing the massive drain of citizens as the result of criminal Western actions of enticement. Refugees who were detained came to expect harsh retribution, and the GDR government finally took the ultimate step of cutting East German territory off from the West. On the night of August 12, 1961, units of the East German police force, the National People's Army, blocked the border between the eastern and western sectors of Berlin. Authorities began to erect a forty-five kilometer stone and barbed-wire wall around West Berlin and declared the following day that anyone who attempted to leave the GDR would be detained with force.[198] Within weeks, the Berlin Wall was completed, and troops were ordered to shoot at anybody who tried to leave. The year 1961 represented a deep caesura in the history of Germany, with most Germans abandoning any remaining hopes for reunification. For the East German state, however, the closing of its territory stopped the population drain, and a period of political and economic stabilization began. Khrushchev dropped his threats, and Berlin ceased to be the flashpoint of crisis that it had been between 1958 and 1961. Tellingly, the Jazz Salons discontinued after the building of the Wall, however, and the activities of the NJCB ceased as well – suggesting that, confirming STASI paranoia after all, they were intended not just to propagate jazz, but to draw East Germans to the West.[199] Trips such as Herbert Flügge had made were, for many, now a thing of the past (Figure 3.14).

---

[196] Deutscher Jazz-Salon Berlin 1961 der Deutschen Jazz-Föderation e.V., "Vorläufiges Veranstaltungsprogramm" (1961). "Kein Jazz aus der DDR. Die Verpflichtung der Dresdner Tanzsinfoniker, Leitung Günter Hörig, zum Deutschen Jazz-Salon, wurde von höchster Stelle im Ministerium für Kultur der DDR untersagt."

[197] Hermann Weber, *Geschichte der DDR* (München: Deutscher Taschbuch Verlag, 1985/1999), 295.

[198] Ibid., 297.

[199] Lange, *Jazz in Deutschland*, 156. According to Lange, the building of the Wall in 1961 was the reason for the end of these jazz events trying to connect East and West. In 1962, the NJCB disbanded.

Figure 3.14   Advertisement of the film *Jazz an einem Sommerabend* (Jazz on a
Summer's Night) from Herbert Flügge's jazz diary (1961). Flügge's entry reads: "My last
visit to the movies in West Berlin before the building of the wall." Private collection of
Flügge, used by permission

Conclusion

In the 1950s, the Marxist view of jazz constructed an origin-myth that explained jazz history as a history of the exploitation and repression of African Americans. According to the East German jazz discourse of this era, the New Orleans style represented the music's primordial variant, uncorrupted by commercial interests. Communist parties had used African American folk music as a tool of propaganda since the 1920s, but over time, the recruitment of jazz music for the socialist cause had lost effectiveness for two reasons. First, while the Marxist interpretation had championed "true jazz" as valuable humanist music, socialist-realist conceptions of culture revived a musical nationalism that undergirded an increasingly hostile reception to jazz in the Stalinist years utilizing a rhetoric reminiscent of the Nazi era. Second, jazz culture in postwar Germany had developed its own dynamics that transgressed norms of gender and race and that collided with bourgeois conceptions of culture and conduct. To counteract such developments – which East German officials regarded as infiltration by an imperialist enemy – those officials sought to enforce a dance culture that invoked German national traditions and dignified comportment. The Stalinist STAKOKU attempted to implement guidelines for proper dancing and tried to subdue sexuality in dances that were termed "hoten." Yet young people regarded STAKOKU's interference, which was justified as socialist education, as an unwarranted invasion of their private sphere. The ways STAKOKU interfered in youth entertainment reveals the cultural chasm that existed between political bureaucrats and working-class youth and exposed the state to ridicule and undermined its authority in the wake of the 1953 uprising. In this context, it is now clear that jazz dance culture harbored political valences that reinforced other discontents.

Marxist theories of jazz approved of its "primordial" pedigree and denounced its commercialization by the profit-oriented music industry, complicating the ideological streamlining of the music through policy-making. The multitude of popular music styles in the 1950s perceived as "jazz" both by the general public and by state officials resulted in genuine confusion, leading to inconsistent policies that irritated fans. On the one hand, STAKOKU's campaign for a "national dance culture" brought repressions against dance styles perceived as transgressive and disreputable, but on the other hand, it did engender an exchange of views between "above" and "below" that engaged officials, jazz fans, and the general public during the post-Stalinist years. The debates in the late 1950s sought to ameliorate sweeping judgments against jazz and, in many ways, succeeded.

Overall, these forums sought to correct a distorted image of the music back toward the idea of jazz as the music of the people.

In the late 1950s, the East German press presented jazz as humanist music, linking it to *Hausmusik*. As time went on, musicians and fans internalized socialist-realist dogma to reinterpret modern styles of jazz that theorists had denounced earlier in the decade, bifurcating music into authentic/commercial or real/fabricated. As jazz gradually became acculturated, the music fell increasingly into line with Marxist views of history and was therefore portrayed as a valid and valuable contribution in the process of building a humane society. A broader acceptance of jazz also occurred when rock 'n' roll swept over popular youth culture; a genre jazz advocates took pains to denounce as *Unkultur* (non-culture).

Both superpowers used the divided city of Berlin as a forum to propagate their respective cultural attainments. While the East showcased art and music understood as socialist realism, the West propagated works in which modernist trends were predominant. After an initial period of ambivalence toward jazz, American foreign policy recognized its importance by the end of the 1950s. As previous scholars have detailed, the US State Department began sponsoring worldwide jazz tours, sending musicians directly into Cold War hot spots.[200] Supported by Western funds, "Free Berlin" turned into a mecca for jazz fans, featuring concerts and educational events that attracted fans in the eastern sectors to the western sectors. In the GDR, repression against jazz clubs in the late 1950s was not directed against jazz music itself, with officials claiming rather that such interventions were politically necessary during the Berlin Crisis. Facing high numbers of refugees defecting to the West each month, the MfS sought information about these activities and planted informants such as Werner Sellhorn into the jazz scene. Sponsoring his connections between East and West, the STASI both benefitted Sellhorn's career and simultaneously expanded their capacity to conduct dragnet investigations.

Despite the music's increasing adoption in this decade, jazz did not lose its countercultural American appeal, yielding ambivalent reactions across the board. While it now began to represent socialist music culture, it was still associated with the class enemy. As a result, state authorities linked a preference for jazz to ideological instability, which is why they sought to monitor its adherents. As the next chapter details, after the building of the Berlin Wall, STASI informants and agents would continue to spy for years to come. Yet the 1960s would see further transformations in the acceptance and spread of the genre, transformations that revealed jazz's growing presence within socialist society.

---

[200] von Eschen, *Satchmo Blows Up the World*; Monson, *Freedom Sounds*.

CHAPTER 4

Jazz Behind the Wall, 1961–1971

Introduction

On the night of October 23, 1962, Ronald Mooshammer (1937–2017) was hiding near the freeway connecting Berlin-Hannover near Potsdam, on East German soil, waiting for a green Volkswagen Beetle coming from West Berlin. He had information that a suitcase would be dropped off in that location. The driver of the car would be Erhard Kayser, a young student of theology from Münster, West Germany, who was on one of his clandestine delivery tours from the West to supply East German jazz fans with records. Kayser had initiated this activity of delivering jazz records since the late 1950s, but following the building of the Wall, the undertaking of the two young men was highly illegal, and each one risked imprisonment. That particular night he waited in vain for Kayser's Volkswagen, but instead an East German police car stopped and took him into custody. Under normal circumstances his risk was lower, as Mooshammer knew a sympathetic policeman at the border near Potsdam who would tell him when it was safe to drop off and pick up a delivery. On this occasion, though, he was forced to fabricate a story when questioned about his intentions and was released. The next night, Kayser dropped off suitcases successfully, which Mooshammer quickly hid under nearby bushes before escaping as fast as he could. He returned to the location an hour later and took them to his home in Prenzlauer Berg, East Berlin, where he distributed them to a secret list of recipients.[1]

Driven by an urge to provide as much jazz material as he could obtain to East German jazz fans, Kayser contacted record companies and book publishers, begging for donations for his private aid program aptly called the "Jazz Lift." Over time, Kayser was able to amass an unparalleled amount

---

[1] Interviews with Ronald Mooshammer (2010) and Erhard Kayser (2013, 2017).

of materials he personally drove into East German territory to deliver. Another strategy was distribution by mail. Because direct postal deliveries were not possible from West Germany, Kayser drove to the Netherlands, used sender addresses he copied from telephone directories, and sent them from there to East German recipients. It was due to his initiative that thousands of records and books made their way to East Germany and were distributed by Mooshammer among jazz fans, who had established a network throughout the country. From today's perspective, in the age of unlimited access to information, it is hard to imagine how much it meant for people behind the Iron Curtain to receive a record with music they desired. Recipients of the Jazz Lift were overjoyed and expressed their gratitude in long letters to Kayser.[2] Mooshammer, who in 1962 had moved into an old bakery in Prenzlauer Berg, furthermore made his collection available to the jazz community. His apartment at Sonnenburgerstraße No.76 was open to music aficionados functioning as an extended library and jazz center for anyone who was interested. For musicians in the GDR, Mooshammer's collection was essential in their experience to explore jazz history and to catch up on its recent developments. In the 1970s and 1980s, his center served as a contact point and drop-in center for the GDR jazz scene as well as for Western visitors, among them musicians, producers, and officials from the West German diplomatic office who helped to extend the collection (Figures 4.1–4.3). After the re-unification of Germany, Mooshammer read his STASI file and realized that most of these activities were recorded by the agency, who chose not to interfere in order to expand their surveillance of the jazz community.[3]

Kayser and Mooshammer were not alone in their efforts, as a similar initiative arose from across the Atlantic. Music publications such as the American magazine *Down Beat* called out for donations of jazz records to be sent to recipients in the Eastern Bloc: "Donate Jazz LPs For Free Distribution Behind The Iron Curtain, Jazz-Lift, BOX 980, Battle Creek, Michigan."[4] As recent interviews indicate, records arrived by mail from private senders in the United States. Both Karlheinz Drechsel and Gerhard Hopfe received such precious packages, but they never learned how the

---

[2] Unfortunately, Kayser discarded these letters in the 1960s. Interview with the author, 2013.

[3] Interview with the author, 2010. Another reason the STASI held back was that a friend of Mooshammer's, Dieter Wagner, was informing the agency about his activities, and the flow of information was too valuable to compromise. See Ronald Mooshammer, "Geschichten vom Jazz in der DDR," *Horch und Guck* (4/1993).

[4] "Jazz-Lift," *Down Beat Magazine* (September 19, 1968).

Figure 4.1   Werner Gasch, Ernst-Ludwig Petrowsky, Ulrich Türkowsky, Joachim Kühn, Manfred Blume, Roland Mooshammer in Karl-Marx-Stadt, today Chemnitz, who shared jazz records illegally supplied by Erhardt Kayser (1962). Private collection of Ronald Mooshammer, used by permission

Figure 4.2   Erhard Kayser playing jazz violin, late 1950s/early 1960s. Private collection of Erhard Kayser, used by permission

Figure 4.3   Ronald Mooshammer's flat on Sonnenburgerstraße No. 76 (East Berlin) housing an informal jazz library, early 1970s. Jost Gebers seated at right. Private collection of Ronald Mooshammer, used by permission

senders got hold of their addresses.[5] For about fifteen years, from 1965 until 1980, Drechsel received about two records per year from various senders in the New York City area, one of whom was musician Paul Winter. Drechsel kept quiet about these postings, so as to not arouse any attention. Even one of America's "Jazz Ambassadors," Dave Brubeck, promoted such initiatives. In the late 1950s, during Brubeck's tour in Poland, the scarcity of recordings for Polish musicians and jazz fans left a profound impression on him, and he eagerly engaged in propagating and organizing a Jazz Lift from the States.[6]

Ironically, the growing isolation of East Germany from the West that culminated in the building of the fortified border induced increased jazz activities as well as a tighter networking of the jazz scene. The confinement to GDR territory bound jazz fans closer together, depending on one another to provide access to their beloved music. The activities of this community compelled officials to take measures toward the centralization of the jazz scene as well as its organization and observation. In 1962, mere months after the building of the Wall, the ZK took the step of articulating a central jazz resolution to streamline its political position on the music.

---

[5] Interview with Hopfe (2013). He remembered the sender's name, Theo Grievers. The package was imprinted with "This is a gift from the jazz lift."

[6] Keith Hatschek, "The Impact of American Jazz Diplomacy in Poland During the Cold War Era," *Jazz Perspectives* 4, no. 3 (2010): 291–94.

This resolution set the direction for a future incorporation of jazz into socialist state culture, as well as the incorporation of the jazz scene into government bodies. This chapter examines the trajectory of jazz during the 1960s, from the building of the Berlin Wall in 1961 to the end of the decade, a trajectory formed at various turns by informal and autonomous listener movements, by official state directives, by socio-political upheaval in the United States, by a pivotal visit by legendary musician Louis Armstrong, and by a resurgence of interest in jazz at the close of the decade.

Jazz behind the Iron Curtain

After the Berlin Wall went up in August 1961, jazz activities in the GDR were thrown into disarray. With fans and performers no longer able to travel easily between East and West, the flow of music, information, and records slowed considerably. The closure of the border effectively trapped East German citizens within the GDR. In the immediate aftermath of the closure, jazz activities increased mainly at places of higher education, which the higher ranks of SED leadership construed as sites of enemy agitation – indicating the degree of paranoia among government officials who had barely survived the uprisings just a few years earlier in 1957. Now, facing opposition from within the enclosed country, party leadership was forced to reckon with dissent from members who were no longer able to emigrate or escape to the West.

Shocked by the state's measure of building the Wall, jazz fans attempted to make their voices heard, sending out letters of protest to organizations such as the state Writers Association (*Deutscher Schriftstellerverband*, DS) to draw attention to their situation. In November 1961, students at the Humboldt University, who had founded an active jazz club prior to the building of the Wall, sent out circulars typed on university stationery to imply a formal appeal, which set officials on alert.[7] These letters were addressed to diverse party organizations (including the association of composers) demanding solidarity among friends of jazz. The students' proclamation did not explicitly protest the Wall; in fact, it did not even directly mention the enclosure of the country.[8] Instead, the authors gestured to

---

[7] The students had formed a club, *Arbeitsgruppe für Jazz*, hosting jazz events featuring Andre Asriel, Jens Gerlach, Manfred Krug, and Gerry Wolf. The club was registered with the FDJ Berlin Mitte and counted as members music historians and writers such as Asriel, Gerlach, and Heinz Bernstein. See "Nicht im eigenen Saft schmoren" (unauthored article), *Berliner Zeitung*, May 3, 1961.

[8] In interviews conducted for this book, several contemporary witnesses even indicated their acquiescence to the construction of the Wall.

the fortification of the border only as the "new situation."[9] Claiming to represent the leadership of a "jazz movement," the students stated that the "new situation" had created new problems that had to be solved. Calling for allies in the press and other organizations, they proclaimed a central organization demanding the abolition of restrictive measures concerning jazz. The students' indignation reflects their sudden isolation from the Western jazz world, and it seems that these feelings of abandonment prompted them to call for solidarity.[10]

The Ministry for Culture knew who the authors of the circular were. One of them was secret informant Werner Sellhorn, or IM Zirkel.[11] As noted in the last chapter, in 1961, Sellhorn's regular meetings with the STASI had been interrupted for six months. It was not until November, when the next meeting occurred, that Sellhorn vehemently denied any complicity with the Humboldt University student's "jazz movement" and the distribution of the circular letters.[12] In fact, Sellhorn suggested that the group had counterrevolutionary intents, particularly since a former student of West Berlin's Freie University was involved in the agitation, which substantiated officials' suspicions of subversive Western influences under the pretext of jazz.[13] In this November meeting, the STASI instructed Sellhorn to temper his activities in jazz organizations, reasoning that "other friends of jazz might orientate themselves according to the [Humboldt University's] subversive agitation, evolving into a movement which he [Sellhorn] did not want. . . . "[14] He was further advised to concentrate only on jazz broadcasting

---

9 Zentralrat der FDJ, "Beratung über Jazz am 15.12.1961," BArch/DY 24/1804 (April–December 1961).

10 The Ministry for Culture called for a meeting about jazz activities after the building of the Wall, including Uszkoreit, Brattke, Groß (Ministry for Culture) Gluck and Gützner (Ministry of Education), Jahn (Secretary of Higher Education), and Helmut Diller (Central Committee, FDJ). Diller's report to Horst Schumann on December 18, 1961, summarized the Humboldt students' complaints: "Four to six weeks ago these two people [Sellhorn, van Spall] sent letters to various organizations including that of the composers with the following content: 'Because of the new situation we have now larger tasks. We took the movement into our hands and want to solve the following problems: countrywide organizing, abolishment of the 60:40 decree, questions of dance and entertaining music, lectures, and questions of fees. Signed with jazz greetings [Jazz-Grüßen].'" Zentralrat der FDJ, "Beratung über Jazz am 15.12.1961," BArch/DY 24/1804 (April–December 1961).

11 Zentralrat der FDJ, "Beratung über Jazz am 15.12.1961," BArch/DY 24/1804 (April–December 1961).

12 BStU, MfS, "Zirkel," pp. 110–16.

13 Zentralrat der FDJ, "Beratung über Jazz am 15.12.1961," BArch/DY 24/1804 (April–December 1961). These STASI reports as well as Diller's 1961 report to Schumann both mention a student from the Netherlands named van Spall, who registered first at West Berlin's Freie University and then in East Berlin's Humboldt University. Karlheinz Drechsel remembered van Spall as a jazz musician (email to the author dated January 17, 2014).

14 BStU, MfS, "Zirkel," p. 115.

and lectures, which would help to educate society about jazz. That way, the STASI argued, Sellhorn would not become a spokesman for "negative forces."[15] Sellhorn must have understood the indirect threat and, as discussed below, functioned as an informer on the GDR jazz scene only off and on until the 1980s.[16] Although Sellhorn's work as a STASI informant was only made public after 1990, most friends and admirers seemed to have been aware of it long beforehand and did not take much offence at his complicity.[17] As noted in the introduction to this book, at his funeral in June 2009, a large crowd gathered to commemorate him as one of the most significant figures of jazz in the GDR. Many of the mourners present had been close friends as well as subjects of his denunciations to the STASI.[18]

In any case, government officials observed that after the enclosure of GDR territory, grassroots jazz activism intensified. Hans Georg Uszkoreit, head of the Ministry for Culture's music department at the time, issued a report noting that jazz clubs had "mushroomed," particularly in Berlin, pointing at Humboldt University, which he suspected as the seedbed of the alleged "jazz movement."[19] Officials took this increasing activity – not only in the capital – seriously, scrutinizing institutions of higher education across the country. They found that in Leipzig, concerts in the Karl-Marx-University's dining hall were presented weekly, and the local FDJ featured regular jazz events.[20] Halle's Martin Luther University and the College for Electro-Technology also showed increased activism. The city of Eisenach even sought to organize a three-day jazz festival.[21] In larger cities such as Berlin and Leipzig, numerous jazz circles had formed at FDJ clubhouses

---

[15] Ibid.

[16] Ibid. See also: BStU, MfS, XV/3356/72, "Zirkel" (1972–1980). From here on out, references to Zirkel's earlier file (1958–1967) will be referred to simply as "Zirkel," whereas references to his later file will include the later date range.

[17] Werner Sellhorn, "Meine Kontakte zur Stasi," *Horch und Guck*, no. 13 (1994). In a recent interview (2011), Jürgen Schitthelm suspected Sellhorn's complicity with the STASI before it became public knowledge.

[18] As noted in the introduction, the author of this book attended Sellhorn's funeral.

[19] Uszkoreit led the briefing on jazz on December 15, 1961, including members of the FDJ, Ministry for Culture, and Ministry for Education. The report was sent to Horst Schumann, Ministry for Culture. See Zentralrat der FDJ, Abteilung kulturelle und sportliche Massenarbeit, "Beratung über Jazz am 15.12.1961 an Genossen Horst Schumann beim Ministerium für Kultur." BArch/DY 24/1804 (April–December 1961).

[20] Zentralrat der Freien Deutschen Jugend, Sekretariat Fritz Kirchhof, Schriftwechsel mit Horst Schumann (Sekretär des Zentralrates der FDJ). "Bericht über die Durchführung von Jazz-Konzerten, deren Einfluß auf die Jugend und die Schlußfolgerungen für den Jugendverband." BArch/DY 24/2439б (1961–1963).

[21] Zentralrat der FDJ, "Beratung über Jazz am 15.12.1961," BArch/DY 24/1804 (April–December 1961).

or at venues of other mass organizations without any official involvement or incentive.[22] All this activity occurred behind the Wall, where people attempted to pursue their musical passion in the newly confined space.

Concerned by these developments, officials in both the Ministry for Culture and the ZK formed a swift opinion of the situation, believing that increased jazz activities after 1961 were caused by Western agitation and suspecting that a "jazz movement" here posed a danger greater even of that in the previous decade led by Reginald Rudorf.[23] Ultimately, as discussed below, these concerns would lead to the central jazz resolution, but in the meantime, reports of the Ministry for Culture as well as the FDJ between August and December of 1961 not only show how differently officials assessed the increased activity and responded to it, but also disclose miscommunication and mistrust between the FDJ, governmental departments, and higher levels of leadership.[24] It seems that even within the FDJ opposing perceptions showed discrepancies both on a local level and between higher and lower ranks of the organization's hierarchy. Although Horst Schumann, first secretary of the FDJ, had generally endorsed jazz concerts, he ordered that the FDJ should be prevented from organizing such events in their local clubhouses.[25] Such decisions indicate that the youth organization's leadership mistrusted local functionaries in dealing with jazz activities and tried to curtail jazz at the grassroots level, which would become part of a broader attempt to centralize control over the scene.

In contrast to the assessments of Ministry officials, it seems that lower-rank officials in the FDJ, who were closer to the scene, were less worried about subversive jazz activism allegedly stirred from the West. In fact, in October 1961, these lower-rank functionaries of the FDJ had moved to incorporate jazz activities into its youth educational programs. Proponents

[22] "Without the involvement of the FDJ, jazz fans have formed jazz circles in clubhouses not only of the FDJ itself but also at schools and universities." Zentralrat der FDJ, Sekretariat Fritz Kirchhof, Zusammenarbeit mit den Abteilungen Kultur bzw. kulturelle und sportliche Massenarbeit, "Bericht von Fred Müller." BArch/DY 24/24373, 1961–1962.

[23] Zentralrat der FDJ, "Beratung über Jazz am 15.12.1961," BArch/DY 24/1804, April–December 1961.

[24] Zentralkomitee der SED. "Zur Beschäftigung mit dem Jazz in der DDR." BArch/DY 24/1804, BArch/DR 1/8668 (January 1962). Hereinafter referred to as "1962 ZK Jazz Resolution." As referred to in Ministerium für Kultur, Sekretariat des Ministers Hans Bentzien, "Auftrittsverbot für Rivertown Jazzband," BArch/DR 1/8668 (1962–1965).

[25] Sekretariat Fritz Kirchhof Zentralrat der Freien Deutschen Jugend, Schriftwechsel mit Horst Schumann, 1. Sekretär des Zentralrates der FDJ, BArch/DY 24/24396, "Brief vom 6.11.61" (1961–1963).

of jazz – mainly academics between the ages of twenty-five and thirty – represented themselves according to bourgeois norms of respectability by displaying sophisticated manners, conduct, and attire.[26] Their lectures at FDJ clubhouses contained educational components presenting music that strongly delineated such jazz from contemporary dance events. Officials acknowledged that "they appear in proper clothes (no leather jackets or the like) and behave accordingly and concert-like (*konzertmässig*). . . . People who were expecting thuggishness at such events were disappointed and did not return in the future."[27] Members of jazz circles differentiated themselves from the rock 'n' roll scene not only by musical preferences, but also by educational and class differences. By appearing in "concert-like" attire to their meetings, it seemed that they consciously emphasized the intellectual, bourgeois approach to the music to avoid attracting volatile crowds (cf. Figure 3.13). They actively pushed for jazz to be accepted in the realm of middle-class respectability, informed by the idea of jazz as the "music of the people." By the early 1960s, jazz fans not only distinguished the music from perceived commercialized derivatives, but also from contemporary dance music such as rock 'n' roll, which was labeled as outside the realm of culture. According to their perceptions of cultural hierarchy, rock 'n' roll was branded as non-culture (*Unkultur*), thereby using similar terminology as was deployed in the early 1950s for jazz.[28]

FDJ officials positively noted the jazz fans' sensible judgment, intellectual approach, and devotion to the music, and the fact that zero incidents of provocation arose. This reckoning prompted them to conclude that such events that appealed to the youth should be continued.[29] By supporting jazz events, FDJ officials sought to achieve two objectives: first, such events drew young people to the organization when it was difficult to encourage adolescents to participate in local FDJ activities;[30] second, a serious preoccupation with jazz fulfilled both educational and ideological objectives when put into a social context. Seeing the potential for cooperation, the FDJ suggested that jazz fans could be motivated to engage in

---

[26] Zentralrat der FDJ, Kirchhof mit Schumann, "Bericht über die Durchführung von Jazz-Konzerten," BArch/DY 24/24396 (1961–1963).

[27] Ibid.

[28] Ibid.

[29] Ibid. Report dated October 30, 1961.

[30] Zentralrat der FDJ, Abteilung kulturelle und sportliche Massenarbeit, "Bericht an das Büro des Zentralrats über die Arbeit im Wohngebiet und den Stand der kulturellen und sportlichen Massenarbeit." BArch/DY 24/1804 (April–December 1961). The file documents the FDJ briefing on this problem.

other forms of educational work. The liberal approach toward jazz in the second half of the 1950s, when the FDJ aspired to consider the needs of the youth by staging youth forums, was taken a step further by incorporating jazz into FDJ activities. FDJ officials who had insight into grassroots activity refrained from ideological laments about the destructive influences of class enemy infiltration or decadent jazz styles; instead, they seemed to have respected the pursuit of jazz. But in the eyes of party leadership such liberal approaches served as evidence for the FDJ's inability to recognize the perils of class enemy infiltration. From the standpoint of party leadership, jazz activities within the FDJ portended that the class enemy was attempting to create political outposts.[31]

Similar fears arose in meetings of ministry officials headed by Uszkoreit. He had been active in the Ministry for Culture's predecessor organization, STAKUKO, until its closure in 1953. When the STASI recruited him in 1961, he was the head of the department of music at the Ministry for Culture. The STASI praised him as a qualified associate as well as a reliable informant both on the GDR jazz scene and on the ministry itself. He had even received the code name "Amiga" because of his position at the East German record label.[32] In contrast to the in-depth reports of the FDJ, protocols of ministerial discussions headed by Uszkoreit disclose the Ministry's superficial knowledge of the jazz scene. Their ignorance and helplessness confronting the "problem" are revealed in phrases such as: "It is difficult to say where the positive side of jazz ends and the negative side begins." It seems that officials were over-stretched in assessing the increase in jazz activities, for the term "jazz" encoded too many meanings, irritating policymakers as they sought measures of tolerating or repressing jazz in the GDR's musical life. By repeating notions such as "stereotypical interpretations of jazz create craziness, trance, and aggressions," it appears that officials had simply consulted Meyer's *Musik im Zeitgeschehen* from 1952.[33] And by remarking, "One should not mix up jazz with the jazz movement," they at least acknowledged that the music itself ought to be differentiated from an alleged subversive movement, seen as orchestrated by the West. It seemed that within this discussion the term jazz functioned as a code for a multitude of associations including juvenile aggression, enemy subversion,

---

[31] 1962 ZK Jazz Resolution.

[32] In 1963, Uszkoreit became president of the Carl-Maria von Weber Conservatory in Dresden. For his file as STASI informant see BStU, MfS, 5225/77, "Amiga" Hans-Georg Uszkoreit, Band [Vol.] I and II.

[33] Zentralrat der FDJ, Kirchhof mit Schumann, "Bericht über die Durchführung von Jazz-Konzerten," BArch/DY 24/24396 (1961–1963).

and ideological accordance. It is not surprising therefore that the outcome of this confusion was a set of directives bolstering state authority, ordering strict prohibitions against any form of jazz organizations such as the founding of new clubs.[34]

Officials at the Ministry for Culture and the FDJ agreed on the imperative to defend state authority. They strictly denounced the perceived undermining of state authority in the form of organized sectarianism and stressed the point that jazz should not represent an exceptional position within the GDR's musical life. But they acknowledged the valid position of jazz within socialist music culture generally and refrained from prohibiting officially registered jazz events.[35] Nevertheless, it seems that the ministry representatives around Uszkoreit acknowledged a lack of information and were not aware of, or simply ignored, FDJ reports. Miscommunication between governmental departments resulted in discrepancies of restrictive measures, annoying musicians and fans. Although there was a general consensus on refraining from the prohibition of jazz concerts, other examples of repression in the 1960s do arise, but even these did not represent arbitrary repression against jazz in general. In withdrawing the performance license from the Rivertown Jazz Band at the Humboldt University in February 1962, the Ministry for Culture most likely referred to the student club's agitation in 1961 in the aftermath of the country's lockdown. The band's members – students of the Berlin Conservatory – were ordered to a "talk" in which they were admonished to participate in a conventional dance ensemble, "to lead their music enthusiasm in the right direction."[36]

Nevertheless, these repressions grew in visibility and scope. The position of jazz clubs legally organized with mass organizations had already been fragile in the early 1960s, with repression typically taking the form of prohibiting club meetings from using public venues. Leipzig offers an excellent example: like the jazz clubs in Berlin discussed in the last

---

[34] Zentralrat der FDJ, "Beratung über Jazz am 15.12.1961," BArch/DY 24/1804 (April–December 1961).

[35] Ibid. See also Zentralrat der FDJ, Kirchhof mit Schumann, "Bericht über die Durchführung von Jazz-Konzerten," BArch/DY 24/24396 (1961–1963).

[36] Ministerium für Kultur, Sekretariat des Ministers Hans Bentzien, "Auftrittsverbot für Rivertown Jazzband," BArch/DR 1/8668 (1962–1965). *Das Verbot wurde durch den Prorektor für Studienangelegenheiten Genossen Krug ausgesprochen. Er bekam durch die Abteilung Musik folgende persönliche Informationen: "1. Er wurde über das Grundsätzliche der Beschäftigung mit dem Jazz in der DDR entsprechend der Information durch die Kulturabteilung des Zentralkomitees unterrichtet. 2. Er erhielt den Auftrag, eine Aussprache mit dem betreffenden Studenten durchzuführen mit dem Ziel, sie für ein Tanzmusik-Ensemble innerhalb der Hochschule zu gewinnen, um die Musizierfreude so in richtige Bahnen zu lenken."*

chapter, jazz circles in Leipzig, after being prohibited from gathering at an FDJ clubhouse, were forced to regroup and hold meetings in other venues registered with different mass organizations, namely, the DSF.[37] Indeed, the Leipzig Bessie Smith Club, organized with the FDJ since 1959, had endured constant suppression, which eventually prompted them to express their grievances. The members – mostly students and academics – were serious about their jazz studies and seemed to be concerned about the music's social significance, exemplified by the choice of the name "Bessie Smith." (According to contemporary accounts, the blues singer's tragic death was a consequence of racist policies in the state of Mississippi.[38]) Like the majority of East German jazz clubs, the club in Leipzig represented only a small circle of academics and students who were "happy when young people had the opportunity to learn about jazz.[39] (After all, jazz was far from being the dominant music for young people, as by the 1960s, beat music had become the new musical fad despite its associations with youth dissents – especially since the 1965 Leipzig riots after the notorious "Beat-Ban."[40])

In any case, to call attention to their grievances, jazz fans protested vocally, and negotiations between jazz clubs and the FDJ appear in open letters addressed to the organization's central council. The Bessie Smith Club sent a letter to the headquarters of the FDJ, the House of the German Youth (*Haus der Deutschen Jugend*), Unter den Linden, Berlin in May 1961.[41] Additional copies were sent to the editors of the *Junge Welt*, the FDJ-affiliated magazine, hoping to inform a larger audience about their grievances and possibly to solve problems within the collective. In their letter, the jazz fans not only argued for the music's position in East Germany's cultural life, but also provided constructive suggestions about resolving conflicts with authorities. They believed that more information about their music would help to further overcome ignorance and prejudice

---

[37] In fact, on the initiative of club members, they improved their new venue by renovating its clubhouse and beautifying the adjacent garden.

[38] Theo Lehmann, *Blues and Trouble* (Berlin: VEB Lied der Zeit, 1981). See p. 50 in particular for the accounts of Smith's death. The original edition was published in 1966.

[39] "*Wir sind immer wieder froh darüber, wenn unsere Jugend Gelegenheit hat etwas über den Jazz zu erfahren.*" Zentralrat der Freien Deutschen Jugend, Letter from Bessie Smith Club to Horst Schumann, Erster Sekretär, dated May 5, 1961. "Offener Brief an den Zentralrat der Freien Deutschen Jugend." BArch/DY 24/3893.

[40] Mary Fulbrook, *A History of Germany, 1918–2014* (Oxford: Wiley Blackwell, 2015), 130–31. See also Michael Rauhut, *Beat in der Grauzone: DDR-Rock 1964 bis 1972, Politik und Alltag* (Berlin: Basis Druck, 1993).

[41] Letter from Bessie Smith Club to Horst Schumann, 1961.

on an administrative level. "We believe that it is necessary to abolish or at least reduce the general ignorance of jazz. Our youth should not be confronted with adult cultural functionaries who deprecate jazz."[42] Doubting the FDJ's competence to deal with young people's musical preferences, the authors advised that juveniles should not be confronted with state authority represented by an older generation of officials, being somewhat inept in dealing with youth culture. They argued for jazz as a tool of musical education hoping to win more young people over to the "jazz camp," pulling them away from "decadent" pop and dance music.

> We have to say that we love this music deeply in our hearts, but we have experienced many times that our beloved music is not appreciated at all.... Jazz is not taken seriously and is rejected mostly because the responsible functionaries are uneducated about it. ... Jazz is still confused with rock 'n' roll and dance music.

Taking their point even further, the writers provided an analogy by stating "Real jazz is as different from dance music as symphonic music is from *Kaffeehausmusik.*"[43] In this analogy, they attributed artistic value to jazz equal to that of symphonic music and strictly delineated it from dance music, arguing more qualified knowledge about the genre would in fact help to foster adolescent discriminatory musical judgment and to expose the simplicity of pop music (*Schlagermusik*). Jazz used as an educational tool would enable the youth to reject *Schlagermusik*, debunking it as "decadent," especially "the sort of music being broadcasted by the Western Radio Luxembourg."[44] Such arguments advanced an exceptional position for jazz, countering socialist notions of the genre as one equal among others in the pool of the world's folk traditions.[45]

In November 1961, Klaus Hesse, one of the members of the Bessie Smith Club and a signatory of the open letter, was ordered to a "talk," or *Aussprache* in party terminology.[46] He was informed that a public discussion about the issues raised in the letter was not desirable; therefore, the

---

[42] Ibid.

[43] Ibid. "*Echter Jazz ist von der Tanzmusik genauso so weit entfernt, wie die Sinfonik von der Kaffeehausmusik....*"

[44] Ibid. "*Wir sind immer wieder froh darüber, wenn unsere Jugend Gelegenheit hat, etwas über den Jazz zu erfahren. Derjenige junge Mensch, wird die Tanzmusik und ihre Auswüchse mit vernünftigen Maßstäben beurteilen und allen dekadenten Erscheinungen, wie sie uns z.B. über das Radio Luxemburg entgegenschallen, ablehnen. Der Jazz ist also nicht zuletzt ein Erziehungsmittel.*"

[45] 1962 ZK Jazz Resolution.

[46] The German term suggests a discussion in which differences between the two parties will be resolved. The talk is summarized in: Zentralrat der FDJ, "Bericht von Fred Müller." BArch/DY 24/24373 (1961–1962).

letter's publication was rejected, with which Hesse seemed to have agreed. The Leipzig scene and in particular the Bessie Smith Club had been observed by FDJ official Fred Müller, who seems to have had friendly relationships with its members. Müller reported on several private visits to Hesse, who was working at the time as a scientific assistant at a pharmaceutical company. Müller evaluated him as a fanatical jazz fan who possessed detailed knowledge of the jazz scenes in Berlin as well as other cities. Such observations may well have added to the suspicion that the jazz scene intended to organize itself, as his reports stand in stark contrast to the FDJ assessment discussed above. Müller's report harbors no talk of tolerance and cooperation; instead, he viewed the jazz scene as a potential adversary. The language he uses in his reports echoes that of a military observer rather than that of a youth worker.[47] Müller was convinced that in jazz clubs juveniles gathered without a clear position on party and state and were therefore predisposed for enemy infiltration. His report concluded with the recommendation of the prohibition of clubs in general.

Müller noted that incidents of aggression toward authorities occurred when the jazz concerts produced by the Bessie Smith Club attracted large crowds. He seemed to deliberately withhold information about the turmoil's instigators, thereby revealing what he did not want to include in his report. Aggressive juvenile conduct was likely not instigated by the few genteel members of the Bessie Smith Club, but by adolescents of blue-collar background who were more interested in mass events and loud music. Instead, he disclosed detailed information about the activities of the Bessie Smith Club. The majority of the members were academics and students, "who meet and listen to records or tapes, lead discussions about jazz and are deeply devoted to their music." While he depicted their studies with begrudging respect, he also added that they were considered as "failed existences" (*verkrachte Existenzen*), who had "connections to the West and even to the US, from where they received jazz" via records and broadcasts. Suspicious to the end, Müller condemned club members as politically unreliable, arguing that "it would be easy for reactionary forces under the cover of jazz to utilize them for their own goals."[48]

---

[47] In his report, Müller utilizes military terms such as: "listening to transmitters," "build up a group," and "take up quarters": *Sender abhören, Gruppe aufbauen, Quartier beziehen, auf 30 Mann angewachsen, verzogen sich in das Kulturzentrum*. See Zentralrat der FDJ, "Bericht von Fred Müller." BArch/DY 24/24373 (1961–1962).

[48] Ibid.

Like other FDJ officials, Müller repeatedly noted the paucity of working-class youth in these meetings, concluding that there was "no public interest" in jazz; therefore, jazz activities did not deserve the support of the FDJ.[49] Such allegations were vehemently denounced by the Bessie Smith Club members who had integrated working-class youth, though officials suspected that the small number of workers had been recruited by the academics during their obligatory work at factories, recruitments that fulfilled quotas of working-class participation. Because of the small numbers and the alleged absence of workers, Müller argued that jazz circles did not serve public or working-class interests and therefore should not be supported by mass organizations. In retrospect, it is possible that the deeper cause for such reasoning lay elsewhere: that the pursuit of jazz was less offensive than the fact that intellectuals gathered in meetings with a conspiratorial aura. Small groups of students and academics devoted to Western music, distracted from the commitment to socialism, raised suspicions of intellectual sectarianism. Such attitudes reveal the state's mistrust against intellectuals.

Overall, in examining the initial years after the Wall was built, it seems the enclosure of GDR territory ironically increased the activities of a close-knit jazz community. Nervous high-ranking officials felt compelled to take measures toward the centralization of the jazz scene as well as its organization and observation. Enduring years of tangible repression, inconsistent measures, and selective tolerance, the jazz fans' collective protests indicated their intent to negotiate with policymakers in the GDR, even as FDJ and ministry officials concocted divergent and contradictory assessments over jazz activities after August 1961. FDJ officials made liberal propositions to include jazz music's intellectual potential into the work of the youth organization, as well as measures that repelled jazz circles for their perceived intellectual sectarianism. The main task was to prevent any form of jazz organization outside of state structures, as the state's prerogative of organizing society was not to be infringed. Indeed, within a few months after the construction of a fortified border, the ZK had introduced directives that further determined its position toward jazz in the GDR, a directive examined in more detail below.

---

[49] Ibid. Müller acknowledged: "*Es gibt keine Arbeiterjungens.*"

The Jazz Resolution of the Central Committee

The jazz scene's self-assertion around 1960, and especially after the building of the Wall in August 1961, prompted the SED leadership to streamline its position on jazz. In the winter of 1961–1962, for the first time since the founding of the state in 1949, the East German government issued a resolution concerning jazz, specifically outlining its position within socialist society.[50] While pronouncing measures of centralization and micromanagement, the resolution constituted a basic tolerance of jazz with a considerable number of caveats and expectations for the genre attached.

In this resolution, the ZK both recriminated the West for increasing jazz infiltration after the fortification of the West German-East German border and denounced the FDJ for their incompetence in dealing with the situation. As much as the paternalistic tone reflected the party leadership's belief in its own infallibility, it also reveals its disconnectedness from realities on the ground: "It is conspicuous that jazz events and other forms of occupation with jazz after August 13, 1961, increased rapidly. Various occurrences indicate that this rapid increase of jazz propaganda in the GDR can be ascribed to influences of the class enemy."[51] According to the ZK, the people's pursuit of jazz in East Germany was the making of Western agitation. This claim was disputed by the West German press, which had stated that West Berlin jazz events had not been profitable after August 1961 because audiences from the East had been absent. The ZK believed that since the lockdown of GDR territory, the West threatened to direct jazz propaganda on a larger scale against the East. "This scheme," they suspected, "was not detected fast enough by some leaders of our mass organizations," indirectly blaming the FDJ, who not only "had tolerated but also even supported and incorporated jazz events."[52] The ZK not only feared that increased activism was the outcome of Western agitation, but also that FDJ leaders were ignorant of this peril, claiming that "with the popularization of Western culture the enemy is trying to establish political outposts in our territory," a clear suspicion of American plans for world domination.[53] Based on Meyer's cultural criticism, the

---

[50] 1962 ZK Jazz Resolution. The text was printed on two pages, which had been separated from a periodical or brochure and added to the FDJ files used for this research.

[51] Ibid.

[52] Report. See also Zentralrat der FDJ, Kirchhof mit Schumann, "Bericht über die Durchführung von Jazz-Konzerten," BArch/DY 24/24396 (1961–1963).

[53] "Der Gegner versucht, über die Verbreitung 'westlicher Kultur' sich bei uns politische Stützpunkte zu schaffen." 1962 ZK Jazz Resolution.

resolution enunciated the evolution of jazz music as a history of exploitation of genuine folk tradition by capitalism.

> Jazz is a complex musical phenomenon. It developed from the folklore of the Negroes in the US, and had in its beginnings characteristics of folklore and social-critical features. But its decay began even in its emergence, wherein jazz was exploited by the fast-developing capitalist music industry changing its social function and character. More and more, jazz lost its connection with the vital interests of the Negroes, and became a tool of the so-called American way of life supporting their ambitions of imperialist domination. The enemy is trying to exploit this contradistinctive development of jazz. He is invoking true folklore elements of jazz to smuggle in anti-humanist tendencies, and therefore decadent conduct and thuggishness, into our country. Through our best work we must prevent the empowerment of enemy forces in the jazz movement.[54]

Consistent with communist jazz interpretations, officials condemned the corruption of Ur-Jazz. The exploitation by the profit-driven industry had obscured the social function of "the people's music," with African American creativity used to produce commercialized music sold for entertainment, here derided as "the American way of life." In the process, the social function of music – to serve the people's vital interests – had been estranged from its purpose. Corrupted by the industry, jazz no longer served as a means for African American self-determination and, in the communist view, did not sustain the class-struggle.

From this perspective, jazz of the era exemplified such estrangement, not representing an "artistic expression of modern life, but that of a dying class."[55] Contemporary jazz opposed the socialist philosophy of life, for it gave a "chaotic, depressive impression, and lost its democratic quality because it was put into service of American imperialism."[56] Such music

---

[54] 1962 ZK Jazz Resolution. *Der Jazz ist eine komplizierte musikalische Erscheinung. Er entwickelte sich aus der Folklore der Neger in den USA, hatte anfänglich folkloristischen Charakter und trug in manchem auch sozialkritische Züge. Doch mit dem Entstehen des Jazz begann der Prozess seiner Dekadenz, in dem der Jazz von der sich immer stärker entwickelnden kapitalistischen und imperialistischen Musikindustrie ausgenutzt wurde und dabei seine Funktion und seinen Charakter änderte. Er verlor mehr und mehr seine Verbundenheit mit den Lebensinteressen der Neger und wurde ein Motto der Propagierung der sogenannten Amerikanischen Lebensweise im Interesse der Weltherrschaftspläne des US Imperialismus. Diese widersprüchliche Entwicklung des Jazz versucht der Gegner auszunutzen. Er knüpft an echte folkloristische Element im Jazz an, um auch alle antihumanistischen Tendenzen des Jazz und die damit verbundenen dekadenten und rowdyhaften Verhaltensweisen bei uns einzuschmuggeln und zu verbreiten. Durch unsere richtige Arbeit muss verhindert werden, daß gegnerische Kräfte in der Jazzbewegung unterschlüpfen und Wirkungsmöglichkeiten finden.*
[55] 1962 ZK Jazz Resolution.
[56] Ibid.

disturbed the endeavor toward collective harmony essential for the transformation into socialism that promised liberation from the shackles of
human history. According to the ZK resolution, modern jazz was a tool
to either depress or deceive: "One part of modern jazz expresses feelings
[of fear and senselessness] and produces a chaotic impression and depressive moods, and another part [of jazz] intends with the help of hectic
'impulses' to belie the pessimistic perspective of life in the West." What
is here termed "hectic impulses" likely refers to fast, upbeat music interpreted as a strategy of deception distracting listeners from the bleakness of
life under a profit-seeking society. This music, so the ZK argued, became
the vehicle for the enemy to propagate "anti-humanist tendencies, decadence and thuggishness."[57]

The ZK stated explicitly that jazz events should *not* be prohibited, but
at the same time should not take on a predominant role in the musical
life of the GDR or be treated as equal to other genres, stating jazz should
be "rightfully integrated in our musical life."[58] It was acknowledged that
German popular music had assimilated elements of jazz for years, such
as in the Dixieland rhythms or in conventional dances like the foxtrot. But only as long as such elements enriched the ("our") German
national music culture was such incorporation permissible. Overall, the
resolution vehemently opposed the incorporation of jazz elements as a
major means of creativity in ("our") new socialist music. As much as
East German leadership proclaimed its support of primordial jazz, they
demanded that the genre should represent only "one part within the
manifold cultural offerings in our cultural space."[59] By repeatedly referring to and emphasizing "our" cultural space, the resolution implied
that a perceived "German cultural space" penetrated by a transnational
and transracial cultural assimilation hereby indirectly marginalized
the music of the racial other. Although ideologically amenable as part
of the world's folk traditions, jazz – or rather its ideologically correct
derivatives – was not to dominate the German cultural sphere, lest it
interfere with perceptions of German musical (e.g. national) identity.
As is clear, such a view stood in stark contrast to those arguing for an
exceptional role for jazz, as expressed in the letter from the Bessie Smith

[57] Ibid.
[58] Ibid.
[59] Ibid. *"Die Beschäftigung mit dem Jazz sollte lediglich in den Organisationsformen der gesam-
ten Musikpflege und als Teil der sehr reichhaltigen Kulturprogramme in unseren Kulturräumen
geschehen."*

Club – the idea of jazz as equal to European music, or as a tool of musical education to elevate people's discriminatory judgment, violated such perceptions of a Eurocentric cultural hierarchy.

Adopting the ZK's resolution in 1966, composer and national laureate Andre Asriel, a disciple of Meyer, published *Jazz: Analysen und Aspekte*, one of the first histories of jazz in the GDR. In his foreword, he wrote that he intended to abolish misconceptions about jazz in order to ensure the appreciation it deserved due to its "real qualities."[60] Moreover, he told the story of jazz according to Meyer's ideological blueprint, dividing the genre into three major categories: folkloric, commercial, and snobbish. While his categorizations sought to bring a musicologist's order to the genre, they more likely added to the confusion surrounding it. Asriel's preference for what he called "folkloric" (alternately *volkstümlich, authentisch,* or *klassisch*) over later styles was fully in line with party doctrine. Only the music that had its genesis in the creativity of the people was authentic, analogous to what was understood as the classical form. According to Asriel, classic jazz was not manipulated by commercial interest and was best represented by the New Orleans and Chicago styles until 1928: his examples here included King Oliver's Creole Jazz Band, Louis Armstrong's Hot Five, and Jelly Roll Morton's Red Hot Peppers. He attributed the term commercial (*kommerziell*) to swing and snobbish (*snobistisch*) to bebop. Interestingly, in later editions of the book that were published in the 1970s and 1980s, Asriel distanced himself from such categorizations.[61]

According to the ZK, jazz was not to be banned but channeled, preventing any organizing and activism outside of governmental structures. The party denounced every organization and association pursuing the sole cultivation of jazz: "Therefore so-called jazz cellars or cultural centers which only feature jazz are inappropriate."[62] Jazz events were now to be incorporated within state cultural organizations, actually permitting the founding of jazz circles or clubs within the FDJ. At the beginning of 1962, there seems to have been a general consent among officials that such circles or clubs organized within a mass organization should be less prohibited than observed.[63] The STASI, the so-called sword and shield of

---

[60] Andre Asriel, *Jazz: Analysen und Aspekte* (Berlin: VEB Lied der Zeit, 1966).

[61] *Jazz: Analysen und Aspekte* (Berlin: VEB Lied der Zeit, 1977). See also *Jazz: Analysen und Aspekte* (Berlin: VEB Lied der Zeit, 1980) and *Jazz: Analysen und Aspekte* (Berlin: VEB Lied der Zeit, 1985).

[62] 1962 ZK Jazz Resolution.

[63] BStU, MfS, 5225/77, "Amiga" Hans-Georg Uszkoreit, Band [Vol.] I and II. See also BStU, MfS, XX 18520, Operativ-Vorlauf "Jazzer" and BStU, MfS, P XII 2716/62, "Sander" Günter Sommer.

the SED, executed this order by systematically extending their network of informants within the jazz scene. The recruitment of nineteen-year-old Günter Sommer in December of 1962 is but one example: Sommer, a music student at the Carl Maria von Weber Conservatory in Dresden, was an easy catch. In need of planting informants among the students, the STASI officers targeted the young drummer on whom they possessed compromising information. While initially resistant, when the STASI threatened to have him expelled from the conservatory, Sommer agreed to cooperate.[64]

Moreover, echoing the STAKOKU era in the 1950s, the resolution advised methods of micromanaging music. While jazz improvisation was accepted as attributing musical vitality, the ZK demanded that improvised music include themes and melodies of German provenance or of the socialist bloc. Therefore, the ZK insisted on compliance with the "60:40 Act" for musical performances, stipulating the ratio between compositions of Eastern and Western origin. The resolution furthermore recommended the orchestras of Alfons Wonneberg in Berlin and Günter Hörig in Dresden as examples for the appropriate treatment of jazz: both bandleaders, who had received top state awards for their artistic prowess, had made brilliant careers in the GDR.[65] With these guidelines, officials believed they had resolved the inconsistencies in the treatment of jazz and aimed "to reach the appropriate integration of jazz into our musical life," overcoming its orientation toward the West as well as the need for Western jazz materials.[66]

Furthermore, according to the resolution, the ZK sought to support that particular kind of jazz seen as expressing the social struggle of the progressive forces in the United States. Reaching out to those engaged in the fight

---

[64] BStU, MfS, "Sander," p. 23: *Unter den Studienjahren der Musikhochschule sind bisher noch keine IM vorhanden. Die Absicherung ist unbedingt notwendig zur Aufklärung von negativen Personen und Gruppierungen. Er soll besonders zur Aufklärung der Anhänger des Jazz eingesetzt werden.* The cooperation lasted from December 5, 1962 until 1968. The reason for the end of Sommer's cooperation was his irregular attendance at meetings with his handlers.

[65] Cf. "Die Dresdner Tanzsinfoniker. Die Geschichte eines prominenten Orchesters in 5 Folgen," *Melodie und Rhythmus* (22/1961).

[66] Zentralrat der FDJ, "Beratung über Jazz am 15.12.1961," BArch/DY 24/1804 (April–December 1961). "… *auf diese Weise erreichten wir die richtige Einbeziehung des Jazz in unser Musikleben, daß die Orientierung auf den Westen überwunden wird und für die Jazzpflege von dort her keine Schallplatten usw. besorgt werden. Die Musikbegeisterung kann also in richtige Bahnen gelenkt werden.*"

for civil rights, the East German leadership explicitly sought to promote music identified with ongoing social revolution. They proclaimed:

> Along with the claims that American imperialism manipulated jazz and caused the loss of its democratic character, the inherent social criticism in Negro folklore should be elevated and linked to the support of the fight of democratic forces in the US, specifically the Communist Party of America. That way we can reach a genuine partisanship with the truly democratic forces in America and their music.

Implied here is that a lost, primordial quality of the music was to be recovered and tied to the music's political *brisance* of the 1960s. By announcing such a specific position, the ZK sought to encourage and support the class struggle (the *Klassenkampf*) as embodied in the civil rights movement and social-revolutionary organizations such as the CPUSA. Granted, whether the CPUSA in the 1960s represented a feasible organization to support was questionable, when according to historian Harvey Klehr, its political significance had diminished.[67] It was hardly a force to count on in the fight for social liberation. But what is more important here is that the resolution signaled a shift in jazz propaganda away from one as predominantly discredited as enemy infiltration and toward one of protest in the cause of African American equality. Jazz as a tool in the fight for social progress enjoyed renewed significance when the United States was riven by racial unrest throughout the 1960s.

In sum, in their 1962 resolution, the ZK recriminated the West for increasing jazz infiltration after the country's lockdown and denounced the FDJ for its incompetence in coping with the peril of Western agitation. The ZK also opposed any organizational efforts for jazz outside state organizations and strongly recommended surveillance of the scene. It explicitly decreed that jazz events ought not to be prohibited because the music constituted a genuine folk tradition, but at the same time, jazz music should not play a predominant role within East German musical life. The German cultural space was to be guarded from transnational and transracial cultural influx. Pronouncing measures of centralization, micromanagement, and selective tolerance, yet again the state understood that the only way to monitor the activities of its citizens was to use them against one another, as again exemplified in the career of one of the GDR's most celebrated enthusiasts.

---

[67] Harvey Klehr, *The Soviet World of American Communism* (New Haven, Conn.: Yale University Press, 1998).

Jazz und Lyrik with "Josh"

As party officials responded both to the implications of a country enclosed behind the Wall as well as to the new jazz resolution put forth by the ZK, agencies at all levels began to explore these new realities. While in some cases this meant establishing new channels of observation and documentation, in others it meant reopening relationships with prior informants. Collecting personal data was imperative for the STASI after the resolution, which had called for a strict containment of jazz organizations outside of state institutions.[68] The STASI apparatus followed these guidelines, acquiescing in general to smaller, localized jazz activities, but still vigilantly observing the scene. On a wider scale, the ZK resolution, although it had given jazz its ideological blessing, still in many cases enabled the unpredictable and sporadic repression of individual jazz activities.[69]

As discussed above, the STASI had maintained an ambivalent, on-again, off-again relationship with Werner Sellhorn, a relationship that had been on hold since late 1961. In 1962, the needs of the ZK resolution required them to reach back out to their informant. Within the halls of the STASI, this decision was not universally welcomed, for Sellhorn had acquired a reputation that did not endear him to his handlers: STASI officers had repeatedly criticized his indolent lifestyle, had accused him of pursuing his affiliation with the agency solely for personal gain and not for the advancement of state security, and viewed his claims of loyalty to the SED as essentially untrustworthy.[70] But despite these reservations, Sellhorn was too valuable for the STASI to cut off the relationship entirely. His many connections in the West and East German jazz worlds and his insight into the scene had made him irreplaceable.

The STASI expanded its net of informants within the newly enclosed country, with Sellhorn summoned to help.[71] More than once he handed over long lists of names, professions, and physical characteristics of individuals to STASI officers.[72] Apart from their interest in the identification of individuals involved in the jazz scene, STASI officers were also eager to monitor overall political morale, especially during times of high international tension such as the Cuban Missile Crisis. Sellhorn, who meanwhile

---

[68] 1962 ZK Jazz Resolution.

[69] BStU, MfS, "Amiga," p. 49. The prohibition of a concert at a College in Ilmenau is one of numerous examples in the Uszkoreit files.

[70] BStU, MfS, "Zirkel," p. 66. Evaluation dated June 1, 1959.

[71] For surveillance of the scene in Dresden, Leipzig, and Berlin after 1962, see BStU, MfS, "Amiga," pp. 30–60. See also BStU, MfS, Operativ-Vorlauf "Jazzer."

[72] BStU, MfS, "Zirkel," p. 183.

had a steady position at the publishing house Volk und Welt, was urged to instigate discussions about the "American aggression" among his friends. One STASI officer, Reinhardt, ordered Sellhorn to immediately telephone him personally in case of noteworthy occurrences.[73]

After roughly five years of collaboration, interrupted only briefly in 1961, Sellhorn decided in October 1963 to withdraw from the STASI for good. During his meetings with officers, he had become increasingly reluctant to inform on his friends and acquaintances, particularly as his cooperation with the agency was voluntary, not coerced. Despite reassuring Reinhardt of the importance of his work as a security officer, he repeatedly admitted doubt that his contributions could help state security. According to Sellhorn, his decision to withdraw his involvement was based on personal reasons of conscience. Reinhardt did not believe him. The final report about IM Zirkel, dated July 1965, reveals his officer's lasting discontent:

> The informant is politically and ideologically unreliable, is descending more and more into a slovenly lifestyle, and he seems to give a more negative impression than one we can work with constructively. His present conduct and his understanding of morals are no basis for cooperation with the Ministry but are instead dangerous for us. For these reasons, the file on this informant is hereby closed and deposited in the archives.[74]

In this report, Reinhardt reveals his powerlessness over Sellhorn, whose cooperation was imperative for the officer's work. Reinhardt's patience, which over the years had suggested the manner of a parent attempting to educate their child, here yielded to anger about his prize contact, blaming the social environment at the publishing house where Sellhorn had obtained a marketing position.[75] It seems that Sellhorn withdrew his loyalty fearing neither consequences nor personal disadvantages. Despite his refusal to cooperate with the STASI, his career as a jazz impresario and writer was progressing: his position at Volk und Welt provided financial stability and widened his social network, which made him independent from STASI support. Following the lockdown of East German territory, spying for the STASI became much less appealing because traveling to

---

[73] Ibid., p. 168.

[74] BStU, MfS, "Zirkel" [1972–1980], p. 11. Schlußbericht über den GI "Zirkel" 10350/60: ... *Der GI ist politisch-ideologisch abgelitten und beginnt mehr und mehr zu versumpfen und tritt vielmehr negativ in Erscheinung als positiv mit ihm gearbeitet werden kann. Sein gegenwärtiges Auftreten, seine Haltung und Moralauffassung bieten keine Gewähr für eine Zusammenarbeit mit dem MfS sondern stellen vielmehr eine Gefahr dar. Der GI wird aus diesen Gründen im Archiv der Abt. XII zur Ablage gebracht.*

[75] BStU, MfS, "Zirkel," p. 143.

West Berlin, participating in its jazz life, and spending Western currency were no longer part of the game.

During his employment at Volk und Welt, Sellhorn found new creative outlets. Among his friends were high-profile intellectuals and performing artists such as Wolf Biermann, Manfred Krug, and singer Ruth Hohmann; thanks to these associations, Sellhorn formed the idea to combine jazz and other arts, which, as discussed in the previous chapter, he had already put into practice during lectures in the East Berlin Jazz Club in the 1950s. He was able to persuade these celebrities to cooperate on the project *Jazz und Lyrik,* presenting jazz in combination with political protest songs and poetry readings. *Jazz und Lyrik* offered texts of writers such as Pablo Neruda, Erich Weinert, Samuil Marshak, and Kurt Tucholsky accompanied by Dixieland jazz performed by the band Jazz Optimisten. The journal *Melodie und Rhythmus* granted glowing reviews of such "sophisticated entertainment," and the show, first conceived simply as a public-relation event to draw attention to the publications of Volk und Welt, continued for years (Figures 4.4 and 4.5).[76] In fact, the state

Figure 4.4   *Jazz und Lyrik,* held at Kongreßhalle, Alexanderplatz, East Berlin, November 1, 1965. Sellhorn at left, Manfred Krug playing guitar, Ruth Hohmann at right. Bundesarchiv: 183-B1101-0010-001

[76] "Jazz und Lyrik," *Melodie und Rhythmus* (1/1965).

Figure 4.5   The ideal jazz audience: attentively listening to jazz as sophisticated entertainment. Publicity photo for *Jazz und Lyrik*, Freibad Pankow, May 30, 1964. Bundesarchiv: 183-C0531-0006-004

record label VEB Deutsche Schallplatten planned to release a live album on Amiga, but by December 1965, when the record was in the process of distribution, political activist Biermann had been banned from performing.[77] The record featured one of his compositions: what alarmed officials was not the piece itself, which was ideologically germane, but the fact that Biermann had been silenced prior to its release. Consequently, authorities tried to seize the production, but most of the albums had already been sold. This mishap caused heated debates between party leadership and those bearing responsibility.[78] The album was officially censored and not rereleased until after the fall of the Wall.

[77] Amiga 850048, December 1965. See Mathias Brüll, *Jazz auf Amiga: Die Schallplatten des Amiga-Labels von 1947 bis 1990* (Berlin: Pro Business, 2003), 185.
[78] "Zentralkomitee der SED," BArch/DY 30/IVA2/906 (1965). These documents dated December 10–22, 1965, contain correspondence between the ZK (Peter Czerny, Siegfried Wagner), the VEB Deutsche Schallplatten (Siegfried Köhler), and the Ministry for Culture (Kurt Bork) concerning the release of the live record *Jazz und Lyrik* in December 1965, recorded at the Kongreßhalle in East Berlin on November 13, 1964.

But apart from poetry and music, something else about *Jazz und Lyrik* fascinated audiences, namely, what remained unspoken or read only between the lines. And that was Sellhorn's gift. Sellhorn was what historian Thomas Lindenberger has called "a specialist of public communication, who in the realm of symbolic [artistic] representation continuously had to deal with limits of transgressions."[79] An anonymous STASI report referring to a sold-out *Jazz und Lyrik* show on November 13, 1964, spotlights Sellhorn's role as the master of ceremonies. On this occasion, Sellhorn announced the 1920s Tucholsky ballad "About the Fat Cats" (*Über die Bonzen*), stating that the criticism found in the song four decades earlier was still relevant even then in the 1960s. At this moment, an audience member could have interpreted this remark as an affront against East German authority; however, after a short pause, Sellhorn added, "... but only in West Germany."[80] According to the STASI report, only a small part of the audience, mainly young people, students, and artists, applauded such provocative ambiguity. For the most part, "the audience acted decently during the entire show. ... Only a minority showed negative reactions."[81] Suggesting that the audience expected "clear political statements" from the performances and wanted to be entertained by crowd favorite Manfred Krug, the anonymous observer noted that neither Biermann – who sang lines such as "If I feel like it, I'll go to hell and treat Stalin to a beer" – nor Sellhorn himself earned the undivided approval of the crowd.

In these turbulent years, conflicts between performers and state officials continued. On October 30, 1965, Biermann, whose ban from performing had come not long before, was arrested while trying to attend the sold-out *Jazz and Lyrik* show in East Berlin's new assembly hall at Alexanderplatz. According to actor Manfred Krug, the entire ensemble refused to perform until Biermann was freed, while on stage, Sellhorn offered the excuse that "technical problems" had delayed the beginning of the show. News of Biermann's arrest had spread in the audience, with concertgoers remaining in their seats for almost an hour applauding Sellhorn's repeated "apologies." The fact was, of course, that Biermann's attempt to attend the show, even as a mere audience member, equaled a public appearance and therefore a provocation of state authority. But by arresting Biermann, state

[79] Thomas Lindenberger, ed. *Herrschaft und Eigensinn in der Diktatur* (Köln Weimar Wien: Böhlau Verlag, 1999), 35.

[80] BStU, MfS, BV Berlin AKG 710, "Bericht über die Veranstaltung Jazz und Lyrik am 13. Nov. 1964 in der Kongreßhalle."

[81] Ibid.

officials overstepped the bounds of legitimacy, inciting resistance to their acts among the audience – which, despite the excuses, was well aware of what was actually happening. After about an hour, the people won the wrestling match with state authority: backstage the STASI told the ensemble that Biermann was freed, and the show began as though nothing had ever happened.[82]

But this time, Sellhorn had gone too far. After the Biermann incident, he lost his position at Volk und Welt, though such loss harmed neither his career as a freelance writer and jazz impresario, nor the continuation of his bohemian lifestyle lacking steady employment – an extraordinary feat in the East German state. The *Jazz und Lyrik* shows went on without him, and Sellhorn continued organizing concerts and writing about jazz. Among his achievements was an article on Louis Armstrong published in a high-profile venue: the epilogue to *My Life in New Orleans*, the long-awaited 1967 Armstrong biography.[83] Sellhorn even managed to have the editors include a reproduction of a photograph of himself with Armstrong in the book.

In these years, Sellhorn was still observed by the STASI, who, remarkably, planned once more to renew their relationship with IM Zirkel. It seems that STASI officers had resigned themselves to his unconventional lifestyle and gave up urging him to seek steady employment. From now on, to the Ministry, Sellhorn would be the "philosopher" or "jazz impresario."[84] In November 1972, the STASI found that IM Zirkel was "suited as a secret informant for the disclosure of enemy activity because of his varied connections and contacts to individuals in the artistic realm."[85] Sellhorn's file returned from the archives to yet another officer's desk, and soon he was attending regular meetings with his handlers once again.

In sum, Sellhorn's cooperation with the STASI after the building of the Wall illuminates the agency's methods of surveillance in the enclosed country. Prior to August 1961, the STASI documented the efforts of Western jazz propaganda across geographic sectors to establish relations with East German citizens. After August 1961, however, the STASI redoubled its efforts in its own territory. In relationships that could last for decades, informants were asked to fulfill various functions: in Sellhorn's

[82] Werner Sellhorn, *Jazz, DDR, Fakten* (Berlin: Neunplus1, 2005), V-IV.
[83] Louis Armstrong, *Mein Leben in New Orleans* (Berlin: Henschelverlag, 1967).
[84] BStU, MfS, "Zirkel" [1972–1980], p. 12.
[85] Ibid., 10.

case, he collected extensive data on the jazz scene as well as monitored overall political morale, detailing the opinions and positions of the artistic and intellectual realms that intersected with that scene. This observation took place both in times of political crisis as well as in response to party leadership's cultural directives more generally. Showing his capacity to move in rarefied circles as well as among everyday jazz fans, Sellhorn informed on high-ranking officials such as Karl Eduard von Schnitzler, propagandist and television moderator, and Gerhardt Eisler, the brother of Hanns Eisler and president of the GDR state broadcasting service.[86]

As should be clear, by the mid-1960s relations between state authorities and jazz fans continued to evolve, as state authorities bent to the realities of public appetites for jazz in concert halls and auditoria. Certainly, prominent individuals such as Sellhorn and Krug played a role in shifting these positions by degrees – but following the visit of one legendary Western musician to the country, jazz in the GDR would undergo yet another evolution in its development.

"It's a Wonderful World": Louis Armstrong in the GDR

The headlines proclaimed the news loud and clear: "Louis Armstrong has arrived!" "He is one of the most prominent representatives of the 'other America.'"[87] "His world-wide recognition strengthened the self-confidence of the American black population and its fight for emancipation and civil rights."[88] Even weeks before his arrival in East Germany's capital on March 19, 1965, such announcements heralded the "King of Jazz"[89] and indicated the great political significance of Armstrong's upcoming tour of the Eastern Bloc. In the GDR, Armstrong's presence met an unprecedented media spectacle, overshadowed only by the sensational news of the first successful extravehicular spacewalk by Soviet cosmonaut Aleksei Leonov, conducted that same week.

As noted above, on the other side of the Atlantic, beginning in the mid-1950s, the US State Department had included jazz in cultural outreach

---

[86] Interestingly, according to Sellhorn's reports, Gerhardt Eisler did not endorse the rejection of progressive jazz (jazz that departed from traditional or Dixieland styles). See BStU, MfS, "Zirkel," p. 124: *Gen. Eisler brachte zum Ausdruck, daß wir auch die guten Seiten dieser Musik zu unserer Bereicherung verwenden und pflegen und ein Ablehnen des fortschrittlichen Jazz falsch ist.*

[87] *Berliner Zeitung*, February 27, 1965.

[88] *Berliner Zeitung am Abend*, February 27, 1965. This text is repeated in multiple times in various papers.

[89] *Berliner Zeitung*, March 20, 1965.

programs in regions of American political interest. The scholars Penny von Eschen, Ingrid Monson, and Lisa Davenport have all examined how the US State Department utilized jazz as a form of cultural diplomacy.[90] Integrated jazz ensembles sought to project the democratic, multiracial coexistence that had engendered the American art form, encapsulating universal values that the United States promoted during the Cold War. Armstrong had already participated in such outreach programs in the early 1960s in South America and Africa, and the tour to the Eastern Bloc was most likely also initiated by the US State Department (although no published sources attest to this fact).[91] The sole account suggested that American involvement came from Karlheinz Drechsel, who accompanied the All-Stars in the GDR as their tour manager. In a recent interview, he claimed that the State Department had engaged a Swiss agency to cover up any American connections.[92] The reason for withdrawal from official sponsorship may have been the protests against voter discrimination, represented by the civil rights marches from Selma to Montgomery, Alabama, in the spring of 1965. Jazz presented in official State Department outreach programs to project achievements of democracy would have been implausible at the time, at least until President Lyndon Johnson signed the Voting Rights Act in August of that year, which outlawed discriminatory voting practices adopted in many Southern states during the Jim Crow periods following the Civil War.[93]

Whatever the State Department's decision in 1965 was, the GDR immediately turned Armstrong's visit back against American jazz propaganda: while American jazz diplomacy intended to project democracy and racial harmony, the GDR projected jazz as a music leveling grievances against the capitalist system. Armstrong's music was seen as a weapon in the fight for human dignity, as a "musical expression of an episode of suffering and fighting, of hope and confidence of his people. ... The music is his sword with which he fights for decent conditions for his coloured brothers and

---

[90] Penny M. von Eschen, *Satchmo Blows Up the World: Jazz Ambassadors Play the Cold War* (Cambridge, Mass.; London: Harvard University Press, 2004); Ingrid Monson, *Freedom Sounds: Civil Rights Call Out to Jazz and Africa* (Oxford University Press, 2007); Lisa E. Davenport, *Jazz Diplomacy Promoting America in the Cold War Era* (Jackson: University Press of Mississippi, 2009); Iain Anderson, *This Is Our Music* (Philadelphia: University of Pensylvania Press, 2007).

[91] Monson, *Freedom Sounds*, 124–25.

[92] Interview with the author, 2009. Cf. Stephan Schulz, *What a Wonderful World: Als Louis Armstrong durch den Osten tourte* (Berlin: Neues Leben, 2010), 33–39; Drechsel.

[93] William J. Cooper and Thomas E. Terrill, ed. *The American South: A History, Volume II*, 4th ed. (Rowman & Littlefield, 2009).

Figure 4.6   Louis Armstrong interviewed upon his arrival in Berlin, March 1965.
Werner Sellhorn at right in rear of image (partially obscured, head only). Picture
Alliance, reference# 23467185

sisters and for the friendship amongst people."[94] Armstrong was celebrated
as the ambassador representing the "true" America, confident in its socialist
destiny.

Armstrong's tour included twenty-one concerts in five cities – Berlin,
Leipzig, Erfurt, Magdeburg, and Schwerin – from March 20 to April 8,
1965, with press conferences attached to many of the performances
(Figure 4.6).[95] While in country, the GDR press equally celebrated his
musicianship as much as it propagated his roots in slavery and segregation and his engagement in the fight for black freedom. This politicized

---

[94] *Für Dich*, Illustriert Frauenzeitschrift, April 1, 1965.
[95] Armstrong played twenty-one concerts in twenty days. Two concerts per night in Berlin,
   Friedrichstadt-Palast on March 20–22; two concerts per night on March 23–24 in Leipzig,
   Messehalle 3; a TV appearance in West Germany on March 25th; two concerts on March 26th in
   Berlin; two concerts on April 2nd in Leipzig; two concerts on April 5th in Berlin, Friedrichstadt-
   Palast; two concerts on April 6th in Magdeburg, Hermann-Gieseler-Halle; two concerts on April
   7 in Erfurt, Thüringenhalle; and one concert on April 8 in Schwerin, Sport-und Kongresshalle.

image defied Western perceptions of a comparatively nonpolitical black entertainer who was rarely outspoken about his view on race relations in the United States. Whereas in East Germany he was presented as a socially conscious proponent of black freedom engaging in political discussions, the West German media drew an image of the compliant entertainer who showed "no political interest."[96] His appearance on *Der Goldene Schuß*, a popular West German television comedy-variety show out of Frankfurt, reinforced this image.[97] Armstrong's image in the East German press, however, was predominately informed by perceptions of his political consciousness, which constituted his accomplishment and fame as much as his musicianship. One headline proclaimed "Louis Armstrong: a star of human greatness."[98] It was not only his music, but also his "staunch position on racial politics and his solidarity with the poor in his country [that] contributed to his immense popularity all over the world."[99]

In the 1960s, the East German media had frequently reported about racial inequality and aggression against blacks, including Ku Klux Klan atrocities and clashes between civil rights protesters and authorities, comparing the racist violence in the United States to that of the Nazi regime. One headline cites an alleged remark of Martin Luther King. "Bloody pogrom in Alabama. Dr. King: Barbarism as in Hitler's Germany."[100] Such reports served to portray socialist societies in a brighter light: America was denounced for its double moral standards, including the country's declaration of colonial independence in 1776, which was labeled hypocritical.[101] Performing arts critic Matthias Frede commented:

> While the king of jazz lifts our spirits with his show, his colored brothers in the southern United States are not allowed to visit the same schools as whites, they are not allowed to take the same bus or spend the evening together in a bar. Magdeburg does not know such racial fanaticism. In Dallas, Texas, this is a daily occurrence, mocking the American Declaration of Independence from 1776 which says: "All men are equal created equal, they are endowed by their creator with certain unalienable Rights that among these are Life, Liberty and the Pursuit of Happiness."[102]

[96] *Spandauer Volksblatt*, March 23, 1965. "Louis Armstrong will von Politik nichts wissen." Contrast with an interview about his tour in the East: Dan Morgenstern, *Living with Jazz* (New York: Pantheon Books, 2004), 56.

[97] Schulz, *What a Wonderful World*, 123–25.

[98] *Der Morgen*, March 20, 1965.

[99] *Volksstimme Magdeburg*, March 23, 1965.

[100] "Blutiger Pogrom in Alabama. Negerpfarrer Dr. King: 'Barberei wie in Hitler Deutschland'," *Neues Deutschland* (May 23, 1961).

[101] Matthias Frede, "'Satchmo' und die Südstaaten," *Liberal-Demokratische Zeitung Halle* (April 6, 1965).

[102] Ibid.

On the contrary, in socialist Germany African Americans did not have to endure racial segregation, as a concert program of Armstrong's performances at Berlin's Friedrichstadt-Palast declared: "It was his most important experience when he entered the 'Old World' that there was no racial discrimination."[103]

In the weeks immediately surrounding Armstrong's visit, racial conflict in the United States intensified, for the civil rights movement had entered a pivotal phase. On February 21st, Malcolm X, founder of the Organization of Afro-American Unity, was assassinated, which triggered the radicalization of the Black Power movements.[104] A few weeks later, on March 7, state police violently stopped protestors on a march toward Montgomery, causing the hospitalization of dozens of marchers. When Armstrong came to the GDR two weeks after that, the visit of the "emissary of the good America" served as the ideal opportunity to demonstrate East Germany's solidarity with the black social revolutionary movement.[105] This solidarity manifested itself in the extraordinary treatment of the African American artist as a political celebrity. As the ZK had just proclaimed in its resolution in 1962 that jazz in the GDR ought to be connected to the "real democratic forces" in the United States to support their fight, this was the moment to do so.[106] Armstrong's tour was presented as a celebration of unity with an America that firmly believed in overcoming racism through socialist-revolutionary changes. The reality of the tour for Armstrong, however, who was not in good health, meant that, on top of his tight performance schedule, he had to endure a marathon of press conferences and receptions at city halls, from autograph signings to photo shoots where he even had to pose with products of East German manufacturing.[107]

During this tour, Armstrong met with many local jazz enthusiasts. As noted above, Karlheinz Drechsel was appointed to accompany Armstrong and his band throughout the GDR, often serving as his master of ceremonies (Figure 4.7). His account of an incident in the city of Genthin, near Magdeburg, sheds light on the multiple facets of Armstrong's personality, challenging Western images of the artist as a nonpolitical entertainer.

---

[103] Program of Armstrong's concerts in Berlin, Friedrichstadt-Palast, March 20–22, 1965. Author: Karlheinz Drechsel. See also: Karl Heinz Drechsel, "Louis Armstrong," *Melodie und Rhythmus*, no. 11–14 (1964).

[104] Peniel E. Joseph, ed. *The Black Power Movement: Rethinking the Civil Rights-Black Power Era* (New York: Routledge, 2006).

[105] *Neues Deutschland*, March 22, 1965.

[106] 1962 ZK Jazz Resolution.

[107] Schulz, *What a Wonderful World*, 178–82.

Figure 4.7   Karlheinz Drechsel with Louis Armstrong in the Hotel Deutschland in Leipzig (March 24, 1965). Private collection of Karlheinz Drechsel, used by permission

During a brief rest in this village, the musicians were surrounded by excited schoolchildren seeking Armstrong's autograph. Armstrong obviously enjoyed this moment and took his time to sign his name for each child. Fearing delays, the white American tour manager, Pierre Tallerie, shouted at Armstrong to get on the bus. With an unusually aggressive outburst, Armstrong replied: "We are not in the United States here. And even there you won't be able to boss us around much longer. Get out. Slavery is over once and for all. We're not leaving here before I have signed the last autograph."[108] Known for his smiling and accommodating onstage persona, this incident reveals Armstrong's awareness of the significant differences in racial dynamics between the two countries.

Two years later, in Corona, New York, Armstrong sat down during a break from his exhausting schedule to write an eight-page letter to Drechsel (**Appendix**). In April 1967, the letter reached Drechsel in Adlershof, East

---

[108] Interviews with Karlheinz Drechsel, 2008 and 2009. For a slightly different version, see ibid., 144–45.

Berlin. In this letter, Armstrong noted that he would always remember his visit to East Germany, and he thanked Drechsel profusely for the way he introduced the band on stage:

> The trip I made in your country will live in my memories for ever. I will never forget. Especially the way you brought us on the stage. My wife Lucille often speak[s] of the wonderful moments – and also think you are the finest and the sharpest 'M.'C. I have ever had.[109]

Armstrong was particularly grateful that Drechsel emphasized the historical context and musical significance of Armstrong's art. What might have differentiated Drechsel's introductions from those of other emcees was the fact that Drechsel, a specialist on early jazz, provided not only a detailed history of each individual musician, but also the historical context of the music, to which audiences listened intently. Drechsel's approach elevated the character of Armstrong's playing from mere entertainment to a sophisticated level of performance, thereby representing jazz as a musical experience equal to that of European concert music.

Outside these in-person encounters, the majority of newspaper reviews reveal the state's influence on the East German press. A headline of *Neues Deutschland* proclaimed: "Armstrong: 'I support my brothers,'" which conjured his solidarity with the Civil Rights movement as well as his political conviction.[110] Armstrong appeared as the representative of the "other" America, which was imagined as the America of "progressive, democratic forces" and oppressed minorities.[111] Alluding to the violent confrontations in Alabama, one account pointed to the musician's mental preoccupation with racial upheaval, emphasizing his social consciousness: "Louis Armstrong, acknowledged king of jazz, performs this weekend in the capital of the GDR. But his thoughts indeed are in Selma and Montgomery, where the fight against racial segregation culminates."[112] Armstrong was considered to have expressed "fierce outrage" about the "gruesome racist terror" against the freedom marchers in the South.[113] According to articles in numerous outlets, he was supposed to have commented on the Alabama violence: "When he witnessed police brutality on the TV screen against the demonstrators in Selma, he felt physical pain. So far, he had supported the fight of his colored brothers with monetary donations. But

[109] Louis Armstrong's letter to Karlheinz Drechsel, dated April 10, 1967.
[110] *Neues Deutschland/Berliner Ausgabe*, March 26, 1965.
[111] Cf. 1962 ZK Jazz Resolution.
[112] *Wochenpost Berlin*, March 20, 1965.
[113] *Berliner Zeitung*, February 27, 1965.

now that might be not enough."[114] GDR media thus suggested that if up to then he had been a passive supporter of civil rights, facing such injustices Armstrong would take a more active role.

According to these outlets, Armstrong had shared his political views all along. Wrote one commentator: "Armstrong has never remained silent about the civil rights movement. He made his positions clear, which provoked fierce reactions from white racial fanatics."[115] He was portrayed as an active supporter of those who risked their lives for the cause of freedom: "The evening before the day of the demonstration of the civil rights fighters in Montgomery, Louis Armstrong tells journalists that he would do anything he could to support these fighters through concerts and foundations. With great seriousness he assured: 'I will do the best that I can.'"[116] Other accounts point out that for years Armstrong had repeatedly denounced racial segregation in public. "Already in 1957 in his American homeland, he pledged himself to the fight of the colored people against injustice."[117] Alluding to racial violence in Little Rock, Arkansas, ignited by educational integration, this account stressed Armstrong's fury. Reports also repeated the notion that "thereafter somebody committed a bomb attack against Armstrong and his orchestra in Tennessee."[118] To further emphasize Armstrong's political involvement, he was quoted as saying: "Some people have the opinion that I am too soft on the question of race. Many have accused me that I would be a kind of 'Uncle Tom' and not aggressive. How can they say that? I have done pioneer work for desegregation."[119]

Predictably, Armstrong's music was recruited to advance socialist realism. Grounded in party doctrine, the central party organ *Neues Deutschland* interpreted Armstrong's playing as standing in a musical tradition "based on and fed by plebeian sources" presenting "popular melodies, brilliantly and perfectly played."[120] Notions of socialist-realist aesthetics informed such rhetoric, echoing writings such as Meyer's in the early 1950s. For *Neues Deutschland*, Armstrong was the "embodiment of the so-called classical

---

[114] Various periodicals repeated this claim, such as *Tribüne, Ausgabe Groß-Berlin*, March 19, 1965; *Wochenpost Berlin*, March 20, 1965; and *Berliner Zeitung*, March 27, 1965.

[115] *Liberal-Demokratische Zeitung Halle*, April 6, 1965.

[116] *Norddeutsche Zeitung Schwerin*, March 28, 1965.

[117] *Berliner Zeitung*, March 20, 1965; *Berliner Zeitung am Abend*, March 19, 1965.

[118] *Liberal-Demokratische Zeitung Halle*, April 6, 1965.

[119] *Wochenpost Berlin*, March 20, 1965.

[120] The articles reflect the rhetoric of the 1962 ZK Jazz Resolution. See "Hier liegt der Kern ihres volksnahen Musizierens," *Neues Deutschland*, March 22, 1965.

jazz with collective and solo improvisation," perceived as "the essence of music close to the people" (*volksnah*) and fused with the highest artistic standards.[121] For *Neues Deutschland* as for the majority of the GDR press, Armstrong's musical persona embodied the imagination of a socialist-realist artist. The reviews suggested a sincere relation between his musical persona and audience, informing a quality of musical experience that was allegedly lost through commercialism. One unsigned editorial suggested that the Armstrong concerts represented a togetherness of musicians and audiences, beyond the parameters of entertainment as purchasable items of show business. "Only very seldom is an artist given such a warm welcome."[122] Armstrong: "We have enjoyed every minute of our togetherness."[123] When the tour in the GDR was interrupted because of the engagement in Frankfurt, West Germany, the Eastern press depicted the continuation of the tour in the East as a "comeback," which Armstrong supposedly initiated himself because of his enthusiastic, loving audiences in the East.[124]

Armstrong was regarded as a proponent of traditional jazz, staying "true to his origins, the New Orleans tradition," namely, the "principle of primordial vital music."[125] Such accounts echo socialist-realist notions of jazz from the 1950s, determining the ideological foundation for a selective jazz tolerance that enabled a political acceptance of traditional or New Orleans jazz styles called Dixieland.[126] (As discussed later, the Dixieland Festival in Dresden, founded in 1971 and headed by Karlheinz Drechsel, would become one of the first jazz festivals in the GDR and still held to date.[127]) Moreover, reflecting the socialist-realist notion that socialism had overcome musical hierarchies, the GDR press celebrated the embrace of popular and classical music. The reviews projected the affinity of Louis Armstrong toward the world of classical music and vice versa: "Armstrong loves the music of Mozart."[128] One comment in a Leipzig paper aimed to establish a direct connection between Armstrong and the city's famed orchestra: "He was pleased to receive LPs with recordings of Beethoven, Haydn, and Schumann of the Gewandhausorchster."[129] The world of

---

[121] Ibid.
[122] *Berliner Zeitung am Abend*, March 20, 1965.
[123] *Norddeutsche Zeitung Schwerin*, March 28, 1965.
[124] *Nationalzeitung Berlin, Brandenburgische Neueste Nachrichten, Norddeutsche Neueste Nchrichten*, March 22, 1965.
[125] *Neue Zeit Berlin*, March 21, 1965; *Sächsisches Tageblatt*, March 25, 1965.
[126] Cf. Meyer; "Anti Jazz?," *Neues Deutschland* (April 5, 1951); DEFA Film: *Vom Lebensweg des Jazz*.
[127] www.dixielandfestival-dresden.com/.
[128] *Neue Zeit Berlin*, March 25, 1965.
[129] *Leipziger Volkszeitung*, March 24, 1965.

classical music, according to the East German press, seems to have had appreciated Armstrong's musicianship and showed no fears of contact: not only did Toscanini befriend him, but "the famous American conductor Leopold Stokowski invited Armstrong and his All Stars to a concert with the New York Philharmonic Orchestra."[130] According to another account, Armstrong was supposed to join a performance conducted by Stokowski: "Armstrong wants to play solo trumpet with the Boston Philharmonic Orchestra conducted by Leopold Stokowski in a performance of a trumpet concerto of Darius Milhaud."[131]

Such comments intended to dissipate notions of cultural hierarchy, dismantling barriers between the cultural spheres of popular and "art," or *ernste Musik*. "Proletarian" jazz, perceived as being born in the black ghettos of New Orleans, represented the vital creativity of the people and was honored by the musical elite. The chasm between popular music and art could thus be overcome with Armstrong's musical persona, a persona that bridged both worlds due to his versatility in many genres.[132] Here, jazz and the classics were not antithetical; in fact, Armstrong's playing was perceived as a fusion of both, presenting a "baroque art of improvisation" and calling for jazz as an "an emancipated art form in international musical life."[133] Music and theater critic Matthias Frede offered an even more assertive position, listening to musical phrases that he believed expressed more than just popular melodies: "The music Satchmo stands for functions as protest. The furious, vicious musical riffs of modern jazz are equivalent to the revolts of poets such as Langston Hughes in contemporary America. The era of the Negro clown such as Uncle Tom is definitely over. The shocking effect on the white racists is intended."[134] In his report, Frede saw Armstrong's playing as shunning the mask of the servile jester, marking the arrival of a new era in jazz determined by social consciousness and social obligation: "This manifests his social obligation, which also Armstrong has understood, of which the Belgian tenor saxophone player Bobby

---

[130] *Neue Zeit Berlin*, March 25, 1965; *Leipziger Volkszeitung*, March 22, 1965.

[131] *Neue Zeit Berlin*, March 25, 1965.

[132] Ibid.

[133] *Thüringische Landeszeitung*, March 26, 1965; *Volksstimme Magdeburg*, April 4, 1965.

[134] *Liberal-Demokratische Zeitung Halle*, April 6, 1965. *"Die Musik die Satchmo vertritt hat ihre Protestfunktion. Die rasenden bösen musikalischen Läufe des Modernen Jazz sind als Parallele zum Aufbegehren vieler Dichter, wie Langston Hughes und Maler im heutigen Amerika zu verstehen. Die Zeit des negroiden Spaßmachers, wie Onkel Tom ist endgültig vorbei. Die Schockwirkung auf die weißen Rassisten ist beabsichtigt."*

Jaspar said: 'Jazz which is played without a moment of protest loses its sig-nificance.'"[135] For Frede, Armstrong's music expressed a rebellious stance, consciously rejecting compliant melodic structures and dance rhythms, thus engaging an intellectual reception to evoke social consciousness.

Contrary to the majority of the reviews, Frede's critique represents an exceptional position, what he called "vicious riffs," contrasted sharply with the accounts of "popular melodies" described in *Neues Deutschland*.[136] Indeed, Frede's position was in line with socialist perceptions of jazz, for he saw it as informed by the socio-political upheaval of the 1960s, repre-senting resistance against oppression, but simultaneously inducing shifts in socialist-realist aesthetics. The interconnectedness of politics and musical appreciation that associated Armstrong's music with modern jazz of the 1950s and 1960s loosened the rigidity of socialist-realist dogma toward more unrestricted forms of melody, harmony, and improvisational expression. In that sense, the Armstrong tour represented a turning point toward the acceptance of unrestricted forms as an expression of social protest.

At this same time, musicologist (and founding member of the VDK) Harry Goldschmidt praised Armstrong's jazz as a new art form within the century of the people's emancipation, as if the emergence of jazz was the musical equivalent of socialist upheaval in the twentieth century. Goldschmidt saw Armstrong's performance as a "natural phenomenon which triggered an avalanche, setting new standards and establishing new proportions...."[137] He regarded jazz as "an enrichment and renewal of musical world culture radiating beyond the entertaining arts into the serious realms of music."[138] Interestingly, such perspectives had appeared before: not only did they date to the Weimar era, when jazz was perceived as a fresh ingredient to loosen up rigid European musical traditions, but like Meyer, Goldschmidt regarded "the chasm between art and entertain-ment" as the "sad heritage of capitalism" and praised jazz for having saved the world from this grievance.[139] Goldschmidt asked: "Where do we find [this chasm] playfully and so thoroughly overcome as within jazz, whereby most sophisticated art unifies so naturally with the highest level of mass effectiveness?"[140] Armstrong, the "classicist of modern folk art" (*Klassiker*

---

[135] *Liberal-Demokratische Zeitung Halle*, April 6, 1965.

[136] Frede described "vicious riffs" in *Liberal-Demokratische Zeitung Halle*, April 6, 1965; "popular melodies" were celebrated in *Neues Deutschland, Berliner Ausgabe*, March 22, 1965.

[137] Harry Goldschmidt, "Klassiker moderner Volkskunst," *Berliner Zeitung* (March 24, 1965).

[138] Ibid.

[139] Ibid.

[140] Ibid.

moderner Volkskunst), appeared as the embodiment of the socialist-realist artist able to unite mass entertainment and art and was lauded as the vanquisher of the crisis of music in capitalist systems, which had estranged artists from society.[141]

In sum, Armstrong's tour constitutes a turning point in the trajectory of jazz history in the GDR. The highly politicized event contributed to shifts toward a greater social acceptance of jazz in the East German state. The East German press presented Armstrong as the role model of a socialist-realist artist and subsequently as a model for jazz musicians. Critics interpreted his music as breaking down cultural barriers and informing political agitation through forms of expression that simultaneously expanded conceptions of socialist-realist music. While US jazz diplomacy had attempted to project the achievements of American democracy, the GDR continued to propagate jazz as music informed by grievances against the capitalist system. Defying Western perceptions of a nonpolitical person, Armstrong was described as actively involved in the fight for African American rights. As the ZK's jazz resolution in 1962 had called for the music's politicization to support the Civil Rights movement in the United States, the Armstrong concert tour in East Germany here appeared as a celebration of unity with a "progressive" America on its way to its socialist destination. Armstrong's music was considered a musical weapon against oppression, recalling the COMINTERN's position on African American music as propaganda in the 1920s but repurposed for the era of racial upheaval in the 1960s.

Moreover, the politicization of Armstrong shifted the rigid musical templates of the 1950s. While some critics adhered to the strict socialist-realist rhetoric of that time, others interpreted Armstrong's music as an expression of protest reflecting social consciousness, suggesting that Armstrong rejected the role of the popular entertainer for a more political role. Such views opened the perceptions of jazz toward more unrestricted forms of expression, bringing about tolerance and acceptance of modern forms of jazz, which just a few years before officials had labeled as "anti-humanist" and "decadent."[142] Critics now presented jazz as an emancipated art form equal to those performed in concert halls and opera houses. If a few years earlier the ZK's jazz resolution alluded to fears of racial transgression, in 1965, critics presented the music of the racial other as emancipated within

---

[141] Meyer, *Musik im Zeitgeschehen*.
[142] 1962 ZK Jazz Resolution.

the German "cultural space."¹⁴³ Here, jazz was given an unconditional position in the GDR's *Kulturlandschaft*. In that sense, the Armstrong tour codified the affirmation of East Germany's own history in particular and communism's historical trajectory in general.

A Jazz Resurgence, 1965–1971

In examining East German cultural politics of the decade, it is important to remember that jazz was not the only musical form on offer. Indeed, the 1960s as a whole were marked by the diversity of styles permeating German audiences – not just jazz and rock 'n' roll, but now beat and surf – a process that would see noted shifts in party policy by the close of that decade and the opening of the next. After years of countless meetings discussing guidelines for a national dance music, the national association of composers, the VDK, declared in 1961: "We have our own dance music, even if the bosses of the Western hit industry don't want to believe it!"¹⁴⁴ The 1960s had seen plenty of popular music original to the GDR, including a newly created dance, the *Lipsi,* to counter the preference for Western musical trends among East German youth.¹⁴⁵ The VDK was convinced that East German dance music represented a more sophisticated tradition, synthesizing world folklore while simultaneously preserving German national qualities such as a "Germanic melody" or a "Germanic intonation."¹⁴⁶ As noted above, respected music journals vilified Western pop music as an capitalist attempt to dull the masses through cheap entertainment and the corruption of tradition and cultural identity. West Germany's popular culture was a favorite target, charged equally with having abandoned its national identity and having capitulated to Americanization. In these publications, critics accused West Germany of functioning merely as

---

¹⁴³ Ibid.
¹⁴⁴ "10 Jahre VDK – 10 Jahre Entwicklung einer neuen Tanzmusik," *Melodie und Rhythmus* (6/1961).
¹⁴⁵ The *Lipsi* was first performed during the Tanzmusikkonferenz in Lauchhammer, GDR, in January 1959. Following Ernst Hermann Meyer's suggestions that jazz rhythms could enliven popular music in the East, the *Lipsi* incorporated syncopated rhythms and was regularly presented at VDK meetings. "Ein neuer Tanz: Lipsi," *Melodie und Rhythmus* (1959/2); Hugo/ Schneider, "Heute tanzen alle jungen Leute," in *Helga Brauer und die Flamingos, Rundfunk Tanzorchester Leipzig, Leitung Kurt Henkels* (Berlin: AMIGA, 1959); "Eine Tanzmusik-Konferenz, drei Kapellen, ein Tanzabend," *Melodie und Rhythmus* (10/1959).
¹⁴⁶ "Tanzmusik als Spiegel der Zeit," *Melodie und Rhythmus* (10/1959). "Ein Novum: Komponisten, Textautoren und Musikwissenschaftler berieten gemeinsam Fragen der Tanzmusik," *Melodie und Rhythmus* (3/1964).

America's "hit colony," whereas East Germany stood fast as the custodian of a German national culture.[147]

In truth, however, state-controlled offerings could not compete with, let alone counter, the rapidly developing styles and the technological refinement of Western popular music. When in the 1960s Elvis and rock 'n' roll gave way to a new sound of bands such as the Beatles, the Beach Boys, and the Rolling Stones, East German officials faced yet another revolution in popular music. In 1963, the last year of Khrushchev's premiership, and the last year of the so-called Thaw of reformist politics, the SED in its *Jugendkommuniqué* presented a more liberal approach toward adolescent musical preferences.[148] This new course triggered a rapid expansion of an East German "beat music" scene (*à la* the Beatles), so that by the mid-1960s hundreds of GDR beat bands were followed by thousands of teenage fans enthusiastic about the "Liverpool sound." Reformist policies under the slogan "trust in youth, and youth's responsibility" encouraged open discussions regarding the Western orientation of the GDR youth culture.[149]

Orchestra leader Alfons Wonneberg, who in the early 1950s had been involved in the East Berlin Jazz Club's activities and befriended Werner Sellhorn, was aware of the volatility of Western pop music and its trendsetting impact on GDR youth.[150] In the summer of 1964, in a candid statement in *Melodie und Rhythmus*, he wrote that: "Fashion is as capricious in the realm of dance music as it is in the realm of apparel. A professional dance musician is exposed to international competition. It is no secret: the guitar fad, the so-called Liverpool sound is the call of the day."[151] In his statement, Wonneberg indirectly conceded the failure of state policy to prevent the influence of Western trends, further revealing the occasional liberalism of those years that made such criticism even possible. In a recent interview, Wonneberg reflected on his career, recalling from his experience as a practicing bandleader that pleasing audiences was of first importance. Aware of the shortcomings of obtaining up-to-date technology in a Soviet-style command economy, he publicly urged that modern equipment was

[147] "Der Weg des Verderbens," *Melodie und Rhythmus* (7/1960).
[148] Ulrich Mählert and Gerd-Rüdiger Stephan, *Blaue Hemden, Rote Fahnen: Die Geschichte der Freien Deutschen Jugend* (Opladen: Leske und Budrich, 1996), 152–53.
[149] "Das Vertrauen der Jugend und ihre Verantwortung." Kommunique des SED-Politbüros vom 17. September 1963 as cited in: ibid., 150–52.
[150] Interview with the author, 2009.
[151] Alfons Wonneberg, "Wo bleiben unsere modernen Gitarren und Verstärkeranlagen?," *Melodie und Rhythmus* (16/1964).

needed for GDR musicians to be able to compete with the "modern and international" trends in popular music.[152] What Wonneberg meant, of course, were Western trends.

The GDR's liberal bent toward the beat movement became tangible for thousands of young people from East and West during the Deutschlandtreffen, a festival for youth in Berlin in May 1964. A newly installed radio program called "DT64" regularly broadcast beat music by East German bands, such as The Sputniks, inspired by the surf rock and garage band styles popular at the time. Furthermore, to help shed the dogmatic image of the youth organization, officials such as FDJ President Horst Schumann publicly danced the fashionable American twist.[153] Such signs of reform as well as a generational shift in FDJ leadership trying to distance itself from the repressive practices toward youth culture of the early 1950s were further exemplified by the Felsenkeller events in Leipzig. During this three-day festival in 1964, the borders of divided Berlin were opened to West Germans, with innumerable beat concerts presenting an open and confident East German state.

This period of liberalization came to an end the following summer. In 1965, Erich Honecker, at the time the second-most important official under head of state Walter Ulbricht, instigated a change in cultural politics. (Ulbricht would remain in power until 1971, but many of these changes in policy arose from Honecker.) Whatever his reasons might have been – his disapproval of Western popular music or his ambitions for state leadership – Honecker set about undermining Ulbricht's course of reform and succeeded in reversing liberal policies. First, he undertook a drastic step against the beat movement by withdrawing the performing licenses of beat and guitar groups. As a result, in late October of that year, a demonstration of beat fans spread through the inner city of Leipzig, a mass gathering that resulted in many charges and convictions of "youth criminality."[154]

At the time, party rhetoric denouncing the beat movement echoed that toward jazz in the 1950s by the STAKOKU, and it escalated to a new phase of crackdown spearheaded by Honecker and decreed at the Eleventh Plenum of the ZK on December 16–17, 1965.[155] The Eleventh Plenum represented some of the most vigorous interventions into artistic

[152] Ibid. Interview with the author, 2009.
[153] Ulrich Mählert, *Kleine Geschichte der DDR*, 5th, 2007 ed. (München: C. H. Beck, 1998), 105.
[154] Fulbrook, *A History of Germany, 1918–2014*, 130–31. See also Rauhut, *Beat in der Grauzone*.
[155] Mählert and Stephan, *Blaue Hemden, Rote Fahnen*, 167.

processes and intellectual debates to date, interventions that paralyzed intellectual life in the GDR.[156] Numerous writers, filmmakers, and theater producers who had criticized the SED's path to socialism were attacked during the Plenum that winter. Literary works, theatrical productions, and feature films – almost all of the film productions of an entire year – were denounced and banned. These measures affected many high-profile actors, some of whom were part of the jazz scene: feature films and television productions starring actors such as Manfred Krug and singer Ruth Hohmann, for instance, were withdrawn from public life. As a result, some performers left the GDR entirely, whereas others yielded to the pressure, silencing their criticism and comporting themselves with party ideology. Because of his popularity, Krug was able to emigrate to West Germany, while Hohmann succeeded in making a career change. The realm of jazz was a safe haven for those stigmatized for partaking in artistic productions that grappled with the realities of socialist everyday life. Following her work on screen, Hohmann became a well-established jazz vocalist in the GDR.[157]

Despite the cultural crackdown in the final Ulbricht years from 1965 to 1971, the jazz scene managed to survive. Far from reverting to a musical wasteland, the late 1960s in the GDR were the years of the founding of jazz festivals and concert series, the granting of state awards to jazz musicians, the rise of amateur jazz bands, the publication of academic jazz histories, the rehabilitation of ostracized genres of jazz, the regular broadcasting of jazz, and the implementation of jazz programs at schools and music conservatories – all topics discussed in the next chapter. One of the pillars of the GDR jazz scene was represented by amateur bands, which had arisen in force some years earlier – partly as a result of state policy. The cultural programs established in 1959 and 1964 during the Bitterfeld conferences had encouraged amateur workers to partake in creative processes, which were guided by professional artists.[158] The programs coined as the *Bitterfelder Weg* (way/path) represented a further attempt to push for the idea of socialist art, in which professionals and amateurs joined in the process of creating art for the people.

As one component of the *Bitterfelder* programs, critics and observers saw jazz as a genre potentially giving a boost to East German dance

---

[156] Günter Agde, ed. *Kahlschlag: Das 11. Plenum des ZK der SED 1965* (Berlin: Aufbau Verlag, 1991).
[157] Interview with the author, 2008. Hohmann referred to an operatic drama called *Hete*, produced for TV by Harry Kupfer.
[158] "Lebendige Verbindung zwischen Komponisten und Arbeitern," *Melodie und Rhythmus* (22/1959).

music and urged amateur musicians to participate in courses to expand their artistic abilities.[159] Apart from the purpose of advanced training, such programs also served the mechanisms of control and ideologization, often of those individuals who had theretofore eschewed political conformity. Officials had called for the intensified incorporation of amateur jazz bands in work collectives and to share experiences and increase social cohesion.[160] Yet jazz musicians, more so than musicians in other genres, were reluctant to respond to such calls and did not attend meetings as they should have. It seems that despite the legitimacy newly bestowed on these ensembles, the tendency to preserve the countercultural ambience of the jazz scene remained. Even so, compliance was rewarded, with musicians who complied receiving public recognition and appreciation. Jazz amateurs were regularly featured at festivals competing with professionals in so-called "shows of excellence," and their achievements were recognized in the media[161] (Figure 4.8). Distinguished bands had the opportunity to exchange ideas with high-profile professionals, and in one celebrated case, a band had the chance to meet and learn from celebrity bandleader Klaus Lenz.[162]

In 1968, *Musik und Gesellschaft* predicted a glorious future for jazz in the GDR. Jürgen Elsner, a noted musicologist at the Humboldt University of Berlin, declared that jazz of all styles enjoyed an irrevocable position in the cultural landscape of socialist Germany. In his article, he welcomed the prolific future of jazz development in East Germany and stated that in the GDR's new socio-economic system "institutions, musicians and audiences bid farewell to the coercions of the capitalist music world, to satisfy their true musical needs in the GDR's humanized cultural creativity."[163] Such a prediction was fulfilled partly by the encouragement of amateur bands, but also by the creation of new institutional entities to showcase jazz. In 1971, three years after Elsner's prediction (and the

[159] "Vier Schwerpunkte der künftigen Arbeit der Amateurtanzmusiker," *Melodie und Rhythmus* (2/1968). "Neue Lehrgänge in Sondershausen," *Melodie und Rhythmus* (3/1966). For more on the Bitterfeld policies, see Gerd Dietrich, *Kulturgeschichte der DDR* (Göttingen: Vandenhoek&Ruprecht, 2018).

[160] "Vier Schwerpunkte der künftigen Arbeit der Amateurtanzmusiker," 106.

[161] Karlheinz Drechsel, "Treffpunkt Jazz," ibid. (7/1968); "Fahrkarten nach Magdeburg," ibid. (8/1970).

[162] "Erfolgsgeheimnis-Konzeption und Kontinuität: Amateurcombo Swingtett 67," *Melodie und Rhythmus* (5/1968).

[163] Jürgen Elsner, "Gedanken zum Thema Jazz angeregt durch Publikationen des VEB Deutsche Schallplate," *Musik und Gesellschaft* (8/1968): 558.

Figure 4.8　Program for the Berlin Jazz Amateurs competition, November 23, 1963.
Private collection of Katja Deim, used by permission

year of Louis Armstrong's death), the longest-lived jazz festival in East
Germany was founded in Dresden, a festival dedicated entirely to New
Orleans' jazz culture – as represented by Armstrong, King Oliver, Kid
Ory, and Sidney Bechet. Indeed, the Dixieland Festival established a tradition that persisted long past the existence of the East German state. One
of its founders was Dresden native Karlheinz Drechsel, who (as discussed
in Chapters 2 and 4) experienced the city's firebombing in 1945 as a child
and who was deeply involved in the postwar grassroots jazz scene. By the
early 1970s, Drechsel was nationally known for his jazz radio programs
and his role as the master of ceremonies at major jazz events, such as the
Armstrong tour in 1965. For decades, Drechsel served as the Dixieland
Festival's organizer and announcer: held every year in early summer, the
festival transformed Dresden into a place celebrating Dixieland and New

Orleans' musical culture, with events spread through the entire city, in concert halls, churches, restaurants, clubs, and city squares, as well as on the promenades and the riverboats of the river Elbe. Far from a modest local effort, the festival's significance was complemented by coverage in national broadcasts as well as productions on the Amiga record label. Reaching attendance of up to 90,000 at its peak in the late 1980s, it became one of the most popular events in the GDR. Like many modern musical festivals, tickets became so popular that Dixieland fans camped out in tents at sales offices days in advance of their opening (Figures 4.9 and 4.10).

As part of its programming, the festival featured international artists as well as East German Dixieland bands, most of them amateur musicians. During the festival, participants took part in New Orleans traditions such as the parading of "second lines" behind a marching jazz band carrying umbrellas and led by a Grand Marshal. The presentation of music on riverboats followed the tradition of entertainment on boats along the Mississippi River, where Louis Armstrong performed early in his career.

Figure 4.9   New Orleans Style second line procession during Dixieland Festival in Dresden (undated image, probably early 1980s). Private collection of Otto Sill, used by permission

Figure 4.10   Celebrating music for world peace: crowds at the Dixieland Festival
in Dresden, May 1986. Picture-alliance / ZB-Ulrich Hässler

These performances meant more than just fond memories: such a whole-
sale adoption of jazz culture offered a form of escapism, a way to imagine
life in a place beyond the Iron Curtain. While festivalgoers lived out their
imaginations of New Orleans, the festival nevertheless demonstrated its
political conformity to socialist ideology by perpetuating the myth of the

people's music. Socialist views of the genesis of jazz exemplified in the writings of Ernst Hermann Meyer and jazz historians such as Andre Asriel were visibly manifest in the proceedings, which celebrated "old time jazz" as a music of "proletarian vitality, alarming for the bourgeoisie, a music of the poor, which evinced the power of the people."[164] For at the end of the 1960s, as at their beginning, socialist ideologues continued to interpret American jazz as emblematic of the exploitation of the people's creativity under capitalism. In this view, compelling stories such as King Oliver's could have not happened under socialism. Werner Sellhorn wrote about the native Louisianan musician: "And now began King Oliver's tragic story. Like many of his colleagues he was helpless in the commercial entertainment industry, and missed his chance.... Yet he did not want to give up, could not accept that his struggle in a society that put profit above all had to fail."[165] In East Germany, so went the narrative, jazz was liberated from the coercions of the profit-oriented music industry; here it could not just survive, it could thrive.

Conclusion

The era from the building of the Berlin Wall in 1961 to Ulbricht's abdication in 1971 witnessed the incorporation of jazz into socialist state culture, a process shaped by a variety of factors, including the dialectic between American racial politics and the socialist jazz reception in the GDR. At first, the period immediately surrounding the building of the Wall saw a disparity of opinions about jazz activities. These opinions encompassed liberal propositions to include the intellectual potential of jazz fans into youth organizations, as well as those that repelled jazz circles for their intellectual sectarianism, allegedly excluding the working class. Such disparity complicated policymaking. In general, the ZK, which most likely ignored or selectively read such reports, attempted to consolidate its control over the jazz scene and came up with ideological-phrased directives expressing a deep mistrust of the music and its proponents.

In December 1961, the ZK, feeling pressured by the growing popularity of jazz, took the first measure toward the cultural incorporation of jazz by decreeing a resolution only a few months after the lockdown of the country. The enclosure of GDR territory had increased jazz activity for

---

[164] Asriel, *Jazz: Analysen und Aspekte*, 101. In all of the editions of Asriel's *Jazz: Analysen und Aspekte* from 1966 to 1985, the author's verdicts on *Volkstümlicher Jazz* never changed.
[165] For example: Werner Sellhorn, "Joe 'King' Oliver," *Melodie und Rhythmus* (6/1966).

various reasons, which alarmed high-ranking officials who feared the loss of ideological control, class enemy infiltration in youth organizations, and spontaneous, autonomous organizing of the scene. The proclamation of the 1962 jazz resolution was a tactical decision toward the centralization and observation of the jazz scene in order to consolidate party authority over jazz. It explicitly decreed that jazz events ought not to be prohibited because they represented ingenious folk music and therefore were in accordance with party ideology. However, they should not be allowed to proliferate unchecked. Authorities recognized that outlawing or eliminating jazz would not be just unwise, but also infeasible, and moved instead to control it. Draconian measures such as the interventions into dance events initiated by STAKOKU were relics of the Stalinist past, but nevertheless up to the mid-1960s, the ZK's jazz directive still prompted limitations. While those affected might have taken these limitations as repressions on jazz specifically, they were in fact exerted to protect the state's monopoly on organizing its citizens.

After the lockdown of the GDR territory, East German authorities expanded and refined their mechanisms of surveillance and control. First, the incorporation of amateur jazz bands within the framework of the Bitterfeld programs (which had begun in the late 1950s) served both purposes of education and purposes of control. Despite jazz's ideological conformity, American music still codified countercultural tendencies, standing outside the social mainstream. Through inclusion into the Bitterfeld programs, amateur jazz bands were given the potential for further guided education, hereby subjecting them to authoritative control. Second, after August 1961, the STASI began to build up networks of informants who submitted data on the jazz scene nationwide. The long-lasting deployment of informant Werner Sellhorn exemplifies the methods of STASI surveillance, choosing key figures well-acquainted with the scene and informed about its players.[166] In the case of agent IM Zirkel, the STASI tolerated (and ultimately profited from) his bohemian persona, which in fact contradicted the ostensible "ideal" socialist citizen. It is possible that the STASI nurtured this persona because it assured his conspicuous position in a scene, attracting intellectuals and artists who exchanged ideas and criticism about state policies. The STASI granted their informant room to maneuver, creating a sphere of the "alternative" lifestyle and culture whose observation was of vital interest for state security.

---

[166] For other recruits, see BStU, MfS, Cottbus AIM 681/81, "Thomas," Ulrich Herbert Blobel, Band [Vol.] I (1972–1981) and II (1982–1984). See also BStU, MfS, "Sander."

In the mid-1960s, the political dimensions of jazz's revolutionary potential became of recharged significance when state authorities used it as a vehicle to propagate the GDR's solidarity with the African American civil rights movement. The ZK's resolution in 1962 had proclaimed the support of jazz as social protest against racial oppression, a proclamation that culminated in the presentation of Louis Armstrong's visit in 1965.[167] While the US State Department's jazz diplomacy attempted to project the achievements of American democracy, the GDR propagated jazz as music informed by failures of the American socio-economic system. Defying Western perceptions of a nonpolitical person, Armstrong was presented as a political individual actively involved in the fight for African American civil rights. Armstrong's reception did not feature comments in terms of national or racial cultural delineations; to the contrary, jazz was assigned an unconditional position in the GDR's socialist culture. Seen as breaking down cultural barriers and sweeping away notions of cultural hierarchy, Armstrong, the "classicist of modern folk art" (*Klassiker moderner Volkskunst*), was celebrated as the embodiment of the socialist-realist artist.[168] In that sense, Armstrong's tour constituted a turning point in the trajectory of jazz in the GDR, for this event induced shifts toward a greater acceptance of the music in the East German state.

Even after a widespread crackdown on culture and the arts in 1965, propelled in part by the notorious Eleventh Plenum, jazz continued to thrive in East Germany. Only a few short years after the jazz polemics of the late 1950s that debated the *raison d'être* of the American music in the GDR, by the late 1960s, leading critics and officials consented to grant the genre greater freedom to develop. Theorists such as Jürgen Elsner predicted that locally made jazz had a bright future: liberated from a profit-oriented system, the "people's music," whose genesis and history was inextricably intertwined with capitalist oppression, would freely unfold in socialism to satisfy the true needs of the people.[169] Quickly it became apparent which styles of jazz would represent the GDR in the decades to come: the Dixieland movement (and its festival in Dresden) was devoted to re-imagining early forms of jazz, which attracted the masses celebrating the myth of the people's music.

However, a new form of jazz was beginning to take shape. As the next chapter will show, the other major pillar of GDR jazz was represented by

---

[167] 1962 ZK Jazz Resolution.
[168] Harry Goldschmidt, "Klassiker moderner Volkskunst," *Berliner Zeitung* (March 24, 1965).
[169] Elsner, "Gedanken zum Thema Jazz angeregt durch Publikationen," 1968.

those who sought to explore free forms of jazz, not least because they aimed to connect to American developments in the 1960s. In contrast to the amateur musicians of the Dixieland style, most of these performers were academically trained at conservatories and in jazz programs, such as at the Dresden Conservatory that graduated its first class in 1967.[170] Over the next twenty years, free jazz or "new jazz" – a predominantly non-verbal musical expression – flourished. Finally adopting jazz as a truly national form, state authorities strongly supported the free jazz scene, promoting festivals and events and showcasing key figures of the scene on global stages. In a stark contrast to the trajectory of years before, when jazz was a genre to be feared and controlled, in the final two decades of the GDR, jazz would be championed as symbolic of an open and progressive East German state.

[170] "Diplom Tanzmusiker aus Dresden," *Melodie und Rhythmus* (12/1967).

CHAPTER 5

The Rise of New Jazz, 1971–1979

Introduction

In the last decades of the GDR, the policies of East and West Germany under *détente* were the primary shapers of the trajectory of jazz. In 1969, West Germany launched its *Ostpolitik* programs under Chancellor Willy Brandt, negotiating controversial treaties with Moscow and East Berlin. These treaties, which continued into the early 1970s, recognized each Germany's independence, thus normalizing relations between the two states.[1] Yet the GDR continued to demand formal recognition of full sovereignty, which West Germany for constitutional reasons could not grant, leading the ZK to denounce West Germany for thwarting the process.[2] In 1973, both West and East Germany joined the United Nations as full members and, in the following year, established diplomatic outposts in their respective capitals: the so-called "permanent representations" (*Ständige Vertretungen*) in Bonn and in East Berlin. Furthermore, after participating in the Conference on Security and Co-operation in Europe (CSCE), both states signed the 1975 Helsinki Accords, adding further legitimacy to the East German regime. At the time, such a move served equally to solidify the division of Germany and to consolidate the recognition of postwar borders – leading Brandt's political opponents to blame him for "selling out" Germany's most deeply held national interest: the reunification of Germany.

---

[1] See Julia von Dannenberg, *The Foundations of Ostpolitik: The Making of the Moscow Treaty between West Germany and the USSR* (Oxford University Press, 2008). M.E. Sarotte, *Dealing with the Devil: East Germany, Detente and Ostpolitik, 1969–1973* (Chapel Hill: University of North Carolina Press, 2001).

[2] ZK der SED, "Protokoll der 6. Tagung des Zentralkomitees, parteiinternes Material." BArch/ DY 30/IV2/1/458 (1972). See also Helga Haftendorn, "The Unification of Germany, 1985–1991," in *The Cold War, Volume III: Endings*, ed. Melvyn P. Leffler and Odd Arne Westad (Cambridge University Press, 2010), 335.

Despite the controversy with Brandt's slogan "Change through rap-prochement" (*Wandel durch Annäherung*), *Ostpolitik* strengthened West Germany's ties to the East and began to transform the stalemate between the two German states.[3] Yet what was touted internally in the East as Chairman Honecker's greatest political success in foreign policy – recognition of the GDR as an autonomous state – was, in fact, a delicate web of compromises. A minister in Honecker's administration, skeptical of the deal, assessed the ramifications of *Ostpolitik* as Western "aggression in felt slippers."[4] While these diplomatic agreements between East and West did, undeniably, smooth the path toward the GDR's international recognition, they also set preconditions for the controlled and gradual opening of the GDR, rendering the Iron Curtain increasingly permeable. The principles embodied in the 1975 Helsinki Accords gave citizens who dared to criticize their regimes in Eastern Europe – as *Ostpolitik* chief negotiator Egon Bahr would later remark – "a framework that they could refer to and that allowed them to operate a little more freely."[5]

The closer the GDR came to its goal of formal statehood, SED politics toward the West and in particular toward West Germany (*Westpolitik*) sought two main ends: the cultural demarcation of the East German state from its Western counterpart and the enforcement of the German parti-tion. While in the Ulbricht era, ideologues had backed the position of the GDR as "a socialist State of a German nation" and supported the state's role as the advocate and defender of an all-German national culture, by the early 1970s, such positions on nationhood had shifted.[6] According to party ideologues, the worker's and peasant's state had transformed into a new type of nation and, by 1971, had entered the phase of "developed socialism."[7] Contrary to Brandt, who had claimed that two states existed within one broader German nation, SED chief ideologists saw the two Germanies as two separate nations pursuing opposing social systems.[8]

---

[3] Jussi M. Hanhimäki, "Détente in Europe, 1962–1975," in *The Cold War, Volume II: Crisis and Detente*, ed. Melvyn P. Leffler and Odd Arne Westad (Cambridge University Press, 2010).
[4] Otto Winzer (1902–1975), Minister für Auswärtige Angelegenheiten, 1965–1975. See Egon Bahr, *Bulletin of the German Historical Institute* Supplement I, 2004 (2003).
[5] Ibid., 137.
[6] Wolfgang-Uwe Friedrich, "SED und die deutsche Frage," in *Lexikon des DDR-Sozilaismus*, ed. Rainer Eppelmann (Paderborn: Ferdinand Schöningh, 1997), 579.
[7] Udo Margedant, "Staat," in *Lexikon des DDR-Sozialismus*, ed. Rainer Eppelmann (Paderborn: Ferdinand Schöningh, 1997), 787–91.
[8] Friedrich, "SED und die deutsche Frage," 575–80. Friedrich cites ZK member Albert Norden (1904–1982).

At a 1972 ZK meeting, these ideologues denounced West German political leaders for holding on to the idea of a continuation of unified German culture, which they rejected. Rather, according to the Marxist-Leninist view of history as class warfare and continual revolution, a unified German culture never existed.[9] These ideologues further argued that there was no joint economy, no mutual contemporary culture, and that ideas of history and tradition between the two Germanies were strictly opposed. On this hard-line view, the socialist system in East Germany had allegedly created a new personality with psychological and moral characteristics distinctive from its Western counterpart.[10] This divorce took place in key markers of national identity: in the early 1970s, policymakers even attempted to eliminate the terms *deutsch* and *Deutschland*. The former German broadcast was renamed to "The Voice of the GDR" (*Stimme der DDR*), phrases in the national anthem alluding to the unity of Germany were excluded, and in the new 1974 Constitution passages that related to the German nation were erased.[11]

The fact was, however, that these treaties granted significantly increased interaction between the citizens of the two Germanies. After years of separation, telecommunication between East and West Berlin was reinstalled, and after a six-year moratorium, West Berliners were allowed to stay in the East for up to thirty days. Overall, visits of West Germans to the GDR increased considerably, tripling between 1969 and 1975.[12] Information flowed through Western journalists who could now be accredited in the East, and Western goods became more readily available for those who spent hard currency. While the black market was still in effect, East German citizens were now allowed to purchase certain Western goods at the so-called Intershops.[13] By the mid-1970s, the purported lockdown of East German society was proving increasingly difficult, and by the end of the decade, large numbers of GDR citizens, including members of the jazz scene, justified their claims for freedom of choice of residency by citing these same Helsinki Accords from 1975 – increasingly applying for the

---

[9] ZK der SED, "Protokoll der 6. Tagung des Zentralkomitees, parteiinternes Material." BArch/DY 30/IV2/1/458, 1972.

[10] Jochen Staadt, *Die Geheime Westpolitik der SED, 1960–1970* (Berlin: Akademie Verlag, 1993), 13; Friedrich, "SED und die deutsche Frage," 579.

[11] Cf. Friedrich, "SED und die deutsche Frage."

[12] Ulrich Mählert, *Kleine Geschichte der DDR*, 5th, 2007 ed. (München: C.H. Beck, 1998), 131.

[13] www.bpb.de/geschichte/zeitgeschichte/deutschland-chronik/131850/25-berlin-regelung-und-berlin-politik-1971-1982.

permission to leave the GDR. Erich Mielke, the longtime head of the MfS and STASI chief, had warned against the looming "negative political-ideological ramifications" of *détente* and gave orders for STASI agents to remain on alert.[14] During the Honecker era, the STASI – "the swords and shield of the party" – bolstered its workforce to over 90,000 employees and doubled the number of unofficial informants to about 190,000. Such enormous surveillance was intended to forestall dissent and to prevent any challenges to the SED's claim to power. In this effort, party leadership and the STASI remained close collaborators.[15]

Following a decade of upheaval and change, this chapter examines the development of jazz in the GDR in the 1970s. In what follows, Section One ("Satchmo and the Black Panthers") examines views of jazz reflecting social upheaval and black nationalist sentiment in the United States, and how it was co-opted by East German political strategists in the early 1970s. Section Two ("Bach and Coltrane: Free Jazz in the GDR") chronicles how the East German jazz world received and understood the new genre of free jazz, nascent during this time period, and how free jazz furthermore participated in the creation of a national socialist state culture. Chronicling the experience of a key informant on the jazz scene active in the 1970s and early 1980s, Section Three ("The STASI at Woodstock") explores the creation of a new, grassroots free jazz festival in the context of the STASI's continued methods of surveillance, and Section Four ("Jazz as Diplomacy and *Jazz Now*") details the way in which jazz again became a tool for diplomacy throughout these critical years.

Satchmo and the Black Panthers

Throughout the 1970s and 1980s, just as he had in the 1950s and 1960s, Werner Sellhorn remained active in continuing to promote and lecture on jazz. In the spring of 1973, he was touring the eastern GDR provinces accompanied by an American journalist and collaborator who was a member of the CPUSA. In a lecture on February 12th, at the "Forum K" in Cottbus, the American journalist – whose name was unfortunately redacted in STASI files – spoke on the Black Power movement in the

---

[14] Jens Gieseke, *Der Mielke-Konzern: Die Geschichte der Stasi 1945–1990* (Stuttgart; München: Deutsche Verlags-Anstalt, 2001), 86.

[15] Gieseke (*Der Mielke-Konzern*, pp. 70–72, 86–89) argues that the expansion of the STASI apparatus was an indirect reaction to *détente*.

United States, accompanied by Sellhorn's selection of jazz music.[16] In this presentation, they adopted positions that had arisen within East German jazz discourse in the late 1960s and 1970s, positions that associated the American free jazz movement with radical leftist groups such as the Black Panther Party (BPP). As noted above, in the socialist view, this music served as a tool in the struggle of class warfare: with the emergence of militant black organizations in the 1960s contesting the social order in the United States, jazz was regarded not only as an emblem of protest and a means of demand for socio-political change within the system, but also as a music that by its nature expressed opposition against the system itself.

The groundwork for these views had been laid years before. For in its jazz resolution of 1962, the ZK had outlined the dissemination of educational materials through channels such as the Society for the Propagation of Scientific Knowledge (*Gesellschaft zur Verbreitung wissenschaftlicher Erkenntnisse*, later shortened to URANIA), an organization that dated to the late nineteenth century and recalled the traditions of liberal education. During the Nazi years, URANIA was prohibited, but in the 1950s, the East German state revived it by instrumentalizing its traditions and reputation to spread popular scientific knowledge, including that of arts and culture, on behalf of socialist education. In its new incarnation, URANIA cooperated with other mass organizations as well as East German media, and by the 1980s, the organization enjoyed more members than the Kulturbund, organizing up to 400,000 events annually with 10–12 million participants.[17] In this context, URANIA's influence as a multiplier of propagandistic party directives, such as the one on jazz, cannot be overstated.

Urania, the organization's periodical, propagated links between jazz and radical black liberation movements by publishing materials that presented jazz in the context of militant organizations such as the BPP. In 1972, the publication featured an image of Louis Armstrong on its front page, published alongside articles that attempted to construct historical continuities between styles of jazz and their function as tools of self-determination and class warfare. Although not directly argued, the combination of visual and textual materials implied an ideological alliance between Armstrong and the Black Panthers' socialist-revolutionary aims (Figure 5.1). Moreover, in his

---

[16] BStU, MfS, "Thomas" Band I, p. 44. For jazz and the Black Power movement, see Phillipe Carles and Jean-Louis Comolli, *Free Jazz/Black Power* (Jackson: University Press of Mississippi, 1979/2015); Eric Porter, *What Is This Thing Called Jazz? African American Musicians as Artists, Critics and Activists* (Berkeley: University of California Press, 2002).

[17] Gerd Dietrich, "Kulturbund," in *Die Parteien und Organisationen der DDR: Ein Handbuch*, ed. Gerd-Rüdiger Stephan et al. (Berlin: Karl Dietz Verlag, 2002), 817–20.

Figure 5.1 *Urania*, the periodical of the Society for the Propagation of Scientific Knowledge, featured Armstrong on its February 1972 cover. Private collection of Jan Eikermann, used by permission

article in the magazine, author, pianist, and composer Hans Rempel proclaimed that jazz, "which triumphed around the world" due to its "general humanist content," was to be cherished and supported in the GDR in its "classical" form.[18] The term "classical jazz" had permeated East German jazz discourse since the Armstrong tour in 1965 and alluded to notions of "true" humanist, non-commercial jazz seen in Armstrong's music. Rempel wrote in *Urania*: "A primordial, vital, artistic realization, the [socialist] engaged attitude of life preserves [jazz's] vitality and connects it with the audience. Indeed we are in a position to listen to and understand jazz, however, not in the manipulated form of the American way of life."[19] Indeed, such socialist-realist notions of jazz articulated by theorists such as Meyer and his disciples such as Elsner and Asriel (over three editions of his seminal treatise), as well as still being proclaimed at party meetings throughout the 1970s, would continue to inform the jazz discourse even until the 1980s.[20]

Critics such as Rempel saw East German jazz as purified from capitalist manipulation by preserving it as a music representing a socially conscious position. As noted, this ideal was represented by music such as Armstrong's, whose birthplace, New Orleans, was associated with the style of collective improvisation. Such constructs of jazz as "the people's music" had permeated the jazz discourse since the 1950s, indicating the state's tolerance of and later support for Dixieland. Now in the 1970s, however, Rempel, a proponent of the GDR free jazz scene, would argue for strict historical continuity for the genre. In 1971, he declared in *Urania*: "For about ten years the collective invention of melody has predominated jazz. Because of the revaluation of collective melodic improvisation, in which solo parts recede, the style of the recent years [the 1960s] reveals a surprising affinity to the classical style of jazz."[21] Rempel detected musical parallels in these styles between the allegedly uncorrupted forms such as Armstrong's "classical" jazz and the African American jazz of the 1960s (declining to name his exemplars). While the former was seen as an expression of black self-determination, the latter was understood as an expression of revolution. This revolutionary effort in the United States was described by the American correspondent for *Neues Deutschland*, Klaus Steiniger (1932–2016), who was convinced of

---

[18] Hans Rempel, "Jazz: Woher – Wohin?" *Urania*, no. 2 (1971), p. 7.
[19] Ibid.
[20] The third and final edition was published in 1985. Asriel, *Jazz: Analysen und Aspekte*. See also Jürgen Elsner, "Gedanken zum Thema Jazz angeregt durch Publikationen des VEB Deutsche Schallplate," *Musik und Gesellschaft* (8/1968): 553–58. Additional material can be found in BArch/ DY 30 IV2/1/458 ZK der SED, "Protokoll der 6.Tagung des Zentralkomitees."
[21] Rempel, "Jazz: Woher – Wohin?"

the efficacy of leftist militant groups pushing global revolution forward – the son of Peter Alfons Steiniger, who had helped draft the first GDR constitution in 1949, Klaus had witnessed the trials of Angela Davis in the United States. In *Urania*, he noted that the leaders of the Black Panthers have "no doubt, that the USA, the prison of the people, could be only forced open by a socialist revolution."[22] On this view, profound social change was not to be achieved within the capitalist system but only through revolution and the installation of socialism, for which the Panthers fought. Interracial communist agitation, the union of black and white in class warfare, was considered to be the driving force of black liberation. Channeling the views of earlier Socialists, Steiniger stated: "The Party of the Black Panthers and that of the Communists in the US are the backbone of the African American liberation movement."[23]

Importantly, according to this ideology, black liberation was as much a matter of class as it was of race. In *Urania*, Steiniger denounced black-nationalist separatist movements as "reactionary" given that their proponents rejected interracial cooperation and stoked an increasing social awareness amongst the masses of the black oppressed class: "As a matter of fact," he wrote, "one has to talk about the unparalleled rise of the African American liberation movement, whose primary criteria is its growing class consciousness."[24] In this context, both Steiniger in particular and East German critics in general, who were writing about social upheaval in the United States in the 1960s, focused on individuals such Marxist activist Angela Davis. For Davis, who pursued Marxism over black nationalism, the battle lines were clear. Quoted in the *Berliner Zeitung*, she argued that

> The reason that we are forced to carve out our miserable existence in the lowest level of American society is connected to the nature of capitalism. If we are willing to cast off our repression and destitution, if we no longer want to be the target of racist thinking of police, we have to destroy the American capitalist system.[25]

---

[22] Klaus Steiniger, "Black Panther: Schicksal und Kampf, Weg zum Ziel," *Urania*, no. 2 (1971): 40–43. Translated from the original German: "While the political organizations of African Americans perceive themselves as adjuncts of the bourgeoisie and unfold their activism in the framework of the imperialist two-party system, the BPP declared uncompromising war on the existing structures of power. ... Their leaders have no doubt that the prison of the people called the USA will only be forced open by a socialist revolution" (p. 41).

[23] Ibid.

[24] Ibid., 43. See also *Angela Davis: Eine Frau schreibt Geschichte* (Berlin: Neues Leben, 2010). Davis visited Berlin in 2010 as an honorary guest of the *Fest der Linken* at the Kulturbrauerei.

[25] *Berliner Zeitung*, September 26, 1971. *Über Probleme des Schwarzen Amerika. Der amerikanische Rassismus - vor allem eine klassenmäßige Erscheinung.* The article originated from *Meshdunarodnaja Shisn*, Moscow.

And that fight between "capital" and "work" could only be achieved through the united effort of black and white, which would be the "key towards victory."[26] Interestingly, Davis' imprisonment for her activism generated an enormous international solidarity effort, to which the GDR contributed by engaging schoolchildren to participate in the "one million roses for Angela Davis" campaign. After her release in 1971, Davis accepted several invitations to the GDR, where she was celebrated as a political figure representing the "other" America – the same role Paul Robeson and Louis Armstrong had played just a few years earlier. Demonstrating solidarity between socialist Germany and the American left, in the Eastern Bloc, socialist leaders bestowed Davis with numerous honors, ultimately awarding her the Lenin Peace Prize in Moscow in 1979.

In the East German view, the BPP represented a significant threat to those in power in the United States. According to Steiniger in *Urania*, the BPP held "powerful meetings of combat" (*gewaltige Kampfmeetings*), they triggered "a wave of combative mass activity" (*Welle der Massenaktivität*), and they induced a changing social consciousness among the African American working class, which prompted the "ultra-right Nixon regime of murderers to develop violent and deadly strategies."[27] The graphic rhetoric utilized in these propagandist writings alluded to the imagery of both the Holocaust and slavery, combined with a fascination with American exotic urbanity. According to these articles, President Nixon's "regime of murderers ... intends to kill Angela Davis in the Californian gas chamber"; heavily armed police forces "chained young African Americans like slaves"; and American authorities organized "Panther hunts in the jungle of concrete in the American metropolises."[28]

Yoked to the forthcoming revolution, then, African American jazz such as the music of Ornette Coleman was understood not only as signaling protest and resistance against racial discrimination, but also as expressing solidarity with the Communist Party internationally. East German critics interpreted leftist militant agitation as the sign both of an escalating class consciousness among African Americans and an increasing willingness among workers to take part in the revolutionary process. At long last African Americans had left the path of peaceful resistance and had chosen the means of violent struggle for change. Jazz critics such Andre Asriel, Hansgeorg Mühe, Hans Rempel, and Werner Sellhorn interpreted free

[26] Steiniger, "Black Panther: Schicksal und Kampf, Weg zum Ziel," p. 41.
[27] Ibid.
[28] Ibid.

jazz as a revolutionary expression. The socio-political background for this music, according to Asriel, was the "changing international situation" that meant the ongoing revolution. The "aggressive, brutal, shrill, haunted, exorbitant, and orgiastic" music of American free jazz sounded in Asriel's ears as a call to combat against the ruling powers of the imperialist West – an imperialism demonstrated most recently in the conflict in Vietnam. Conjuring communist solidarity with an African American revolutionary movement, Asriel cited Archie Shepp: "Our revenge will be black, as our suffering is black, as Fidel is black, as Ho Chi Minh is black."[29]

In that sense, musicologists such as Mühe, professor at the Musikhochschule Franz Liszt in Weimar, saw Coleman's free jazz as a musical expression of that imminent revolution, as a "valve of class warfare."[30] Mühe called it an "outcry of the oppressed race" but simultaneously understood it to express "optimism and triumphal confidence," implying Coleman's belief in the superiority of socialism.[31] By comparison, the sound of "leftist" West German Peter Brötzmann sounded like "infuriated scolding." Mühe asked: "Does this not sound as if this would be an expression of somebody who was outcast by the capitalist society, an expression of the hopeless?"[32] Rather, the father of free jazz – just as Sellhorn had assessed Coleman – "led the way and others followed." And the ranks of these soldiers were deep: among the other artists Sellhorn listed in his "chapter on free jazz" were Anthony Braxton, Marion Brown, Eric Dolphy, Pharoah Sanders, Paul and Carla Bley, Cecil Taylor, Sun Ra, and John Coltrane.[33]

In this sense, American free jazz represented a form of modern agitprop, a music representing and championing a social-revolutionary process.[34] American "power-holders" (*Machthaber*) thus had an interest in mitigating the revolutionary potential of the music. If capitalism had been blamed for corrupting the music by commercializing it, then East German critics now accused industry executives of falsifying the music and diminishing its combative quality. "The capitalist society utilizes jazz in its commercial form not only to profit from it but rather to diffuse it,"

---

[29] Asriel, *Jazz: Analysen und Aspekte* (1977), 180–181. For black leftist activism and jazz, see Porter, *What Is This Thing Called Jazz?*.
[30] Hans Georg Mühe, "Jazz in der DDR (III): Bemerkungen zur Entwicklung und Gesellschaftlichen Funktion," *Musikforum* (6/1977): 28.
[31] Ibid.
[32] Ibid.
[33] Werner Sellhorn, "Ein Kapitel in Free Jazz," *Kassette 1. Ein Almanach für Bühne, Podium und Manege* (1977).
[34] Ibid.

Rempel declared.[35] The metaphor of "jazz at a crossroads"[36] thus epitomized the split East German view of the music as a means of protest and solidarity for the socialist cause, on the one side, and as opposition to capitalist exploitation and political diffusion, on the other. Indeed, these two ideological views of the music – a tradition deeply rooted in folk styles and a tool of ongoing class warfare – would undergird the state's later overt support of the genre discussed below.

In sum, at the beginning of the 1970s, many of the old debates regarding the role of jazz in socialist society resurfaced in the GDR but with heightened attention to events and developments regarding class consciousness in the United States. As discussed in Chapter 1, in the 1920s, the COMINTERN had first propagated African American folk songs to raise black self-determination and stoke social protest. Fifty years later, according to party ideologues, African Americans had finally developed their class consciousness and were directly engaged in class warfare, hastening the imminent world revolution. But the genre would still have room for organic growth and development even within these larger political trends. Indeed, during this decade, East German jazz would come to comprise two main separate subgenres: Dixieland, represented mainly by amateurs, and free jazz, represented mainly by academically trained professionals. This subdivision of styles paved the way for a new freedom of experimentation for those who made a name for themselves as representing East German free jazz.

Bach and Coltrane: Free Jazz in the GDR

During the 1970s, the jazz discourse in the GDR developed further ideas about uniquely East German styles of contemporary jazz. Such debates over the genre's autonomy (*Eigenständigkeit*) did not arise in a vacuum, however. Rather, they arose within the specific framework of shifting positions on East German nationhood and national culture. With the public declaration at the Eighth Party rally in 1971 that socialism in the GDR had reached a new stage – reaching a form of maturity not seen in its earlier incarnations – the question naturally arose how the GDR would now represent itself on the world stage not just politically, but culturally. In this process, jazz, one of the dominant "national" art forms – a remarkable title – would play a key role. Ultimately, however, amid the effort to

---

[35] Rempel, "Jazz: Woher – Wohin?" p. 7.
[36] Ibid.

define this East German cultural identity, jazz itself would diversify and see the growth and development of the subgenre of free jazz; a subgenre novel to the East German community of performers, listeners, and critics.

As in years past, these debates involved a variety of stakeholders – musicians, musicologists, broadcasters, and journalists, as well as everyday listeners and fans – and again focused on the music's function within the socio-political order. Musicologists Hansgeorg Mühe and Jürgen Elsner had both dated the emergence of an autonomous GDR style to around 1960 and claimed that "New Jazz" in socialist European countries differentiated itself from that in the United States.[37] Unlike American jazz associated with the Black Power movement that allegedly expressed opposition to the capitalist system, these critics took East German jazz as generally expressing consensus with socialism.[38] Mühe proclaimed in *Musik Forum*:

> New Jazz in socialist European countries does not only differentiate itself from American free jazz in style, but also in function: it is an intellectual expression of a debate about the problems of our construction of socialism. It is not the expression of opposition, but the articulation of a position within our society.[39]

In this sense, the social function of jazz was not to challenge an undesirable system, but to contribute positive constructive positions that advanced the socialist cause.

In accordance with this view of jazz's social function, East German critics and observers altered their terminology for jazz. Scholars, journalists, and musicians established the term "New Jazz" in contrast to the American term "free jazz," although the terms "free jazz" or "contemporary jazz" continued to pervade the GDR discourse.[40] In the United States, Ornette Coleman had first used "free jazz" as the title for the LP in 1961, and as

---

[37] Hans Georg Mühe, "Die Improvisation im Jazz (II): Anregungen für Instrumentalisten," *Musikforum* (5/1979): 28. Regrettably, Mühe does not support his assumptions with harmonic, melodic, or rhythmic analysis, and gives no specific examples of differences between American and East German styles. Rather, he believed in a national intonation that differentiated GDR jazz. Cf. "Improvisation im Jazz (III): Anregungen für Instrumentalisten," *Musikforum* (6/1979). Cf. also Elsner, "Gedanken zum Thema Jazz angeregt durch Publikationen des VEB Deutsche Schallplate."

[38] See also, Mühe, "Jazz in der DDR (III)."

[39] Mühe, "Die Improvisation im Jazz (II)."

[40] Mühe, "Jazz in der DDR (III)." Bert Noglik and Heinz-Jürgen Lindner, ed. *Jazz im Gespräch* (Berlin: Verlag Neue Musik, 1978); Bert Noglik, *Jazzwerkstatt International* (Berlin: Verlag Neue Musik, 1981). Within the GDR jazz discourse, protagonists used terms such as free music (*freie Musik*), contemporary music (*zeitgenössische Musik*), or free jazz when addressing music, which was predominantly based on free improvisation.

discussed in the previous chapter, within East German jazz discourse that term carried a political-ideological as well as a black-nationalist connotation.[41] The term *New Jazz*, however, dissociated jazz made in the GDR from such connotations and signaled consensus with the socialist system, incorporating phrases such as "collective melodic invention" or "creative collective co-creation," replacing common Western jazz terminology and its politically loaded concepts such as "individual expression" and "solo improvisation."

This distinction was key to understanding the reception of the form. While Western notions of jazz typically associated the music with expressions of individuality and freedom of expression, East German notions associated it with a larger collectivism, within which individual expressiveness was integral. *New Jazz* represented an art form of a collective process that granted individual creativity. As Hans Rempel explained in *Urania*: "Jazz is … the impulsive collaboration of a collective, simultaneously granting the highest degree of free development to the individual in order to realize an artistic idea."[42] Accordingly, musical ideas were realized through the interdependence between the collective and the individual, thereby granting artistic freedom to the individual player.[43]

Critics, scholars, and audiences alike identified many key players who had made a name for themselves in the GDR and the Eastern Bloc. In 1980, *Musik und Gesellschaft* identified the following musicians as representing the GDR free jazz scene: saxophonists Ernst-Ludwig Petrowsky, Friedhelm Schönfeld, Manfred Schulze, and Günter Fischer; trombonists Konrad Bauer and Hubert Katzenbeier; pianists Ulrich Gumpert and Hans Rempel; trumpeter Hans Joachim Graswurm; percussionist Günter Sommer; bassist Klaus Koch; and vocalists Uschi Brüning and Regine Dobberschütz.[44] Most of these musicians had enjoyed a solid musical education, either at music schools or conservatories, in contrast to the amateur players primarily of the Dixieland style, and formed various

---

[41] Scott DeVeaux and Gary Giddens, *Jazz*, 2015 ed. (New York; London: W.W. Norton & Company, 2009), p. 409. The title was *Free Jazz: A Collective Improvisation by the Ornette Coleman Double Quartet* (Atlantic 1364).

[42] Rempel, "Jazz: Woher – Wohin?"

[43] For Mühe's writings, see Hans Georg Mühe, "Jazz in der DDR (I): Zur Entwicklung und gesellschaftlichen Funktion in der DDR," *Musikforum* (4/1977). "Die Improvisation im Jazz (II)." "Jazz in der DDR (III)." "Improvisation im Jazz (III)." For Noglik, see Bert Noglik, "Spontaneität und Konzeption – zur Jazz-Szene in der DDR," *Musik und Gesellschaft* (3/1980) and his edited collection with Lindner (1978). Elsner also covered this point: Jürgen Elsner, "Gedanken zum Thema Jazz angeregt durch Publikationen des VEB Deutsche Schallplate."

[44] Noglik, "Spontaneität und Konzeption – zur Jazz-Szene in der DDR."

bands as they developed. One of the most popular bands was Synopsis, later called *Zentralquartett*, which Petrowsky noted in a 1991 interview caused "a furor."[45] The band celebrated its debut at the 1973 Jazz Jamboree in Warsaw and enjoyed a steady fan base for many years after the fall of the Berlin Wall, only giving a farewell concert in 2015.[46] Importantly for the time, however, these free jazz musicians were granted opportunities for experimental music-making with few limitations, pushing the acoustic boundaries of their instruments and engaging in genre-crossing projects. Bauer, for instance, explored the possibilities between sound and noise (*Geräusch*). Gumpert fused spontaneous processes with known musical fragments, utilizing folk and trivial music. Schönfeld's music combined arrangements with free improvisation and Sommer abolished fundamental rhythms in favor of accentuated arcs of suspense.[47] Nor did jazz musicians eschew the cooperation with proponents of other musical genres: Manfred Schulze, for example, fused contemporary jazz with elements of contemporary chamber and symphonic music. One of the most extreme (if later) examples came when percussionist Sommer and organist Hans Günter Wauer released *Verschränkte Konstruktionen* on Amiga in 1986, which was praised as a project fusing diverging traditions of African American and German sacral heritage and combining sounds of percussion with the Ladegast organ of the Dome in Merseburg.[48] Writing in the liner notes for this record, musicologist Bert Noglik saw a historical continuity between J.S. Bach's improvisational talents, Franz Liszt's *Präludium und Fuge über B-A-C-H*, and John Coltrane's *Ascension*. For Noglik, this experiment mediated such divergent traditions in order to create new dimensions of contemporary sound, transcending mere incorporation into GDR state culture: rather, as a work that was new, innovative, and future-oriented, yet expressly intended to resolve cultural hierarchies and emancipate musical forms, *Verschränkte Konstruktionen* could only be understood as specifically socialist and German.

Literacy in the genre grew quickly among serious fans, and bandleaders and performers became celebrities in their own right. For live performances, however, the context was a critical part of the experience of *New Jazz*. *New Jazz* was aimed at what was called a Workshop, or *Werkstatt*

---

[45] Interview Radio, *Erinnerungen an den Jazz in der DDR. Siegfried Schmidt-Joos im Gespräch mit Ernst-Ludwig Petrowsky* (Sender Freies Berlin, October 3, 1994).

[46] "Jazz Jamboree '73," *Melodie und Rhythmus* (January 1974).

[47] Noglik, "Spontaneität und Konzeption – zur Jazz-Szene in der DDR."

[48] Günther Sommer and Hans Günther Wauer, *Verschränkte Konstruktionen* (Berlin: VEB Deutsche Schallplatten, Amiga 856134, 1986).

setting, in which the audience also enjoyed creative agency.[49] Historically, the term "Jazz Workshop" had been used by African American musicians such as Charles Mingus since the late 1950s. Mingus' Jazz Workshop operations, what he called "the creative interaction of individuals on the bandstand," sought to signal his independence from commercialism and the recording industry.[50] In the GDR in the 1970s, the concept of free improvising interaction was taken a step further: a "collective moment" informed audience reaction, which directly responded to and influenced subsequent performances.[51] Mühe explained in *Musik Forum*:

> If a good jazz ensemble in countless performances comes to a maximally satisfying communal solution, and if a composition is created through collective improvisation, then one cannot speak about improvisation any longer—this is real jazz, because everyone involved was part of the final creation.[52]

In that sense, ideologues argued the term "jazz improvisation" was inappropriate: indeed, *New Jazz* in the GDR was understood instead as a "creative collective co-creation."[53]

At the time, critics such as Noglik emphasized the perpetual creative process during these workshops, in which musical ideas took shape from the interdependence of musicians, audiences, time, and space.[54] He argued furthermore that the engagement in collective musical creation represented an indispensable educational tool in the GDR's cultural life: "Jazz reception sharpens the aesthetic sensibility and activates creativity while still retaining its aspect of entertainment. *New Jazz* has personality-building qualities and therefore has a vital essential function in the cultural life of our society."[55] Noglik interpreted the function of *New Jazz* according to socialist-realist dogma, as a music that simultaneously appealed to a broader spectrum of audiences (*unterhaltend*), uplifted the intellect, and helped to forge the socialist self.

---

[49] Noglik, *Jazzwerkstatt International*. Both English and German terms were used. See programs of 1. Jazz Tage der DDR, 1985. Mühe, "Jazz in der DDR (III)," 27. Cf. also Bert Noglik, "Rezeptionsästhetische Aspekte des zeitgenössischen Jazz," *Informationen der Generaldirektion beim Komitee für Unterhaltungskunst*, no. 5 (1986).
[50] Scott Saul, *Freedom Is, Freedom Ain't: Jazz and the Making of the Sixties* (Cambridge, Mass., London: Harvard University Press, 2003), 149.
[51] Rempel, "Jazz: Woher – Wohin?"
[52] Mühe, "Jazz in der DDR (I)," 29.
[53] Ibid., 29–30.
[54] Noglik, "Spontaneität und Konzeption – zur Jazz-Szene in der DDR."
[55] Ibid., 159.

Such claims explicitly invoked the discourse about the socialist experiment. Perpetual jazz workshops reflected a society that was concordant with socialism: within a communal effort, individuals sublimated their egos in order to create, even as within that creative act the individual found self-fulfillment. Individuality expressed itself without overpowering other players and without interfering with the "common melody created through collective interplay."[56] In this respect, *New Jazz* embodied the ideal socialist society in which collectivism and individualism were not antitheses: the individual's obligations toward the collective and the collective's obligations toward the individual were not mutually exclusive. On the contrary, individual positions offered constructive correctives to the collective, thereby improving the socialist project. Detached from the crude realities of real existing socialism, the music created in these workshops functioned as a tangible way to live out a socialist utopia.

The view of a uniquely national GDR jazz culture was not just limited to theorists; however, jazz musicians themselves pursued it too. Around 1973, the first professional jazz musicians, trained in East Germany's most prestigious conservatories, broke away from the yoke of dance-hall and popular music-making.[57] What they later recalled as a "professionalizing of jazz" began in the first half of the 1970s and encompassed state-sponsored free jazz activities, including rehearsals, recordings, and tours, making them financially independent and providing them the freedom of unrestricted experimentation, particularly in pursuing free forms of improvisation.[58] Reflecting on this era, musicians themselves acknowledged the political nature of these developments, keeping their eyes on past and present alike. Saxophonist Petrowsky saw his music as both emulating American jazz and combining it with music of the Weimar era: "We try to work with material we know. Free jazz gave us a chance to work independently with the music of Monk and Mingus as well as with the socially relevant music of Eisler and Dessau."[59] Hanns Eisler's musical heritage remained throughout

---

[56] Mühe, "Jazz in der DDR (I)"; "Jazz in der DDR (III)."
[57] Martin Linzer, "Jazz, zeitgenössisch: Meinungen zu Standort und Perspektive einer Kunstgattung," *Kassette 6: Ein Almanach für Bühne, Podium und Manege* (1982): 209.
[58] Noglik, "Spontaneität und Konzeption – zur Jazz-Szene in der DDR," 159; Rolf Reichelt, "Zur gegenwärtigen Repräsentanz des Jazz in der DDR," *Informationen der Generaldirektion beim Komitee für Unterhaltungskunst* (2/1979); Linzer, "Jazz, zeitgenössisch."
[59] Ernst-Ludwig Petrowsky (born 1933), 1956 Conservatory Franz Liszt in Weimar, 1957–60 Orchester Eberhard Weise, 1960–61 Tanz-und Schauorchester Max Reichelt, 1962–70 Manfred Ludwig Sextett, from 1967 Jazz Ensemble Studio IV, from 1968 international concert tours with various ensembles. 211.

the 1970s and 1980s a touchstone for GDR jazz musicians, exemplified in projects such as the Eisler commemoration concerts in 1988 featured at Jazzbühne in Berlin.[60] Elsewhere, Friedhelm Schönfeld, musical manager of the theater in the Palace of the Republic, explained his music in a similar way, as standing within a specific European tradition, connected to the modernism of Schönberg and Eisler as well as to German folklore. Writing at the time, he reflected that

> The Schönfeld Trio feels obliged to the 1960s' free jazz movement, which gave European musicians the chance to find ways based on our own tradition and to break away from American role models. We understand free jazz as a free play in a framework of concepts and as the utilization of musical elements of folklore and contemporary music.[61]

In perhaps one of the most succinct claims on record, pianist Ulrich Gumpert formalized the emancipatory process of GDR jazz in these words: "We cannot just divest ourselves of something [old], we must also create something new. This is a revolutionary principle."[62]

This conscious identification with German musical heritage manifested in multiple ways. In their recordings and performances of the 1970s, musicians combined elements of the pool of German musical tradition with jazz. Sommer's contribution with Bach and Liszt, described above, was but one example. As the title suggests, Gumpert based his compositions of *From German Lands – Suite based on Themes of German Folk Songs (Aus Teuschen Landen – Suite nach Motiven Deutscher Volkslieder)* on German *Volkslieder* dating back to the 1500s, choosing as well to use the eighteenth-century spelling of *Teutschen* rather than *Deutschen*.[63] This particular recording was used as educational material from 1983 on the Schola label, aimed at secondary school students, and featured traditional

---

[60] GDR broadcast commissioned pianist Hanes Zerbe to write a piece for Eisler on what would have been his ninetieth birthday. For a review, see Rainer Bratfisch, "12. Jazzbühne," *Musik und Gesellschaft* (8/1988); "Hanns-Eisler-Projekt: Jazzbühne Berlin '88 des Rundfunks der DDR," *Der Morgen* (May 30, 1988); Jan Eik, "Jazzbühne '88: Eisler und schwarze Klassik," *Weltbühne* (1988/27).

[61] Theater im Palast Palast der Republik, BArch/DC 207/657, "Jazz und Neue Musik" (1976); Interview with the author, 2010.

[62] Linzer, "Jazz, zeitgenössisch," 211.

[63] Vinyl record: Amiga 855 549, "Retrospective 100x Jazz in der Kammer, Jazz in der Kammer Nr. 48," 1977. See Mathias Brüll, *Jazz auf Amiga: Die Schallplatten des Amiga-Labels von 1947 bis 1990* (Berlin: Pro Business, 2003), 260. Performed by the Jazz-Werkstatt-Orchester and directed by Rolf Reichelt, Gumpert's piece was recorded on September 4, 1972, during the 48th concert of the series "Jazz in der Kammer" at the Deutsches Theater in East Berlin by the Rundfunk der DDR and was released by Amiga in 1977.

versions of folk songs alongside the free jazz version of Gumpert's compositions, suggesting, as Noglik had above, an unbroken continuity of music history in socialist Germany.[64] To further demonstrate emancipation from American role models, free jazz recordings and ensembles of this era used predominantly German names and titles: one of Petrowsky's ensembles was titled Bergisch-Brandenburgisches-Quartett, a pun on Bach's *Brandenburgische Konzerte*.[65] As Martin Linzer, one of the leading jazz journalists at the time, and cofounder of the series *Jazz in der Kammer*, stated

> The emancipation of GDR jazz was accomplished through the appropriation of contemporary or free jazz, not as style but as method, whereby our own national tradition was included in the finding of identity: medieval folklore all the way up to the music of the twentieth century such as Schönberg, Weill and Eisler.[66]

The uniquely East German nature of the music carried other dimensions. According to its musicians, GDR jazz was not subject to Western commercial trends. Petrowsky assured his listeners: "We do not borrow phony, insincere styles and elements from the West, such as are embodied in jazz rock and fusion music, even if they are more commercially workable (exploitable)."[67] Such a statement by one of the most respected musicians in the GDR reflected the position that East German free jazz did not depend on a simple, crowd-pleasing melodic or rhythmic structure. As discussed in previous chapters, the tendency to denounce commercialism stemmed from the jazz discourse of the 1950s and 1960s, in which escapism and stupefaction of the people were identified as the products of the Western musical industry. Indeed, critiques of "commercial" music delineated GDR free jazz from Western styles throughout the 1970s and 1980s, exemplified by jazz rock ensembles such as *Weather Report* or productions of the West German label ECM.[68]

The freedom to experiment was further nurtured by state sponsorship guaranteeing the musicians' livelihoods. Observing this shift, pianist Ulrich

[64] Schola 875123 VEB Deutsche Schallplatten, *Zum Jazz. Musikalische Beispiele für die Behandlung der Stoffeinheit 5 (Der Jazz als Ausdruck der Protesthaltung gegen Ausbeutung und Rassenunterdrückung), Klasse 10* (1983).

[65] Bergisch-Brandenburgisches-Quartett, Amiga 856031, February 1984. Titles include compositions such as: *Ohne Telefonbücher, Empfindungen und Nachempfindungen, Die Kuh mit den zehn Litern, Neapolitanische Schwermut*. See Brüll, *Jazz auf Amiga*, 312–13.

[66] Linzer, "Jazz, zeitgenössisch," p. 211.

[67] Ibid., 213.

[68] See Bert Noglik, "5. Leipziger Jazztage," *Melodie und Rhythmus* (September 1980).

Gumpert remarked: "What is happening musically under our conditions, in our social and cultural setting, has unique characteristics."[69] Gumpert here alluded to the belief that state-sponsored culture, independent from market coercion, maximized artistic freedom. Similarly, Petrowsky, conscious of his privileged position as a state artist, declared:

> In my opinion, one characteristic of the situation of our jazz musicians is the fact that the state takes them so seriously. We have a close relationship to our state, which has become for us so natural and mutual. Since I have spoken to musicians from abroad, I know that this situation would be unthinkable in the West … we live in a very different reality, and cultural politics in our country addresses the needs of all groups of society. Here, jazz is an emancipated genre in the ensemble of the arts.[70]

Petrowsky, who received the GDR art award in 1982, was one of the few who was allowed to engage with the international jazz scene including that of North America (his travels to the West had included a performance organized by his friend and mentor Karl Heinz Deim at the 1968 Montreux festival). These players realized their position only after exchanges with colleagues abroad and came to appreciate the privileges of their artistic lives in the GDR, including travel across the Iron Curtain. Within the GDR, an increase in opportunities to participate on international stages, and the growing exchange with Western bands in the 1970s was in some cases seen as a positive step on the path to determine a national musical identity. Gumpert himself stated that if "we want to reach world-class levels, we have to grapple with the world's standards. Since we have begun to perform internationally, critics recognize our music as GDR jazz … the increasing internationalization pushes us to define our position."[71]

If these ideas about a uniquely East German style of free jazz were discussed in the standard venues for jazz discourse – newspapers, commentary, and broadcast outlets – they also showed up in the performance venues themselves. As noted above, the Deutsches Theater hosted *Jazz in der Kammer* featuring modern and experimental jazz as an integral part of its programming. Since 1965, these events were strictly oriented toward contemporary jazz, namely jazz made in the GDR, jazz from other socialist countries, and jazz from the European West. Moreover, international stars also appeared at the Jazzbühne Berlin – arguably the most sensational jazz event in the GDR, held at the new Friedrichstadt-Palast – with concerts

[69] Linzer, "Jazz, zeitgenössisch," 213.
[70] Ibid., 209.
[71] Ibid., 213; Likewise, see Noglik, "Spontaneität und Konzeption – zur Jazz-Szene in der DDR," 163.

featuring players from abroad, such as Ornette Coleman, Art Blakey, and Dizzy Gillespie. Of course, these venues and others were critical to the dissemination of free jazz in the GDR, but no venue was more visible, prominent, or symbolic than the Palace of the Republic (*Palast der Republik*) in Berlin. The Palace was a symbol of state power as well as state culture, housing the people's parliament and staging SED party conventions, which were celebrated with cultural presentations. For the public, it functioned as a house with music, art, theatre, and gastronomy. The Palace's theater was called TIP (*Theater im Palast*) and was directed by Vera Oelschlegel, who was ambitious to meet the expectations of East Berlin as the GDR's cosmopolitan capital. TIP featured plays and performances by internationally known artists from both sides of the Iron Curtain, such as composers Luigi Nono and Alfred Schnittke, singer Bulat Okudshawa, and writers Boris Polewoi, Stanislav Lem, Friedrich Dürrenmatt, Anna Seghers, Günter Grass, Ernst Jandl, and Elfriede Mayröcker.[72] This claim to global cosmopolitanism was complemented by celebrating the work of the founding fathers of GDR culture, such as Hanns Eisler, Paul Dessau, and Berthold Brecht. Critically, from its start in 1976 under the direction of Friedhelm Schönfeld, cultural offerings at the Palace included a jazz series, *Jazz International*, featuring concerts that included international experimental jazz, fusing German musical heritage with modern experimentalism. Ultimately, while an entire history just of this performance series could well be written, one thing is clear: if free jazz had been searching for legitimacy, no greater cultural credibility could be gained than by its appearance in the beating heart of the East German political body (Figure 5.2).

In the 1970s, critics and musicians saw free improvised jazz made in the GDR as exemplifying a uniquely socialist German art form, on multiple levels. First, from a sociological perspective, the music was conceived within a collective in which individual expression could thrive. While inspired by American role models, it enjoyed consensus with the socialist system but did not serve (as in the United States) as an instrument of class warfare. Second, from a historical perspective, it linked medieval folk traditions to Weimar modernity as well as to the founding fathers of German socialist music in an unbroken chain of continuity. Third, from a socio-economic perspective, free jazz remained independent from market coercion in its sponsorship by state agencies. Musicians enjoyed mutually beneficial relationships with the state, in which they could both freely

---

[72] "Theater im Palast: Die zweiten 5 jahre" (Berlin: Theater im Palast, 1986).

Figure 5.2   Palast der Republik (demolished), regularly featuring contemporary
jazz performances. Photograph by Hubert Link, October 3, 1979.
Bundesarchiv: 183-U1003-024

create and function as representatives of a German socialist culture. Yet despite the growing popularity of the form and its ideological harmony with socialism, in the 1970s and 1980s, jazz still demanded the close scrutiny of the East German state. *New Jazz* festivals that required monitoring and control were popping up all over the country, as evidenced by the case of a young jazz enthusiast and STASI informant in the small town of Peitz.

The STASI at Woodstock

In late September 1972 in the eastern district of Cottbus, MfS officers Henoch, Fritzsche, and Vogel of Department XX decided to recruit a twenty-two-year-old man in the village of Peitz, near the Polish border.[73]

---

[73] State Security Department XX was responsible for cultural affairs, alternative social groups (*Untergrund*), as well as churches.

Figure 5.3   Jazz entrepreneurs Peter Metag (center left) and Ulrich Blobel (far right) with pianist Alexander von Schlippenbach (center), at the Peitz Festival in 1982. Photo by Otto Sill, used by permission

Ulrich Blobel (Figure 5.3), an employee at the optician Thoma-Optik and the leader of the town's youth club, had come to the officers' attention due to his involvement in the jazz scene. That year, Blobel had attempted to found a jazz club in Cottbus. Although Blobel's initiative had some support among officials, the city did not initially grant him the required permissions. According to declassified files, it seems that local functionaries did not exactly trust the ideological aims of Blobel and his friends, suspecting that they were primarily interested in organizing musical events that, in the past, had attracted large crowds.[74] Accordingly, these functionaries stigmatized Blobel and his friends, who sported long hair and blue jeans, as "hippies and tramps."[75] Such signs of Western decadence (*Dekadenz*) did not coincide with the image of jazz in the GDR that had projected

[74] BStU, MfS, "Thomas" Band I, p. 29.
[75] Ibid., 11–13. For a discussion on social profiling in the SED state, see Rauhut, *Ein Klang - Zwei Welten: Blues im geteilten Deutschland* (Transcript Verlag, 2016).

the cultural ascendency of socialism. Such events, dedicated to the sounds of free jazz, conflicted with the image of jazz as a respected art form in socialist society, as exemplified by *Hausmusik*, discussed in Chapter 3. Nevertheless, Blobel was eventually given permission to pursue his free jazz events in Cottbus and Peitz under the series title *Jazzwerkstatt*.

According to STASI officers, Blobel was an "intelligent and eloquent man," with excellent organizational abilities.[76] He operated an extended network of contacts and produced performances with bands such as Pantha-Rei, SOK, Modern Soul, the Friedhelm Schönfeld Trio, Klaus Lenz, Uschi Brüning, and Etta Cameron.[77] Both Blobel and his companion Jimi Metag (nicknamed "Peter" in his STASI file) were familiar with bureaucratic processes, negotiations with artists, and the organizational necessities of these events. STASI agents noted that Blobel showed mastery in handling logistical procedures, whereas Metag took the role of musical adviser, but both seemed to have been genuinely fascinated by the music and shared a deep passion for experimental jazz. STASI informants marveled how Blobel's normally business-like attitude transformed into that of a pure aficionado: observing that "[his] sovereign demeanor as promoter stands in stark contrast to his manners during a live jazz concert: here he trembles and convulses and moves more or less freely to the rhythm of the music."[78]

The STASI meticulously planned his recruitment, tightening the net around Blobel by activating informants in his vicinity, leading toward the final step of direct contact. According to agent Vogel, November 1, 1972, was the first meeting between Blobel and the STASI. The officers applied a routine of intimidation and relief that went as follows: that day, Blobel was charged to "clarify an issue" at the local police station, which set him deeply ill at ease, given that he was unaware of the reason for the charge. There, Vogel disclosed his identity as a STASI officer and explained that Blobel was, in fact, not charged with any misdoings at all. Instead, Vogel invited him to an informal conservation over beer in a local pub. The change of venue combined with the relief of avoiding police charges must have eased Blobel's mind, for he accompanied Vogel to the pub, and listened "receptively and attentively" to what the officer

---

[76] BStU, MfS, "Thomas" Band I, p. 27. Blobel was aware of the formalities necessary for the production of concerts: *1. Genehmigung des ABV; 2. Genehmigung Abteilung Kultur, Rat des Kreises; 3. Genehmigung Abteilung Preise, Rat des Kreises; 4. Genehmigung Volkspolizei.*

[77] Ibid., p. 47.

[78] Ibid., p. 39.

had to say. Under the pretext of problems concerning youth and controlling crime, Vogel won Blobel's consent and the two agreed to follow-up meetings.

Even so, to ensure that the young man of "decadent attire with long hair and full beard" would function as a dependable informant, the STASI conducted a thorough background check, investigating his *vita*, family ties, and political convictions.[79] Then, on May 8, 1973, Blobel waited at a predetermined location, where agents Vogel and Fritzsche picked him up and drove to a secluded area. As they had done before, they reiterated the dependency of the GDR's security on the cooperation of its citizens, and that the bonds between the STASI and regular citizens were based primarily on trust and camaraderie. According to the officers, Blobel was outspoken and conscientious and wrote out his commitment by hand, becoming IM Thomas.[80] Small though his signature may have been, this "contract" granted Blobel *carte-blanche* to pursue his grand ambitions, enabling him to launch an unparalleled international music promotion business over the course of the next decade, which would in turn make the small city of Peitz a place of legendary reputation in the history of GDR jazz.

As noted above, the partial opening of the GDR after the West German-East German treaties in the early 1970s was part of the diplomatic trade-off of *Ostpolitik*. From 1972 onward, the border between East and West grew increasingly porous, keeping security officials on alert. Nevertheless, despite their caution, the STASI acted according to Honecker's new course in foreign policy, with local agents tolerating Blobel's international networking in music production and granting him an almost unrestrained flow of information across the Iron Curtain. Taking advantage of this newly opened window, one of the first people Blobel contacted was Joachim Ernst Berendt in Baden-Baden in West Germany. Berendt, who just had ended his position as producer of the Berliner Jazz Tage (West), replied to Blobel's request for contacts with valuable information.[81]

---

[79] Ibid., pp. 53–57. Vorschlag zur Werbung eines IMS, Cottbus, den 8.5.1973. The STASI approved of his family's working-class background and general socialist leanings, which probably helped with his recruitment.

[80] Ibid., pp. 59–62: *Bericht über die erfolgte Verpflichtung der in der VA. IM VI/1012/72 erfaßten Person.* Blobel's handwritten commitment as follows: *"Hiermit verpflichte ich mich auf freiwilliger Basis mit dem Ministerium für Staatssicherheit zusammen zuarbeiten. Ich werde alle Handlungen, die gegen die DDR und das sozialistische Lager gerichtet sind ehrlich und unverzüglich dem MfS mitteilen. Über diese inoffizielle Zusammenarbeit mit dem MfS werde ich zu jeder Zeit und gegenüber jeder Person strengstes Stillschweigen bewahren. Zur Abdeckung meiner inoffiziellen Tätigkeit wähle ich mir den Decknamen 'Thomas.'"*

[81] Letter from Berendt to Blobel, February 11, 1974. Ibid., pp. 67–68.

These contacts formed the core cell of his musical network that, under the watchful eye of the STASI, he would soon expand across Europe. The STASI, on the other hand, ordered a comprehensive observation of Blobel himself involving dozens of informants and the diligent monitoring of his mail to and from the West. Indeed, few letters went unread, and few packages went unopened and their contents recorded, before they reached their recipients. And in those instances when Blobel had not previously informed the STASI about a posting, which had been part of their agreement, the officers rebuked him for his dereliction and, in some cases, punitively interfered in his correspondence.[82]

The monitoring of Western contacts was of the utmost importance for the STASI. Comparisons with Werner Sellhorn here are revealing: like Sellhorn fifteen years earlier, Blobel was recruited as an informant for just this reason. Both Sellhorn (IM Zirkel) and Blobel (IM Thomas) were familiar with the jazz scene in East and West, and both were recruited in crucial phases of state political history, when the STASI sought to combat the danger of Western ideological infiltration. Sellhorn had become an informant in 1958, when Western jazz propaganda was staged primarily in West Berlin (until the Wall was built in 1961), and Blobel had joined in 1973, when the border became permeable once more. Both informants were able to supply STASI officers with enough information to ensure the identities of those involved in the jazz exchange between East and West, and furthermore, just as Sellhorn eventually withdrew from STASI cooperation in the early 1960s when it ceased to benefit him, so Blobel did later on. Both cases reveal the degree of leeway the STASI could give an individual, having established their integrity, but such leeway did not necessarily mean lifelong collaboration: following his involvement, Sellhorn pursued a career as a jazz entrepreneur and emcee within the GDR, and Blobel was eventually able to leave altogether in 1984.

As revealing of state practices as such comparisons are, however, the differences between Sellhorn and Blobel are also instructive. While Sellhorn's career was determined by the parameters of the enclosed society within the Wall after 1961, Blobel, from the beginning of his cooperation with state officials, envisioned his operations extending beyond the physical limitations of the Iron Curtain. The changes in GDR foreign policy in the early 1970s inspired the twenty-year-old to widen his radius of action

---

[82] In one of his letters to the West, Blobel claims to his correspondent that he "never had problems" with his mail, a dubious claim at best, and one that in fact indirectly admits to STASI cooperation. Ibid., p. 138.

beyond political borders, connecting Eastern and Western jazz scenes in two key ways. First, Blobel managed to bring Western bands to Peitz from 1976 onward, such as OM from Switzerland, an early guest of the club.[83] The incentive for the young entrepreneur might have been to increase his ticket sales, but nevertheless, he relentlessly pursued encounters between East and West on the grassroots level. Second, the fact that in 1973 both Germanies had joined the United Nations motivated Blobel to engage in correspondence with international organizations such as the jazz federations in Vienna and Warsaw. As a result, in 1976 Blobel registered the Peitz club with the International Jazz Federation and, from then on, received publications of the jazz organization from Warsaw.[84] This jazz club (Jazz Werkstatt Peitz) would go on to sponsor one of the most important free jazz events and open air festivals in the region, the festival at Peitz, first held in 1979.

The Peitz festival seems to have appealed to a broad spectrum of people, not necessarily all drawn by free jazz. Students and academics as well as white- and blue-collar workers undertook the pilgrimage in June for a festival that sought to represent the range of the European avant-garde (Figure 5.4). Some participants indulged in the melodic sounds of guitar, flute, or jaw harp, singing along to such Western hits as Neil Young's *Heart of Gold*, and yet others, in the evening hours after beer and wine, preferred German *Volkslieder*.[85] What united all festivalgoers in Peitz, though, was its nonconformist ambience. For jazz connoisseurs as well as for others, the festival served as a space in the enclosed society in which to imagine alternatives in entertainment and lifestyle. Although the *Jazzwerkstatt* series and its corresponding festival were produced within the state's institutional framework, and by the mid-1970s were receiving rave reviews in the state press and periodicals, contemporaries often praised the festival's autonomy and semilegality.[86] Such perceptions were

---

[83] Ibid.

[84] On October 15, 1976, IM Hubert Franke informed the agency that Blobel had begun the registration process, as well as that Blobel had privately criticized party authorities. (Ibid., p. 287.) On August 17, 1977, IM Frank Kröber further informed the STASI that the International Jazz Federation had sent its publications to the youth club Forum K. in Cottbus. BStU, MfS, "Thomas" Band II, p. 13.

[85] *Woodstock am Karpfenteich: Die Jazzwerkstatt Peitz* (Bundeszentrale für politische Bildung, 2011), 109. See also Bert Noglik, "Peitz und der Feuerschlucker vom Centre Pompidou," in *Woodstock am Karpfenteich: Die Jazzwerkstatt Peitz* (Bundeszentrale für politische Bildung, 2011).

[86] Frank Starke, "Beliebte Montagstreffs mit Gesprächen und Jazz: Cottbuser Veranstaltungen für Mittzwanziger," *Neues Deutschland* (August 26, 1977). Noglik, "Peitz und der Feuerschlucker vom Centre Pompidou."

Figure 5.4   Jazz workshop with Petrovsky on saxophone and welders on stage at Peitz
Festival. Photo by Otto Sill, used by permission

generated by the fact that *Jazzwerkstatt* arose from a grassroots initiative, and that Blobel and cofounder Jimi Metag were well-established in the local scene. Furthermore, the absence of state enforcers such as police or mass organizations like the FDJ contributed to the festival's reputation as an autonomous event. However, the omnipresence of the STASI apparatus was beyond the immediate perception of festival participants, and only their tight grip on the scene via Blobel as an informant enabled their tolerance toward an event on that scale. Nevertheless, until 1982, this "Woodstock on the carp lake" attracted thousands of attendees and grew to become one of the most prominent international free jazz events in the country (Figure 5.5).

Young people attracted to Peitz came seeking an alternative experience on the periphery of East German society, building tents and settling on the meadows surrounding the central amphitheater each summer. The audience there, around the theater, was the core of the free jazz scene at Peitz. Here, one paid serious, critical attention to the music. As one contemporary put it, "a tacit ban on laughter dominated the audience," a notion that becomes clear when examining photographs depicting the

Figure 5.5   Audience at the 1981 Peitz Jazz Festival, including critic Bert Noglik (center left, in jacket). Photo by Matthias Creutziger, used by permission

faces of earnest young jazz enthusiasts.[87] These were the people who worshipped the GDR's free jazz scene and knew its music, as well as its history and literature, by heart.[88] Recalling the ambience of the festival years later, jazz critic and writer Bert Noglik described the meaning of the music to its listeners: "What this music was really trying to say remained vague. In any case it produced a feeling of being alive. One could find protest and despair. In the course of this interplay, free of conventional rules, one could also see a new art of social communication."[89] Noglik's perspective in hindsight echoes others: many contemporary accounts express similar effects on the audience during the live performances.[90] It seems that the experience of a live performance intended to engage a nonverbal dialogue that fascinated audiences with its chaotic, anarchic qualities, allowing for tension, conflict, contradiction, and disharmony. On these grounds, it is equally possible to see how the fascination of this music lay in the friction

---

[87] Noglik, "Peitz und der Feuerschlucker vom Centre Pompidou."
[88] Ulrich Steinmetzger, "Das richtige Leben im falschen," in *Woodstock am Karpfenteich: Die Jazzwerkstatt Peitz* (Bundeszentrale für politische Bildung, 2011).
[89] Noglik, "Peitz und der Feuerschlucker vom Centre Pompidou," 40.
[90] Interviews with the author: Martin Linzer, 2010, and Rolf Reichelt, 2009.

it projected onto a society that felt the need to permanently reaffirm harmony and consensus on its journey to a socialist utopia.

In 1978, five years after his recruitment, an internal evaluation of IM Thomas revealed the STASI's increasing frustration with its informant. In an anonymous report, a STASI officer lamented Blobel's recent unreliability and how still, after so many years, Blobel refused to report in a politically compromising manner on his friends and acquaintances. STASI agents had often asked Blobel about his friends' political standpoints or possible subversive acts and ultimately labeled him with the unwelcome charge of "political blindness." The following quote reveals the officer's position on the ideological frontlines, and the need to avert cultural infiltration from the West: "[IM Thomas] is acquainted with a large number of people which are of great interest for the MfS, because they represent in the cultural realm a potential reserve of the enemy."[91] Yet Blobel's refusal to report on such matters hindered neither his music promotion business nor his networking on the international level. On the contrary, his Western contacts remained of great interest to state officials: the screening of his correspondence did not just serve to monitor IM Thomas but provided the STASI access to the Western jazz network; thus, the opportunity to expand its net of observation in enemy territory.

Blobel's cooperation with the STASI came to an abrupt halt when in April 1980 authorities denied him the status of the "travel-cadre" (*Reisekader*). His application to accompany the Conny (Konrad) Bauer Quartet to the West was rejected because he was supposed to function as a "contact person to people in West Germany, who were in contact with the West German Ministry for Inter-German Relations."[92] It seems that STASI officers had reason to believe that Blobel might have had intended to function as a double agent. Blobel did not refrain from expressing his anger about this turn of affairs and threatened municipal authorities with complaints to the Department of Culture at the ZK. These events were typical of a pattern of action, wherein a regional authority blocked movement across the Iron Curtain, but because of the political ascendance of artists and jazz entrepreneurs in the state's hierarchy of power – an ascendance discussed below – Blobel and Bauer were in a greater position to put pressure on those regional offices. In this particular case, however, it was to no avail: the Conny Bauer Quartet traveled without him.[93] In 1981, another application to travel to the West, with guitarist Uwe Kropinski,

[91] BStU, MfS, "Thomas" Band II, p. 70.
[92] Ibid., p. 155.
[93] Ibid., p. 121.

met the same fate. This time, Blobel addressed a letter directly to the STASI headquarters in Berlin, complaining vehemently about the prohibition. Illustrating the importance of his stature in the GDR jazz scene, he asked whether such treatment was the reward for his loyalty to the state.[94] From that time on, he continuously avoided contact with the STASI, and flaunting his distaste for state authorities, he was increasingly outspoken about his political opinions of the GDR.[95]

In truth, however, another fact had annoyed Blobel that might have prompted him to dissent. Shortly before the fourth Peitz festival in 1982, officials withdrew both Blobel's and Metag's financial and organizational authority, an authority that they had enjoyed for over ten years. Since 1972, the STASI had known about the promoters' corrupt handling of festival finances as well as illegal acts circumventing formal procedures and had nonetheless tolerated it. As Blobel remarked in a 2009 interview, it was possible to earn a considerable private income within the communist economy, even if during this interview he did not specify how he managed to do so. His STASI file, though, discloses his and Metag's procedures for cheating local and regional authorities. In some cases, Blobel circumvented the state's tour management company (Konzert- und Gastspieldirektion, KGD), which owned the monopoly on importing artists from abroad. Blobel simply did not officially announce his events but instead sent out tickets privately and invited the musicians (including some from the West) on a private basis. With black market prices reaching 100 marks (in comparison, the rent for the venue was only 200 marks), combined with the practice of underreporting how many tickets had been sold for various concerts, Blobel and Metag were able to pocket a great deal of money.[96]

---

[94] BStU, MfS, AS 202/85, Letter from Blobel to MfS dated December 21, 1981.

[95] Assessment, IM Thomas, October 1, 1980. See BStU, MfS, "Thomas" Band II, pp. 135–136.

[96] BStU, MfS, "Thomas" Band I, p. 27: Bericht über die Person Blobel vom 13.10.1972. *"Bei diesen Instituten ist es jedoch möglich etwas zu mogeln. Bei der Preisgenehmigung kann man Punkte, wie zum Beispiel Saalmiete höher veranschlagen als nötig. Weiterhin mehr Personen zulassen als genehmigt."* Band I, pp. 241–42: Bericht über die Jazzwerkstatt Nr. X in Peitz vom 19.11.1975. *"...Das Bemerkenswerte war auch, daß die Veranstaltung nirgends publiziert wurde. Die Karten wurden von Blobel und Metag persönlich vertreiben bzw. verschickt....Eine Person hat sich über die Kartenverteilung und den Preisen zur Jazzveranstaltung beschwert, die im Forum K. praktiziert wurde. Metag hatte dort die Karten von einer Rolle verkauft, nur 1. bis 6. Reihe des Peitzer Kinos."* Band II, pp. 38–39: Theaterkontrolle im Filmtheater Peitz, 25.2.1978: *"Durch den Ordnungsdienst wurde uns mitgeteilt, dass nach Beginn von Jugendlichen noch 100 Mark für den Erwerb einer Karte geboten wurde."* Band I, p. 118: Bericht zum Jazzklub Peitz vom 23.12.1974: *"Doch die angewandte Praxis - Ansprechen vom Musikern im Ausland, ohne die KGD oder Künstleragentur einzubeziehen, ist ungesetzlich. Auch ist die Frage der Verrechnung der Honorare und der Steuerabrechnung durch den Klub nicht bekannt. Der Klub sollte sich an das Kreiskabinett Cottbus/Land wenden, um seiner Arbeit endlich einen legalen Ausdruck zu geben."*

All this was known and tolerated by the STASI as long as Blobel was a cooperative informant, but in April 1981, his handlers wrote a final report about IM Thomas that ended the relationship with their unpredictable informant.[97] Subsequently, in March 1982, the state's financial auditors investigated Blobel's and Metag's illegal dealings and removed their authority. After all, the coming festival in June was already under the control of the regional authorities of Cottbus.[98] Blobel finally left the GDR in January 1984 and settled in Wuppertal, where he continued his music promotion business via his extended network. He managed to fund his activities through cultural institutions such as the Kulturamt Wuppertal but also through the American Embassy in East Berlin.[99] Ironically, within a short time, he was able to establish himself as a jazz promoter in the West, orchestrating tours and events featuring many of the same artists with whom he had worked back home in the East. To this day, he is a successful jazz promoter receiving funds from the Federal Republic of Germany.

To conclude, just as Sellhorn's cooperation with the STASI had launched his career as one of the most prominent figures in East German jazz, it also granted Blobel an outstanding career in jazz promotion, which he was able to continue even after he had settled in West Germany. Both individuals' activities as informants fundamentally altered their own professional lives, but they also influenced significant developments in East German jazz. There is no doubt that neither Blobel's nor Sellhorn's activities would have reached the scales they did without STASI involvement, which suggests that the STASI did indeed represent a power in the realm of culture beyond the mere means of repression. In some respects, the position of jazz in the GDR cultural landscape had remained uncontested since 1962, with its scene mainly just observed and documented. But what is interesting here is that the mutual dependency of the STASI and its informants created a dynamic that directly shaped the cultural landscape, in that the STASI hereby manipulated the development of live jazz in the GDR. Nor were Sellhorn and Blobel alone: other declassified state files

---

[97] Abschlußbericht zum IM-Vorgang THOMAS, REG.-NR. VI/1012/72. BStU, MfS, "Thomas" Band II, p. 168.

[98] BStU, MfS, Cottbus, AGK 123 Nr. 52/82, Information über geplante Veranstaltungen der Jazz-Werkstatt Peitz am 26–27 Juni 1982.

[99] BStU, MfS, HA II 21578, Blobel's letters from West Germany to the US Embassy in East Berlin. As well as containing his correspondence, this file contains lists of the bands he is managing from West Germany. Prior to his departure in January 1984, he had assisted the US Embassy in organizing jazz events (pp. 49–50).

suggest the complicity of even more jazz informants.[100] But despite such manipulations from one area of state control, as the 1970s waxed on, jazz took on yet another role in state diplomacy, a role examined below.

Jazz as Diplomacy and *Jazz Now*

In the summer of 1972, West Berlin jazz entrepreneur Jost Gebers, the cofounder of Free Music Production (FMP), an internationally acclaimed free jazz label, received a curious phone call. The caller, allegedly a representative of the Berliner Rundfunk, expressed great interest in the West Berlin jazz scene and in FMP's work and asked for a meeting with the West German producer.[101] At first, Gebers did not fully understand to whom he was speaking, until the caller suggested that they meet near Bahnhof Friedrichstraße, in the eastern sector of the city. In a recent interview, Gebers recalled: "As we were first talking, I did not at all realize that this man was calling from East Berlin. He introduced himself as a man from Radio Berlin, and asked if we could meet and I just said, 'yes, sure, where and when.'" Once Gebers had understood that the caller was from the East, however, he tensed up. "At that point I was on full alert. It was a little spooky, because I did not usually get calls from the East, and I thought people there were not allowed to make Western contacts."[102]

As noted above, in the early 1970s, it had become easier for West Berliners to travel to the eastern part of the city. A few days after the phone call, Gebers undertook the short journey from his residence in Charlottenburg to Friedrichstraße, to the other side of the Wall. When he arrived, he met two men: Rolf Reichelt, a musician and journalist trained at the Dresden Conservatory and producer for the show *Jazzwerkstatt* at the GDR Berliner Rundfunk, and the jazz bandleader and saxophonist Ernst-Ludwig Petrowsky. Reichelt was keen to connect with a kindred spirit, who would be able to provide Western jazz records such as those of FMP, where Gebers had been producing records and free jazz shows since the late 1960s. That day, Gebers brought samples of the latest FMP productions, including sought-after Western vinyl.[103]

---

[100] Cf. BStU, MfS, "Sander."
[101] See reviews of records: www.fmp-label.de/.
[102] Interview with the author, 2009.
[103] Gebers had founded the label on the initiative of musician Peter Brötzmann; in the early 1970s FMP had featured musicians such as Brötzmann, Manfred Schoof, Alexander von Schlippenbach, Gunter Hampel, Peter Kowald, and Sven-Åke Johansson.

After an inspiring discussion about jazz in East and West, Reichelt suggested he take Gebers to a nearby jazz session. On Prenzlauer Berg at Kulturhaus Erich Franz (the same place where the jazz club met in the 1950s, then the location of the DSF) under the leadership of pianist Ulrich Gumpert, a large ensemble was preparing for a concert. Gebers was delighted with this unexpected experience, and soon thereafter, on September 4, 1972, he returned to East Berlin to attend a performance of the longstanding series *Jazz in der Kammer* at the Deutsches Theater. There, Gumpert's Jazz-Werkstatt-Orchester presented concert No. 48 of the series, whose musicians included Petrowsky, Manfred Schulze, Ulrich Gumpert, and Günter "Baby" Sommer.[104] Gebers had been aware of these names, having known their music through GDR Radio jazz programs received in West Berlin, but the opportunity to experience the music in a live setting was a markedly different experience – and, as this section explores, would in fact influence the history of jazz in both countries. For what followed Jost Geber's musical encounters in East Berlin that summer was a close cooperation between Free Music Productions and the East German free jazz scene that would involve not only proponents of the respective scenes, but high-ranking officials and diplomats on both sides of the Wall as well.

For Gebers, this meeting was only the beginning. For nearly two decades following this encounter, between 1973 and 1989, FMP would produce dozens of records of East German free jazz, and by the late 1970s, East German musicians would be performing at FMP's various concert series as well as at other venues throughout West Germany. Gebers recalled:

> After I met Reichelt and Petrowsky, I came to know Karlheinz Deim, a broadcast functionary, who was a good friend of saxophonist Ernst-Ludwig Petrowsky. We met in Petrowsky's weekend house and got terribly drunk. Deim told me exactly how to proceed in this matter, namely to write a letter to the Ministry for Agitation and Propaganda headed by Werner Lamberz, in which I outlined my goal of producing records of East German jazz.... Deim said that I would get an answer within two days. I was highly doubtful, telling Deim that the ministry would not even receive the letter in two days. But it happened just as Deim had predicted. I had an answer from Lambert's office exactly two days later. It was unbelievable! Usually a letter to the GDR took at least a week!"[105]

[104] Program of concert provided by Wolf "Assi" Glöde. The series ran from 1965 to 1990; concert No. 48 was recorded by Radio DDR. Walter Cikan, "Jazz-Dokumentation, Jazz in der Kammer: 1966–1990," ed. Rundfunk der DDR.
[105] Interview with the author, 2009.

Figure 5.6   Petrowsky Sextet in Studio 4 at Rundfunk der DDR on Nalepastraße where the first FMP record, *Just for Fun*, was recorded. Ernst-Ludwig Petrowsky, saxophone; Hans-Joachim Graswurm, trumpet; Hubert Katzenbeier, trombone; Eberhard Weise, piano; Klaus Koch, bass; Wolfgang Winkler, drums. Photographer unknown. Private collection of Katja Deim, used by permission

The letter Gebers received included all the necessary information, including contacts of people who would handle formalities such as licensing and payments, which Gebers was obliged to pay in Western currency. Shortly thereafter, on April 29, 1973, Gebers was granted access to the recording facilities of Radio DDR, East German state radio, on Nalepastraße in East Berlin, and directed his first sessions with Petrowsky, Konrad Bauer, Klaus Koch and Wolfgang Winkler. The first FMP record featuring GDR musicians was entitled *Just for Fun*[106] (Figure 5.6).

From Gebers' point of view, the speed of the bureaucracy was surprising. But in retrospect, there was more to the story. What Gebers might not have realized was that his request was handled with the utmost priority: he had not contacted a low-level East German office, but rather Karl Heinz Deim, a senior broadcast functionary who had traveled with the

---

[106] Ernst-Ludwig Petrowsky Quartett, *Just for Fun*, FMP 0140.

Jazz Ensemble Studio 4 to the Montreux jazz festival in 1968 and who made the connection. Deim instructed Gebers to send his letter to the office of Werner Lamberz (1929–1978), who since 1967 had served as the ZK secretary for Agitation and Propaganda (AGITPROP).[107] This agency was well-established: Lamberz had succeeded Albert Norden (1904–1982), who had conducted secret operations in West Germany to manipulate West German politics and public discourse toward socialist ideals.[108] The direct handling of Gebers' request through AGITPROP, and the high priority Lamberz's office placed upon it, suggests that the GDR intended to utilize the FMP records of GDR jazz as a propaganda tool in West Germany. This collaboration (and indeed, the following sixteen years of FMP/AGITPROP/Radio DDR coproductions, from 1973 to 1989) must then be understood within the larger context of *Ostpolitik*, as well as the East German state's attempt to connect to and support "progressive artistic forces" in the West. In their belief in a socialist world revolution, ZK members declared in 1972 that

> The changing balance of power between socialism and imperialism as well as the growth of the anti-imperialist movement is bringing about the enforcement of socialist elements of the culture in imperialist countries. There are cultural ambitions in all realms which express in their work a true humanist concern.[109]

From this perspective, the "German jazz rapprochement" more accurately illustrates the complexity of a German-German cultural project across the Iron Curtain, in which all agents involved pursued their own objectives.

Gebers was no stranger to the politics of music, and its place in broader cultural debates. After all, he and saxophonist Peter Brötzmann had initiated one of the first FMP events in the basement of the Delphi Palace in Berlin in 1968, the same venue in which Rex Stewart had given his legendary "air lift" performance in 1948. Twenty years later, however, Berlin was once more the stage for tense ideological confrontation, which generated fierce street violence and set the context for his subsequent work. By

---

[107] Lamberz was head of the department Agitation and Propaganda from 1966 to 1971; Cf. www.argus.bstu.bundesarchiv.de/dy30bla/index.htm.

[108] From 1960 to 1979, Norden was head of the Commission-West at the Politburo of the ZK. Cf. www.bundesstiftung-aufarbeitung.de/wer-war-wer-in-der-ddr-%2363%3B-1424.html?ID=2533. See also Jochen Staadt, "Westarbeit der SED," in *Lexikon de DDR-Sozialismus: Das Staats- und Gesellschaftsystem der Deutschen Demokratischen Republik, Band 2: N-Z*, ed. Horst Möller, Rainer Eppelmann, Günter Nooke, and Dorothee Wilms (Paderborn: Ferdinand Schöningh, 1997).

[109] ZK der SED, "Protokoll der 6. Tagung des Zentralkomitees, parteiinternes Material." BArch/DY 30/IV2/1/458, 1972, p. 40.

the late 1960s, the leftist student movement had rejected the established values of West German society and its NATO allies and demanded anti-authoritarian renewal from the ground up, citing key issues such as coming to terms with the Nazi past, the influence of the right-wing press, the educational system, and the Vietnam War. Student leaders applied Marxist theories of political science and sociology to the social reality of West Germany, rejecting a life organized around the profit motive, careerism, and consumerism. Such notions invoked the teachings of the Frankfurt School, whose social scientists such as Herbert Marcuse, Theodor Adorno, and Max Horkheimer had criticized capitalist consumerism.[110]

Despite these tensions, the student protests had been mainly peaceful until June 1967 when an innocent bystander, Benno Ohnesorg, was shot by a West German policeman, Karl-Heinz Kurras.[111] About a year later, in April 1968, Rudi Dutschke, the movement's most prominent spokesman, was critically wounded by an anti-Communist activist. These events propelled the radicalization of the movement and resulted in street violence not seen since WWII. What the public did not know at the time, however, was that Kurras, the police officer who had killed Ohnesorg, was in truth a STASI agent, a fact not revealed until 2009. In hindsight, such revelations about this *Westarbeit,* the direct involvement of the SED and STASI manipulating public opinion as well as supporting terrorist acts in West Germany, sheds light on to what degree the SED sought to strengthen the West German leftist movement and thereby influence West German politics. After Ohnesorg's death, West German student activists intensified their denunciation of West Germany as a fascist state, echoing what East German propaganda had claimed since its founding. In the course of the student movement's radicalization, the STASI cooperated with and supported terrorist organizations such as the Rote Armee Fraction (RAF), seeking ultimately to destabilize West German society.[112]

---

[110] Belinda Davis, Martin Klimke, Carla MacDougall, and Wilfried Mausbach, *Changing the World, Changing Oneself: Political Protest and Collective Identities in West Germany and in the US in the 1960s and 1970s* (New York; Oxford: Berghahn Books, 2010). As cited in: Timothy Scott Brown, *West Germany and the Global Sixties: The Antiauthoritarian Revolt, 1962–1978* (Cambridge University Press, 2013), 8. In his essay "Résumé über Kulturindustrie," Adorno had criticized *Massenkultur,* a critique that later oriented leftist intellectual concerns about popular culture. See Theodor W. Adorno, "Resume über Kulturindustrie (1963)," in *Texte zur Theorie des Pop,* ed. Charis Goer, Stefan Greif, und Christoph Jacke (Stuttgart: Reclam, 1963/2013).

[111] Later revelations showed that Kurras was a STASI agent. Cf. Sven Felix Kellerhof, *Die Stasi im Westen. Der Kurras Komplex* (Hamburg: Hoffmann und Campe, 2010).

[112] Ibid.

In examining the activities of the West German anti-authoritarian movement of the 1960s and 1970s, Timothy Brown has suggested that these efforts were directed against establishment forces, in general, and that they were part of young people's "multi-faceted assault on the strictures governing artistic and personal expression."[113] Young people initiated a large range of projects and activities to make their voices heard in the so-called "alternative public sphere," which Brown argues was "posited by student activists as an antidote to the deforming power of the mass media."[114] It was thus in this spirit that Gebers and Brötzmann were inspired to launch their project of Free Music Production (FMP). In November of that year, they launched an attack on the jazz establishment with what they called a "Total Music Meeting. " The magazine *Neue Musikzeitung* stated: "It began in 1968, at the first anti-festival organized by Berlin musicians, which was a heated battle-cry against the official Berlin Festival. Its place of birth was the underground pub Quartier des Quasimodo."[115]

This first event provided a forum for what FMP initiators called "free music," liberated from commercial and traditional restraints.[116] What differentiated FMP events from those of the alleged establishment, however, was the audience's strict demand for free forms of improvisation. Here, musicians were verbally criticized (booed) when playing to cantilena, melodic, harmonic, or swing rhythms.[117] According to some critics, musicians were liberated from fulfilling an audience's habitual expectations of listening patterns, after having been "conditioned" by the music presented at official events such as the Berlin Jazz Festival at the Philharmonie, the home of the Berlin Philharmonic Orchestra.[118] Here, in the cellar at Quasimodo's in the basement of the Delphi Palast, by contrast, music critic Werner Panke noted that "stars such as Sonny Sharrock and Pharoah Sanders were able to let go and improvise freely in these long nights."[119] Reviewers applied a conspiratorial ambience to the venue, serving as an underground alternative to above-ground

[113] Brown, *West Germany and the Global Sixties*, 139.
[114] Ibid., 139.
[115] Werner Panke, "Mit eigenen Platten gegen mächtige Krämer: Die Free Music Production macht ihrem Namen alle Ehre," *Neue Musikzeitung* (December 1975/January 1976).
[116] Dieter Zimmerle, *Jazz Podium* (December 1968). According to Zimmerle, FMP producers protested the underrepresentation of free jazz at the Berlin Jazz Festival.
[117] Wolfgang Burde, "Alternative: Total Music Meeting," *Tagesspiegel, Berlin* (November 5, 1972).
[118] Panke, "Mit eigenen Platten gegen mächtige Krämer." Klaus Achterberg, "Wo sich jeder Freispielen kann," *Kulturanzeiger* (April/May 1976).
[119] Panke, "Mit eigenen Platten gegen mächtige Krämer."

concert halls, and as a means of breaking the shackles on self-expression. According to the *Frankfurter Rundschau*, FMP attacked the capitalist music world, liberated jazz from commercial coercion, and provided a forum for the genre that, within a profit-oriented system, could not find an outlet otherwise.[120] Panke reflected that "FMP arose as a needful alternative. Because the business of music could not go on like this any further. The German avant-garde musicians were totally ignored by those mongers who only bargain with this art form."[121] Bolstered by sympathetic views in the left-wing press, FMP styled itself as an alternative to the commercial jazz world represented by major recording labels, offering instead a liberating experiment, which was "to learn and to practice aesthetic and social emancipation in a hostile capitalist environment."[122] Indeed, this experiment was so ideologically amenable to left-wing activists on both sides of the Wall that by 1980 FMP would release the first jazz record, *Touch the Earth*, featuring both East and West Germans on one recording.[123]

On the other side of the Iron Curtain, Marxist cultural theorists interpreted these socio-political developments in West Germany as history in the making. According to chief propagandist Albert Norden, Western leftist intellectuals and artists had finally acknowledged the virulence of the capitalist system and had connected with the social power of the worker's movement.[124] In 1972, at the 6th party meeting of the ZK, Norden explained that awareness of East German cultural life in the West had increased "in literature, political lyrics, political song, in graphics, in record production, and in theater, all of these cultural genres mirror influences which radiate from the GDR."[125] As an illustration of his claim, the ZK trumpeted that in 1971 alone, 530 ensembles and 2,300 soloists had traveled to the GDR from abroad, and 78 ensembles and 1,200 soloists had traveled abroad from the GDR.[126] At long last, Norden and other

[120] Wilhelm E. Liefland, "Der Weg zu uns," *Frankfurter Rundschau* (January 24, 1976).

[121] Panke, "Mit eigenen Platten gegen mächtige Krämer."

[122] Ralph Quinke, "Die Berliner Free Music Production: Musikalische und gesellschaftliche Emanzipation," *Musik und Bildung* (October 1977).

[123] FMP 0730, Leo Smith (trumpet), Peter Kowald (bass), Günter Sommer (drums), recorded at the FLÖZ club, West Berlin, November 13–14, 1979, produced by Jost Gebers. Cf. www.fmp-label.de/fmplabel/index.html.

[124] Albert Norden, "Protokoll der 6. Tagung des Zentralkomitees, BArch/DY 30/IV/2/458" (Zentralkomitee der SED, 1972).

[125] Ibid.

[126] ZK der SED, "Protokoll der 6. Tagung des Zentralkomitees, parteiinternes Material." BArch/DY 30/IV2/1/458, 1972, p. 41.

ideologues believed that socialist culture was finally making an impact on the West. In meetings of the ZK, party leadership proclaimed the superiority of the communist model and cultural production. Norden declared that "in a historically short time" the GDR had "accomplished the birth of a new socialist-national culture, ever growing," precisely because "the means of production are in the possession of the people."[127]

In this context, the SED's course in the early 1970s explains the willing collaboration of Lamberz's office with a West Berlin record label such as FMP. Socialist culture – in this case free jazz, praised by the Western press as a world-class art form – was to function as an ideological tool in the West, projecting openness and tolerance, and was furthermore to espouse countercultural projects based on leftist paradigms. Both East and West free jazz scenes shared more ideological similarities than differences, an accord that motivated their members and supporters to pursue intra-German jazz projects across the Iron Curtain. Proponents of both scenes believed in an anti-capitalist position allowing unrestricted forms of expression emancipated from market conditions. Furthermore, proponents of both scenes saw themselves as insiders active in a counterculture.[128] Proponents of free jazz in the West saw themselves as protesting against commercialism and establishment forces, and those in the East saw themselves as involved in a stimulating alternative cultural scene "under the radar of state authority."[129] Both scenes advocated concepts of "workshop" settings, where music was not so much performed as composed instantaneously, involving musicians and listeners in a collective act. Audiences were tolerant of such experiments and were likewise intolerant of traditional musical parameters such as melody and harmony.[130]

Following Gebers' proposal, Lamberz's AGITPROP effort simultaneously launched the careers of East German musicians in the West and offered these musicians opportunities to produce records as well. Yet the state-owned record company VEB Deutsche Schallplatte, which operated the labels Eterna and Amiga, was reluctant to make free jazz records.[131]

[127] Norden, "Protokoll der 6. Tagung des Zentralkomitees, BArch," 30.
[128] E.g. Martin Linzer, cofounder of *Jazz in der Kammer*. Interview with the author, 2010.
[129] Linzer, interview with the author, 2010.
[130] See the West German *Jazzpodium* "Free Music Workshop in Berlin," *Jazz Podium* (June 1970). The East German *Melodie und Rhythmus* praised the fusion of audience and stage at a performance of the Wilhelm Breuker Kollektiv. Martin Linzer, "Gäste aus Holland," *Melodie und Rhythmus* (June 1977).
[131] Brüll, *Jazz auf Amiga*. One of the first productions in the genre of free jazz was *Synopsis* (1974), Amiga 855395, featuring Ernst-Ludwig Petrowsky, Konrad Bauer, Ulrich Gumpert, Günter Sommer, and appearing shortly after *Just for Fun*.

According to former Amiga producer Jürgen Lahrtz, there were several key reasons for this reluctance, and two stand out. First, within the genre of jazz, Amiga offered selections of traditional, swing, and modern jazz titles, most of them licensed from Western companies. Within the East German listenership, certain styles were simply better known and more popular. Jazz classics, such as recordings by Louis Armstrong, Oscar Peterson, or Ella Fitzgerald, usually sold out within days, whereas free jazz was far more difficult to market.[132]

Second, and more importantly, socialist central economic planning determined Amiga's politics of publishing. State-allocated contingents of raw materials, such as those for printing and vinyl production, the latter imported and available only with Western currency, strictly determined production numbers. Therefore, Amiga primarily printed music that was marketable whether in the GDR or beyond, including in capitalist countries. Ironically, the Deutsche Schallplatte in communist East Germany represented an international market-oriented enterprise grossing large sums of foreign currencies. Its classical label Eterna routinely profited from East Germany's acclaimed orchestras, choirs, and soloists, but producing a free jazz record was clearly not in the market-oriented interests of the label.[133] The fact, though, that the West German label FMP published the first record of GDR free jazz in 1973 put Amiga in an awkward position: left-wing German media outlets reviewing Petrowsky's FMP album *Just for Fun* cheered the music of what they saw as the Eastern anti-establishment players. The West German *Frankfurter Rundschau* stated: "It is remarkable how here [at FMP, in West Berlin] musicians from over there [in the GDR] reach world-class levels in the realm of jazz, which GDR functionaries would have rather seen in East German pop music."[134]

It is almost certain that East German bureaucrats were aware of such critiques, but sources do not indicate their reaction. Either way, with its review, the Western *Frankfurter Rundschau* implied that world-class GDR jazz was deprived of the chance to fully flourish, and that the lack of native records had kept the music from international recognition (a situation remedied only by Western intervention). Furthermore, the newspaper

---

[132] Interview with Jürgen Lahrtz, 2009.
[133] Interviews with Jürgen Lahrtz, Walter Cikan, and Volkmar Andrä, 2007–11.
[134] Lucas Cramer, *Frankfurter Rundschau* (October 6, 1973). *"Erstaunlich ist, wie hier Musiker von drüben ausgerechnet auf dem Gebiet des Jazz Weltniveau entwickeln, das die DDR-Funktionäre aus Absatzgründen lieber im Schlagerbereich erwartet hätten."*

took a jab at Amiga's pop music productions, claiming that they fell short in competing with Western popular music trends, and that their acts failed to attract the same level of audiences. In any case, the collaboration between FMP and AGITPROP/GDR broadcasters to release *Just for Fun* put enormous pressure on Amiga executives, pressure that showed results: just a year later, Amiga, too, produced a record with Petrowsky and friends. In April 1974, the band Synopsis (mentioned above) – featuring Petrowsky, Bauer, Gumpert, and Sommer – recorded at the Amiga Studios in East Berlin and published a record under the same name.[135] In the years that followed, Amiga and FMP regularly competed to produce GDR free jazz, characterized largely by Amiga trying to keep up with FMP's busy release schedule.[136]

These newfound "collaborations" between East and West were not just limited to record production, however. AGITPROP functionaries as well as West German diplomats pursued German-German jazz projects, which were nurtured from both sides of the Wall and which served divergent propagandistic aims. In its propaganda effort, West Germany followed the guidelines of *Ostpolitik*, namely, to nurture cultural exchange between the two Germanies: jazz was used as a diplomatic tool to initiate dialogue between the two states. In May 1974, the Permanent Representation of the Federal Republic, (*Ständige Vertretung der Bundesrepublik*, STÄV) opened under the umbrella of the Federal Ministry for Intra-German-Relations (*Bundesministerium für innerdeutsche Beziehungen*, BMiB) and regularly featured jazz music as part of its cultural activities.[137] Such events were embedded in diplomatic receptions, such as one on April 28, 1976, when the Manfred Schoof Quintet from West Germany was hired to perform. Rainer Haarmann (Figure 5.7), cultural attaché at STÄV at the time, recalled in a recent interview:

> Günter Gaus [head of STÄV, 1974–1981] had given the signal to put on a cultural event in the garden house, and so it took place disguised as a diplomatic reception in April 1976. We planned an evening of jazz, and invited the Manfred Schoof Quintett from West Germany with Jasper van't Hof, Michel Pilz, Günter Lenz and Ralf Hübner. The Haus was full, the

[135] Brüll, *Jazz auf Amiga*. Amiga 8 55 395, 1974.
[136] According to Gebers, FMP produced twenty-six LPs of East German free jazz until 1989.
[137] The work of the Ständige Vertretungen in Bonn and Berlin (Ost) began on May 2, 1974. "Zeittafel," in *DDR Handbuch* (Köln: Bundesministerium für innerdeutsche Beziehungen, 1985), 1590.

Figure 5.7   Rainer Haarmann (left) and Christo (right), at the Ständige Vertretung, East Berlin, 1976, during the planning phase for Christo's projected wrapping of the Reichstag. Private collection of Rainer Haarmann, used by permission

diplomatic corps and many, almost all of the GDR jazz musicians came, but also many artists of other disciplines from West and East Germany. I had heard that beforehand GDR officials and security were considerably nervous. Since some musicians were state-employed, they considered preventing them from participating. But in the end, they all came.[138]

Forearmed, the STASI had their agents well in place at Chausseestraße 131, to which almost everyone of importance in the GDR jazz scene had received an invitation. Informants Blobel and Sellhorn were in attendance, and Sellhorn's subsequent STASI report – his cooperation with the agency had recently been reactivated yet again – listed the following people as present that evening: jazz musicians Petrowsky, Sommer, and Gumpert; orchestra leader Wonneberg; writers Wolfgang Harich and Klaus Schlesinger; singer-songwriter Bettina Wegener; Amiga executive H.P. Hofmann; Karl Heinz Deim from Radio DDR; and Karl Heinz Gerstner from GDR television.[139] The building boasted a new annex,

[138] Email from March 28, 2016 to the author. Translation by the author.
[139] BStU, MfS, "Zirkel" [1972–1980], pp. 45–47.

a pavilion called the Gartenhaus, in which about 250 people enjoyed West German jazz as well as West German refreshments. Sellhorn reported: "For the jazz concert of the Schoof band not enough chairs were available, so part of the audience sat on the floor and some remained in the back room drinking. The ambience was very casual and not formal at all." He further expressed his surprise that nobody was asked to show their invitations, and practically anybody was able to enter the STÄV building.[140] What is clear in retrospect, however, is that STÄV officials had aimed to include as many people as possible that evening, ostensibly in support of *Ostpolitik*.

For many East Germans, this was a rare – if not first – tangible experience of the West, but the real excitement took place shortly after midnight, after the reception was over and the doors of STÄV had closed. What happened then was reminiscent of the intrazonal Rex Stewart sessions in Berlin in 1948, when German musicians had jammed with Stewart by candlelight until late into the night. In the early morning hours in the nearby Bar Möve, the East-West encounter continued in a new way, with East and West German musicians jamming together before a large audience.[141] The fact that German musicians from both sides of the Iron Curtain were playing together was, at that time, unheard of: as noted above, *Touch the Earth*, the first recording featuring musicians from both Germanies would not appear until 1980. Haarmann would later recall: "That was in fact a very special occurrence, and a truly unforgettable experience. One must be aware that at that time, it was taboo, if not illegal, to engage in such German-German encounters or even to organize them. Such acts would break a political taboo." The world-class talent in this clandestine performance notwithstanding, what made this encounter truly special in the eyes of West German diplomats was its symbolic meaning: it proved that there was a form of communication possible despite the seemingly insurmountable differences between the two political camps. This jam session, brief though it may have been, bridged two diverging ideological worlds through the universal language of jazz.

Overall, the availability of East German music in the Western market served diplomatic efforts on both sides of the Wall. So, too, did the increased representation of East German jazz on international stages. Beginning in the late 1970s, East German musicians, many of whom had

---

[140] Ibid.
[141] Interview with Rolf Reichelt, 2017.

made their name performing at festivals in the Eastern Bloc such as the Jazz Jamboree in Warsaw, were granted permission to travel to the West.[142] With rare exception, Petrowsky's jazz ensemble, not least due to his friendship with Karl Heinz Deim, was one of the first bands that was allowed to perform in the West, playing the Montreux Jazz Festival in 1968.[143] Ten years later, the West German Norddeutscher Rundfunk in 1978 invited Petrowsky's trio to Hamburg to produce a show for West German broadcasting, where journalist Michael Naura featured them on his show *Jazz Workshop* (not the same production as the *Jazzwerkstatt* above) in November 1978.[144] The following year, the Ulrich Gumpert Workshop Band played at the Jazz Festival in Moers, in North-Rhine Westphalia.[145] In time, the East German free jazz export became an increasingly common feature on West German stages. Networking efforts of the West German Ministry for Intra-German Relations pushed for opportunities to stage GDR musicians, and STÄV repeatedly procured invitations from West German producers to East German musicians to perform in the West. At the same time, STÄV attachés in East Berlin pushed East German authorities to allow musicians to accept the invitations. In a 2009 interview, Haarmann recalled:

> We can admit now that we pushed Western producers to invite East German artists. It was part of our diplomatic strategy. Our motto was "constant dripping will wear the stone". Once the invitation was official, we would immediately show up at the GDR Ministry for Foreign Affairs and push for the granting of travel permits.[146]

Over time, such persistent exposure of GDR jazz to Western ears created an environment for its recognition and appreciation. The West German Ministry for Intra-German Relations even allocated generous grants to stage free jazz events. The FMP concert series *Jazz Now* featured a festival

---

[142] See "Zeitgenössischer Jazz. Probleme und Ausblick," *Melodie und Rhythmus* (December 1972). Other festivals included *Jazz nad odra* in Wroclaw, Poland, and the jazz festival in Slany, Czechoslovakia.

[143] See Montreux Jazz Festival program, June 13, 1968, Jazz Ensemble Studio Vier. Claude Nobs also featured the West German Manfred Schoof Sextett that year (correspondence with Nobs' office courtesy of Katja Deim).

[144] Werner Burkhardt, "Nichts Fremdes. Petrowsky-Trio zum ersten Mal in der Bundesrepublik," *Die Zeit*, November 10, 1978. The lineup was Petrowsky on sax, Sommer on drums, and Klaus Koch on bass.

[145] Wilhelm E. Liefland, "Deutschland ein Improvisationsmärchen. In der FMP-Workshop-Reihe 'Jazz Now': Die DDR Avantgarde," *Frankfurter Rundschau* (August 16, 1979).

[146] Interview with the author, 2009.

in 1979 presenting exclusively East German bands, remarkably, on the weekend just prior to the anniversary of the building of the Wall on August 13, 1961. This particular event was generously supported by the Ministry for Intra-German Relations and took place at West Berlin's Akademie der Künste, an exhibition hall large enough for nearly 1,000 people.[147] For this festival – which in the eyes of AGITPROP was free propaganda – GDR officials granted travel visas to over two dozen musicians to perform at the modern building complex on Hanseatenweg, near Schloss Bellevue. Over three days, *Jazz Now* drew about 3,000 visitors from West Germany, a sold-out event that received the close attention of Western press and offered a chance for East German cultural functionaries to witness the appreciation of the form from across the border. From contemporary accounts, most of them seem to have been impressed by what they saw and heard. Jost Gebers later recalled: "There were these functionaries of the GDR Artist Agency (*Künstleragentur*) and the Ministry for Culture who approached me and told me that they had been not aware of the hidden musical treasures in the GDR."[148]

Indeed, Western journalists praised the *Jazz Now* project – held on FMP's tenth anniversary – as a small but significant sign of rapprochement between the two Germanies, despite their remaining divisions. West German regional and national press uniformly praised the virtuosity and creativity of the East German musicians and noted the fusion of European musical traditions and contemporary jazz. The magazine *Jazz Podium* and the daily newspaper *Frankfurter Rundschau* observed the convergence of styles evoking the Second Viennese School, as well as baroque, classical, and folk traditions that together diffused the borders of jazz and European art music (*Kunstmusik*).[149] The Berlin *Tagesspiegel* regarded these approaches as representing the search for new paths in the improvisational arts.[150] One year later, FMP released a double LP entitled *Snapshot*,

---

[147] www.fmp-label.de/freemusicproduction/projekte/p_sp_1979_d.html, "Jazz Now" (August 1979). This West Berlin Academy of the Arts was a separate entity from the ADK created in the GDR in 1950.

[148] Interview with the author, 2009.

[149] Lothar Jänichen, "Jazz Now. Jazz-Austausch mit der DDR," *Jazz Podium* (October 10, 1979); Jürgen Engelhardt, "Musik auf der Werkbank. Zweiter und dritter Tag bei 'DDR-Jazz Now'," *Frankfurter Rundschau* (August 16, 1979).

[150] Liefland, "Deutschland ein Improvisationsmärchen"; Engelhardt, "Musik die nicht rostet: Jazz aus der DDR in der Akademie der Künste," *Der Tagesspiegel* (August 14, 1979).

presenting a selection of *Jazz Now* concerts accompanied by a forty-eight-page booklet. East and West cooperated in this as well: East German pianist and composer Hans Rempel, music journalist Rolf Reichelt, and West German musicologist Jürgen Engelhardt all contributed texts with musical analysis, texts that largely mirrored socialist views of East German jazz culture. For example, referring to the autonomy of East German jazz and its relation to German folk art, Engelhardt stated: "The folk song was simultaneously the subject, source, and catalyst for contemporary GDR jazz at the beginning of the 1970s, and provided a means of extracting GDR jazz from the aesthetic diction of the American prototype in an independent and authentic way."[151] Such views, a familiar refrain for music theorists of the day, once again reinterpreted the German folk song as the backbone of "authentic" GDR jazz.

Despite their praise for the event, these Western publications did not miss the chance to remind readers that the musicians from the East crossed a border dividing two Germanies with two divergent worlds.[152] But ultimately, *Jazz Now* put the spotlight onto East German free jazz, bolstering its recognition from both political camps, and some leading GDR officials to see new value in the music. Apart from its propagandistic value, East German musicians were also earning hard currency, a portion of which went to the East German state.[153] Yet despite these opportunities, the granting of visas to musicians also represented a risk for East German authorities, who issued them only to those individuals who were considered to be "able to travel" (*reisefähig*) – a term that in GDR lingo meant these people were most likely loyal enough to return to their homeland. Indicators for such status were family ties, professional careers, and the degree of popularity in the countries of the Eastern bloc.[154] Those who decided to stay in the West, whether illegally or through the torturous process of legal emigration – such as musicians Klaus Lenz and Friedhelm Schönfeld, respectively – were

---

[151] www.fmppublishing.de/freemusicproduction/labelsspecialeditions/snapshot_engelhardt_d.html.

[152] Liefland, "Deutschland ein Improvisationsmärchen"; Engelhardt, "Musik die nicht rostet." Engelhardt's writings were supported in the leftist *Argument Verlag*, for example "Eislers Weg vom Agitprop zum Lehrstück," in *Hanns Eisler*, Argument Sonderbände (Berlin: Argument-Verlag, 1979).

[153] Musicians in all genres, including rock, who performed abroad were obliged to hand over a portion of their earnings to the state. See Rauhut, *Rock in der DDR* (Bundeszentrale für politische Bildung, 2002), 57.

[154] From 1978 to 1981, guitarist Helmut Sachse repeatedly applied for a visa to travel to the West and perform with fellow musicians such as Conny Bauer, yet his status as "*nicht reisefähig*" negatively impacted his career. See BStU, MfS, ZMA/KUL 97/5 Abt. XX.

stripped of their status and prestige and, in most cases, were unable to establish themselves in the West in the field of music. A rare exception is represented by the case of Joachim Kühn, who was able to build a career in the West. As noted, musicians who were allowed to travel, such as Petrowsky, Sommer, Bauer, and Gumpert, belonged to the fortunate ones, enjoying relatively privileged lives in the East.

It is important to remember that while the two Germanies participated in a vibrant free jazz exchange on an official diplomatic level, both Germanies participated in this exchange for their own reasons: West Germany sought rapprochement (if not reunification, in a distant future), and East Germany sought autonomy and the spread of socialism, two opposing agendas that were served by any means necessary, including jazz. The dismantling of walls and the building of cultural bridges between states was not a task that could be completed overnight, and even in the culture sector, the conflict between opposing ideologies could take a militaristic tone. On a tour in 1983, for example, the Manfred Schoof Big Band received an icy welcome from the GDR. Around this time, Rainer Haarmann's office at STÄV was ordered to present suggestions for cultural exchange projects during a proposed meeting between the two German heads of state, Erich Honecker and Helmut Kohl. One suggestion arranged a tour for the West German ensemble to East German cities including Berlin, Rostock, and Meerane, but when Schoof's band reached Neubrandenburg, GDR officials countered their presence with the presence of its military. The auditorium was filled with soldiers of the National People's Army (*Nationale Volksarmee*, NVA), who did not applaud the performance and who at the end marched out of the auditorium in silence.[155] Journalist Werner Burkhardt, who accompanied the tour for the *Süddeutsche Zeitung*, chose to omit this chilly reception in his review, instead praising the effort to build bridges via jazz with the people of the GDR.[156] The following year, Haarmann (who had recently left STÄV in East Berlin for the BMiB in Bonn) managed to coproduce an Amiga record featuring excerpts of Schoof's live performances in the GDR.[157]

[155] Interview with Tom van der Geld, 2018.
[156] Werner Burkhardt, *Klänge, Zeiten, Musikanten* (Waakirchen: Oreos Verlag, 2002), 155–60.
[157] Brüll, *Jazz auf Amiga*, 317–18. Amiga 85606; Manfred Schoof Orchester featuring Albert Mangelsdorff, Wolfgang Dauner, and Eberhard Weber.

In sum, all actors involved harbored an interest in and, in one way or another, profited from the free jazz exchange between East and West in the 1970s. Selected East German musicians were granted opportunities to extend their performing radius across the Iron Curtain and increasingly gained recognition in the West. Their links with Western free jazz musicians influenced their direction as artists, which on the one hand advanced notions of an autonomous GDR style and, on the other, heightened the awareness of their privileged position as state-sponsored artists. On the same token, West German musicians performing on East German stages enjoyed their status as sought-after imports of talent, often drawing considerable crowds, and capitalizing on their increased caché. For FMP promoter Jost Gebers, this jazz rapprochement put the spotlight not just on his own music company and his stable of artists, but on the genre of contemporary free jazz as a whole. One may wonder what the history of East German jazz would have looked like without these collaborations and partnerships. However, one thing remains true that on a diplomatic level in the eyes of West German proponents of *Ostpolitik*, such jazz exchanges were helping to build cultural bridges between the two Germanies in the era of *détente*. From the perspective of the East, such as for AGITPROP functionaries, such jazz exchanges fulfilled the task of the dissemination of East German culture into the West to further unite and foment leftist "progressive forces," which would ostensibly bring worldwide socialism on its way. Both East and West Germany utilized the jazz exchange as a tool in cold war politics, just with divergent objectives.

Conclusion

The decade of the GDR's formal international recognition saw the emergence in both theory and practice of an autonomous jazz style unique to East Germany. Ideologues outlined a fundamental difference regarding the music's socio-political function, expressing harmony with socialism, as opposed to its critique of the system in capitalist countries. Associated with the Black Power movement, American free jazz was seen as an expression of the social revolutionary process in which it functioned as a political tool. In the GDR, a state which had ostensibly overcome class struggle, jazz was in consensus with society. In the era of real existing socialism, critics interpreted the music as a collectivism within which individual expressiveness was integral, thus representing an art form created in a collective process that granted individual creativity.

Moreover, musicians and critics alike claimed that GDR jazz had broken away from American role models, connecting instead to German traditions. East German jazz incorporated twentieth-century elements, as well as those of the German *Volkslied*, and fused sacred traditions with experimental. Such claims lent credibility to the notion of jazz as specifically GDR-born, or as socialist *and* German. As well as looking to the past, the jazz discourse stressed the music's position within a historical trajectory that included the twentieth century. On this view, East German jazz's emancipatory process from American role models was informed by the musical influences of Schönberg, as well as the ideologically motivated works of Eisler, Weil, and Dessau. Jazz had transformed under socialist conditions – contrary to its Western counterpart, freed from market coercion – into a new and authentic form of music. At the same time, cultural theorists also claimed free jazz as a tool for education. Engaging with experimental jazz was a way to enhance the public's intellectual faculties, enabling the discrimination between the sophistication and simplicity of a musical form. As a result of this belief, by 1983, East German jazz was a key part of music education in schools.

In retrospect, members of the jazz scene often spoke of their fascination with the experience of live music, in particular the countercultural quality of free jazz. Here, the chaotic sounds and the communicative friction of the music transcended life in a society dominated by the official consensus of the socio-political system. A free jazz event functioned as a realm beyond the verbal in which to dispute and disagree. The Peitz jazz events and its festival evolved out of a grassroots initiative, organized and produced within the framework of municipal authority by young people and local enthusiasts. Nevertheless, it resembled a subcultural event outside the reach of state tutelage and paternalism, featuring Western bands and drawing increasing numbers of adolescents each year. In the 1970s, state authorities acquiesced in such alternative gatherings to grant a degree of self-determination, yet such "tolerance" was from the beginning accompanied by thorough state surveillance. The account of Ulrich Blobel, or IM Thomas, provides a case study of STASI methods of infiltration such as the recruiting of a prominent figure in the scene, monitoring Western contacts, and control through third parties, up to the informant's neutralization.

Finally, the GDR's so-called *Westarbeit* pursued the goal of destabilizing West German society. Such activism ranged from direct support of terrorist acts to the widespread propagation of a positive image of the GDR. Such aims were exemplified by the free jazz coproduction between the FMP record label and East German functionaries. This cooperation across the Iron Curtain benefitted all players involved and served a variety of interests, not least GDR state propaganda. With its support of free jazz, the SED state projected tolerance and openness, just as the cooperation benefitted the Western strategy of rapprochement: increasingly, by the end of this decade, East German musicians were allowed to perform in the West to extend their reputation beyond the Wall. In order to bring this story to a close, the next section will examine jazz in the last decade of the GDR, in which jazz activities were increasingly streamlined under state authorities but, before the Wall would come down, would still see their own surprising turns.

CHAPTER 6

"A National Treasure": Jazz Made in the GDR, 1980–1990

Introduction

In March 1989, the year of the fortieth anniversary of the founding of the GDR, Jörg Wicke, secretary of the Kulturbund (KB) Leipzig, urgently wrote to his superior in Berlin pleading for help.[1] The Jazztage, the annual festival that had featured contemporary and experimental jazz since 1976, was in jeopardy over its major venue, the Kongreßhalle, in which decades of neglect had finally taken their toll. In 1988, building inspectors had considered it necessary to close the building due to its pending collapse.[2] Wicke's letter was one of numerous such missives exchanged between Kulturbund functionaries, Leipzig's municipal officials, and representatives of the Jazz Club Leipzig, and that year, even on such an important anniversary, time was running out.[3] In their letters to state authorities, festival organizers stressed the event's national and international significance.[4] They argued that only through the diligent work of countless volunteers and the strong support of Leipzig's jazz community had the festival grown to flourish by the late 1980s. The event, whose only external support came from relatively low state subsidies, largely covered its own

[1] Bundesekretariat Kulturbund der DDR, BArch/DY 27/9500, "Jörg Wicke, Bezirkssekretär Bezirksleitung Leipzig, Kulturbund an Dieter Zänker, Bundessekretariat, Sekretariat des Präsidiums, Abt. Kunst und Literatur, Kulturbund" (March 31, 1989).
[2] "Leitungsmitglied des 'jazzclubs leipzig' an SED Bezirksleitung Mayer" (April 8, 1989).
[3] Letter of March 31, 1989, from Jörg Wicke, Kulturbund der Deutschen Demokratischen Republik, Bezirksleitung Leipzig an Kulturbund der DDR Bundessekretariat des Präsidiums, Abt. Kunst und Literatur, Berlin, z.H. Gen. Zänker. Thereafter the KB in Berlin pressured Leipzig authorities. See Letter to Stadtrat für Kultur, Dr. Fischer, dated May 9, 1989. Letter dated May 25, 1989, from Prof. Dr. K.-H. Schulmeister, 1. Vizepräsident u. 1. Bundessekretär, Kulturbund der DDR Bundessekretariat des Präsidiums, Abt. Kunst und Literatur, Berlin an Rolf Opitz Vorsitzender des Rates des Bezirkes Leipzig. "Tätigkeit der Arbeitsgruppe Jazz der Zentralen Kommission Musik beim Präsidialrat des Kulturbundes" (1980).
[4] "Helga Lützkendorf and Bernd Seidel" (February 22, 1989).

costs, attracting more than 10,000 visitors each year.[5] A festival on that scale, organizers argued, required the coproduction and financial support of state institutions.[6] Their desperation was such that they even considered reusing a circus tent for a venue, as they had done the year before when the visiting Circus Busch was able to help out.[7] Ultimately, after a lengthy administrative struggle, the festival finally took place in the fall of 1989. But by that point, Leipzig's citizens were engaged in an event far larger than a music festival: by that autumn, tens of thousands of people were openly protesting a political leadership that they claimed was oppressive. Indeed, the peaceful revolution that began in Leipzig – prior to its culmination in Berlin – was the beginning of the end of the German Democratic Republic.

As this chapter details, such an outcome, even just a few years earlier, was unthinkable, and the political and economic context of these changes is key to their unfolding. In the early 1980s, few observers foresaw the dramatic shifts unfolding at the end of the decade that would finally crumble the Eastern Bloc and bring the Cold War to an end. For in the 1970s, the GDR had become the second-most powerful industrial state in the Eastern Bloc, and its populace enjoyed relatively high standards of living compared to other socialist countries.[8] But despite these achievements, discontent among the people was growing. In the late 1970s, living standards faltered, and the East German economy seemed to stagnate. Though costs of living were low and basic needs such as health care and housing were readily available, the "bottleneck economy" of the time increasingly jeopardized the flow of supplies, severely affecting everyday life. Many goods were only available for inflated prices, with Western currency, or through bartering. By contrast, images of West Germany evoked a land of abundance and prosperity. Despite state attempts at economic demarcation and centralized efforts to contravene Western cultural influences with GDR-made productions, large parts of the East German populace took advantage of their access to West German television and enjoyed

[5] "Konzeption zum Programm der 11. Internationalen Leipziger Jazztage 1986." *Anlage 3. Finanzplanung.* According to the 1986 financial plan, projected income covered about 70 percent of expenses. Additional expenses were funded by regional and municipal authorities.
[6] "Jörg Wicke, Bezirkssekretär Bezirksleitung Leipzig, Kulturbund an Dieter Zänker, Bundessekretariat, Sekretariat des Präsidiums, Abt. Kunst und Literatur, Kulturbund."
[7] The *Arena-Zelt* was also considered as a venue in 1989. Bundesekretariat Kulturbund der DDR, BArch/DY 27/9500, "Information für den Stadtrat für Kultur, Dr. Fischer" (March 31, 1989). See also Kulturbund der DDR, "Helga Lützkendorf and Bernd Seidel."
[8] Mary Fulbrook, *A History of Germany, 1918–2014* (Oxford: Wiley Blackwell, 2015), 179.

its programs nightly, exposure that contributed to the conception of an alternative model for society.

Though party propaganda tried to burnish the GDR's economic health, the reality was that the East German economy was deeply troubled at the beginning of the 1980s. Comparable, if not worse, was the situation in the Soviet Union. Because the Soviet Union faced enormous difficulties providing its populace with basic supplies, it was forced to sell oil contingents to the West in order to finance desperately needed imports of grain. Thus, Soviet leadership reduced the flow of oil to its satellite states – including the GDR – in the early 1980s, which infuriated the SED leadership and forced Honecker to challenge Brezhnev over whether "two million tons of oil would be worth it to destabilize the GDR."[9] By 1982, the GDR had reached fiscal insolvency and had no choice but to take credits of nearly a billion marks from West Germany; not once but twice in 1983 and 1984.[10] Indeed, despite these stopgap efforts, the challenges facing the East German economy were greater than mere temporary measures could fix.

Again, historical context is key to understanding the fortunes of the GDR in these years, both for the country as a whole and for culture, music, and jazz in particular. Though in retrospect it might seem disconcerting, many political players across East Germany aligned themselves with the status quo, regardless of the crises facing the country. During SED rallies and May Day demonstrations, party leadership presented confidence and optimism, and in its last decades, the GDR underwent a new boost of institutionalization.[11] Growing membership numbers for mass organizations and for the party itself suggest the general disposition of the populace to abide by state and system.[12] Membership in the Cultural Alliance (Kulturbund, KB) increased by over a third between 1970 and 1985, the number of events the KB organized increased by over 40 percent from 1975 until 1985, and the number of participants at those events doubled during that same time.[13] The efforts of the jazz community in those years to centralize and organize its members exemplifies this

[9] Andreas Herbst, Gerd-Rüdiger Stephan, and Jürgen Winkler, eds., *Die SED: Geschichte-Organisation-Politik* (Berlin: Dietz, 1997), 752.

[10] Charles S. Maier, *Dissolution: The Crisis of Communism and the End of East Germany* (Princeton: Princeton University Press, 1997), 62.

[11] Gerd Dietrich, "Kulturbund," in *Die Parteien und Organisationen der DDR: Ein Handbuch*, ed. Gerd-Rüdiger Stephan et al. (Berlin: Karl Dietz Verlag, 2002), 542.

[12] Compare FDJ and DSF membership numbers in: Ibid.

[13] Ibid., 558–59.

overall trend, as did the belief of its members that stronger state affiliation would benefit their cause. This belief would only partially prove true. But until then, the story of jazz in the last years of the GDR can partly be told through the story of the Leipzig and Weimar festivals, two of the most visible and significant events in late East German history.

The Leipzig Jazz Festival

For decades, jazz activities in Leipzig had garnered official attention from the GDR. The days of the Felsenkeller in the early 1950s, the rise and fall of activist Reginald Rudorf, the closing of jazz clubs by Honecker's order in the mid-1950s, and the resurgence of jazz fans in the Bessie Smith Club in the early 1960s all illustrate the ambivalent relationship of authorities toward the music. But in the last years of the GDR, the Jazz Club Leipzig (JCL), founded in 1973, enjoyed the status of a well-established cultural organization. A large and vibrant group, the JCL harbored some of the same members of the jazz scene who had been active in the Bessie Smith Club in the early 1960s, such as Klaus Hesse, whose activities were discussed in Chapter 4.[14] Throughout the year, lectures at club meetings accompanied live performances at venues throughout the city, including the historic Felsenkeller, featuring mainly contemporary jazz and hosting such globally recognized artists as Sun Ra.[15] Three years after its founding, over the weekend of June 10–12, 1976, the club presented its first festival, the I. Leipziger Jazztage in the Wintergarten Cinema (*Kino Wintergarten*). Quickly growing in popularity, the festival was soon extended to four days and moved into its signature venue, the Kongreßhalle, just outside the historic center of town.[16]

The artistic concept of the festival showcased modern and experimental jazz, with a stated emphasis on providing new musical experiences that expanded the listening expectations of the audience. Performers came both from the GDR and, by the late 1970s, from international scenes: in 1985 festival organizers could boast that musicians from over 25 countries

---

[14] Other founding members were Gerd Gleßmer, Steffen Hempel, Wofhard Röhlig, and Sigurd Rosenhain. See Jazzclub Leipzig, *15 Jahre "jazzclub leipzig", Versuch einer Chronik* (Leipzig, 1988).

[15] Jazzclub Leipzig, *Jubiläumsausgabe Jazzreport - 10 Jahre Leipziger Jazztage* (Leipzig: Kulturbund, 1985).

[16] Ticket sales rose from 3,900 in 1977 to 9,700 in 1985. See letter from head of JCL G. Schulz dated June 11, 1986 to Kulturbund der DDR, Bundessekretär Zänker. Bundessekretariat Kulturbund der DDR, BArch/DY 27/9500 (1980–89).

had participated at the Jazztage. Among the many noted artists who made the Leipzig Festival a mecca for the avant-garde were the Phalanx Quartet with James Blood Ulmer, formerly the guitarist for Ornette Coleman; saxophonist George Adams, known for his work with Charles Mingus; Sam Rivers, who worked with Miles Davis; trumpet virtuoso Woody Herman Shaw; bassist Peter Warren; and drummer Andrew Cyrille, bandmember for Cecil Taylor.[17] Drummer Tony Oxley, trombonist Paul Rutherford, and pianist Irene Schweitzer came from Western Europe. The Eastern Bloc was represented by greats such as Polish trumpeter Thomasz Stańko and Hungarian bassist Aladár Pege. The GDR itself was represented by musicians such as Petrowsky, Bauer, Gumpert, and Sommer, who along with other East German musicians were able to regularly exchange with foreign artists in jam sessions.

Producers generally agreed upon a "noncommercial" quality for the festival, a principle that excluded – in critic Bert Noglik's words – "trendy, easily consumable music."[18] For these organizers, for whom sophistication was a high ideal, the purpose of music was not just to entertain, but to edify and enlighten. As Noglik observed:

> Leipzig is not as much a showcase (*Schaufenster*) but a workshop (*Werkstatt*). And the audience is able to participate in this creative process—agreeing, disagreeing, selecting. Undoubtedly Leipzig's audiences are changed through the music the Jazz Club selected. They are more competent and tolerant, as well as more discerning.[19]

The key difference for the jazz workshop, then, was the emphasis on the experiment as opposed to the showcase. While the so-called "shows of excellence" (*Leistungsschaus*) that occasionally characterized events featuring East German jazz (and other genres) aimed to highlight the achievements of socialist culture, the Jazztage offered audiences a chance to expand their abilities to comprehend and appreciate music, creating an experience for performer and recipients that went beyond mere consumption or spectacle.[20] Alongside the goal of enrichment, the Jazztage

---

[17] Program of the tenth festival, collection of the author.
[18] Leipzig, *15 Jahre "jazzclub leipzig"*.
[19] Ibid.
[20] In contrast, KfU regulations demanded the production of *Leistungsschaus* for all sections of the entertaining arts. BArch/DR 101/3c Komitee für Unterhaltungskunst der DDR, "Geschäftsordnung" (1988), 52–55. See also Thomas Wilke, "Diskotheken im Vergleich. Abendunterhaltung im Rampenlicht des sozialistischen Wettbewerbs," in *Heißer Sommer – Coole Beats: Zur populären Musik und ihren medialen Repräsentationen in der DDR*, ed. Sascha Trültzsch and Thomas Wilke (Frankfurt a. M.: Peter Lang, 2010).

also aimed to join other musical events that honored the musical heritage of the city. At the tenth annual festival in 1985, the city of Leipzig declared: "Leipzig is a center of socialist music culture of international stature, and we feel obliged to foster all genres."[21] The festival took place alongside the events commemorating Bach and Händel, as well as Leipzig's opera and the Gewandhaus, in a year that also marked the fortieth anniversary of the end of Hitler's fascist rule. With an eye on the city's musical past, and a focus on contemporary performers and modern styles, the Jazztage exemplified an innovative socialist culture of the day, emancipated alongside other genres of German musical heritage.

Such exemplification was carefully constructed. Early on, the JCL leadership, headed at the time by Heinz-Jürgen Lindner, had pushed for an affiliation with the KB and suggested the formation of a transregional jazz committee within the agency. Pursuing greater political leverage, the JCL proposed that established East German jazz clubs as well as amateur jazz musicians ought to be centrally organized under the umbrella of the KB.[22] These efforts arose for several discrete reasons, including the fact that a closer affiliation with high-ranking decision makers would generate more political clout, whether through the prospect of financial support or career opportunities for individuals. A 1980 communiqué between Lindner and Werner Danneberg, head of the department of music at the KB (*Sektorenleiter für Musik im Bundessekretariat des Kulturbundes*), developed the following three objectives. First, the incorporation of East German jazz clubs under the umbrella of the Kulturbund. According to the communiqué, as of 1979 about twelve clubs with an estimated 1,000 members were affiliated with the KB, while over a dozen clubs were affiliated with other mass organizations, such as the FDJ. Second, Lindner noted the continued upsurge of interest in jazz among young people, a fact requiring the attention of the KB. Third, he suggested they draw up guidelines to ensure the proper instruction of club leadership, which was often comprised of inexperienced youth. For instance, in Weimar, because one club leader was unaware of the "principles of leadership" – likely legal and fiscal responsibilities, as had been the case elsewhere – local authorities had withdrawn the club's funding. To achieve these goals, Lindner proposed the founding of a general jazz committee (*Jazz AG*) analogous to

---

[21] Leipzig, "Jubiläumsausgabe Jazzreport."

[22] In the early 1980s, several jazz clubs were housed in mass organizations other than the KB. Bundesekretariat Kulturbund der DDR, BArch/DY 27/9500, "Werner Danneberg, Sektorenleiter Musik an Bernd Dorn" (April 19, 1984).

other KB committees, such as the one for church organ music within the Central Commission for Music (*Zentrale Kommission für Musik*, ZKM).[23]

As a first step toward this centralization, in March 1981, the KB sent out invitations to the heads of jazz clubs throughout the GDR for a meeting during the jazz festival in Leipzig that June. Labeled as an "exchange of experiences" to increase the socio-political effectiveness of their work, this meeting included lectures about the role of jazz in socialism by critic Bert Noglik, and its participants even debated becoming a permanent committee of the KB.[24] The KB agreed to finance the JCL's centralizing efforts and allocated funding for meetings, accommodation, and catering. Although the tone of correspondence was informal, suggesting warm relationships between those involved – official letters were signed "keep swinging" instead of "with socialist greetings" – such support cannot be seen as a purely friendly gesture to the club.[25] Rather, this centralization of jazz initiatives from below, and their incorporation into the mass organization of the KB, met the recent political proclamations concerning the consolidation of socialist society at the tenth SED party gathering in April 1981. At this gathering, party leadership had demanded strength and ideological consensus at a time of political upheaval in Poland in the previous fall, taken as another sign of the instability of the Eastern Bloc. As such, the gathering of the jazz club leaders in Leipzig was held alongside that rally in which 2,700 delegates reelected Honecker as general secretary, who both reiterated the uncontested central authority of the SED and demanded higher standards from mass organizations to ensure the ideological stabilization of the working class.[26] Lindner took such injunctions seriously and wrote to jazz club leaders on the last day of the rally asking them to consider "how after the tenth party rally the effectiveness of jazz clubs could be optimized within

[23] *Vorschläge zur Unterstützung der Tätigkeit der Freundeskreise Jazz im Kulturbund der DDR* (Ergebnisse des Gespräches mit Dr. Heinz-Jürgen Lindner, Leiter des Jazzclubs Leipzig im Kulturbund der DDR am 17.7.80). Page 3, 1. *"Es wird – analog der Arbeitsgruppe Orgel in der Zentralen Kommission Musik – eine Arbeitsgruppe Jazz gebildet. Diese Arbeitsgruppe erarbeitet – ähnlich wie die AG Orgel – Richtlinien für die Tätigkeit der Freundeskreise Jazz im Kulturbund der DDR."* Document signed by Werner Danneberg, Bundessekretariat des Kulturbundes der DDR. See "Tätigkeit der Arbeitsgruppe Jazz der Zentralen Kommission Musik beim Präsidialrat des Kulturbundes."

[24] *Zur Rolle des Jazz in der sozialistischen Musikkultur,* Dr. Bert Noglik. "Einladung an die Leiter von Jazzclubs der DDR aus Berlin, gez. Heinz-Jürgen Lindner, Christiane Leonhardt, Hans-Peter Klausnitzer, Werner Danneberg" (May 17, 1981).

[25] "Tätigkeit der Arbeitsgruppe Jazz der Zentralen Kommission Musik beim Präsidialrat des Kulturbundes." See Letter from IG Jazz Dresden to Kulturbund der DDR, Bundessekretariat, Abt. Kunst und Literatur, Werner Danneberg. Dated July 11, 1985.

[26] Hermann Weber, *Geschichte der DDR* (München: Deutscher Taschbuch Verlag, 1985/1999), 423–27.

East German social life."[27] Such zeal came to fruition: three years after their dialogue opened, the jazz committee of the KB was established at the ZKM on April 15, 1983 in Berlin.[28] Not long afterward, in 1984, Lindner moved to Berlin to take a position at the Ministry for Culture and became head of that very committee he first sought to form.[29]

The power of the jazz bloc in the KB manifested in different ways, including its ability to appeal to the ZK for funding for jazz-related initiatives and efforts.[30] Moreover, over the course of the 1980s, these efforts produced comprehensive lists of East German jazz clubs, describing the demographics of members (gender, age, and profession), their activities, and their preference of jazz styles. Indeed, by the mid-1980s, the KB began publishing lists of jazz clubs, which both enabled the flow of information between above and below and served as reference guides for fans and amateur performers.[31] The KB also supported the publication of programs that illuminated the vibrant jazz scene during the 1980s in cities such as Leipzig, Magdeburg, and Berlin, which typically offered several live events per day.[32] Furthermore, by the late 1980s, the "Festivalkalender" in the *Berliner Jazzblatt* not only publicized events in East Berlin and the GDR, but also those across the Iron Curtain, which at the time remained out of reach for a spontaneous visit for most East Germans and, moreover, could be understood as a subtle criticism of the dogmatic superiority and isolationism of GDR musical culture.[33]

---

[27] Letter to the leaders of jazz clubs, from Kulturbund Bezirkssekretariat Leipzig, signed by Dr. Heinz Jürgen Lindner. See Bundesekretariat Kulturbund der DDR, BArch/DY 27/9500, "Heinz Jürgen Lindner an die Leiter von Jazzklubs" (April 16, 1981). For the X. SED party rally see Weber, *Geschichte der DDR*, 425.

[28] Bundesekretariat Kulturbund der DDR, BArch/DY 27/9427, "Protokoll der konstituierenden Sitzung der Arbeitsgruppe Jazz im Kulturbund der DDR am 15. April 1983 in Berlin" (April 15, 1983).

[29] Konzeption des Seminars für die Vorstände Interessengemeinschaften Jazz im Kulturbund der DDR vom 3.–5. April 1987 in Dresden. Lindner is mentioned as discussion leader, holding the position of "Leiter der Jazz AG der Zentralen Kommission für Musik." Bundesekretariat Kulturbund der DDR, Abteilung Kunst und Literatur, BArch/DY 27/9404 (1986–1987). See also: Note from Immo Fritzsche to Wolfgang Brauer, dated June 19, 1984. Bundesekretariat Kulturbund der DDR, Abteilung Kunst und Literatur, Tätigkeit der Arbeitsgruppe Jazz der Zentralen Komission Musik beim Präsidialrat des Kulturbundes, BArch/DY 27/9500 (1980–1989).

[30] BArch/DY 27/9500 Kulturbund der DDR, "Kulturbund an ZK, Abteilung Kultur, Jürgen Hagen" (May 6, 1986).

[31] The KB was frequently asked to send such lists to its members. Cf. correspondence between Danneberg and Christian Ebert, dated May 28, 1986, in which Danneberg promised to send the 1987 list. Kulturbund der DDR, "Tätigkeit der Arbeitsgruppe Jazz der Zentralen Kommission Musik beim Präsidialrat des Kulturbundes."

[32] Jazzclub Magdeburg, "Arbeitsgemeinschaft Jazz Magdeburg beim Kulturbund der DDR," *Jazz-Nachrichten*, 1982. See also Jazzclub Berlin, "Berliner Jazzblatt" (Berlin: Kulturbund der DDR, 1980–1989).

[33] "Berliner Jazzblatt." BArch/DY 27/11519 (Berlin: Kulturbund der DDR, 1981–1985). These calendars can be found in issues such as October–December 1988.

Interestingly, the information the KB acquired did indicate a rising interest in contemporary jazz. According to their data, the majority of jazz clubs in the GDR had been founded after 1980, and their members preferred contemporary home-grown jazz, facts that KB functionaries wove into their cultural-educational mission: this growing interest in "sophisticated" entertainment was to be nurtured. Furthermore, jazz was drawing not only young intellectuals, but young workers as well. KB officials saw it as their duty to protect and nurture these needs and delegated the jazz committee to actively shape club life.[34] To aid in this effort, Danneberg called for a conference, the first annual Jazzpodium, during the tenth Leipzig Festival in 1985, to optimize this new *Jazzarbeit*.[35] Beforehand, he challenged presenters with questions reminiscent of the 1950s such as "What conditions lead to a high impact of jazz on the audience? Do other popular genres dumb down the jazz audience? Do discotheques spoil them either?"[36] A small personal spat emerged in this discourse: Noglik, who had been invited to participate, strongly doubted that such an approach would bear fruit, which he made clear to Danneberg – questioning the bureaucrat's intentions and exposing such proceedings as effectively spouting empty rhetoric for personal gain.[37] Doubting the effectiveness of the conference, Noglik eventually withdrew from participation, but despite this criticism, KB bureaucrats continued to produce ideological assessments on how to foster jazz in the GDR's cultural life. A 1986 statement

---

[34] Bundesekretariat Kulturbund der DDR, Abteilung Kunst und Literatur, DY 27/9422, "Konzeption: Jazzpodium I, 'Der Jazz und sein Publikum' Positionen-Fragen-Diskussionen am 29.9.1985 in Leipzig" (May 9, 1985). *1. Anliegen: Der Beschluß des Präsidiums des Kulturbundes vom 23.11.1978 "Zur Verbreitung und Aneignung von Kunst" weist in Abschnitt 1.2. auf die stärkere Einbeziehung der populären Kunstgattungen in der kunstpropagandistischen Arbeit des Kulturbundes. In den 70ger und 80ger Jahren haben sich im Kulturbund zunehmend Jazzklubs gebildet, die einem anspruchsvollen Unterhaltungsbedürfnis Rechnung tragen und vorwiegend junge Werktätige und junge Intelligenz an sich ziehen. Die Belange dieser Jazzklubs werden durch die Arbeitsgruppe Jazz der zentralen Kommission für Musik vertreten, so daß sie über die Organisationsgrenzen des Kulturbundes hinaus wirksam wird. Zur Wahrung dieser Verantwortung richtet die Jazz AG im Auftrag der ZKM Veranstaltungen aus, die Vorsitzende der IG Jazz zur Gestaltung eines intensiven und territorial wirksamen Klublebens befähigt. Diese Überlegung begründete die Nummerierung der Jazzpodien.*

[35] This term, coined here for this purpose, refers to the work of state and local authorities toward jazz, whether to support the activities of local clubs or to finance events such as festivals.

[36] Bundesekretariat Kulturbund der DDR, BArch/DY 27/9422, "Den Referenten des Jazzpodiums 'Der Jazz und sein Publikum'" (September 17, 1985).

[37] In a letter to Danneberg, Noglik wrote: "Many times when the KB and other organizations talked about jazz in a cultural-scientific terminology, I could not resist the feeling that there was a considerable distance from our real jazz life. Sometimes it is difficult to differentiate between a real concern and the occupation of empty rhetoric [*Alibifunktion*]." See "Bert Noglik to Werner Danneberg, Kulturbund, Bundessekretariat Abteilung Kunst und Literatur" (April 9, 1985).

illustrates the emptiness of the rhetoric he had criticized, with its mantra-like formula: "Jazz is part of the socialist music culture of the GDR. Jazz contributes to the development of the socialist way of life and accommodates the entitlement of the working class to sophisticated entertainment and sociability as well as musical education."[38] Yet Noglik remained involved in the work of the KB and the centralization process in order to help the wider cause, continuing to address the real needs of the jazz community, such as financial problems and the lack of sufficient venues.[39]

Bureaucratic politics aside, the Leipzig Festival did ultimately prove a benefit to its performers, organizers, and attendees in ways that directly shaped the reception and expansion of jazz in the GDR. Indeed, as passionate as its fans were for its music and culture, the festival has – unlike others, which were short-lived – outlived many of its comparable events by a significant degree and still takes place today. But even at the time, the interest in jazz that the KB documented showed its continued vitality in many regions of the GDR, well into the 1980s. Yet the obstacles that jazz faced did not disappear simply because of its increased popularity. Indeed, internal tensions within the jazz community as well as divergent state structures that supported it continued to complicate the history of the genre throughout the 1980s – for even as the festival in Leipzig celebrated its tenth anniversary in 1985, a new festival nearby would add a further dimension to the politics of jazz.

Jazz Nationalized: The Weimar Festival

The Weimar Jazz Festival, officially known as the *Erste Jazztage der DDR*, took place from December 6–8, 1985, and showcased 220 musicians, including 120 professionals and 100 amateurs. The sold-out event hosted about 8,000 spectators, among them journalists, cultural functionaries, concert producers, and guests from abroad – including journalists from across the Iron Curtain, who according to *Neues Deutschland*, had the "unique opportunity to experience the internationally recognized East German jazz scene in its stylistic diversity."[40] To present East German jazz

---

[38] BArch/DY 9500 Bundesekretariat Kulturbund der DDR, "Hinweise zur Pfelge des Jazz im Kulturbund der DDR" (November 11, 1986).

[39] BArch/DY 27/9427 Kulturbund der DDR, "Auswertung der Angaben, die die im Kulturbund der DDR organisierten Jazzklubs in Form augefüllter Informationsbögen gemacht haben" (September 20, 1987).

[40] Hugo Elbe, "Eine Nationale Festivalpremiere: Erfolgreiche 1. Jazztage der DDR," *Berliner Zeitung* (December 14, 1985).

as a whole, the original idea of the organizing committee to present solely contemporary jazz was rejected in favor of showcasing the entire spectrum of styles that the country had to offer.[41] Among the styles featured were traditional/Dixieland, free jazz, electronic jazz, gypsy swing, big band jazz, and jazz rock, though the genres of Dixieland and free jazz comprised the majority of the events. Leading musicians performed alongside emerging talent across all these styles, and genre-crossing projects such as fusing jazz, which improved with German musical traditions, as well as combinations of music, dance, action painting, and children's shows were also featured.[42] The broad spectrum of events, running from morning to well after midnight each night, clearly reveals the producers' attempt to attract a diverse audience, catering to all ages and musical tastes, and even to those not particularly interested in jazz. Here, attendees could encounter styles of music outside their normal listening habits within the framework of a public festival (*Volksfest*) (Figure 6.1).

Figure 6.1 Performance with dancer Fine Kwiatkowski at the Festival *Jazztage der DDR*, 1985 in Weimar. Photo by Matthias Creutziger, used by permission

[41] Ministerium für Kultur, "Problemspiegel in der Auswertung der Zentralen Tagungen der Arbeitskreise des Komitees," BArch/DY 43/1350 (February 27,1984).
[42] For a detailed listing of performers see Martin Linzer, "1. Jazztage der DDR in Weimar: Kritische Reflexionen über ein nationales Festival," *Unterhaltungskunst* (2/1986).

The official organizers of the festival were the Committee for the Entertaining Arts (*Komitee für Unterhaltungskunst,* KfU), the county of Erfurt, and the city of Weimar, whose statement read: "For the first time with this festival, we are creating a national forum to present the internationally acclaimed jazz of the GDR.[43] This national approach, showcasing jazz made exclusively in East Germany, was praised by the press as a "national festival premiere."[44] Cultural functionaries ordered extensive media coverage to ensure nationwide attention on Weimar, explicitly directing that these broadcasts projected the party's support of jazz as an integral part of East German cultural identity.[45] Moderators were instructed to convey firstly that "East German jazz is a vital part of the musical politics of the SED and is acknowledged and supported accordingly," and secondly, that "for the first time a festival gives the opportunity to extensively assess the level of achievement (*Leistungsstand*) of GDR jazz."[46]

The increasing significance of jazz in the state's cultural canon as a national art form was furthermore visible in the choice of Weimar as the location for the first "national" jazz festival. This choice was not random. Rather, "Weimar" encoded a spectrum of cultural and historical meanings. First, it was the cradle of the German classics, such as the literature of Goethe and Schiller that represented an integral part of the humanist education socialists sought to deliver. Therefore, jazz in Weimar constituted an ideological choice challenging cultural hierarchies: as a musical form allegedly rooted in capitalist oppression, jazz appeared in the city of Goethe and Schiller as an emancipated art form that both surmounted divisions in culture and reflected the triumph of the socialist society. Second, Weimar symbolized the modernity of the German Republic of the interwar years, to which East German critics warmed in the 1970s and 1980s, informing a demarcation from previous American role models wherein performers invoked a German cultural history embracing early twentieth century modernism. Thus, the choice of Weimar for a national

---

[43] Komitee für Unterhaltungskunst der DDR, "1. Jazztage der DDR. 6.12 – 8.12.1985" (1985).

[44] Elbe, "Eine Nationale Festivalpremiere."

[45] GDR TV broadcast the festival performances in December 1985 and throughout the following year. See "Fernsehen Aktuell. Aktuelle Kamera: Jazz aus Weimar, aus Konzerten der '1. Jazztage der DDR'," ibid. "Fernsehen: 1. Jazztage der DDR. Hermann Naehring. Übertragung aus dem 'Saal im Palais' Weimar," *Neue Zeit* (August 14, 1986).

[46] Rundfunk der DDR, "Chefredaktion Musik, K.-D. Hendrik. Sendekonzept zu "Jazz in Weimar – ein Bericht von den '1. Jazztagen der DDR' 14.12.1985, 23.30 Uhr, 1.Pr. (90')," (Collection Jan Eik.1985). "*Absicht: Dem Zuschauer soll verdeutlicht werden, – daß der DDR-Jazz enger Bestandteil der Musikpolitik der SED ist und dementsprechend anerkannt und gefördert wird; – daß mit dem Festival erstmalig die Möglichkeit geschaffen wurde, den Leistungsstand des DDR-Jazz umfangreich zu erfassen und darzustellen.*"

jazz festival legitimized, at least in part, the construct of an original East German socialist and national culture in which its own homegrown jazz was a key facet.

Unlike its counterpart in Leipzig, the Weimar Festival did not face financial difficulties, nor did it suffer a lack of venues in the small, picturesque Thuringia town. Produced and backed by the KfU, the festival took place in venues throughout the city.[47] The KfU, a governmental body at the Ministry for Culture, had been founded in April 1973 with the task of "optimizing the potential of East Germany's own entertaining arts."[48] At its inception, the committee sought "a critical scientific analysis of such developments, analyzing trends in the entertaining arts in the GDR and in the socialist brotherlands, as well as in the Western capitalist countries."[49] Backing such rhetoric was a call to equip East German artists performing in popular genres to meet international standards in competition with Western pop and rock music, genres which remained a trendsetting presence in the East. (To give but one example, when Bruce Springsteen performed in 1988, over 160,000 young East Germans attended the concert, a fact that did not go unnoticed by party leadership.[50])

Prior to that point, however, leading up to the creation of the Weimar Jazz Festival, the KfU had encouraged the artistic community to gather input from its members to "raise the standards of the entertaining arts,"

---

[47] The KfU allocated 190,000 Marks for the festival, with venues including the Weimarhalle; FDJ Studentenklub Kasseturm; Cinema "Haus Stadt Weimar"; and the Music Conservatory, Saal im Palais. BArch/DY 43/1350 Komitee für Unterhaltungskunst der DDR, "Protokoll der Beratung des Sekretariats des Komitees am 25. Januar 1985" (1985).

[48] KfU general director was Peter Czerny, with the following members: Horst Fliegel, state committee for broadcasting; Harri Költzsch, director of VEB Deutsche Schallplatten; Siegfried Meisgeier, state committee for television and director of the department of music; Werner Thomas, *Künstleragentur der DDR*; Gunther Schröder, artistic director of the DEFA Filmstudio; Otto Netzker, general director of VEB Zentral-Zirkus; Herbert Täschner, director, Verlag Lied der Zeit; Fritz Natschke, dance music editor at Harth-Musik-Verlag; Hans Bugenhagen, director of VEB *Konzert- und Gastspieldirektion*. "Der Minister für Kultur konstituierte das Komitee für Unterhaltungskunst," *Melodie und Rhythmus* (June 1973).

[49] Gespräch mit dem Generaldirektor des Komitees für Unterhaltungskunst Genosse Peter Czerny in: "konkret," *Unterhaltungskunst* (June 1973). See also Unauthored article, "Der Minister für Kultur konstituierte das Komitee für Unterhaltungskunst," *Melodie und Rhythmus* (June 1973).

[50] This concert was organized and funded by the FDJ; unsurprisingly, authorities co-opted Springsteen's working-class background representing the "other" America to promote leftist ideology just as they had with Louis Armstrong back in the 1960s. "Große Stunden mit Bruce Springsteen," *Neue Zeit* (July 21, 1988); "160000 kamen zum Konzert mit Bruce Springsteen," *Neues Deutschland* (July 20, 1988); Claus Michael Bartsch, "Rockrebell mit rauher Raspelröhre," *Neue Zeit* (July 16, 1988). For a discussion of rock in East Berlin, such as Springsteen and Joe Cocker, see Michael Rauhut, *Rock in der DDR* (Bundeszentrale für politische Bildung, 2002), 105–108.

which were articulated within specific committees (*Arbeitskreise*). These genres included dance, dance musicians, singer-songwriters, disco, rock, and jazz, and represented interest groups that effected an extension of official KfU responsibilities beyond its initial tasks at the time of its founding.[51] Over the course of the 1980s, the governmental body took on multiple responsibilities, including mentoring professional independent artists; establishing a legal basis for salaries, retirement, and copy and performing rights; offering training opportunities; and, naturally, providing ideological guidance.[52] In addition to practical support concerning the working welfare of artists, ideologization was considered a key goal in the growth of achievement and attainment in the arts. To showcase its achievements to the public, the KfU regularly produced competitions and *Leistungsschaus* that were organized by the committees of their respective genres.[53] It was under this aegis that the Weimar Jazz Festival was produced, functioning as a "public show of excellence" to demonstrate the country's achievements in jazz.[54] In this, the conceptualization of the Weimar festival differs from the Leipzig one in two key ways: first, Weimar's concept was nationally oriented, featuring jazz music in its diversity contrasting Leipzig's international orientation toward contemporary jazz; and second, Weimar was understood as a showcase presenting the level of national achievement, whereas Leipzig was conceptualized around the idea of the workshop setting. Here, audiences were seen in dialogue within the musical process, whereas in Weimar, audiences were to marvel at socialist musical accomplishment, feeding into the myth of the superiority and progress of socialism.

The KfU jazz committee, founded in 1978, was headed by composer, arranger, and bandleader Walter Kubiczek.[55] Its members included Uschi Bruning, Günter Sommer, Konrad Bauer, Karlheinz Drechsel, Martin

---

[51] Ministerium für Kultur, "Entwurf. Richtlinie für die Tätigkeit der Arbeitskreise des Komitees für Unterhaltungskunst," BArch/DY 43/1350 (November 7, 1983).

[52] BArch/DR 101/3/c, "Statut des Komitees für Unterhaltungskunst der Deutschen Demokratischen Republik" (1984). Neufassung /Entwurf 1988, Geschäftsordnung, Punkt 2. This paragraph includes also nonprofessional artists eligible for membership.

[53] BArch/DR 101/3/c, "Geschäftsordnung der Sektion des Komitees für Unterhaltungskunst der DDR/Neufassung März 1988" (1988). For *Leistungsschaus* in other genres of popular music see Wilke's article in Sascha Trültzsch and Thomas Wilke, ed. *Heißer Sommer – Coole Beats. Diskotheken im Vergleich. Abendunterhaltung im Rampenlicht des sozialistischen Wettbewerbs* (Frankfurt a. M.: Peter Lang, 2010).

[54] Gabriele Oertel, "Weimar lädt zu den 1. DDR-Jazztagen ein: 120 Musiker wirken mit," *Neues Deutschland* (October 16, 1985).

[55] BArch/DY 43/1350 Ministerium für Kultur, "Arbeitskreis Jazz, Inhalt und Ergebnis der zentralen Tagung am 16. Dezember 1983" (December 16, 1983).

Linzer, Ernst-Ludwig Petrowsky, Rolf Reichelt, and Bert Noglik, all figures who have already entered prominently in this history.[56] Most of the regular members – whose numbers increased to over 100 by the late 1980s – were professional musicians who were primarily eager to lobby for their own advancement, including by sharing their grievances with the state. A detailed list of these grievances from 1984 reveals insight into the difficult working conditions of performing artists as well as these artists' criticism of other state agencies. Tools necessary to function as an independent artist, such as telephone lines and cars, were scarce. Also lacking was a catalog of professional jazz musicians analogous to the one for rock music, which had been published in the early 1980s.[57] Unlike their counterparts in rock, jazz musicians here complained about insufficient opportunities to perform and requested numerous forms of compensation: subsidized tours, the establishment of a venue in Berlin that would permanently feature jazz, and a national jazz festival, all of which would elevate the status of jazz in the GDR.[58] Such engagement with the agency offered the prospect of political leverage not just with the KfU, but with the KGD and the Künstler-Agentur der DDR as well, the two agencies that held the monopoly on contracting all artists, whether foreign or domestic. Regular KfU committee meetings provided a forum in which jazz musicians openly criticized the high fees of the KGD as well as the inefficiency of the artists' agency to process contracts for performances abroad.[59]

Despite the issues pervading the KfU, its musicians were nonetheless eager to perform at such a prominent event as the Weimar festival. The press, too, lauded the event, emphasizing the mutually beneficial relationship between the authorities and the jazz community. In a stark contrast to its ambivalence of twenty years earlier, the *Berliner Zeitung* crowed that "this national music forum [was] possible because of the level of accomplishment of our musicians in our country, as well as the supporting role of enthusiastic producers, jazz fans and journalists."[60] To ensure the widest possible exposure, radio and television stations repeated their broadcast

---

[56] Ministerium für Kultur, "Die Mitglieder der Arbeitskreise des Komitees für Unterhaltungskunst," BArch/DY 43/1350 (1984).

[57] BArch/DY 43/1350 Komitee für Unterhaltungskunst der DDR, "Informationen über die Tätigkeit der Arbeitskreise des Komitees für Unterhaltungskunst" (January 25, 1984), 79.

[58] Kultur, "Problemspiegel in der Auswertung der Zentralen Tagungen der Arbeitskreise des Komitees, BArch/DY 43/1350."

[59] Ibid.

[60] Elbe, "Eine Nationale Festivalpremiere."

Figure 6.2 Album cover of *Erste Jazztage der DDR, Weimar 1985* (Amiga 8 56 216).
Released 1986. Permission by Sony Records

of performances and commentaries throughout the following weeks.
A year later Amiga published a record to commemorate the "1. Jazztage
der DDR" (Figure 6.2).[61] Plaudits aside, however, the impacts of the festival were significant: in its wake came the founding of the National Jazz
Orchestra, further cementing jazz in the East German cultural canon
(Figure 6.2). Though larger events would subsume its establishment, plans
for this orchestra included for it to be led by a new conductor each year
and to perform commissioned works by leading musicians of the scene.

[61] "1. Jazztage der DDR," *Berliner Zeitung, TV Program* (December 6, 1989); "1. Jazztage der
DDR," *Neue Zeit, TV Program* (December 15, 1989); "1. Jazztage der DDR," *Berliner Zeitung, TV
Program* (December 14, 1989); "1. Jazztage der DDR," *Berliner Zeitung, TV Program* (December
5, 1985).

Furthermore, the KfU and the KB set in motion projects such as the publication of a national jazz guide (*Jazzführer DDR*) as well as a book-length history of GDR jazz.[62] When in 1986 a reporter asked Karlheinz Drechsel, then vice president of the jazz section at the KfU, about the prospects for the next festival, he answered: "Well, we will have to wait and see what the first one offers us. We would be happy if, in the future, the national jazz festival would find a solid position within East German cultural life."[63] But the subsequent years would prove to be more unpredictable than Drechsel or anyone at that point could predict. Indeed, by the time Weimar organizers were preparing for the second national festival four years later, they would be overrun by the dramatic events that would sweep the entire country. The fate not just of jazz, but of the entire GDR, was about to change.

Gorbachev, Liberalization, and the Road to 1989

On March 11, 1985, Mikhail Gorbachev became general secretary of the Central Committee of the Communist Party of the Soviet Union and proceeded to reform the Soviet system as it then stood. Though his changes aimed to stabilize the superpower, historian Archie Brown has argued that at the point of Gorbachev's election, neither members of the Politburo, the Central Committee that elected him, nor Gorbachev himself could have foreseen the anticipation of events in the following years, of which "the greatest unintended outcome was the disintegration of the Soviet Union."[64]

As a reformer, to address the grievances of a dysfunctional political and economic system, Gorbachev pushed for openness and transparency of the political system as well as for freedom of information, ideas famously circumscribed with the slogan *glasnost*. Accelerating these policies of openness that Gorbachev had envisioned was a sudden catastrophe: the nuclear meltdown at Chernobyl a year after his election. The initial reaction of his administration to the disaster – which was first detected

[62] See Komitee für Unterhaltungskunst der DDR, "Informationen über die Tätigkeit der Arbeitskreise des Komitees für Unterhaltungskunst." For the proposed history of jazz, see Bert Noglik, "Konzeption (erste Überlegungen) zu einem für 1989 geplanten Semiar zur Geschichte des Jazz, BArch: DY 27" (June 2, 1988).

[63] Cristine Wagner, "Jazztage der DDR. Erstmals in Weimar," in *Profil: Methodik zur Tanzmusik 5* (Leipzig: Zentralhaus-Publikation, 1986).

[64] Archie Brown, "The Gorbachev Revolution and the End of the Cold War," in *The Cambridge History of the Cold War*, ed. Melvin P. Leffler and Odd Arne Westad (Cambridge University Press, 2010), 248. See also *The Gorbachev Factor* (Oxford University Press, 1997).

in the West, not in the Soviet Union – was, perhaps unsurprisingly, a security lockdown and the negation of *glasnost*. But both the Soviet public and the international community demanded answers for this irresponsible cover-up, which made Chernobyl a turning point in the development of greater openness.[65] Even spurred by this crisis, however, it was primarily Gorbachev's divergent outlook from his predecessors that produced an innovative foreign policy to end the Cold War. The long-standing arms race between superpowers was, as Gorbachev put it, "not a normal condition of international relations, since it constantly carried within itself a military threat."[66] Given the fact that in the event of nuclear confrontation between superpowers, central European territory would have been the battlefield, Gorbachev spoke to the hearts and minds of millions of Europeans, many of them organized in peace movements in the West and in the East, by declaring that "Europe is our common home and not a theatre of military operations." Indeed, during his leadership, both the Soviet Union and the United States recognized the need to eliminate the nuclear threat and signed far-reaching agreements for mutual disarmament.[67]

Moreover, regarding Moscow's relation to Soviet satellite states such as East Germany, Gorbachev was determined that the Soviet Union should undertake no further armed interventions. This brought an end to the doctrine of "legitimate interference," a position that historically had facilitated the military suppression of the East German uprising in 1953, the Hungarian Uprising in 1957, as well as the Prague Spring in 1968. The leaders of such satellites could no longer rely on Moscow's intervention as the ultimate guarantor of their power.[68] Furthermore, regarding Soviet hegemony, Gorbachev announced the free choice of economic system. At a speech at the UN in December 1988, Gorbachev declared that each country would not only have the right to political independence, but also economic independence, and the right to choose its own economic system. US President Ronald Reagan's secretary of state, George Shultz, noted the full extent of Gorbachev's words by stating "if anybody declared the end of the cold war, he did in that speech."[69]

---

[65] Zhores Medvedev, "Chernobyl': A Catalyst for Change," in *Milestones in Glasnost and Perestroyka: Politics and People*, ed. Edward A. Hewett and Victor H. Winston (1991). Cf. Brown, *The Gorbachev Factor*, 163.

[66] M.S. Gorbachev, *Izbrannye rechi I stat'i* [Collected Speeches and Articles], 5 vols. (Moscow: Politizdat, 1987), vol. II, 75–198. As cited in: "The Gorbachev Revolution and the End of the Cold War," 246.

[67] Ibid., 265.

[68] Ibid., 253. Cf. *The Gorbachev Factor*, 212–51.

[69] "The Gorbachev Revolution and the End of the Cold War," 253–54.

Disdaining Gorbachev's ideas, the hard-line East German leadership attempted to repress information about the new Soviet course. For the first time in the history of the GDR, the SED leadership openly demonstrated disloyalty against Moscow and showed a growing disapproval of Soviet reforms.[70] When, in his welcome speech at the eleventh SED party rally on April 17–21, 1986, Gorbachev claimed that "self-criticism is imperative for success," East German Chairman Honecker spoke confidently of the "unshakable relation of trust between his party and the people of the GDR."[71] Honecker's inability (or refusal) to discern the signs of the times and his strict adherence to the status quo offended more progressive SED loyalists and intellectuals and would ultimately lead to his forced resignation, discussed in more detail below.[72]

Amid such national developments, the culture sector could not remain unaffected, and sources show increasing criticism of party leadership from without and within. About six months after Gorbachev's election, the KfU held a meeting on November 6, 1985, led by lyricist and then president Gisela Steineckert. Attendees presented their activities and future projects, such as the second national jazz festival in Weimar, as well as events of the East German peace movement, such as "Rock für den Frieden" and the Friedensfest at the Volksbühne. The rest of the conference was devoted to events surrounding the eleventh party rally the following April – the one in which Gorbachev was slated to appear. The KfU was responsible for the production of the accompanying events in Berlin, such as a gala and ball in the Palace of the Republic and several revues in the Friedrichstadt-Palast. Committee members anticipated an exciting year and assured themselves of the high artistic standards of KfU events – were it not for one distressing fact: the report of Deutsche Schallplatten executive Hansjürgen Schäfer about Amiga, the record label producing pop, hits, and jazz.

Schäfer's contribution to the conference stands out amid the ideological self-adulation of the KfU, confronting the committee members with a harsh reality. In a report prepared exclusively for the eyes of the committee, Schäfer acknowledged a dramatic decline in the demand of East Germany's own popular music, noting:

> There is an alarming decline in the demand for [GDR] rock and pop. Whereas in previous years our leading rock bands sold 250,000 to 600,000 albums, these numbers now tend to be far below 100,000, sometimes only

[70] Brown, *The Gorbachev Factor*, 249.
[71] Protokoll XI. Parteitag, P.32, 155. As cited in Weber, *Geschichte der DDR*, 451–52.
[72] Ulrich Mählert, *Kleine Geschichte der DDR*, 5th, 2007 ed. (München: C.H. Beck, 1998), 150.

20,000. This problem is much greater in the realm of pop (*Schlager*). The best-selling recording artist in our country is by far not an Amiga artist but our trumpeter Professor Ludwig Güttler, with his recordings of the works of Bach, Händel, Schütz, and their contemporaries.[73]

The public appeal of the GDR's own rock and pop music had declined to a worrisome extent, threatening to make Amiga a failing label were it not for the licensed productions of Western titles. Radio listenership, too, had declined, as by the mid-1980s the vast majority of East German audiences were turning away from homegrown productions, even as Gisela Steineckert repeatedly trumpeted the national significance of the GDR's popular arts.[74] It seems that the majority of audiences did not identify with national products in rock and pop, as they had in the 1970s, and preferred trendsetting Western imports instead. The only exception to this dramatic development, according to Schäfer, was the East German rock band Phudys, who "because of their professionalism could keep their audience in a remarkably pleasant way." In his report, he explained the reasons for the decline, noting:

> Our entertaining arts have to compete with and distinguish themselves from international trends and stars. That is a difficult task. It requires not only quality of production and genuine invention, but also better cooperation between media, live events, and press campaigns as practiced internationally.

Notably, Schäfer did not mention any considerable decline in sales in jazz. Amiga's jazz division represented about ten percent of its entire productions, which suggests that buyers' interest in jazz titles seems to have been stable.[75] Even so, while concealing the fact of declining interest in GDR productions from the public, the KfU continued its propaganda about

---

[73] "*Nur auf einem Gebiet haben wir zunehmend besorgniserregende Probleme: Dem des aktuellen Amiga Angebotes, Rock und Pop und Schlager betreffend: Hier ist ein großer Rückgang des Käuferinteresses am nationalen Angebot zu erkennen.*" BArch/DR/101/3/b, "Hansjürgen Schäfer. 5. Tagung des Komitees für Unterhaltungskunst. Thema: Die Verantwortung des Komitees für Unterhaltungskunst für die Erhöhung der weiteren Wirksamkeit der Massenmedien. Diskussionsbeitrag DS: Zur Interpreten-, Produktions- und Angebotspolitik des DS" (November 6, 1985). According to Schäfer's report, the Deutsche Schallplatte produced 20 million records (LP, MK and singles) in 1985, which satisfied demand. One exception was the repertoire of licensed Western productions. Demand was higher and an increase of such productions depended on the available amounts of foreign currency. Overall, Amiga production comprised 25 percent pop (*Schlager*), 25 percent rock, 25 percent opera and musical (and *unterhaltende Musik*), 15 percent singer/songwriter and folk, and 10 percent jazz.
[74] BStU, MfS, Potsdam HA XX 535, Komitee für Unterhaltungskunst.
[75] Ibid. In his report, Schäfer does not discern between national jazz production and Western titles licensed to Amiga.

East German rock and pop. In February 1989, KfU general director Rainer Heinemann argued in *Neues Deutschland*: "Whoever wants to compete internationally must present their own distinctive art, and must reach top performances. An artist who wants to be accepted by his audience must be determined – yes, I would even like to say, must obsessively strive for the highest accomplishments to realize his artistic intention."[76] The closer the country approached collapse, such rhetoric sounded increasingly frantic.

Sources do not indicate how the committee reacted to Schafer's report, but it was true that throughout the second half of the 1980s the KfU could not reverse the growing disinterest in East German rock and pop. Rather, the committee members (of whom the majority were performing artists themselves) were mostly dedicated to the betterment of working conditions under the mere pretense of being internationally competitive. Their belief in the welfare state as a provider for their needs seems to have weathered any seasonal upswings or downturns in audience desires. Rather than pursue its original goals of coordinating artistic productions, the KfU turned instead into a welfare organization and advocacy group for artists, with increasing demands on the state support system as the years went on. The KfU social commission brought a "catalog of problems" to the Ministry for Culture as late as September 1989, only weeks before the fall of the Berlin Wall. This wish list included such items as new automobiles and vans for artists (the preferred model was a Barka B1000), interest-free credit, apartments in Berlin, special flats suited for artists, tax reductions, recreational facilities, secretaries, and computers.[77] In a country in which scarcity dominated everyday life, with average citizens waiting years for a single vehicle, such demands reveal the belief of these artists that their position within the state hierarchy ensured preferential treatment and amenities.

It is true, however, that a musician's membership in the KfU could positively impact his or her everyday life. Trombonist Konrad Bauer, then head of the KfU jazz section, described in a recent interview how under his leadership many musicians did receive assistance such as adequate living space. Furthermore, KfU membership had other advantages beyond just comfort. During a jazz concert in Cottbus about a month before the Wall came down, musicians put forth a resolution demanding political changes

---

[76] Günter Görtz, "Vor dem Kongreß der Unterhaltungskunst. Damit die Besucher noch mehr Spaß an der heiteren Muße haben," *Neues Deutschland* (February 25, 1989).
[77] BArch/DR 101/5c Komitee für Unterhaltungskunst der DDR, "Problemkatalog" (September 1989).

in the GDR, which local authorities regarded as extremely provocative.[78] When the performers were asked to stop their demonstration, they justified their acts by claiming that the KfU had permitted their resolution, which had allegedly already been public for two weeks, and threatened to complain to Steineckert. After a period of intense questioning, the local authorities relented as it seems that these musicians' affiliation with high-ranking officials safeguarded them from immediate repercussions. While short-lived, this one incident does illustrate how toward the end of the GDR the extension of state power, here exemplified in an unusual alliance of grassroots protesters and high-level state authorities which neutralized executive power, contributed to the implosion of the East German state.

From 1985 on, Gorbachev's reformist notion of the free flow of information increasingly took shape in East German print media, such as the Kulturbund/Jazz Club Berlin publication *Berliner Jazzblatt* (discussed above). This periodical served as a forum for open criticism against state authorities by the jazz establishment in a way that stands out prominently among most of the press coverage. In an article about the Jazzbühne 85, the annual high-profile jazz event in Berlin, one writer described a surprising reaction from audiences, who seemed to have turned against the jazz establishment.[79] Gisela Steineckert's lyrics, commissioned for the Jazzbühne and interpreted by the Brüning and Petrowsky duo, were apparently panned. The writer, who signed his comments only with his or her initials, notes that "Steineckert's *Jazztexte*, which was exclusively commissioned for the Jazzbühne 85, was badly received, and not just because of Brüning's inarticulate presentation." Furthermore, according to this observer, star drummer Günter Sommer miscommunicated with his players, creating a "syrupy tingle." The writer then attacked the producers of the Jazzbühne, claiming that they were unfamiliar with the tastes of young audiences who preferred "hard-core" jazz, and that Sommer's piece led to massive audience desertion during his performances.[80]

While such words can appear somewhat mild in tone today, this open expression of opinion represents a startling example amid the status quo of

---

[78] This resolution was dated September 18, 1989. Cf. BStU, MfS, Cottbus AGK 1704, *Information über das Vorlesen der Resolution der Berliner Unterhaltungskünstler*, October 6, 1989. See also Rauhut, *Rock in der DDR*, 133–35. The protest took place on October 6, 1989, at the *Kulturhaus des Textilkombinates*, Cottbus. The identity of the performers is classified; see also: www.hu-berlin.de/alumni/prominente/interviews/wenzel.

[79] By 1985, Petrowsky, Bauer, and Sommer had received GDR art awards.

[80] "Berliner Jazzblatt," ed. Jazzclub Berlin im Kulturbund der DDR (July 1985), 4–7. The initials of the writer match those of the publisher of the *Jazzblatt*, but it is uncertain whether they are the same person.

publications such as *Melodie und Rhythmus* and *Neues Deutschland*, which almost uniformly praised the artistic achievement of East German jazz. This new tone in the *Berliner Jazzblatt* suggests that Gorbachev's notion of *glasnost* did encourage writers to break away from the ideological mainstream and take the opportunity to speak critically. Indeed, from 1988 on, its "Jazzkalender" regularly noted events taking place in West German cities, events which, as noted above, were at that point still largely out of reach for most East German citizens. GDR jazz fans were not just informed of festivals in Western Europe, such as in The Hague, West Berlin, Moers, and Leverkusen, they also learned about the Western tour dates of Herbie Hancock, about jazz exhibitions such as one in Munich dedicated to Miles Davis, and about Western films such as *Round Midnight* about the life of Charlie Parker.[81] In 1985, cultural scientist Helmut Hanke had argued for just this need – for the GDR to open its doors to international culture – claiming that "we have to absolutely be open to international impulses and achievements in popular arts and entertainment. Often, they come from the other world and evolve out of the commercialization and usurpation of alternative, democratic, and socialist art and culture whether we call it New Wave, Aerobic or Break Dance."[82] By the late 1980s, such seeds of openness would bear fruit.

A Coda for Jazz? The Fall of the Wall

By the end of 1989, the SED leadership faced a dilemma. The Soviet Union would no longer back any forceful measures against public unrest in the GDR, at a time when tens of thousands of citizens were seeking to leave the country. The loosening of travel restrictions in 1988 had granted temporary travel visas to West Germany to almost 2.7 million citizens, a protocol that represented a key source of Western currency for the East German state: the following year, from January to September 1989, 2.2 million private trips to the West had been approved.[83] But many East Germans did not trust such liberalization, choosing instead the risky route of permanent emigration. From November 1988 to September 1989, requests for exiting the GDR doubled to about 160,000. Indeed, this flight from East Germany dramatically accelerated in the summer of 1989

---

[81] "Berliner Jazzblatt," ed. Jazzclub Berlin im Kulturbund der DDR (October–December 1988).

[82] BArch/DY 43/1350 Komitee für Unterhaltungskunst der DDR, "Diskussionsbeitrag auf der Beratung des Komitees für Unterhaltungskunst von Helmut Hanke" (June 6, 1985).

[83] Maier, *Dissolution*, 128.

when East Germans took refuge in West German embassies in Budapest and Prague, as well as in the STÄV in East Berlin. By that September, the numbers of East Germans in Hungary alone had risen to about 150,000, when reformists in the Hungarian government allowed East Germans to legally cross the border into Austria.[84]

But not all East Germans were able or willing to leave, and those who remained demanded more reforms. In the fall of 1989, Leipzig, the second largest city in the GDR and home to the jazz festival described above, had become a center of resistance against state authority, a movement that only later spread to Berlin. As historian Charles Maier documents, this resistance was initially spearheaded by church organizers, via the long-standing Monday prayer meetings in the Nikoleikirche that "provided a pre-exciting nucleus of disaffiliation."[85] He concludes: "Ironically enough it was precisely the opportunity to leave that crystallized the formation of opposition groups among those determined to stay. The growing flight compelled those unprepared to uproot themselves to demand reforms that might justify their remaining."[86] As these tensions came to a head, on Monday, September 25, 1989, the citizens of Leipzig launched the first major demonstration for democratic renewal.[87]

At this point, business proceeded as usual – at first. The Leipzig Festival took place as planned, from September 28 to October 1, 1989, between the first and second Monday demonstrations. The circus tent was ultimately not needed for the festival, with the Capitol Cinema (*Kino Capitol*) serving as the major venue instead, and none other than Werner Sellhorn serving as emcee. At the same time, however, the Berlin ceremonies to celebrate the fortieth anniversary of the founding of the GDR on October 7, 1989, also proceeded as planned with ceremonies attended by Gorbachev, Honecker, and other allied heads of state. Military and FDJ "blue shirts" greeted the dignitaries along Karl-Marx-Allee, but later that day, opposition groups expressed their desire for change by openly addressing Gorbachev. Regrettably, these peaceful – though not officially permitted – demonstrations were violently suppressed by police and STASI forces, but citizens of both cities, Leipzig and Berlin, kept pushing for peaceful change. In examining these volatile days, Maier has argued

[84] Ibid., 120–31. For a discussion on the fall of communism in Eastern Europe, see Gale Stokes, *The Walls Came Tubling Down* (Oxford University Press, 1993).
[85] Maier, *Dissolution*, 139.
[86] Ibid., 136.
[87] Ibid., 137.

that "in effect the fate of the East German regime was decided on the Leipzig Ring on four successive Monday evenings between September 25th and October 16th, then confirmed in Berlin between Saturday, November 4th, and Thursday, November 9th."[88] Indeed, on October 18th, under pressure from Politbüro and ZK, Honecker finally agreed to step down – under the public cover of resigning for health reasons – and was replaced by his protégé Egon Krenz, who promised reforms of the socialist system.[89] Shortly thereafter, to keep the momentum of protest alive, groups such as the *Neues Forum* called for demonstrations in central Berlin on November 4th, which were officially permitted. Over half a million people joined the call and attended the speeches of cultural and party officials on Alexanderplatz, in one of the largest mass gatherings in East German history.[90]

In interviews conducted for this book, many members of the East German jazz community recalled their experiences of these fateful days. Jazz enthusiasts Helmut Eickermann and Gerhard Hopfe described marching that day and attending the Alexanderplatz rally to express their protest at the state system. Others, such as Alfons Wonneberg, Herbert Flugge, and Karlheinz Drechsel lived through those days in very different ways. In recollection, these jazz fans have suggested that they were prepared for anything to happen, but all were surprised just how quickly events developed. For only five days later, on November 9th, SED spokesman Günther Schabowski gave the official order to open the borders.[91] For East German citizens, the world as they knew it had changed forever.

That night, Hopfe, fifty-six years old at the time, was on his way back to Berlin from Leipzig, where he had attended a conference in his career as a librarian. He had heard about the opening of the borders in Berlin while on the train home, where people in disbelief were reassured by those who carried portable radios, shouting, "Schabowski just ordered the borders to be opened." Immediately opening beer bottles, the train passengers began to celebrate right then and there. By the time Hopfe arrived at his home in Marzahn, a little after 10:00 p.m., he saw many people in his neighborhood

---

[88] Ibid., 139.

[89] Helga Haftendorn, "The Unification of Germany, 1985–1991," in *The Cold War, Volume III: Endings*, ed. Melvyn P. Leffler and Odd Arne Westad (Cambridge University Press, 2010), 339.

[90] Speakers that day included Günter Schabowski, Markus Wolf, Christa Wolf, and Stefan Heym. Schabowski, a member of the ZK, gained worldwide fame for a press conference on November 9th wherein he declared that border checkpoints should be opened, on some accounts hastening the fall of the Wall. Markus Wolf, head of GDR counterintelligence, had resigned in 1986 and joined opposition groups from October 1989.

[91] Haftendorn, "The Unification of Germany, 1985–1991," 339.

starting up their Trabants to drive to the checkpoint at Bornholmer Straße. As he recalled, after an exhausting day of meetings and lectures, Hopfe was too tired to join them, so the next day he crossed over the Wall. It had been constructed while he was imprisoned from 1959 until 1962 and had made his parents' home uninhabitable – their property in Falkensee was one of the last ones before the border with West Berlin. On the night of November 9th, Hopfe was not particularly curious about seeing the West, as he was no stranger to it. Every year since 1986 he had applied for a visa to visit his aunt, who also supplied him with Western currency to obtain goods he was unable to get in the GDR.

On the same night, Eickermann, then forty-nine, met with his Maxim Gorky literacy circle that gathered weekly at the DSF in the Palais am Festungsgraben.[92] In previous years, he had been successful as a writer and had quit his job as a radio technician to dedicate his time fully to writing. Every Thursday evening, the circle met to read and discuss their work, which lately had engaged the tense political situation more and more. One of the members, a retired veterinarian, was able to travel regularly and supplied circle members with the Soviet periodical *Sputnik*, which at the time published articles sympathetic to Gorbachev's politics and which had been banned in the GDR in 1988. Afterward, they usually continued over beer at the nearby Domklause located in the upscale Palasthotel, a short walk across the Schlossbrücke. Here, Eickermann and his friends heard about the opening of the border from a GDR state TV report. (In public spaces, Western television was taboo; although many East German citizens watched Western TV in the private sphere, talking about it openly was rare.) This resulted in great excitement among the Domklause patrons, who ordered sparkling wine to celebrate. According to Eickermann, though, many people he encountered, including the Gorky circle, remained relatively calm. On his way home that night via Alexanderplatz to Moldaustrassse, Eickermann did not notice much turmoil, either on the streets or in the underground. At home, his wife Angelika and his daughter were anxiously awaiting his return to share the news, but at that point, it was close to midnight, so they refrained from leaving the house.

The next day, November 10th, after their children returned from school, the Eickermanns drove in their Trabbi near the border checkpoint at Oberbaumbrücke. This was the place where, until August 1961, Eickermann had crossed the border to attend jazz bands in West Berlin,

---

[92] According to Eickermann, leader of the circle since 1986, the circle was founded in 1955.

attending concerts by such performers as Duke Ellington. That afternoon, the area at Oberbaumbrücke was filled with people, all trying to
slip through the narrow opening less than three feet wide. Eickermann
recalled that people were cheerful, but disciplined. A police officer shouted,
"Please be careful, some people already want to come back," a comment
that stirred laughter among those waiting to enter the West. Once on the
other side, hundreds of people waited at a nearby bank teller to receive the
Western "welcome money" of 100 Deutsche Mark. But the Eickermann
family had something more important to do. They took the underground,
traveled to Kurfürstendamm to meet Eickermann's daughter from a previous marriage, and visited a shopping center. While the sixteen-year-old
son bought a lens for his camera, their twelve-year-old daughter was proud
that she was not tempted by the Barbie dolls and afterward told everybody
at home how she did not succumb to the shopping frenzy that many other
East Germans were participating in at that very moment.

Sixty-two-year-old Alfons Wonneberg, who by 1989 could look back on
a brilliant career as a bandleader, was in his office at home in Schöneiche
on November 9th. He had spent the evening writing arrangements for
his orchestra, which was his real passion. His wife, Brigitte, formerly a
singer and dancer with the well-known group Michael Hansen and the
Nancies, heard the news on West German television and told her husband, who, in disbelief, questioned her claim. That night they followed
the dramatic events on TV. The next day, Mrs. Wonneberg, who due to
her profession had also been familiar with the West, crossed the border
at Friedrichstraße by herself and bought three oranges and one tube of
lipstick. As she recalls, Alfons was not overly interested to see the open
border immediately, reasoning that the crowds were too much trouble to
deal with, and besides, the West was familiar to him as well – as the leader
of the Alfons Wonneberg Orchestra he had traveled to dozens of countries across the world, including the United States. A few days later, they
drove their Wartburg to Zehlendorf in West Berlin to visit Wonneberg's
aunt. According to Brigitte, it was an uplifting experience for both of
them to cross the once-divided city from Schöneiche in the northeast to
Zehlendorf in the southwest. As he recalled, Wonneberg was not entirely
surprised when the Wall fell, an event that he had privately anticipated for
several years, but that night it was clear to him that his career as a state-
sponsored bandleader and musical ambassador was over. Although he was
able to find employment as a teacher at the Hanns Eisler Music Academy
in the 1990s, he nevertheless regretted that his life as a performing artist
and manager had come to an end.

Herbert Flügge, then fifty-six, a lifelong teacher who at the time was vice president of a Babelsberg school, lived in Potsdam in the west of Berlin. A trip to East Berlin from Potsdam, which they did not often undertake, was usually time-consuming during the era of the Wall. On November 9th, he and his wife Christel closely followed the reports on TV, stunned at the news. To them, the prospect of an open border to Wannsee, Zehlendorf and the other western parts of Berlin had been inconceivable. Almost three decades had passed since the last time he had been in the West: shortly before the Wall went up, they had seen *Jazz on a Summer's Day* at the Aktualitäten Kino at Berlin Zoo. From then until the autumn of 1989, they had not been in the West at all. As civil servants, they had refrained from applying for visas both because they felt it was inappropriate, and because they were afraid of becoming targets of surveillance. Even after the Wall had fallen on November 9th, they waited several days until the rush to the border had calmed down. When they crossed the border near Potsdam, Flügge was mostly interested in the physical dimensions of the Wall called the Iron Curtain. Inspecting its structure and surface – it was painted white, with barbed wire and glass splinters on top – he recalled wondering about the fragility of the fortification that had divided not just the city but two worlds.

Across town, that night Karlheinz Drechsel was moderating his monthly live radio show *Jazznacht* on Nalepastraße, when a college student in the studio placed a note on his desk, saying that the border to the West had opened. In disbelief he turned on the television and saw that people were crossing checkpoints in droves. Immediately he interrupted his show and announced the news on *Jazznacht*. When he came home to Adlershof, his wife had not yet heard the news, so the next day they crossed over and attended a Dixieland and swing dance in West Berlin at the Funkturm. For Drechsel, such opportunities had been numerous – like Wonneberg, he had traveled as far afield as New York, but for his wife, it was the first time she had ever set foot on Western soil.

In 1989, Rolf Reichelt, then forty-seven, had been living in West Germany for five years after he had chosen to stay in West Germany while on an official trip. The night of November 9th he spent with his fellow music therapy students, who met once a week in Frankfurt am Main to discuss their studies and prepare for their examinations. Suddenly, he recalled, the door opened and one of the participant's spouses shouted, "Quickly, come and see, the Wall in Berlin has fallen." Everybody rushed to a nearby television to watch the live broadcast of the event. His colleagues, all of them West Germans, erupted with joy, but grew irritated when they saw Reichelt's reaction, who expressed neither joy nor excitement. As he recalled, at that moment he was unable to react at all. Rather, he was unable to enjoy the news, as he was emotionally overwhelmed by trying to comprehend both what was happening and what would come. He thought of his friends and colleagues in the GDR, and about those who were imprisoned: the state that he had escaped had at that moment ceased to exist. When he arrived at his home in Darmstadt, his wife, a West German, was not delighted about this historic moment either, expressing her own fears about nationalist movements interfering with a united Europe. Even so, for Reichelt, the time around November 9th was dominated by events less of professional than of personal significance, such as reuniting with his children from his previous marriage, now twenty-one and twenty-three years old, who had escaped via Budapest to West Germany.

On November 9th, Jost Gebers, the producer at FMP in West Berlin, was getting ready to prepare for his trip the next morning to Einbeck, West Germany. It was a sad occasion: his father had passed away a few days earlier, and the funeral was to take place the next day on November 10th. It was about 9:30 p.m. when Gebers, who directed a youth club on Olbersstraße in Charlottenburg and still at his office, received a call from a West German friend informing him of the opening of the Wall. As he recalled, Gebers replied: "You are crazy!" Then he turned on the TV, and seeing the events, thought, "For God's sake, I still have to get to the studio in Wedding, and will have a hell of time with the traffic coming from the East via Bornholmer Straße." He immediately left his office and headed toward Wedding. Indeed, the main axis at Bornholmer Straße/Osloer Straße was at that point flooded with hundreds of Trabants on their way west. Nevertheless, he managed to get across the jammed street to his studio in Wedding. He allowed himself just a few hours of sleep before leaving early the next morning. The transit route via Magdeburg to Hanover was packed with East Germans heading west, but fortunately, he arrived in time to his father's funeral.

East German writer Bert Noglik, then forty-one, was on his way back from Berlin to Leipzig on the afternoon of November 9th. He had produced a contemporary jazz show for Radio DDR II at the Nalepastraße facility, working with his friend and technician Brigitte Orawetz the day before. He recalled that in the railway compartment a person next to him was carrying a portable radio, listening anxiously to headphones. Except for this person, Noglik did not observe anybody acting abnormally, as most people seemingly had no notion of what was unfolding that night in the capital. Noglik, who at that time was living with his parents, arrived at home, had dinner with his parents, then went to bed. After midnight, they woke from their sleep when the telephone rang. It was Orawetz, who was overcome with joy, telling them the Wall had fallen. Noglik and his parents followed the events on West German TV until the early morning hours, and some days later, he crossed the border and visited West Berlin. This experience was not entirely new, as by special permission from GDR authorities, he had attended the Cecil Taylor festival hosted by FMP in 1988. Yet thereafter, he spent his first days in West Berlin primarily visiting friends.

On November 9th, West German cultural attaché Rainer Haarmann was in Leipzig, attending a private view of artworks from North-Rhine-Westphalia in the Georgi-Dimitroff Museum of the Arts. Haarmann had helped to coordinate this event, which was to be personally opened that night by Johannes Rau, then Minister President of North-Rhine-Westphalia from 1978 to 1998 (and later the first president of the reunified country) and, at the time, working at the Intra-German Ministry. The opening was yet another cultural exchange project to nurture relations between the two German states. At the museum's press conference that morning, however, none of the impending changes that were about to happen were discussed. Yet that evening, during the event's opening ceremonies, the spread of the news left attendees at the gallery stunned – especially given that as a result of the news all future projects to sustain communication between the two Germanies were suddenly made obsolete. In a recent interview, Haarmann recalled the night:

> We were overwhelmed, highly emotional, and hugged each other with joy, although the situation had a surreal quality (*Hauch des Unwirklichen*). But the reality was obvious on the streets. The news had spread like wildfire, that everybody could now travel with visa stamps in their passports. And because the GDR was a thoroughly German state, agencies opened up all night for people to obtain such visas. It seemed that the whole city of Leipzig was up and about until deep into the night. And one moment that night will be ineradicably etched in my memory: East German art historian Werner Schmidt magically came up with a giant bouquet of red roses, and distributed them among the exhibition's attendees.

Finally, that same night, Erhard Kayser, pastor of the Friedenskirche in Bergkamen, West Germany – who as a young seminarian had risked imprisonment with the 1960s Jazz Lift – was also in Berlin. For many years in his church position, he had taken educational journeys with his parishioners. Thus far, they had visited East Asian countries and European capitals, but 1989 was the year they had chosen West Berlin as their destination, arriving on the evening of November 9th. Kayser, who had bravely smuggled contraband jazz materials between the two Germanies many times, was able to witness firsthand the opening of the Iron Curtain at the Brandenburg Gate. Here, East German police (*Volkspolizisten*) waved East Germans westward, where West Germans welcomed them enthusiastically. Kayser has recalled an "indescribable excitement" in these moments – years earlier he had sought to help jazz fans in the East, and now at Brandenburg Gate, he knew what he had to do. He managed to obtain hundreds of 5-Mark bills and, in his words, "splashed them around" to those who had just taken their first steps onto Western soil in this new era.[93]

Conclusion

As noted, at the first National Jazz Festival in Weimar in 1985, over 8,000 visitors had attended four days of sold-out events. Planning for the second festival began almost immediately, where none other than the inaugural National Jazz Orchestra of the GDR (*Nationales Jazz Orchester der DDR*) prepared for its debut.[94] Yet when the festival opened on November 23–26, 1989, the scene could not have looked more different: its former crowds were absent, and its ensembles played to sparsely filled halls.[95] Two weeks earlier, the Berlin Wall had fallen. Years later, in an interview, trombonist Konrad Bauer recounted: "I do not think jazz was of any importance at that moment. Fourteen days prior the Wall had opened, and then none of this [the Festival] was of any significance, either for us or for the audience."[96] Nevertheless, like many other musicians, Bauer performed at the festival's opening event as scheduled, despite the lack of attendance. In an article entitled "Superb Performances in Empty Halls," *Neues Deutschland* assured its readers that the apparent flop was not the musicians' fault. Rather, writer Andreas Holgert argued that "Weimar offered a lot of

---

[93] Interview with the author, April 2017.
[94] Bratfisch, *Frei Töne*, p. 202.
[95] Ulf Drechsel, "2. Jazztage der DDR in Weimar," *Journal für Unterhaltungskunst* (2/1990).
[96] Bratfisch, *Frei Töne*, p. 218.

music worth listening to and revealed more than just the musicians' joy of playing, unconcerned with the depressingly empty halls." Furthermore, he noted:

> Nobody had doubted the legitimacy of the second festival. After all, jazz has established itself in our country, and has evolved as an essential part of the remarkable standards in our culture ... But we underestimated that four years had passed [since the last festival] and that those concepts no longer work if they lag behind the *Zeitgeist*. A festival that presents exclusively national music diminishes its appeal. Processes of internationalism [e.g. the fall of the Wall] cannot respond to bigoted traditionalism.[97]

Holgert's perspective, written just after the event, is characteristic for East German observers who were seeking to make sense out of the tumultuous events in the aftermath of the fall of the Wall. Though nobody at the time knew what the new *Zeitgeist*, as he termed it, would consist of, it was clear enough that a period of fundamental social and cultural restructuring was about to dawn.

What happened in the four short years between 1985 and 1989, such that nobody attended the second National Jazz Festival? Was the fall of the Berlin Wall alone a sufficient explanation for this dramatic decline in interest? Examining the dissolution of East Germany at large, historian Charles S. Maier has argued: "What occurred in November 1989, was that the permanent constraints suddenly disappeared. ... The Wall at the frontier had made possible all the walls within; the GDR had been a regime of walls, the most effective being those within its citizens' heads."[98] On this view, the Wall had become "the paradigm for a regime of confined space," so when the physical wall fell, the "walls within" fell too. Maier's metaphor of the "walls within" illuminates the constraints on life determining individual thought and behavior in a society bound by a complex network of dependencies, complicities, and secrecy. Indeed, this society, which Mary Fulbrook has characterized as a "system sustained through myriad micro-relationships of extended power and authority," more closely resembled what she has termed a "participatory dictatorship."[99] Consequently, when

---

[97] Andreas Holgert, "Erstklassiges Spiel vor leeren Sälen: Betrachtung nach dem 2. Nationalen Jazz-Festival in Weimar," *Neues Deutschland* (December 2, 1989).
[98] Maier, *Dissolution*, 56.
[99] Mary Fulbrook, *The People's State: East German Society from Hitler to Honecker* (New Haven, Conn.: Yale University Press, 2005), 236.

the Wall came down, those confined spaces opened up, and with that new perspective came the opportunity to leave one's old life behind. In abandoning the National Jazz Festival in 1989, then, audiences had abandoned any association with socialist culture: not only did audiences not identify with the idea of a "national" event, they no longer even identified with the state as a national entity.

The fall of the Wall did not just open the borders, it also ended the much-lauded citizens' participation in state-sponsored culture, with the dismantling of state institutions and organizations that had been in place for decades. Overnight, all the policies that had defined jazz in the GDR – the 1962 jazz resolution, STASI surveillance under *Westarbeit*, the move toward national centralization of local clubs – began to dissolve, just as did the many different agencies and committees tasked with stewarding music in the state. Not only did the ZK cease to exist, but so did the KfU, which formally dissolved on December 18, 1989, and later, the Rundfunk, the KB, and Amiga (VEB Deutsche Schallplatten). Indeed, after 1990, none of the organizations, platforms, publications, or festivals showcasing East German jazz survived fully intact, if at all. Given that, by the 1980s, many key players in the jazz scene were also high-ranking members of the state arts bureaucracy (as detailed above). These musicians were suddenly forced into major career changes against every expectation or desire – a painful irony that the alleged triumph of free-market capitalism, at that moment, did not necessarily create opportunities for all citizens, but instead meant the end of opportunities for who had made their living by direct involvement in East German state culture. Dramatic as the events of November 9, 1989, were, it is also true that many members of the East German jazz scene – whether musicians, producers, or bandleaders – did not in fact have their lives changed that very day. Rather, their lives and fortunes would change in the weeks and months that followed, as the two Germanies sought the complicated process of reunification.

As noted, many of these players had pursued prestigious careers and gained recognition far beyond the borders of East Germany; envied by their Western counterparts, these performers were well aware of their privileged status as artists and, at the time, openly expressed their appreciation for such a beneficent state. In retrospect, though, after the demise of the SED, many began to retroactively construct a rather different past. In public remarks, interviews, and other venues, high-profile players such as Ernst-Ludwig Petrowsky and Uschi Brüning – to name but two – distanced themselves from the failed socialist state and instead advanced the version of the story of jazz as counterculture and expression of resistance.[100] From the contemporary perspective, as these former East German artists sought to come to terms with their past, a past in which complicity and privilege figured prominently, the fact that such revised narratives would emerge is hardly surprising. Equally unsurprising is that of these revisionists, Werner Sellhorn – one of the key figures of this account, ever adaptive to his surroundings – went perhaps the furthest: in the years surrounding Germany's reunification, Sellhorn joined the public effort to unveil STASI complicity. Remarkably, the former IM Zirkel now took up the role of a civil rights defender, spearheading the initiative to expose former STASI agents: from 1991 to 1994, he served as the editor-in-chief of the publication *Horch und Guck* until the truth about himself came to light. He denied all accusations, and the fact that he informed on most of his friends seems not to have discredited him. Until the end of his life, he remained in favor with the close-knit jazz community, as evidenced by the luminaries who attended his funeral, described in the opening of this book. Granted, not everyone in the scene mourned his passing; in recent interviews, Gerhard Hopfe expressed no desire to attend, and Alfons Wonneberg remarked that he did not want to pay his respects to someone who had not earned them.

But for many members of the East German jazz scene, the collapse of the state that had nurtured their careers meant that now they were forced into professional reorientation. A few individuals – Drechsel, Hopfe, Flügge, and Noglik among them – were able to continue their jazz activities in the reunified Germany, working in fields such as music journalism, performance, or management, but others did not share that same success. Indeed, with a few exceptions, most of the individuals interviewed for this history had to take up new careers. Arranger and bandleader Alfons Wonneberg was forced to take up teaching at the Hanns Eisler Conservatory and, in his retirement, worked on band arrangements that (as he put it) "nobody will ever listen to." Jan Eikermann successfully established himself as an author of crime stories, and Reinhard Heinemann, formerly the director of the KfU, opened a stamp store in Prenzlauer Berg. And those musicians

---

[100] Cf. three radio broadcasts: (1) Ernst-Ludwig and Siegfried Schmidt-Joos Petrowsky, *Erinnerungen an den Jazz in der Zone: Siegfried Schmidt-Joos im Gespräch mit Ernst-Ludwig Petrowsky* (Sender Freies Berlin, SFB 3, October 3, 1994). (2) Ernst-Ludwig Petrowsky and Uschi Brüning, *Schräge Töne aus der DDR: Die Jazzmusiker Uschi Brüning und Ernst-Ludwig Petrowsky erzählen* (Sender Freies Berlin, SFB 3, November 3, 1990). (3) Ernst-Ludwig Petrowsky, Uschi Brüning, and Klaus Lenz, *Wir machten Jazz: Ernst-Ludwig Petrowsky und Uschi Brüning im Gespräch mit Klaus Lenz* (Deutschlandsender Kultur, December 31, 1991).

who had emigrated from the GDR before 1989 subsequently gave up their celebrity status in the West, as citizens of a state that no longer existed. Star trumpeter, bandleader, and arranger Klaus Lenz dedicated his time to restore historic buildings near Cologne, and Friedhelm Schönfeld, who had emigrated to Canada, came back and settled in West Berlin to teach. Music journalist Rolf Reichelt began a new life in the West as a music therapist.

Such narratives of invention and reinvention in German society after reunification are limitless in number and constitute a broader story to tell all its own. That story is a longer story than can be told in this book. Rather, this book has sought to tell the story of jazz primarily within the years of the German Democratic Republic (including, briefly, its predecessors in the Weimar Republic and the Third Reich). Challenging the prevailing scholarly view of jazz in the GDR as a *de facto* oppositional musical genre, this research has shown instead that jazz in its many variations was a central part of East German policymaking, and that at no point in the GDR's history was jazz ever considered merely a musical genre to be enjoyed. Rather, from East Germany's earliest days during the era of Soviet occupation to the end of the GDR, policymakers saw jazz explicitly as an ideological tool. To tell that story, and to understand the complex nature of policymaking in a fraught political and cultural environment, this research has charted the development of jazz at key phases in the history of the GDR, from its origins in the Weimar era, to occupation after WWII, to Stalinism and partition, to *détente, ostpolitik, glasnost,* and cultural liberalism.

To tell this story, this research has unearthed policies on jazz that have never been analyzed in Western scholarship, arguing that the state sought to be flexible and adaptive in response to the changing tastes and aesthetics of its citizens. Not all policies were equally successful in maintaining control: some, like STAKOKU's repressive measures, ultimately led to backlash and failure, while others, such as the 1962 jazz resolution, were far more long-lasting and influential. This book has revealed the deep layers of involvement between musicians, audiences, and state surveillance, exploring for the first time how the state directly shaped jazz life and how collaboration shaped these interactions. For players such as Werner Sellhorn or Ulrich Blobel, who served both their own personal interests as well as those of the state, STASI complicity further engendered interactions between informers, audiences, and performers in far-reaching ways. Even though jazz fans in the GDR were subject to acts of surveillance or censorship, this history refutes the notion that state officials were solely invested in suppressing what they saw as a renegade, countersocialist form. On the contrary, East German officials came to understand that jazz was a musical genre that enjoyed great significance in the lives of their citizens and thus sought ways to integrate it into state ideology. Over time, this dialectic shaped activities and production to the extent that it can now definitively be claimed that party leadership and state security directly influenced the history of jazz in the GDR over the whole of its forty-year lifespan. Writ large, this study has sought to illuminate the dialogic relationship between the state and the citizenry and offer a departure point for future work that explores this relationship in greater detail. It is this author's hope that, with even deeper exploration of declassified files, with continued conversations with the surviving players on the scene, and with a greater understanding of this critical period in twentieth-century history, even more of the story of "a people's music" can one day be told.

Archival Sources

Bundesarchiv, Berlin-Lichterfelde

Stiftung Archiv der Parteien und Massenorganisationen der DDR im Bundesarchiv (SAPMO)

Kleines Sekretariat der SED, BArch/DY 30/J IV 2/3 52 (1949)

Komitee für Unterhaltungskunst der DDR, BArch/DR 101/3 (1984–1988)
Komitee für Unterhaltungskunst der DDR, BArch/DR 101/3c
Komitee für Unterhaltungskunst der DDR, BArch/DR 101/5c
Komitee für Unterhaltungskunst der DDR, BArch/DY 43/1350

Kulturbund der DDR, BArch/DY 24/3893 (1950–1952)
Kulturbund der DDR, BArch/DY 24/1804 (1951–1954)
Kulturbund der DDR, BArch/DY 24/24373 (1952–1953)
Kulturbund der DDR, BArch/DY 27/7527 (1955)
Kulturbund der DDR, BArch/DY 24/392 (1955–1956)
Kulturbund der DDR, BArch/DY 24/24396 (1961–1963)
Kulturbund der DDR, BArch/DY 24/24418 (1964)
Kulturbund der DDR, BArch/DY 27/950 (1980–1989)
Kulturbund der DDR, BArch/DY 27/9500 (1980–1989)
Kulturbund der DDR, BArch/DY 27/6506 (1982)
Kulturbund der DDR, BArch/DY 27/11519 (1982–1985)
Kulturbund der DDR, BArch/DY 27/9427 (1983–1987)
Kulturbund der DDR, BArch/DY 27/9422 (1985)
Kulturbund der DDR, BArch/DY 43/1350 (1985–1989)
Kulturbund der DDR, BArch/DY 27/9404 (1987)
Kulturbund der DDR, BArch/DY 27/8801 (1987–1988)

Ministerium für Kultur, BArch/DR 1/415 (1955–1957)
Ministerium für Kultur, BArch/DR 1/4533 (1955)
Ministerium für Kultur, BArch/DR 1/415 (1955–1956)
Ministerium für Kultur, BArch/DR 1/8668 (1955)
Ministerium für Kultur, BArch/DR 1/243 (1955–1957)
Ministerium für Kultur, BArch/DR 1/239 (1956)
Ministerium für Kultur, BArch/DR 1/19371 (1982)

Palast der Republik, Theater im Palast, BArch/DC 207/657 (1980)
Palast der Republik, Theater im Palast, BArch/DC 207/714
   (1979–1980)

Staatliche Kommission für Kunstangelegenheiten, Hauptabteilung
   Darstellende Kunst und Musik, BArch/DR 1/6133 (1952–1953)
Staatliche Kommission für Kunstangelegenheiten, Hauptabteilung
   Darstellende Kunst und Musik, BArch/DR 1/6138 (1952–1953)
Staatliche Kommission für Kunstangelegenheiten, Hauptabteilung
   Darstellende Kunst und Musik, BArch/DR 1/240 (1952–1954)
Staatliche Kommission für Kunstangelegenheiten, Hauptabteilung
   Darstellende Kunst und Musik, BArch/DR 1/236 (1951–1953)

Zentralrat der Freien Deutschen Jugend, Abteilung kulturelle und
   sportliche Massenarbeit, BArch/DY 24/1804 (1960–1961)
Zentralrat der Freien Deutschen Jugend, Horst Schumann, BArch/
   DY 24/3893 (1961–1962)
Zentralrat der Freien Deutschen Jugend, Sekretariat Fritz Kirchhof,
   BArch/DY 24/24396 (1961–1963)
Zentralrat der Freien Deutschen Jugend, Sekretariat Fritz Kirchhof,
   BArch/DY 24/24373 (1961–1962)

Zentralkomitee der SED, BArch/DY 30/J IV 2/3 52. 52 (1949)
Zentralkomitee der SED, Zur Beschäftigung mit dem Jazz in der
   DDR, BArch/DY 24/1804 (1961–1962)
Zentralkomitee der SED, BArch/DY 30/IV A2/9.06. 163 (1965)
Zentralkomitee der SED, Protokoll der 6.Tagung des
   Zentralkomitees, BArch/DY 30 IV2/1/4581972 (1972)
Zentralkomitee der SED, BArch/DY 30/IV2/458 (1972)

Der Bundesbeauftragte für die Unterlagen
des Staatssicherheitsdienstes der ehemaligen
Deutschen Demokratischen Republik (BStU)

Ministerium für Staatssicherheit, BStU/MfS Leipzig AU 43/57, Reginald Rudorf (1957)

Ministerium für Staatssicherheit, BStU/MfS 13412/65, Zirkel (1958–1963)

Ministerium für Staatssicherheit, BStU/MfS 5496/72, Jazzbrücke (1959)

Ministerium für Staatssicherheit, BStU/MfS P XII 2716/62, Sander (1962–1968)

Ministerium für Staatssicherheit, BStU/MfS AP36747/92, Karl-Heinz Drechsel (1963)

Ministerium für Staatssicherheit, BStU/MfS HA XX 18520, Operativ-Vorlauf "Jazzer" (1964)

Ministerium für Staatssicherheit, BStU/MfS BV Berlin AKG 710, Jazz and Lyrik (1964)

Ministerium für Staatssicherheit, BStU/BVfS Leipzig Abt. II 00279/02, L. Armstrong (1965)

Ministerium für Staatssicherheit, BStUM/MfS XV/3356/72, Zirkel (1972)

Ministerium für Staatssicherheit, BStU/MfS 5225/77, Amiga (1961–1977)

Ministerium für Staatssicherheit, BStU/MfS BVfS Cottbus AGK 123, Thomas (1977–1982)

Ministerium für Staatssicherheit, BStU/MfS HA II 215778, Thomas (1978)

Ministerium für Staatssicherheit, BStU/MfS AS 202/85, Blobel and MfS (1980)

Ministerium für Staatssicherheit, BStU/MfS/BVfS Cottbus/AKG 123/Nr.52/82, Peitz (1982)

Ministerium für Staatssicherheit, BStU/MfS HA XX 535, Unterhaltungskunst (1988)

Ministerium für Staatssicherheit, BStU/MfS BVfS Cottbus AGK 1704, Thomas (1989)

Ministerium für Staatssicherheit, BStU/MfS HA XX 23162, Politische Untergrundtätigkeit (1985)

Ministerium für Staatssicherheit, BStU/MFS HA II 21578, Konsulat der Vereinigten Staaten von Amerika (1984–1985)

Ministerium für Staatssicherheit, BStU/MfS/HA XX/23162, OPK
"Jazz" (1986)
Ministerium für Staatssicherheit, BStU/MfS/HA XX/23162,
Jazzbühne Ost-Berlin (1986)
Ministerium für Staatssicherheit, BStU/MFS BVfS Cottbus AGK
1704 (1989)

Interviews

Volkmar Andrä, 2011
Konrad Bauer, 2009
Ulrich Blobel, 2009
Rainer Bratfisch, 2010
Walter Cikan, 2010–2017
Katja Deim, 2017
Karlheinz Drechsel, 2007–2009
Helmut Eickermann, 2007
Herbert Flügge, 2011
Jost Gebers, 2009
Wolf Glöde, 2010
Josef Graczynski, 2009
Ulrich Gumpert, 2010
Rainer Haarmann, 2011, 2017
Reinhard Heinemann, 2010
Günter Heinz, 2009
Ruth Hohmann, 2009
Gerhard Hopfe, 2010, 2013, 2017
Renate Heinicke, 1996, 2007
Klaus Jürgen Heinicke, 1996
Erhard Kayser, 2013, 2017
Rolf Kühn, 2015
Jürgen Laartz, 2010
Theo Lehmann, 2011
Klaus Lenz, 2010
Martin Linzer, 2010
Meinhardt Lüning, 2010
Roland Mooshammer, 2010
Bert Noglik, 2011
Vera Oelschlegel, 2011
Rolf Reichelt, 2009, 2017

Jürgen Schitthelm, 2010
Klaus Schneider, 2009
Friedhelm Schönfeld, 2011
Gabriele Staamann, 2011
Gerhard Steincke, 2011
Jörg Stempel, 2010
Tom van der Geld, 2018
Wolfgang Winkler, 2018
Alfons Wonneberg, 2009
Brigitte Wonneberg, 2017

Private Matter

Herbert Flügge, Jazz-Tagebücher
Gerhard Hopfe, collection Wolfgang Muth, *Melodia Rhythmiker*
Jan Eikermann, *Sendekonzepte des DDR Rundfunks*, 1985
Klaus Jürgen Heinicke, Jazz-Vorträge, 1958
Alfons Wonneberg, Jazz-Vorlesungen, 1990

Newspapers and Periodicals

Berlin am Mittag, 1947
Berliner Jazzblatt, 1980–1989
Berliner Zeitung, 1955–1989
Berliner Zeitung am Abend, 1956–1961
Bradenburgische Neueste Nachrichten, 1965
Down Beat, 1948–1968 US section
Frau von Heute, 1956
Für Dich, 1965
Jazz Echo, 2013
Junge Welt, 1953–1970
Kassette, 1977–1982
Komintern, 1921
Komsomolskaja Pravda, 1956 USSR
Leipziger Volkszeitung, 1965
Liberaldemokratische Zeitung, 1956–1965
Liberaldemokratische Zeitung Halle, 1965
Märkische Union, 1965

Melodie und Rhythmus, 1959–1989
Melos, 1948 West Germany
Der Morgen, 1965
Melodie und Rhythmus, 1957–1990
Musikforum, 1970–1989
Musik und Gesellschaft, 1952–1989
National-Zeitung, 1959–1965
Neues Deutschland, 1946–1990
Neue Zeit, 1965
Norddeutsche Zeitung Schwerin, 1965
Sächsisches Tageblatt, 1965
Spandauer Volksblatt, 1965
Der Spiegel, 1948 West Germany
Der Tag, 1955–1965
Thüringische Landeszeitung, 1965
Tribüne, 1965
Unterhaltungskunst, 1984
Urania, 1971
USA in Bild und Wort, 1956
Volksstimme Magdeburg, 1954–1965
Weltbühne, 1980-1990
Wochenpost Berlin, 1965

Audiovisual Sources

Alexan, Georg Friedrich. *Ein Sänger Für Den Frieden: Paul Robeson, Die Wahrheit über Amerika.* X150 DRA Babelsberg, December 12, 1951.

Eisler, Hanns. Hanns Eisler Archiv, Akademie der Künste, 7152 Avm. October 25, 1948.

Erinnerungen an den Jazz in der Zone: Siegfried Schmidt-Joos im Gespräch mit Ernst-Ludwig Petrowsky. Sender Freies Berlin, October 3, 1994

Vom Lebensweg des Jazz. Documentary film, DEFA, Berlin. Producer: Heinz Rüsch. 1957.

Wir machten Jazz: Ernst-Ludwig Petrowsky und Uschi Brüning im Gespräch mit Klaus Lenz. Deutschlandsender Kultur, December 31, 1991

Published Government Documents

Ministerium für Auswärtige Angelgenheiten. *Um Ein Antifaschistisches- Demokratisches Deutschland. Dokumente aus den Jahren 1945–1949.* Berlin: Staatsverlag der DDR, 1968.

Verordnung des Ministerrats der DDR zum Schutze der Jugend, Gesetzblatt der DDR, Teil 1, No. 80. September 29, 1955.

LPs

Bergisch-Brandenburgisches-Quartett, AM 856031
Erste Jazztage der DDR-Weimar 1985, AM 856216
Just for Fun, FMP 0140
Rex Stewart's Hot Club Berlin Session, AM 1050
Snapshot, FMP Special Edition
Synopsis, AM 855395
Touch the Earth, FMP 0730
Verschränkte Konstruktionen, AM 856134
Zum Jazz, SCHOLA 857123

Appendix

(1)

"Satchmo"

April 16th, 1967
36-56-107 st
Corona New York
U S A

My Dear Mr Kasheing Drecksel,
"Surprise Surprise" you must have
thought that I had forgotten you.
But I did not. I thought About you
ever since you and I were together
And you were the M. C. of our
Show. And you did a very wonderful
Job. One of the very best that
Int have ever had to M. C. our
Show. I am sorry to have kept you
So long for An (answer to your)
letter — but I have been so very
busy—'Traveling All over the Country
playing 'One Night Stands'— Concerts,
(over)

Appendix Figure   Letter from Louis Armstrong to Karlheinz Drechsel, dated April 10, 1967, courtesy of the Louis Armstrong House Museum, Queens, NY. Minor irregularities have been preserved.

April 10, 1967
3656 107th Street
Corona, New York
USA

My Dear Mr Karlheinz Drechsel,

"Surprise Surprise." You must have thought that I had forgotten you. But I did not. I thought about you ever since you and I were together and you were the M.C. of our show. And you did a very wonderful job. One of the very best that we have ever had to M.C. our show. I am sorry to have kept you so long for an answer to your letter – but I have been so very busy traveling playing 'One Night Stands' – concerts, off my shoes – I am too tired to even look at my mail. (HA. HA.) And by your being in the music game, I am sure you understand. I told my wife and the gang which mean my 'All Stars' that I received a letter from you – and they all told me to tell you <u>hello</u>. Of course we lost our 'piano man,' Billy Kyle. Remember him? He Died about a year ago. He lived in Philadelphia Pennsylvania. We have Marty Napoleon in Billy's place on piano. Marty used to play with us in the early days before Billy Kyle. In fact Billy Kyle was with John Kirby's Band in those days. Our <u>base man</u> Arvel Shaw – And he has been gone a long time. We have a Base man by the name of Buddy Catlett – no Relations to Big Sid Catlett the <u>great</u> drummer who died years ago. Everybody else is <u>still</u> intact. Tyree Glenn – Trombone. (Buster Bailey) is on the Clarinet instead of Eddie Shu. Danny Barcelona–Drums. Jewel Brown–Vocals. Not much changes in the personel. Of course I am still around. We have lost some good Jazz musicians since I returned home. Such as Louis <u>Russell</u> who's band I played and recorded with in the "THIRTIES. Muggsie Spanier a good jazz trumpet man. He died just recently. And Edmond Hall a very good Jazz Clarinet man – <u>passed</u>. Of course there is quite a few more that 'cut out' (DIED) but I mentioned the names that I thought you would recognize 'during during' your History of the Jazz Musician in America. Well–God Bless <u>All</u> of them. We never know when our time will come to go, as for myself–I have had a pretty nice life. So I am ready to go any time the "<u>man</u> up above" (THE LORD) will call me. "<u>Yessir.</u>"

As <u>far</u> as the records that you want me to send to you – I will gladly send as many as I can. But as we say in America – I <u>am up</u> a <u>TREE</u>. (meaning) I don't exactly know – what records to send – who's records to send and <u>ETC ETC</u>.

Anyway – my manager Mr Joe Glaser who keeps a Recording of everybody in his Office – is very Sick at the moment. But, by the time you receive this letter and send me a list of the Recordings you have in mind – I will do my very best to please you my dear Friend. Because I do not want to send to you anything that you already have, I am sure – Mr Glaser will be well by that time. He will have to be operated on for <u>GALL STONES</u>. I am having a <u>two weeks rest</u> at this moment which I really need. Then we will go back again on a long tour. Well – that's show business for you. I really don't know <u>what</u> I would do without it. (Ha. Ha.) Even at my age (67) it is not so bad. In fact – I don't know of anything else that I would like to do. Even if I should retire – I would always be *doing something around music. I guess you feel the <u>same</u> way – Huh? The trip I made in your Country will live in my memories for ever. I will <u>never</u> forget. Especially the way you brought us on the stage. My wife Lucille often speak of the wonderful moments – and also think you are the finest and the <u>sharpest</u> 'M. 'C. I have ever had. I am hoping that times will change so that you can make a trip over here and meet all of the Jazz greats and sing with them and even play with them. It is <u>just</u> that easy once you get over on this side. Maybe you will <u>stay</u> with us awhile, <u>who</u> <u>knows</u>. <u>Anyway</u> you will have a very good time. Because I personally will see to it to you never a Dull moment – I promise you. I <u>still</u> say – when you <u>believe</u> things will come. In other words – Keep the <u>Faith</u> <u>Baby</u>. A <u>True</u> <u>Saying</u>. Don't forget to keep me posted on the kind of recordings that you can use. And – man" I will send to you a record of pretty near 'everybody that ever opened their Big Mouth or played on wax. (Tee Hee LAUGH) For you it will be my pleasure. So write me again – "<u>HEAR</u>? –*

Thanks for the photographs. The one with you and me I am sending back to you with my personal autograph. Some friends of mine came to see me and begged me for the others so I autographed them to them. <u>Well</u> I will close now hoping this letter will find you well – happy and having a lot of fun. When you write to me I will try my best to grant your wish concerning the Recordings as best as I can—

Am Jazzly Yours

<u>Satchmo</u>

Louis Armstrong

Bibliography

Achterberg, Klaus. "Wo sich jeder Freispielen kann." *Kulturanzeiger* (April/May 1976).

Adorno, Theodor W. *Abschied vom Jazz*. Vol. Gesammelte Schriften, Band 18, Musikalische Schriften V, Frankfurt a. M.: Suhrkamp, 1933/1997–2003.

On Popular Music. Zeitschrift für Sozialforschung. ed. Max Horkheimer Vol. IX/1941, München: Kösel-Verlag, originally published by the Institute of Social Research, Morningside Heights, New York City, 1941, 1941/1970.

"Resume über Kulturindustrie (1963)." In *Texte zur Theorie des Pop*, ed. Charis Goer, Stefan Greif und Christoph Jacke. Stuttgart: Reclam, 1963/2013.

Über Jazz. Vol. Gesammelte Schriften Band 17, Musikalische Schriften IV, Frankfurt a. M.: Suhrkamp, 1936/1997–2003.

Zur gesellschaftlichen Lage der Musik. Vol. Gesammelte Schriften, Band 18, Musikalische Schriften V, Frankfurt a. M.: Suhrkamp, 1932/1997–2013.

Agde, Günter, ed. *Kahlschlag: Das 11. Plenum des ZK der SED 1965*. Berlin: Aufbau Verlag, 1991.

Anderson, Iain. *This Is Our Music*. Philadelphia: University of Pennsylvania Press, 2007.

Andreas-Friedrich, Ruth. *Der Schattenmann*. München: Rheinsberg-Verlag, 2000.

Ardamatski, W. "Jazz und Jazz." *Komsomolskaja Pravda* (August 22, 1956).

Armstrong, Louis. *Mein Leben in New Orleans*. Berlin: Henschelverlag, 1967.

Asriel, Andre. *Jazz: Analysen und Aspekte*. Berlin: VEB Lied der Zeit, 1966.

Jazz: Analysen und Aspekte. Berlin: VEB Lied der Zeit, 1977.

Jazz: Analysen und Aspekte. Berlin: VEB Lied der Zeit, 1980.

Jazz: Analysen und Aspekte. Berlin: VEB Lied der Zeit, 1985.

Bahr, Egon. "American Détente and German Ostpolitik, 1969–1972." *Bulletin of the German Historical Institute Supplement I*, 2004 (2003): 138.

Balbier, Uta A., and Christiane Rösch, eds. *Umworbener Klassenfeind: Das Verhältnis der DDR zu den USA*. Berlin: Christoph Links Verlag, 2006.

Bartsch, Claus Michael. "Rockrebell mit rauher Raspelröhre." *Neue Zeit* (July 16, 1988).

Bartsch, Edith "Jazz und Jugend." *Deine Gesundheit* (April 1961): 5,6,19.

Bartsch, Ernst. *Neger, Jazz und tiefer Süden*. Berlin: VEB F. A. Brockhaus, 1956.

Berendt, Joachim Ernst. *Das Jazz Buch*. Frankfurt a. M.: Fischer, 1953.

Berrett, Joshua. *Louis Armstrong & Paul Whiteman: Two Kings of Jazz*. New Haven, Conn.; London: Yale University Press, 2004.

Berry, W. Abner. "Die Zukunft der Negermusik." *Musik und Gesellschaft* (September 1953).

"The Future of the Negro Music." In *The Communist Position on the Negro Question*. New York: New Century Publishers, 1947.

Blobel, Ulli, ed. *Woodstock am Karpfenteich: Die Jazzwerkstatt Peitz*. Bonn: Bundeszentrale für politische Bildung, 2011.

Borneman, Ernest. "Rex Leads by Candlelight: German Jazz Comes Out of Hiding." *Down Beat* (October 6, 1948).

Borstelmann, Thomas. *The Cold War and the Color Line: American Race Relations in the Global Arena*. Cambridge, Mass.; London: Harvard University Press, 2001.

Bratfisch, Rainer. "12. Jazzbühne." *Musik und Gesellschaft* (8/1988).

Frei Töne. Berlin: C.H. Links, 2005.

"Hanns-Eisler-Projekt: Jazzbühne Berlin '88 des Rundfunks der DDR." *Der Morgen* (May 30, 1988).

Brockhaus, Heinz Alfred, and Konrad Niemann, eds., *Musikgeschichte der Deutschen Demokratischen Republik, 1945–1979*, Sammelbände zur Musikgeschichte der Deutschen Demokratischen Republik. Berlin: Verlag Neue Musik, 1979.

Brown, Archie. *The Gorbachev Factor*. Oxford: Oxford University Press, 1997.

"The Gorbachev Revolution and the End of the Cold War." In *The Cambridge History of the Cold War*, ed. Melvin P. Leffler and Odd Arne Westad. Cambridge: Cambridge University Press, 2010.

Brown, Timothy Scott. *West Germany and the Global Sixties: The Antiauthoritarian Revolt, 1962–1978*. Cambridge: Cambridge University Press, 2013.

Brüll, Mathias. *Jazz auf Amiga: Die Schallplatten des Amiga-Labels von 1947 bis 1990*. Berlin: Pro Business, 2003.

Brüning, Uschi and Ernst-Ludwig Petrowsky. *Schräge Töne aus der DDR: Die Jazzmusiker Uschi Brüning und Ernst-Ludwig Petrowsky erzählen*. Sender Freies Berlin, SFB 3, November 3, 1990.

Buchbinder, Dagmar. "Die staatliche Kommission für Kunstangelegenheiten (1951–1953) - eine Kulturbehörde 'neuen Typus'." In *"Die Eroberung der Kultur beginnt!": Die staatliche Kommission für Kunstangelegenheiten der DDR (1951–1952) und die Kulturpolitik der SED*, ed. Jochen Staadt. Frankfurt a. M.: Peter Lang, Internationaler Verlag der Wissenschaften, 2011.

Burde, Wolfgang. "Alternative: Total Music Meeting." *Tagesspiegel*, Berlin (November 5, 1972).

Burkhardt, Werner. *Klänge, Zeiten, Musikanten*. Waakirchen: Oreos Verlag, 2002.

"Nichts Fremdes. Petrowsky-Trio zum ersten Mal in der Bundesrepublik." *Die Zeit*, November 10, 1978.

Butting, Max. *"Tanzmusik Abschlußbericht."* Berlin: Deutsche Akademie der Künste, Sektion Musik, 1952.

Cahn, Peter. *Das Hoch'sche Konservatorium in Frankfurt am Main*. Frankfurt a. M.: Kramer, 1979.

Carles, Phillipe and Jean-Louis Comolli. *Free Jazz/Black Power*. Jackson: University Press of Mississippi, 1979/2015.

Chamberlin, Brewster S., ed. *Kultur auf Trümmern: Berliner Berichte der amerikanischen Information Control Section, Juli-Dezember 1945*. Stuttgart: Deutsche Verlags-Anstalt 1979.

Cikan, Walter. "Jazz-Dokumentation, Jazz in der Kammer: 1966–1990." ed. Rundfunk der DDR.

Conrad, Gerhard. *Kurt Henkels. Eine Musiker-Biographie mit ausführlicher Diskographie*. Hildesheim; Zürich; New York: Georg Olms Verlag, 2010.

Cook, Susan C. *Opera for a New Republic: The Zeitopern of Krenek, Weill, and Hindemith*. Ann Arbor: UMI research Press, 1988.

Cooper,William J. and Thomas E. Terrill, eds. *The American South: A History, Volume II*. 4th ed. Lanham: Rowman & Littlefield, 2009.

Cramer, Heinz von. "Friedensschluß mit dem Jazz. Moderne Musik für zwei Klaviere." *Berlin am Mittag* (April 28, 1947).

Cramer, Lucas. *Frankfurter Rundschau* (October 6, 1973).

Curjel, Hans. *Experiment Kroll Oper*. München: Prestel, 1975.

Dannenberg von, Julia. *The Foundations of Ostpolitik: The Making of the Moscow Treaty between West Germany and the USSR*. Oxford; New York: Oxford University Press, 2008.

Davenport, Lisa E. *Jazz Diplomacy Promoting America in the Cold War Era*. Jackson: University Press of Mississippi, 2009.

Davis, Belinda, Martin Klimke, Carla MacDougall, and Wilfried Mausbach. *Changing the World, Changing Oneself: Political Protest and Collective Identities in West Germany and in the US in the 1960s and 1970s*. New York; Oxford: Berghahn Books, 2010.

DeVeaux, Scott, and Gary Giddens. *Jazz*. 2015 ed. New York; London: W.W. Norton & Company, 2009.

Dietrich, Gerd. "Kulturbund." In *Die Parteien und Organisationen der DDR: Ein Handbuch*, ed. Gerd-Rüdiger Stephan et al., 530–59. Berlin: Karl Dietz Verlag, 2002.

Kulturgeschichte der DDR. Göttingen: Vandenhoek&Ruprecht, 2018.

Drechsel, Karlheinz. "Louis Armstrong." *Melodie und Rhythmus*, no. 11–14 (1964).

Drechsel, Karlheinz. "Treffpunkt Jazz." *Melodie und Rhythmus* (7/1968).

Drechsel, Ulf. "2. JAZZ-TAGE der DDR in Weimar." *Journal für Unterhaltungskunst* (2/1990).

Zwischen den Strömungen. Karl Heinz Drechsel: Mein Leben mit dem Jazz. Rudolstadt: Greifenverlag, 2011.

Dümling, Albrecht, and Peter Girth. *Entartete Musik. Dokumentation und Kommentar zur Düsseldorfer Ausstellung von 1938*. [in de]. Düsseldorf: dkv der kleine Verlag, 1988.

Dussel, Konrad. *Deutsche Rundfunkgeschichte*. Konstanz: Verlagsgesellschaft Konstanz, 2004.

Dymschitz, Alexander. "Über die formalistische Richtung in der deutschen Malerei. Bemerkungen eines Außenstehenden." *Tägliche Rundschau* (November 19 and 24, 1948).

Eik, Jan. "Jazzbühne '88: Eisler und schwarze Klassik." *Weltbühne* (1988/27).

Eisler, Hanns. *Musik und Politik*. ed. G. Mayer, Berlin, 1973.

Elbe, Hugo. "Eine Nationale Festivalpremiere: Erfolgreiche 1. Jazztage der DDR." *Berliner Zeitung* (December 14, 1985).

Elsner, Jürgen. "Gedanken zum Thema Jazz angeregt durch Publikationen des VEB Deutsche Schallplate." *Musik und Gesellschaft* (8/1968): 553–58.

Engelhardt, Jürgen. "Eislers Weg vom Agitprop zum Lehrstück." In *Hanns Eisler*. Argument Sonderbände, 97–110. Berlin: Argument-Verlag, 1979.

"Musik auf der Werkbank. Zweiter und dritter Tag bei 'DDR-Jazz Now'." *Frankfurter Rundschau* (August 16, 1979).

"Musik die nicht rostet: Jazz aus der DDR in der Akademie der Künste." *Der Tagesspiegel* (August 14, 1979).

Eschen von, Penny M. *Satchmo Blows Up the World: Jazz Ambassadors Play the Cold War*. Cambridge, Mass.; London: Harvard University Press, 2004.

Fast, Howard. *Strasse zur Freiheit*. Berlin: Büchergilde Gutenberg, 1950.

Strasse zur Freiheit. Berlin: Neues Leben, 1948.

Finkelstein, Sidney. *Jazz*. Stuttgart: Verlag Gerd Hatje, 1951.

Jazz: A People's Music. New York: The Citadel Press, 1948.

Florian. "Nihilismus mit Boogie Woogie in der 'Badewanne'." *Neues Deutschland*, September 7, 1949.

Foster, William Z., ed. *The Communist Position on the Negro Question*. New York: New Century Publishers, 1947.

Frede, Matthias. "'Satchmo' und die Südstaaten." *Liberal-Demokratische Zeitung Halle* (April 6, 1965).

Friedrich, Jörg. *Der Brand. Deutschland im Bombenkrieg 1940–1945*. Berlin: List Verlag, 2004.

Friedrich, Wolfgang-Uwe. "SED und die deutsche Frage." In *Lexikon des DDR-Sozialismus*, ed. Rainer Eppelmann. Paderborn: Ferdinand Schöningh, 1997.

Fulbrook, Mary. *A History of Germany, 1918–2014*. Oxford: Wiley Blackwell, 2015.

Anatomy of a Dictatorship: Inside of the GDR, 1949-1989. Oxford: Oxford University Press, 1995.

Interpretations of the Two Germanies, 1945-1990. Basingstoke: Palgrave Mcmillan, 2000.

Power and Society in the GDR, 1961-1979: The 'Normalisation of Rule'?. New York: Berghahn, 2008.

The People's State: East German Society from Hitler to Honecker. New Haven, Conn.: Yale University Press, 2005.

Garabedian, Steven. "Reds, Whites, and the Blues: Lawrence Gellert, 'Negro Songs of Protest,' and the Leftwing Folksong Revival of the 1930s and 1940s." *American Quarterly*, no. 57, 1 (2005): 179–206.

Gassert, Philipp. *Amerika im Dritten Reich: Ideologie, Propaganda and Volksmeinung 1933–1945*. Stuttgart: Franz Steiner Verlag, 1997.

Gellert, Lawrence, G.M. Shneerson, and Ernst Busch, eds. *Negro-Songs: Protestlieder des Amerikanischen Negerproletariats*. Berlin: Lied der Zeit, 1949.

Gieseke, Jens. *Der Mielke-Konzern: Die Geschichte der Stasi 1945–1990*. Stuttgart; München: Deutsche Verlags-Anstalt, 2001.

Glaser, Hermann. *So viel Anfang war nie: Deutsche Städte 1945–1949* [in ger]. 1. Aufl. ed. Berlin: Siedler, 1989.

Goebbels, Josef. "Der Rundfunk im Kriege." *Das Reich* (June 15, 1941).

Goldschmidt, Harry. "Klassiker moderner Volkskunst." *Berliner Zeitung* (March 24, 1965).

Görtz, Günter. "Vor dem Kongreß der Unterhaltungskunst. Damit die Besucher noch mehr Spaß an der heiteren Muße haben." *Neues Deutschland*, February 25, 1989.

Haftendorn, Helga. "The Unification of Germany, 1985–1991." In *The Cold War, Volume III: Endings*, ed. Melvyn P. Leffler and Odd Arne Westad. Cambridge: Cambridge University Press, 2010.

Hanhimäki, Jussi M. "Detente in Europe, 1962–1975." In *The Cold War, Volume II: Crisis and Detente*, ed. Melvyn P. Leffler and Odd Arne Westad. Cambridge: Cambridge University Press, 2010.

Hatschek, Keith. "The Impact of American Jazz Diplomacy in Poland During the Cold War Era." *Jazz Perspectives* 4, no. 3 (2010): 253–300.

Haufler, Daniel. "Amerika, hast Du es besser? Zur deutschen Buchkultur nach 1945." In *Amerikanisierung und Sowjetisierung in Deutschland: 1945–1970*, ed. Konrad H. Jarausch and Hannes Siegrist. Frankfurt a. M.; New York: Campus, 1997.

Heimann, Thomas. "Vom Lebensweg des Jazz." In *DEFA Jahrbuch 2000*, ed. Ralf Schenk and Erika Richter. Berlin, 2000.

Herbst, Andreas, Gerd-Rüdiger Stephan, and Jürgen Winkler, eds. *Die SED: Geschichte-Organisation-Politik*. Berlin: Dietz, 1997.

Höffer, Paul. "Jazz-Musik." *Aufbau* (May 1946).

Hoffmann, H. P. "Unsere Kunst in der DDR." *Melodie und Rhythmus* (7/1967).

Holgert, Andreas. "Erstklassiges Spiel vor leeren Sälen: Betrachtung nach dem 2. Nationalen Jazz-Festival in Weimar." *Neues Deutschland* (December 2, 1989).

Jänichen, Lothar. "Jazz Now. Jazz-Austausch mit der DDR." *Jazz Podium* (October 10, 1979).

Jarausch, Konrad H. *Die Umkehr: Deutsche Wandlungen 1945–1995*. München: Deutsche Verlags-Anstalt, 2004.

Jelavich, Peter. *Berlin Cabaret*. Studies in cultural history. Cambridge, Mass.: Harvard University Press, 1993.

John, Eckhard. "Musikbolschewismus: Die Politisierung der Musik in Deutschland; 1918–1938." Metzler, 1994.

Joseph, Peniel E., ed. *The Black Power Movement: Rethinking the Civil Rights-Black Power Era*. New York: Routledge, 2006.

Kaes, Anton, Martin Jay, and Edward Dimendberg. *The Weimar Republic Sourcebook*. Berkeley: University of California Press, 1994.

Käs, Rudolf. "Hot and Sweet: Jazz im Befreiten Land." *So viel Anfang war nie: Deutsche Städte 1945–1949*, ed. Hermann Glaser. Berlin: Siedler Verlag, 1989.

Kater, Michael H. *Different Drummers: Jazz in the Culture of Nazi Germany*. New York: Oxford University Press, 1992.

Kellerhof, Sven Felix. *Die Stasi im Westen. Der Kurras Komplex*. Hamburg: Hoffmann und Campe, 2010.

Klehr, Harvey. *The Soviet World of American Communism*. New Haven, Conn.: Yale University Press, 1998.

Kleßmann, Christoph. *Die doppelte Staatsgründung: Deutsche Geschichte 1945– 1955*. Göttingen: Vandenhoeck und Ruprecht, 1982.

Knauer, Wolfram. In *Jazz in Deutschland*, ed. Wolfram Knauer. Darmstadt: Wolke Verlag Hofheim, 1996.

Knepler, Georg. "Jazz und die Volksmusik." *Musik und Gesellschaft* (1955/6): 181.

Koch, Hans-Jörg. *Das Wunschkonzert im NS-Rundfunk*. Köln; Weimar: Böhlau Verlag, 2003.

Koebner, Franz Wolfgang, ed. *Jazz und Shimmy: Brevier der neuesten Tänze*. Berlin: Dr. Eysler und Co., 1921.

Konen, W. "Legende und Wahrheit über den Jazz." *Musik und Gesellschaft* (December 1955): 391–97.

Koslow, P. Wladimir und Alexandr O. Tschubarjan, eds. *SMAD-Handbuch: Die Sowjetische Militäradministration in Deutschland 1945–1949*. Oldenbourg: Walter de Gruyter, 2014.

Köster, Maren. *Musik-Zeit-Geschehen: Zu den Musikverhältnissen in der SBZ/ DDR 1945–1952*. Saarbrücken: Pfau, 2002.

Kowalke, Kim. *Kurt Weil in Europe, 1900–1935*. Ann Arbor, 1979.

Lange, Horst H. *Jazz in Deutschland*. Colloquium, 1966.

Lauter, Hans. Der Kampf gegen den Formalismus in Kunst und Literatur. Für eine fortschrittliche Deutsche Kultur: Referat von Hans Lauter, Diskussion und Entschließung von der 5. Tagung des Zentralkomitees der Sozialistischen Einheitspartei Deutschlands vom 15.-17. März 1951. Berlin: Dietz, 1951.

Laux, Karl. *Nachklang*. Berlin, 1977.

Lehmann, Theo. *Blues and Trouble*. Berlin: VEB Lied der Zeit, 1981.

Levi, Erik. *Music in the Third Reich*. Basingstoke: Macmillan, 1994.

Levine, Lawrence W. *Highbrow Lowbrow: The Emergence of Cultural Hierarchy in America*. Cambridge, Mass.: Harvard University Press, 1988.

Lieberman, Robbie. *My Song Is My Weapon: People's Songs, American Communism, and the Politics of Culture, 1930–1950*. Urbana: University of Illinois, 1995.

Liefland, Wilhelm E. "Der Weg zu uns." *Frankfurter Rundschau* (January 24, 1976).

"Deutschland ein Improvisationsmärchen. In der FMP-Workshop-Reihe "Jazz Now": Die DDR-Avantgarde." *Der Tagesspiegel* (August 12, 1979).

"Deutschland ein Improvisationsmärchen. In der FMP-Workshop-Reihe 'Jazz Now': Die DDR Avantgarde." *Frankfurter Rundschau* (August 16, 1979).

Lindenberger, Thomas, ed. *Herrschaft und Eigensinn in der Diktatur.* Köln Weimar Wien: Böhlau Verlag, 1999.

Linzer, Martin. "1. Jazztage der DDR in Weimar: Kritische Reflexionen über ein nationales Festival." *Unterhaltungskunst* (2/1986).

"Gäste aus Holland." *Melodie und Rhythmus* (June 1977).

"Jazz, zeitgenössisch: Meinungen zu Standort und Perspektive einer Kunstgattung." *Kassette 6: Ein Almanach für Bühne, Podium und Manege* (1982): 208–14.

Loth, Heinrich. *Das Sklavenschiff. Die Geschichte des Sklavenhandels.* Berlin: Union Verlag, 1981.

Lotz, Rainer E. *Black People: Entertainers of African Descent in Europe and Germany.* Limited ed. Bonn: Birgit Lotz Verlag, 1997.

Lücke, Martin. *Jazz im Totalitarismus.* Populäre Musik und Jazz in der Forschung. Münster: Lit Verlag, 2004.

Luft, Friedrich. *Berliner Theater.* Hannover 1961.

Mählert, Ulrich. *Die Freie Deutsche Jugend, 1945–1949.* Paderborn: Schöningh, 1995.

Kleine Geschichte der DDR. 5th, 2007 ed. München: C.H. Beck, 1998.

Mählert, Ulrich and Gerd-Rüdiger Stephan. *Blaue Hemden Rote Fahnen: Die Geschichte der Freien Deutschen Jugend.* Opladen: Leske und Budrich, 1996.

Maier, Charles S. *Dissolution: The Crisis of Communism and the End of East Germany.* Princeton: Princeton University Press, 1997.

Mann, Erika. "Don't Make the Same Mistakes." In *Zero Hour, A Summons to the Free.* New York; Toronto: Farrar & Rinehart, 1940.

Medvedev, Zhores. "Chernobyl: A Catalyst for Change." In *Milestones in Glasnost and Perestroyka: Politics and People,* ed. Edward A. Hewett and Victor H. Winston, 19–30, 1991.

Merkel, Ina. "Eine andere Welt. Vortsellungen von Nordamerika in der DDR." In *Amerikanisierung: Traum und Alptraum im Deutschland des 20. Jahrhunderts,* ed. Alf Lüdtke, Inge Marssolek, and Adelheid von Saldern. Transatlantische historische Studien. Stuttgart: F. Steiner Verlag, 1996.

Meyer, Ernst Hermann. "Anti Jazz?". *Neues Deutschland* (April 5, 1951).

Musik im Zeitgeschehen. Herausgegeben von der Deutschen Akademie der Künste. Berlin: Verlag Bruno Henschel und Sohn, 1952.

"Realismus - die Lebensfrage der deutschen Musik." *Musik und Gesellschaft* (1951/2).

Miller, Roger G. *To Save a City: The Berlin Airlift, 1948–1949.* College Station: Texas A&M University Press, 2000.

Monod, David. *Settling Scores: German Music, Denazification, and the Americans, 1945–1953.* University of North Carolina Press, 2005.

Monson, Ingrid. *Freedom Sounds: Civil Rights Call Out to Jazz and Africa.* Oxford: Oxford University Press, 2007.

Mooshammer, Ronald. "Geschichten vom Jazz in der DDR." *Horch und Guck* (4/1993).

Morgenstern, Dan. *Living with Jazz*. New York: Pantheon Books, 2004.

Mühe, Hans Georg. "Die Improvisation im Jazz (II): Anregungen für Instrumentalisten." *Musikforum* (5/1979): 23–29.

"Improvisation im Jazz (III): Anregungen für Instrumentalisten." *Musikforum* (6/1979): 9–18.

"Jazz in der DDR (I): Zur Entwicklung und gesellschaftlichen Funktion in der DDR." *Musikforum* (4/1977): 29–30.

"Jazz in der DDR (III): Bemerkungen zur Entwicklung und Gesellschaftlichen Funktion." *Musikforum* (6/1977): 26–30.

Müller-Doohm, Stefan. *Adorno*. Frankfurt a. M.: Suhrkamp, 2011.

Naimark, Norman M. *The Russians in Germany: A History of the Soviet Zone of Occupation, 1945–1949*. Cambridge, Mass.: Belknap Press of Harvard University Press, 1995.

Nenno, Nancy. "Feminity, the Primitive, and Modern Urban Space: Josephine Baker in Berlin." In *Women in the Metropolis: Gender and Modernity in Weimar Culture*, ed. Katharina von Ankum. Berkeley: University of California Press, 1997.

Noglik, Bert. "5. Leipziger Jazztage." *Melodie und Rhythmus* (September 1980).

Jazzwerkstatt International. Berlin: Verlag Neue Musik, 1981.

"Konzeption (erste Überlegungen) zu einem für 1989 geplanten Semiar zur Geschichte des Jazz, BArch: DY 27." June 2, 1988.

"Peitz und der Feuerschlucker vom Centre Pompidou." In *Woodstock am Karpfenteich: Die Jazzwerkstatt Peitz*.: Bundeszentrale für politische Bildung, 2011.

"Rezeptionsästhetische Aspekte des zeitgenössischen Jazz." *Informationen der Generaldirektion beim Komitee für Unterhaltungskunst*, no. 5 (1986).

"Spontaneität und Konzeption – zur Jazz-Szene in der DDR." *Musik und Gesellschaft* (3/1980): 158–64.

Noglik, Bert and Heinz-Jürgen Lindner, eds. *Jazz im Gespräch*. Berlin: Verlag Neue Musik, 1978.

Nolan, Mary. *Visions of Modernity: American Business and the Modernization of Germany*. New York: Oxford University Press, 1994.

Nordau, Max. *Entartung*. Berlin, 1892/1893.

Oertel, Gabriele. "Weimar lädt zu den 1. DDR-Jazztagen ein: 120 Musiker wirken mit." *Neues Deutschland* (October 16, 1985).

Panke, Werner. "Mit eigenen Platten gegen mächtige Krämer: Die Free Music Production macht ihrem Namen alle Ehre." *Neue Musikzeitung* (December 1975/January 1976).

Partsch, Cornelius. *Schräge Töne: Jazz und Unterhaltungsmusik in der Kultur der Weimarer Republik*. M & P Schriftenreihe für Wissenschaft und Forschung. Stuttgart: J.B. Metzler, 2000.

Pawlenko, Pëtr. *Amerikanische Eindrücke*. Berlin: Tägliche Rundschau, 1949.

Peukert, Detlev. *Inside Nazi Germany: Conformity, Opposition, and Racism in Everyday Life*. New Haven, Conn.: Yale University Press, 1987.

The Weimar Republic: The Crisis of Classical Modernity. 1st American ed. New York: Hill and Wang, 1992.

Pike, David. *The Politics of Culture in Soviet-Occupied Germany, 1945–1949.* Stanford: Stanford University Press, 1992.

Poiger, Uta. *Jazz, Rock and Rebels: Cold War Politics and American Culture in a Divided Germany.* Berkeley: University of California Press, 2000.

Pollack, Heinz. *Die Revolutions des Gesellschaftstanzes.* Dresden: Sibyllen, 1922.

Polster, Bernd. *Swing Heil: Jazz im Nationalsozialismus.* Berlin: Transit, 1989.

Porter, Eric. *What is this Thing called Jazz? African American Musicians as Artists, Critics and Activists.* Berkeley: University of California Press, 2002.

Potter, Celia Applegate and Pamela Maxine. "Germans as the 'People of Music': Genealogy of an Identity." In *Music and German National Identity,* ed. Celia Applegate and Pamela Maxine Potter, 1–35. Chicago; London: University of Chicago Press, 2002.

Prieberg, Fred K. *Musik und Macht.* Frankfurt a. M.: Fischer, 1991.

Quinke, Ralph. "Die Berliner Free Music Production: Musikalische und gesellschaftliche Emanzipation." *Musik und Bildung* (October 1977).

Ranke, Winfried, Carola Jüllig, Jürgen Reiche, and Dieter Vorsteher. *Kultur, Pajoks und CARE-Pakete. Eine Berliner Chronik 1945–1949.* Berlin: Nishen, 1990.

Rauhut, Michael. *Beat in der Grauzone: DDR-Rock 1964 bis 1972, Politik und Alltag.* Berlin: Basis Druck, 1993.

Ein Klang - Zwei Welten: Blues im geteilten Deutschland. Transcript Verlag, 2016.

"Ohr an Masse. Rockmusik im Fadenkreuz der Stasi." In *Rockmusik und Politik. Analysen, Interviews und Dokumente,* ed. Peter Wicke and Lothar Müller. Berlin: Ch. Links, 1996.

Rock in der DDR. Bundeszentrale für politische Bildung, 2002.

Raupach, Manfred. "Swing in Görlitz: Ein musikalischer Rückblick auf die ersten Jahre nach dem 2. Weltkrieg." *Der Jazzfreund,* no. September (1996).

"Reges Forum mit dem Thema Jazz." *National-Zeitung* (April 8, 1956).

Reichelt, Rolf. "Zur gegenwärtigen Repräsentanz des Jazz in der DDR." *Informationen der Generaldirektion beim Komitee für Unterhaltungskunst* (2/1979).

Rempel, Hans. "Jazz: Woher - Wohin?". *Urania,* no. 2 (1971).

Robinson, J. Bradford. "Jazz Reception in Weimar Germany." Chap. 7 In *Music and Performance during the Weimar Republic,* ed. Bryan Randolph Gilliam, 107–34. Cambridge; New York: Cambridge University Press, 1994.

Rudorf, Reginald. "Die Tanzmusik muss neue Wege gehen." *Musik und Gesellschaft* (1954/2).

"Für eine frohe ausdrucksvolle Tanzmusik." *Musik und Gesellschaft* (1952/8): 247–52.

"Für eine frohe und ausdrucksvolle Tanzmusik." *Musik und Gesellschaft* (August 1952).

Jazz in der Zone. Köln; Berlin: Kiepenheuer & Witsch, 1964.

Nie wieder Links. Berlin: Ullstein, 1990.

Zu einigen Grundlagen der Ästhetik als Wissenschaft. Leipzig: Staatliche Kommission für Kunstangelegenheiten, Lizenz-Nr. 460 350/7/53, VEB E.A. Seemann, Leipzig, 1953.

Rupieper, Hermann-Josef. *Die Wurzeln der westdeutschen Nachkriegsdemokratie: Der amerikanische Beitrag 1945–1952.* Opladen: Westdeutscher Verlag, 1993.

Saldern, Adelheid von. "Überfremdungsängste." In *Amerikanisierung: Traum und Alptraum im Deutschland des 20. Jahrhunderts,* ed. Alf Lüdtke, Inge Marssolek, and Adelheid von Saldern. Stuttgart: F. Steiner Verlag, 1996.

Sarotte, Mary Elise. *Dealing with the Devil: East Germany, Detente and Ostpolitik, 1969–1973.* Chapel Hill: University of North Carolina Press, 2001.

Saul, Scott. *Freedom Is, Freedom Ain't: Jazz and the Making of the Sixties.* Cambridge, Mass.; London: Harvard University Press, 2003.

Saunders, Frances Stonor. *Who Paid the Piper? The CIA and the Cultural Cold War.* London: Granta Books, 1999.

Saunders, Thomas J. "How American Was It? Popular Culture from Weimar to Hitler." In *German Pop Culture: How "American" Is It?* ed. Agnes C. Mueller. Ann Arbor: The University of Michigan Press, 2004.

"The Jazz Age." In *A companion to Europe, 1900–1945,* ed. Gordon Martel. Malden; Oxford: Blackwell Pub., 2006.

Scheub, Ute. *Verrückt nach Leben.* Hamburg: Rohwolt, 2000.

Schivelbusch, Wolfgang. *Die Kultur der Niederlage: Der amerikanische Süden 1865, Frankreich 1871, Deutschland 1918.* Fischer. Erw. Lizenzausg ed. Frankfurt a. M.: Fischer-Taschenbuch-Verl., 2003.

In a Cold Crater: Cultural and Intellectual Life in Berlin, 1945–1948. Berkeley: University of California Press, 1998.

Schmidt, Siegfried. "Mitteilungen der 'Arbeitsgemeinschaft Jazz' in der FDJ-Organisation der Martin-Luther-Universität Halle." *Jazz-Journal* (February 1956).

Schmidt-Joos, Siegfried. *Die Stasi swingt nicht: Ein Jazzfan im Kalten Krieg.* Bonn: Bundeszentrale für politische Bildung, 2016.

Schroer, Timothy L. *Recasting Race after World War II: Germans and African-Americans in American-Occupied Germany.* Boulder: University Press of Colorado, 2007.

Schulz, Stephan. *What a wonderful world: Als Louis Armstrong durch den Osten tourte.* Berlin: Neues Leben, 2010.

Schwede, Alfred Otto. *Glory, Glory Hallelujah.* Berlin: Union Verlag, 1968.

Sellhorn, Werner. "Ein Kapitel in Free Jazz." Kassette 1. Ein Almanach für Bühne, Podium und Manege. (1977).

"Jazz im Anzug bürgerlicher Sittsamkeit." *forum* (July 23, 1959).

Jazz, DDR, Fakten. Berlin: Neunplus1, 2005.

"Joe 'King' Oliver." *Melodie und Rhythmus* (6/1966).

"Meine Kontakte zur Stasi." *Horch und Guck,* no. 13 (1994).

"Was auch zum Thema Jazz gehört." *Berliner Zeitung* (August 20, 1959).

"Was ist eigentlich Jazz?". *Märkische Volksstimme* (August 12, 1956).

Shirakawa, Sam H. *The Devil's Music Master: The Controversial Life and Career of Wilhelm Furtwängler.* New York: Oxford University Press, 1991.

Shneerson, Grigoriï. *Musik im Dienste der Reaktion*. Musik und Zeit. Halle (Saale): Mitteldeutscher Verlag, 1952.

Siemsen, Hans. "Jazzband." *Die Weltbühne*, 1921, 287–88.

Siminell, E. "Der Ku-Klux-Klan." *Internationale Presse-Korrespondenz, COMINTERN* (November 19, 1921).

Sponheuer, Bernd. "Reconstructing Ideal Types of the 'German' Music." In *Music and German National Identity*, ed. Celia Applegate and Pamela Maxine Potter. Chicago; London: University of Chicago Press, 2002.

Staadt, Jochen. *Die Geheime Westpolitik der SED, 1960–1970*. Berlin: Akademie Verlag, 1993.

"Westarbeit der SED." In *Lexikon de DDR-Sozialismus: Das Staats- und Gesellschaftsystem der Deutschen Demokratischen Republik, Band 2: N-Z*, ed. Horst Möller Rainer Eppelmann, Günter Nooke, and Dorothee Wilms. Paderborn: Ferdinand Schöningh, 1997.

Starke, Frank. "Beliebte Montagstreffs mit Gesprächen und Jazz: Cottbuser Veranstaltungen für Mittzwanziger." *Neues Deutschland* (August 26, 1977).

Starr, Frederick S. *Red and Hot: The Fate of Jazz in the Soviet Union, 1917–1980*. Oxford; New York: Oxford University Press, 1983.

Steiniger, Klaus. *Angela Davis: Eine Frau schreibt Geschichte*. Berlin: Neues Leben, 2010.

"Black Panther: Schicksal und Kampf, Weg zum Ziel." *Urania*, no. 2 (1971): 40–43.

Steinmetzger, Ulrich. "Das richtige Leben im falschen." In *Woodstock am Karpfenteich: Die Jazzwerkstatt Peitz*. Bundeszentrale für politische Bildung, 2011.

Stewart, Rex. *Boy Meets Horn*. The Michigan American Music Series. ed. Claire P. Gordon Ann Arbor: The University of Michigan Press, 1991.

Stokes, Gale. *The Walls Came Tumbling Down*. Oxford; New York: Oxford University Press, 1993.

Sträßner, Matthias. *Der Dirigent Leo Borchard. Eine unvollendete Karriere*. Berlin, 1999.

Thacker, Toby. *Music after Hitler, 1945–1955*. Aldershot; Burlington, Vt.: Ashgate, 2007.

Tibbe, Monika. "Volkstümlichkeit als Problem des Komponierens." In *Hanns Eisler*, 128–40. Berlin: Argument-Verlag GmbH, 1975.

Trommler, Frank, and Joseph McVeigh. *America and the Germans: An Assessment of a Three-Hundred-Year History*. 2 vols. Philadelphia: University of Pennsylvania Press, 1985.

Trültzsch, Sascha and Thomas Wilke, eds. *Heißer Sommer – Coole Beats. Diskotheken im Vergleich. Abendunterhaltung im Rampenlicht des sozialistischen Wettbewerbs*. Frankfurt a. M.: Peter Lang, 2010.

Voit, Jochen. *Er rührte an den Schlaf der Welt: Ernst Busch. Die Biographie*. Berlin: Aufbau Verlag, 2010.

Wagner, Cristine. "Jazztage der DDR. Erstmals in Weimar." In *Profil: Methodik zur Tanzmusik 5*, 35–36. Leipzig: Zentralhaus-Publikation, 1986.

"Was macht den Jazz aus?". *Berliner Zeitung*, March 17/18, 1956.

Weber, Hermann. *Geschichte der DDR*. München: Deutscher Taschbuch Verlag, 1985/1999.

Wilford, Hugh. *The Mighty Wurlitzer: How the CIA Played America*. Cambridge, Mass.; London: Harvard University Press, 2008.

Wilke, Thomas. "Diskotheken im Vergleich. Abendunterhaltung im Rampenlicht des sozialistischen Wettbewerbs." In *Heißer Sommer – Coole Beats: Zur populären Musik und ihren medialen Repräsentationen in der DDR*, ed. Sascha Trültzsch and Thomas Wilke. Frankfurt a. M.: Peter Lang, 2010.

Wipplinger, Jonathan. "The Aural Shock of Modernity: Weimar's Experience of Jazz." *The Germanic Review* (82/2007): 299–320.

The Jazz Republic: Music, Race, and American Culture in Weimar Germany. Social History, Popular Culture, and Politics in Germany. ed. Kathleen Canning. Ann Arbor: University of Michigan Press, 2017.

Wonneberg, Alfons.
"Wo bleiben unsere modernen Gitarren und Verstärkeranlagen?". *Melodie und Rhythmus* (16/1964).

Wood, Ean. *The Josephine Baker Story*. London: Sanctuary, 2002.

Ziemke, Earl F. *The U.S. Army in the Occupation of Germany, 1944–1946*. Army Historical Series. Washington, D.C.: Center of Military History, United States Army, 1990.

Zimmerle, Dieter. *Jazz Podium* (December 1968).

Zur Weihen, Daniel. "Die Kunstkommission und die Komposition zeitgenössischer Musik." In *Die staatliche Kommission für Kunstangelegenheiten (1951–1953) - eine Kulturbehörde "neuen Typus*,*" ed. Jochen Staadt. Frankfurt a. M.: Peter Lang, Internationaler Verlag der Wissenschaften, 2011.

Index

Note: Page numbers in italic refer to figures.